Conflict Displacement and Legal Protection

While the 21st century bears witness to several conflicts leading to mass displacement, the conflict in Syria has again crystallised the need for a solid legal framework and legal certainty.

This book analyses the relevant legal instruments for the provision of a protection status for persons fleeing to Europe from conflict and violence. It focuses on the conceptualisation of conflict and violence in the countries of origin and the different approaches taken in the interpretation of them in the 1951 Refugee Convention, the Recast Qualification Directive of the European Union and the European Convention on Human Rights. It traces the hierarchical order of protection granted, starting with refugee protection status, to subsidiary protection status and finally with the negative protection of non-refoulement. Recent case law and asylum status determination practices of European countries illustrate the obstacles in the interpretation as well as the divergence in the application of the legal instruments.

The book fills an important gap in examining the current practices of key actors, including the United Nations High Commissioner for Refugees and European states, tracing changes in national and international policies and revealing discrepancies towards contemporary approaches to conflicts. It refines the interaction and cross-fertilisation of the different relevant fields of European asylum law, human rights law and the laws of armed conflict in order to further the development of a harmonised protection regime for conflict-induced displacement.

Charlotte Lülf works as a researcher at the Higher Administrative Court of the State of North Rhine-Westphalia. Prior to that she was a postdoctoral researcher at the Institute for International Law of Peace and Armed Conflict in Bochum.

Law and Migration

Series Editor
Satvinder S. Juss, King's College London, UK

Migration and its subsets of refugee and asylum policy are rising up the policy agenda at national and international levels. Current controversies underline the need for rational and informed debate of this widely misrepresented and little understood area.

Law and Migration contributes to this debate by establishing a monograph series to encourage discussion and help to inform policy in this area. The series provides a forum for leading new research principally from the Law and Legal Studies area but also from related social sciences. The series is broad in scope, covering a wide range of subjects and perspectives.

Other titles in this series:

Children's Rights and Refugee Law
Conceptualising Children within the Refugee Convention
Samantha Arnold

Law and Asylum
Space, Subject, Resistance
Simon Behrman

Ethical, Legal and Social Aspects of Healthcare for Migrants
Perspectives from the UK and Germany
Edited by Katja Kuehlmeyer, Corinna Klingler and Richard Huxtable

Environmental Change, Forced Displacement and International Law
From Legal Protection Gaps to Protection Solutions
Isabel M. Borges

Conflict Displacement and Legal Protection
Understanding Asylum, Human Rights and Refugee Law
Charlotte Lülf

For more information about this series, please visit:
www.routledge.com/Law-and-Migration/book-series/LAWANDMIG

Conflict Displacement and Legal Protection

Understanding Asylum, Human Rights and Refugee Law

Charlotte Lülf

Routledge
Taylor & Francis Group
LONDON AND NEW YORK

First published 2019
by Routledge
2 Park Square, Milton Park, Abingdon, Oxon OX14 4RN

and by Routledge
52 Vanderbilt Avenue, New York, NY 10017

First issued in paperback 2020

Routledge is an imprint of the Taylor & Francis Group, an informa business

British Library Cataloguing-in-Publication Data
A catalogue record for this book is available from the British Library

Library of Congress Cataloging-in-Publication Data
A catalog record has been requested for this book

ISBN 13: 978-0-367-66140-3 (pbk)
ISBN 13: 978-1-138-32683-5 (hbk)

Typeset in Galliard
by codeMantra

Contents

List of abbreviations and acronyms vii

1 **Introduction** 1

1.1 A first glance at the book 1

1.2 Context considerations 3

1.3 The European struggle with asylum realities 8

1.4 The structure and the applicable law 11

2 **Refugee protection in the context of conflict and violence** 18

2.1 An introduction to the 1951 Convention as the primary refugee protection instrument 19

2.2 The 1951 Convention and the regional extended instruments 22

2.3 UNHCR – the mechanism of implementation and its position on persons fleeing conflict 26

2.4 Interpreting the 1951 Convention criteria of a conflict-displaced refugee 61

2.5 Intermediate conclusion on the 1951 Convention and persons fleeing conflict and violence 107

3 **European Union asylum law and persons fleeing conflict and violence** 129

3.1 The historical development of a CEAS 131

3.2 Union law instruments and the protection of persons fleeing conflict and violence 134

3.3 Adjudicating asylum law on the supranational level – the role of the CJEU and subsidiary protection 142

3.4 An interpretative overhaul – the (Recast) QD and international humanitarian law 146

3.5 Intermediate conclusion on the (Recast) QD and subsidiary protection for persons fleeing conflict and violence 176

4 European human rights law protection for persons fleeing conflict and violence **187**

4.1 Complementary protection in Europe – turning to the ECHR 188

4.2 The scope of the Convention's Article 3 of non-refoulement 191

4.3 Extraterritorial application of European human rights law 220

4.4 Intermediate conclusion on the ECHR' s non-refoulement and countries in conflict 228

5 Conclusion **239**

5.1 Conflict displacement and the challenge of status determination 239

5.2 Refugee law, Europe's complementary Protection scheme and the role of international humanitarian law 241

5.3 Concluding remarks 249

Index 253

Abbreviations and acronyms

AALCO	Asian-African Legal Consultative Organisation
ACHPR	African Charter on Human and Peoples' Rights
AMISOM	African Union Mission in Somalia
AP	Additional Protocol to the Geneva Conventions
APD	Asylum Procedures Directive
AU	African Union
CEAS	Common European Asylum System
CERD	Convention on the Elimination of Racial Discrimination
CJEU	Court of Justice of the European Union
CNDA	Court Nationale des Droits d'Asile
COI	Country of Origin Information
DIP	Division of International Protection
EASO	European Asylum Support Office
ECB	European Central Bank
EC	European Community
ECC	European Economic Community
ECHR	European Convention on Human Rights
ECJ	European Court of Justice
ECommHR	European Commission on Human Rights
ECOSOC	Economic and Social Council
ECRE	European Council on Refugees and Exiles
ECT	Treaty Establishing the European Community
ECtHR	European Court of Human Rights
ENDF	Ethiopian National Defense Forces
EU	European Union
EURODAC	European Dactyloscopy
IAC	International Armed Conflict
ICC	International Criminal Court
ICCPR	International Covenant on Civil and Political Rights
ICESCR	International Covenant on Economic, Social and Cultural Rights
ICJ	International Court of Justice
ICL	International Criminal Law

ICTR	International Criminal Tribunal for Rwanda
ICRC	International Committee of the Red Cross
ICTY	International Criminal Tribunal for the former Yugoslavia
IDP	Internally Displaced Person
IFA	Internal Flight Alternative
IHL	International Humanitarian Law
ILC	International Law Commission
IO	International Organisation
IOM	International Organisation for Migration
IRO	International Refugee Organisation
IS	Islamic State
KFOR	Kosovo Force
LGBTI	Lesbian, gay, bisexual, transgender and intersexual
MPSG	Membership of a Particular Social Group
NATO	North Atlantic Treaty Organisation
NGO	Non-governmental organisation
NIAC	Non-International Armed Conflict
OAS	Organisation of African States
OAU	Organisation of African Unity
OFRA	Office Francais de Protection des Refugies et Apartides
OHCHR	Office of the High Commissioner for Human Rights
PKK	Partiya Karkerên Kurdistanê
PPLA	Protection Policy and Legal Advice
PYD	Partiya Yekitîya Demokrat
QD	Qualification Directive
RCD	Reception Conditions Directive
RSD	Refugee Status Determination
TEU	Treaty of the European Union
TFEU	Treaty on the Functioning of the European Union
TFG	Transitional Federal Government
TPD	Temporary Protection Directive
UDHR	Universal Declaration of Human Rights
UK	United Kingdom
UN	United Nations
UNCLOS	United Nations Convention on the Law of the Sea
UNGA	United Nations General Assembly
UNHCR	United Nations High Commissioner for Refugees
UNMIK	United Nations Mission in Kosovo
UNO	United Nations Organisation
UNRWA	United Nations Relief and Work Agency
US	United States (of America)
VCLT	Vienna Convention on the Law of Treaties
YPG	Yekîneyên Parastina Gel

1 Introduction

1.1 A first glance at the book

Protracted humanitarian crises, failing states, natural disasters and recent armed conflicts such as those in Syria, Afghanistan, Iraq or Libya have led to extensive mixed migration movements to neighbouring countries and prominent regions of destination. The total number of forcibly displaced persons reached a record high of 68.5 million at the end of 2017.[1] Some of the affected persons flee persecution, some flee the violence of conflict, while others leave for a variety of different reasons. More often than not, they leave because of a combination of these various driving factors. A highly fragmented legal framework attempts to deliver regulation and protection[2] for those displaced in today's world of internal, cross-border and intercontinental mobility. The diverse reasons for flight, however, hinder the application of pertinent legal regimes. To complicate matters

1 Currently the newest overall number for global forced displacement, United Nations High Commissioner for Refugees, *Global Trends. Forced Displacement in 2017* (2018), available online at http://www.unhcr.org/5b27be547.pdf (last visited 1 August 2018).

2 In this book, the term 'protection' is not used with a broader operational understanding but is understood as the allocation of a protection status. This usage reflects the definition of protection in Article 2 of Recast Qualification Directive 2011/95/EU of the European Parliament and of the Council of 13 December 2011 on standards for the qualification of third-country nationals or stateless persons as beneficiaries of international protection, for a uniform status for refugees or for persons eligible for subsidiary protection, and for the content of the protection granted (recast), 20 December 2011: "For the purposes of this Directive the following definitions shall apply: (a) 'international protection' means refugee status and subsidiary protection status as defined in points (e) and (g); (b) 'beneficiary of international protection' means a person who has been granted refugee status or subsidiary protection status as defined in points (e) and (g)." See for a further discussion on the broader concept of protection in refugee related matters, Fortin, Antonio, 'The Meaning of "Protection" in the Refugee Definition', 12 *International Journal of Refugee Law* (2000) 548. Goodwin-Gill, Guy S., 'International Protection and Assistance for Refugees and the Displaced: Institutional Challenges and United Nations Reform' (Paper Presented at the Refugees Studies Centre Workshop, 2006). United Nations High Commissioner for Refugees, *Agenda for Protection* (2003), available online at http://www.unhcr.org/protection/globalconsult/3e637b194/agenda-protection-third-edition.html (last visited 1 August 2018). Steiner, Niklaus, Gibney, Mark and Loescher, Gil (eds.), *Problems of Protection. The UNHCR, Refugees, and Human Rights* (2003).

further, the legal status of those individuals arriving in receiving countries is far from clear-cut or consistent.[3]

While the 21st century bears witness to several armed conflicts resulting in displacement within the affected country or region or across the globe, the ongoing conflict in Syria is the most recent example and source of forced displacement. It has exposed and highlighted the need for a solid legal framework and legal certainty in the application of protection provisions. By mid-2017, over 5.6 million people had fled Syria and been registered as refugees by the United Nations (UN) High Commissioner for Refugees (UNHCR) in the five neighbouring countries alone.[4] Former High Commissioner António Guterres deemed the displacement caused by the Syrian armed conflict "a refugee outflow [...] at such a frightening rate [not seen] since the Rwandan genocide almost 20 years ago", "the largest crisis of forcible displacement in the world, and [...] a growing threat to regional peace and security".[5] Due to the challenging combination of high displacement numbers and, in particular, inconsistent and changing determination practices concerning Syrians seeking protection in Europe, this analysis uses both this conflict and other situations of violence as examples to illustrate the relevant legal bases for status determination.

The 1951 Convention Relating to the Status of Refugees (hereafter the 1951 Convention) and its 1967 Protocol, the fundamental pillars of international refugee law, establish protection for individuals who have crossed an international border, fearing persecution based on religion, race, nationality, political opinion or membership of a social group. The existing legal framework, established in the aftermath of the Second World War, is, however, perceived as failing to address the size, scale and character of modern forced displacement, particularly displacement from conflict and violence.[6] The individualistic focus of the 1951 Convention seems contradictory and inappropriate when applied to mass displacement of citizens from countries in conflict. The occurrence of conflict alone does not trigger the application of the 1951 Convention and its protection framework. It excludes those who are not persecuted individually for the discriminatory reasons codified in the Convention. Does this affect persons fleeing generalised situations of violence?[7] One has to question whether this generally excludes the application of refugee law to situations of conflict. Further, it must

3 Karatani, Rieko, 'How History Separated Refugee and Migrant Regimes. In Search of Their Institutional Origins', 17 *International Journal of Refugee Law* (2005) 517, at 518f.

4 These countries are Egypt, Iraq, Jordan, Lebanon, and Turkey, United Nations High Commissioner for Refugees, *UNHCR Syria Regional Refugee Response* (2017), available online at http://data.unhcr.org/syrianrefugees/regional.php (last visited 1 August 2018).

5 United Nations High Commissioner for Refugees, *UNHCR Chief Urges States to Maintain Open Access for Fleeing Syrians* (2013), available online at http://www.unhcr.org/51e55cf96.html (last visited 1 August 2018). United Nations High Commissioner for Refugees, *Ministerial Coordination Meeting of Major Host Countries for Syrian Refugees in Jordan* (2014), available online at http://www.unhcr.org/536652a39.html (last visited 1 August 2018).

6 United Nations High Commissioner for Refugees, *supra* note 5.

7 United Nations High Commissioner for Refugees, *Summary Conclusions on International Protection of Persons Fleeing Armed Conflict and Other Situations of Violence. Roundtable 13 and*

be addressed to what extent other legal fields trigger protection. Despite the 1951 Convention's salient position in refugee protection, the broader protection framework has evolved through its interrelationship with neighbouring fields of law, such as human rights law, humanitarian law and developing asylum schemes. Their influence and application are particularly relevant for persons fleeing the consequences of conflict in their countries of origin.

1.2 Context considerations

Flight from conflict is one major component of the larger phenomenon of forced displacement and forced migration movements, both internally, i.e. within the affected state's borders, and across the globe. With its increasing effects, not only for the neighbouring region but also for other prominent states of destination,[8] mirrored in increasing numbers of asylum applications, forced displacement is now a significant item both on the international community's agenda and in public and academic discourse.

1.2.1 "Who is Who"? The complexity of mixed migration movements

Migration may be a reaction to deteriorating circumstances in the country of origin, such as 'sudden' disasters, whether natural or man-made. While it may take the form of forced displacement, anticipatory voluntary movement can, but need not, be the reaction to negative changes in living conditions, such as slow onset disasters.[9] International migration is "[u]sually termed regular or authorised migration and principally a voluntary movement of people seeking better economic and social opportunities, as well as different life experiences and lifestyles".[10] However, migration movements are prone to change; drivers of displacement are not constant and patterns of dislocation change rapidly.[11] "[P]eople flee because of multiple causes of violence, exclusion, environmental degradation, competition for scarce resources and economic hardship caused by dysfunctional states. Some leave voluntarily, some flee because there is no other choice."[12]

---

14 September 2012 (2012), available online at http://www.refworld.org/docid/50d32e5e2.html (last visited 1 August 2018).

8 United Nations High Commissioner for Refugees, *Asylum Trends 2014. Level and Trends in Industrialized Countries* (2015), available online at http://www.unhcr.org/551128679.html (last visited 1 August 2018), at 7.

9 OCHA, 'OCHA and Slow Onset Emergencies', 6 *OCHA Occassional Policy Briefing Series* (2011), at 3f.

10 Zetter, Roger, 'Protecting Forced Migrants. A State of the Art Report of Concepts, Challenges and Ways Forward' (Federal Commission on Migration, 2014), at 20.

11 International Federation of Red Cross and Red Crescent Societies, *World Disasters Report 2012* (International Federation of Red Cross and Red Crescent Societies, 2012), at chapter 1, 13f.

12 Parliamentary Assembly of the Council of Europe, 'Environmentally Induced Migration and Displacement: A 21st Century Challenge' (Doc. 11785, 2008), at 2.

Institutionally, as well as legally, the traditional approach to leaving one's country is twofold. One is persecuted for certain reasons and qualifies as a Convention refugee, or one cannot qualify as such and is treated as a migrant instead. The legally clear distinction between refugees and migrants and the need for international protection for the former, in particular, were institutionalised after the Second World War. It was mirrored in the establishment of the UNHCR and the International Organisation for Migration (IOM) and codified in the clearly demarcated regime of refugee protection, excluding the category of voluntary migrants and other categories of forced migrants.[13] The legal distinction between these different types of displaced persons is enshrined in a detailed framework of status determination procedures that aims at ensuring the correct attribution of a specific legal status and an attached set of rights for its legitimate owner: "Refugee law is anchored in a belief in status. It is reflective of the idea that individuals and groups can be identified by falling within a carefully defined legal construct."[14] The reality of migration and flight movements, however, does not follow such clear-cut and distinguishable legal categories. The complexity of forms of persecution and ill-treatment, together with rights violations ranging from civil and political to socio-economic, blurs the lines separating the artificially construed categories of persons. The status determination process is further aggravated by the flight and migration patterns, which are characterised by mixed migration movements.[15] "The increasingly 'mixed' nature of migratory movements, that is of movements whose participants have differing motivations, objectives and needs, necessarily means that refugees and migrants will often be travelling together."[16]

Despite differences in their entitlements, refugees and conflict-displaced persons enjoy no additional access rights or legal channels to enter countries of asylum than migrants. This practice has become apparent in the European states over the last years. Recognition rates for persons originating from certain

13 Bast, Jürgen, 'International Organization for Migration (IOM)' (Max Planck Encyclopedia of Public International Law, 2010). Kugelmann, Dieter, 'Migration' (Max Planck Encyclopedia of Public International Law, 2009).

14 Juss, Satvinder and Harvey, Colin, 'Critical Reflections on Refugee Law', 20 *International Journal on Minority and Group Rights* (2013) 143, at 143.

15 United Nations High Commissioner for Refugees, *Refugee Protection and Mixed Migration: A 10-Point Plan of Action* (2007), available online at http://www.refworld.org/docid/45b0c09b2.html (last visited 1 August 2018). For matters of implementation, United Nations High Commissioner for Refugees, *UNHCR's 10 Point Plan in Central America, Western Africa, Eastern Africa and Southern Asia – A Two Year Project* (2008), available online at http://www.unhcr.org/4aa7a4bd9.pdf (last visited 1 August 2018). Regional conferences were held in Yemen (2008), Senegal (2008), Costa Rica (2009), Tanzania (2010), Kazakhstan (2011) and expert roundtables in Geneva (2008), Tunis (2009), Geneva (2009), Manila (2010). See for a detailed assessment of the UNHCRs work in this regard, Howe, Tim, *Refugee Protection and International Migration: Achievements, Challenges and Lessons Learned from UNHCR's 10-Point Plan Project* (2012), available online at http://www.refworld.org/docid/4f2654362.html (last visited 1 August 2018).

16 United Nations High Commissioner for Refugees, *Refugee Protection and International Migration in West Africa Statement by the Assistant High Commissioner – Protection, UNHCR Regional Conference on Refugee Protection and International Migration in West Africa* (2008), available online at http://www.unhcr.org/en-au/admin/dipstatements/4937e7742/refugee-protection-international-migration-west-africa-statement-assistant.html (last visited 1 August 2018).

countries in conflict have risen, and some European countries have used their discretionary powers to decide that Syrians, for instance, are to be granted protection. However, legal access to Europe, such as with visas issued by embassies, remains closed.[17] This is in line with the increasingly draconian approach of states to the management of immigration, expressed through the restriction of visa applications, enforcement of carrier sanctions and continuous strengthening of external border controls. Refugees and other forced migrants, therefore, have to resort to irregular migration routes to get to Europe and entering without the necessary authorisation. The death toll of the last years is symptomatic of these developments[18]: "Irrespective of the cause of displacement, [people] use similar routes, modes of travel and aim for similar destinations; increasingly resort to organised movement and the assistance of people smugglers".[19]

The current context of mass displacement and mixed mass movements to potential host countries challenges the application of the pertinent legal instruments. Lacking legal access opportunities, refugees and those displaced due to conflict mix with other migrants on their flight routes and further aggravate tensions in the application of the already disputed protection status.

1.2.2 Forced displacement by violence and conflict – challenges to a legal framework

Displacement is rooted in conflict but also begets conflict itself.[20] Sadako Ogata, former High Commissioner for Refugees, emphasised in 1998:

> The root causes of refugee displacement are inextricably linked to conflict, persecution and the denial of human rights. The very existence of refugees and other forcibly displaced people is therefore a barometer of a society's incapacity to resolve its differences by peaceful, rather than violent, means.[21]

17 European Union Agency for Fundamental Rights, *Legal Entry Channels to the EU for Persons in Need of International Protection: A Tool Box* (2015), available online at http://fra.europa.eu/sites/default/files/fra-focus_02-2015_legal-entry-to-the-eu.pdf (last visited 1 August 2018). European Council on Refugees and Exiles, 'Europe: Safe and Legal Access Channels. Ecre's Vision of Europe's Role in the Global Protection Regime' (2017).

18 Zetter, Roger, *supra* note 10, at 25.

19 *Id.*, at 39.

20 The terminology concerning the legal protection of people fleeing violence and conflict must be used with caution as it is characterised by linguistic and interpretative ambiguity. Both on a political level as well as in the pertinent jurisprudence, classifications of situations in the countries of origin vary in the use and meaning of terms of civil war, armed conflict, conflict, or widespread disorder. In this regard, the book starts from the assumption that the term conflict, as used in asylum law matters, is not limited by the terminology and attached conceptualisation of the laws of armed conflict. When necessary in the determination of the scope of legal instruments, the understanding of the term ‚conflict' is analysed in the respective parts of the chapters to mark differences and commonalities from the perspective of the different legal fields applied.

21 United Nations High Commissioner for Refugees, *Statement by Mrs. Sadako Ogata, United Nations High Commissioner for Refugees, to the 54th Session of the United Nations Commission on Human Rights* (1998), available online at http://www.unhcr.org/3ae68fd48.html (last visited 1 August 2018).

UN Security Council resolutions concerning the conflicts of the 2010s have expressed equally the Council's awareness of conflict-induced displacement and its potential to exacerbate violence in both the country and the region.[22] To leave one's home and one's country is a decision seldom taken lightly, even in the case of conflict. The dynamics of displacement reportedly change during the continuation of conflict. The hope of having to leave only temporarily often results in internal displacement or displacement to directly neighbouring countries. With the increasingly protracted character of conflicts, people are forced to seek more permanent or more promising solutions.[23] This results in onward or secondary movement of displaced persons from the region to hopeful countries of destination.[24] The international and regional framework governing these movements, however, struggles to keep up.

The conceptualisation of a refugee and refugee law as such disrupts the generally clear separation between, on the one hand, a state and its citizens and, on the other hand, other states and their distinct sovereign spheres. The concept of 'refugeehood' is based on the flight from one sovereign state into the power and jurisdiction of another and thereby across the borders that normally separate inclusion and exclusion of membership. While the primary responsibility for nationals theoretically remains with the state of origin, the refugee is unwilling or unable to avail her- or himself of protection of the country of origin, which is either the persecutor itself or incapable of protecting its citizens from harm. The first commentary to the 1951 Convention characterised refugeehood primarily through this ruptured bond between a state and its citizens.[25] This ruptured bond makes the refugee a specific kind of foreigner to whom the new destination society owes specific duties.[26] As such, refugee status has and still "represents a privileged form of migration".[27]

Flight from violence and conflict has a distinct and disputed place in the evolution of international refugee and asylum law. Since the 1950s, both the field of law and the notion of who is worthy of protection have expanded. The 1951 Convention was adopted decades ago, and contemporary shortcomings in its

22 United Nations Security Council, 'Resolution 688' (UN Doc. S/RES/688, 1991). United Nations Security Council, 'Resolution 1008' (UN Doc. S/RES/1008, 1995). United Nations Security Council, 'Resolution 1199, The Situation in Kosovo' (UN Doc. S/RES/1199, 1998).

23 Aranki, Dalia and Kalis, Olivia, 'Limited Legal Status for Refugees from Syria in Lebanon', 47 *Forced Migration Review* (2011) 17, at 17.

24 Phillips, Melissa and Starup, Kathrine, 'Protection Challenges of Mobility', 47 *Forced Migration Review* (2011) 27, at 28. For UNHCR's definition of 'protracted refugee situations', see United Nations High Commissioner for Refugees, *UNHCR Global Trends 2014: World at War* (2015), available online at http://www.unhcr.org/556725e69.pdf (last visited 1 August 2018), at 11.

25 Grahl-Madsen, Atle, *Commentary of the Refugee Convention 1951 (Articles 2–11, 13–37)* (1997), available online at http://www.refworld.org/docid/4785ee9d2.html (last visited 1 August 2018), at 73ff. Shacknove, Andrew E., 'Who Is a Refugee?', 95 *Ethics* (1985) 274, at 275.

26 Durieux, Jean-François, 'Three Asylum Paradigms', 20 *International Journal on Minority and Group Rights* (2013) 147, at 148.

27 Zolberg, Aristide R., Suhrke, Astri and Aguayo, Sergio, *Escape from Violence. Conflict and the Refugee Crisis in the Developing World* (Oxford University Press, 1992), at 9.

application might stem from being outdated. While the Convention is still at the centre of global refugee protection, regional refugee instruments have developed and expanded the exclusive concept of the Convention refugee. UNHCR's mandate has broadened in this regard and now covers many more persons of concern – including other *de facto* but not *de jure* refugees. Persecution by reason of the Convention grounds is no longer the essential criterion to distinguish a refugee from other forced migrants in many African, Latin American and Asian countries. The extended refugee definitions specifically cover persons fleeing generalised situations of violence – at least in legal theory. In contrast to those regional instruments containing broader refugee definitions, the EU has preserved the 1951 Convention's terminological distinction between refugees and others. Also, in the EU asylum law scheme, an EU-specific protection status for other categories of forced migrants was constituted in the form of subsidiary protection. Over the last decade, the substantive rights attached to subsidiary protection were constantly aligned with those of refugee protection – reducing the difference between the protection statuses to nearly mere terminology. With the Syrian conflict becoming more protracted, displacement numbers have increased. The receiving host states in the EU, fearing its consequences, have reversed this development.

Nonetheless, beneficiaries of subsidiary protection, sometimes referred to as 'survival migrants' or "persons who are outside their country of origin because of an existential threat for which they have no access to a domestic remedy or resolution",[28] are still – in protection terms – in line behind Convention refugees. Persons fleeing climate change, other forms of natural disasters or economic downfall are clearly at the end of the protection queue. However, once they have reached Europe, their return is equally restricted by the regime of human rights law, while the hardship that would be endured on return is measured by regional human rights law standards.

> States have been gradually trying to fill some of these gaps. But they have been doing so in very particular rather than overarching ways. [...] Sources of 'complementary protection' have emerged to address the grey area between these extremes of 'voluntary, economic migrant' and 'refugee'.[29]

The various existing protection regimes for asylum seekers,[30] including refugees, beneficiaries of subsidiary protection and protégés of *non-refoulement*, struggle with both their own legal status and their application to the contemporary factual

28 To relate to the notion created by Betts, Alexander, 'Survival Migration: Conflicting Refugee Identities in Africa', in S. Kneebone, D. Stevens and L. Baldassar (eds.), *Refugee Protection and the Role of Law: Conflicting Identities* (Routledge, 2014), 174, at 178.

29 *Ibid.*, at 177.

30 Following UNHCR's definition, an "asylum-seeker is someone whose request for sanctuary has yet to be processed", see http://www.unhcr.org/asylum-seekers.html (accessed: 10 March 2017).

displacement situation.[31] The context of violence poses an additional challenge to the application of relevant laws. The determination of status depends on the characterisation of the violence that claimants of protection have encountered.[32] One has to assess whether generalised violence affects civilians as extensive collateral damage and brings about negative consequences of indiscriminate violence occurring during the conflict. Alternatively, such violence may be persecutory and target specific individuals directly, even if it is covered and concealed by the general situation of conflict. Contemporary conflicts and the legal reactions mirror this 'war flaw'[33] – namely the uncertainty in the legal assessment of the conflict and its resulting displacement.

A major challenge in the application of the legal framework remains the complexity and availability of information in conflict contexts. The complexity of conflicts, the multitude of actors involved and their varying composition, motivation and power blur the assessment of military tactics, their objectives and their targets. One, however, needs to have a clear determination, as the distinction between the applications of refugee status or complementary forms of protection depends solely on this distinction between the individual persecuted for certain reasons and the individual affected by general violence in the country.

1.3 The European struggle with asylum realities

Refugees, people in need of international protection and migrants cross borders, the high seas, and travel through different jurisdictions and, accordingly, varying legal cultures. European asylum statistics illustrate that once they have reached the borders of Europe, most people fleeing conflict become involuntary participants in an asylum lottery.[34] It is the result of diverging interpretations of the applicable legislation relating to the question of which instrument to engage and which status to grant. Legal uncertainties are further increased due to the individual Member States' different political incentives and approaches.

31 "[T]here has been no new treaty-based response to the changing refugee situation", Corkery, Allison, 'The Contribution of the UNHCR Executive Committee to the Development of International Refugee Law', 13 *Australian International Law Journal* (2006) 97, at 98.

32 UNHCR: Farrell and Schmitt, 'The Causes, Character and Conduct of Armed Conflict, and the Effects on Civilian Populations, 1990–2010' (UN Doc. PPLA/2012/03, 2012).

33 "The 'war-flaw' is seen to consist in the failure of international protection to analyse claims by persons fleeing armed conflict by reference to the correct international law framework." Storey, Hugo, 'Armed Conflict in Asylum Law: The "War-Flaw"', 31 *Refugee Survey Quarterly* (2012) 1, at 1. See also, Storey, Hugo, 'The "War Flaw" and Why it Matters', in D. Cantor and J.-F. Durieux (eds.), *Refuge from Inhumanity? War Refugees and International Humanitarian Law* (Brill, 2014).

34 Asylum Information Database, *Not there Yet: An NGO Perspective on Challenges to a Fair and Effective Common European Asylum System. Annual Report 2012/2013* (2013), available online at http://www.asylumineurope.org/sites/default/files/shadow-reports/not_there_yet_02102013.pdf (last visited 1 August 2018).

This directly causes inconsistent recognition rates and divergence in the material scope of rights, even for people from the same country of origin.[35]

> While [...] States have abided by their international duty not to deport people to certain conditions, they have tended to be less diligent in looking to international law to define what legal status those people should be given. Accordingly, protection has varied over time from identical rights to Convention refugees, to a tolerated status with protection from refoulement but little more.[36]

Contemporary conflicts, such as in Syria, are chosen as examples and points of reference. They illustrate the diverging interpretations of and state practice in the application of the different fields of law and the obstacles inherent in a system lacking commitment to solidarity between affected states. These conflicts not only challenged the interpretation of the 1951 Convention, the relatively young EU asylum system and their application in the domestic setting, but also marked a shift in the application of the Convention's legal framework and complementary forms of protection. Syrian applications were the first to be subjected to a real distinction between refugee status and, at that time, still quite newly transposed, subsidiary protection status.[37] Since 2013, Syrians have ranked as the number one distinct displaced group from a common country of origin and, since 1992, have likewise constituted the largest group of asylum applicants in Europe.[38] Following the outbreak of the conflict, the alignment of the different status and legal instruments has changed.[39] While at the beginning of the

35 O'Sullivan, Maria, 'The Intersection between the International, the Regional and the Domestic: Seeking Asylum in the UK', in S. Kneebone (ed.), *Refugees, Asylum Seekers and the Rule of Law: Comparative Perspectives* (Cambridge University Press, 2009), 228, at 275. Battjes, Hemme, *European Asylum Law and International Law* (Martinus Nijhoff Publishers, 2006), at 609ff.

36 McAdam, Jane, *Complementary Protection in International Refugee Law* (Oxford University Press, 2007), at 5.

37 European Legal Network on Asylum & European Council on Refugees and Exiles, *Information Note on Syrian Asylum Seekers and Refugees in Europe* (2013), available online at http://www.ecre.org/wp-content/uploads/2016/05/Information-Note-on-Syrian-Refugees-in-Europe-29112013-final_website.pdf (last visited 1 August 2018). Ostrand, Nicole, 'The Syrian Refugee Crisis. A Comparison of Responses by Germany, Sweden, the United Kingdom, and the United States', 3 *Journal on Migration and Human Security* (2015) 255.

38 United Nations High Commissioner for Refugees, *Wars in Syria and Iraq Drive Highest Asylum Numbers in 22 Years* (2015), available online at http://www.unhcr-centraleurope.org/en/news/2015/wars-in-syria-and-iraq-drive-highest-asylum-numbers-in-22-years.html (last visited 1 August 2018).

39 Subsidiary protection rates for Syrians in 2015 in Cyprus were 97.8%, 92.7% in Malta, 90.1% in Spain, and 87.5% in Sweden. Compared to a subsidiary protection rate of 0.06% in 2015, Germany's subsidiary protection rate for Syrian applicants increased to 4.2% in April 2016: Bundesamt für Migration und Flüchtlinge, *Asylgeschäftsstatistik für den Monat Dezember 2015* (2016), available online at https://www.bamf.de/SharedDocs/Anlagen/DE/Downloads/Infothek/Statistik/Asyl/201512-statistik-anlage-asyl-geschaeftsbericht.pdf?__blob=publicationFile (last visited 1 August 2018). Bundesamt für Migration und Flüchtlinge, *Asylgeschäftsstatistik für den Monat*

conflict, subsidiary protection status was granted widely, the authorities later granted refugee status in a majority of cases. Germany offers one example of a changing interpretation, in which the swing of applicable status determination from subsidiary protection to refugee protection was made. Interestingly, since 2016, this development has been reversed. During the first phase of the conflict, the response pointed to a quick allocation of the newly transposed subsidiary protection status: the first instance decisions in the EU28 for Syrian applicants in 2013 allocated to 62% of the successful applicants subsidiary protection status and refugee status to 27%.[40] Throughout the conflict, the assessment changed in favour of an application of the 1951 Convention also to conflict-induced displacement. In 2014, Germany afforded refugee protection to the majority (20,505 Syrian applicants), while only 3,245 received subsidiary protection.[41] The political tension surrounding the Common European Asylum System (CEAS), the Syrian conflict and concerns about future developments and asylum numbers have evidently resulted in policy change. Looking at recent statistics from 2016 to 2018, the high number of Syrian applicants afforded subsidiary protection status rather than refugee status becomes apparent. Across the EU28, 62% of successful applicants were granted subsidiary protection, and only 32% were granted refugee status. In Germany, 24,620 Syrians were granted refugee status, but 46,965 were granted subsidiary protection at the end of 2016. This increased in 2017, when 55,697 received subsidiary protection, while 34,880 were granted refugee protection.[42] Currently, this trend leaves for instance German courts with large numbers of appeals from Syrian applicants contesting their subsidiary protection status.[43] While these data do not claim to provide a

---

April 2016 (2016), available online at https://www.bamf.de/SharedDocs/Anlagen/DE/Downloads/Infothek/Statistik/Asyl/201604-statistik-anlage-asyl-geschaeftsbericht.pdf?__blob=publicationFile (last visited 1 August 2018).

40 Bitoulas, Alexandros, *Asylum Applicants and First Instance Decisions on Asylum Applications: 2013* (2014), available online at http://ec.europa.eu/eurostat/documents/4168041/5948933/KS-QA-14-003-EN.PDF/3309ae42-431c-42d7-99a3-534ed5b93294 (last visited 1 August 2018). That amounted to 9,920 applicants from Syria receiving refugee protection while 22,635 Syrians were granted subsidiary protection.

41 For the EU-28, Syrians were granted 66% refugee status and only 29% subsidiary protection status in first instance decisions in the 4th quarter of 2014, see *id.*, at 20.

42 Eurostat, *First Instance Decisions by Citizenship and Outcome, Selected Member States, 4th Quarter 2016* (2017), available online at http://ec.europa.eu/eurostat/statistics-explained/index.php/File:First_instance_decisions_by_citizenship_and_outcome,_selected_Member_States,_4th_quarter_2016.png (last visited 1 August 2018). BAMF, 'Asylgeschäftsbericht', 2017, at 2, available online at http://www.bamf.de/SharedDocs/Anlagen/DE/Downloads/Infothek/Statistik/Asyl/201712-statistik-anlage-asyl-geschaeftsbericht.pdf (last visited 1 August 2018).

43 See further PRO ASYL, *Neue Asylpraxis beim BAMF: Immer mehr Syrerinnen und Syrer kriegen „nur" subsidiären Schutz* (2016), available online at https://www.proasyl.de/news/neue-asylpraxis-beim-bamf-immer-mehr-syrerinnen-und-syrer-kriegen-nur-subsidiaeren-schutz/ (last visited 1 August 2018). Legal Tribune Online, *Wei-terhin voller Flüchtlingsschutz für Syrer. VG Münster widerspricht OVG* (2017), available online at http://www.lto.de/recht/nachrichten/n/vg-muenster-urteil-14-a-2316-16-a-syrer-fluechtlingsstatus-widerspricht-ovg (last visited 1 August 2018). On the 'upgrade-appeals': Informationsverbund Asyl und Migration,

valid statistical analysis of the overall application outcomes, it reflects the trend in status determination and changes in the allocation of protection status. The need to consistently address conflict-induced displacement, on the one hand, and the evident change and evolution of the applicable laws, on the other hand, highlight the relevance of this book's topic.

1.4 The structure and the applicable law

Most ambiguity in the assessment of claims from persons fleeing countries in conflict is caused by uncertainty regarding the general application of the various pertinent protection instruments, as well as the interpretation of their respective status determination provisions. For this reason, the book employs treaty interpretation of the instruments applicable to people fleeing violence and conflict in accordance with the 1969 Vienna Convention on the Law of Treaties (VCLT), particularly regarding the interpretation of the 1951 Convention and its definition of a refugee. Divergent interpretative practices in the application of the instruments are highlighted in this book in order to question whether one can identify a progressive interpretation of the instruments. In this regard, subsequent state practice in relation to the international and regional instruments and their transposing legislation is examined.[44] The diverging interpretations in the domestic setting, especially by asylum determining authorities and national courts, are illustrative of the deficiencies in the interpretation of the legal bases. Since this book does not aim to provide a comprehensive picture of subsequent state practice, but puts in focus the primary means of treaty interpretation, and the analysis of jurisprudence of the regional courts, reference to domestic jurisprudence is given to illustrate the application of the different interpretations, but not as evidence of uniform practice.[45] When turning to the supranational and European levels, the jurisprudence of a) the Court of Justice of the EU (CJEU) and b) the European Court of Human Rights (ECtHR) must be put in focus. In contrast to domestic jurisprudence, the two courts play a decisive role in the interpretation of the pertinent legal instruments, as they are mandated to lead the interpretation of EU secondary law instruments and regional human rights, respectively. The CJEU, by means of a preliminary ruling, provides binding

Differential Treatment of Specific Nationalities in the Procedure (2018), available online at http://www.asylumineurope.org/reports/country/germany/asylum-procedure/treatment-specific-nationalities (last visited 1 August 2018).

44 "Times have changed. To an extent almost unimaginable even thirty years ago, national courts in this and other countries are called upon to consider and resolve issues turning on the correct understanding and application of international law, not on an occasional basis, now and then, but routinely, and often in cases of great importance." Lord Bingham, 'Foreword', in S. Fatima (ed.), *Using International Law in Domestic Courts* (Hart, 2005).

45 For these reasons, the book also refrains from a breakdown of the different pillars of state practice in asylum matters, for instance by balancing the role of the different determining authorities, ministries involved and asylum courts or chambers and their position in the domestic hierarchy of the judiciary and the state.

interpretative guidance on the Union law instrument in question, while the ECtHR, when delivering a binding judgement against a Member State, evolves the interpretation of the European Convention on Human Rights and Fundamental Freedoms (ECHR).[46] This book provides a comprehensive coverage of the legal developments concerning the protection of people fleeing conflict. Highlighting the changes in the interpretation and the current state of the art in the interpretation and application of the three individual protection pillars is the primary goal of this research.

The structure of this book reflects the hierarchy[47] of the available protection instruments in Europe and the scope of the entitlement of individual claimants from countries affected by conflict and violence. The first legal point of reference in this book is the detailed and most exclusive international refugee law framework. Its application to situations of conflict has been rejected for a considerable time, and only in recent years has this evaluation been subject to change, albeit falling short of eradicating all obstacles pertaining to claimants from countries in conflict. Refugee law and refugee status offer not only the best-established legal framework but also the one with the most substantive protection. The major question at issue is whether the instrument created nearly 70 years ago applies at all and, if so, what hurdles have to be cleared in interpreting its eligibility criteria. The UNHCR, as a subsidiary organ of the UN General Assembly, is the primary protection actor, and its role includes the monitoring of the 1951 Convention.[48] Therefore, its legal nature, as well as the content of its interpretative guidance concerning conflict-induced displacement, is reviewed. The second part of the first chapter concerns the interpretation of the 1951 Convention in the context of conflict. The application of the Convention in general to conflict-induced displacement is considered first. Second, the conflict-sensitive interpretation of

46 As an additional subsidiary means of interpretation, this book examines the position of the UNHCR and its interpretative guidance, and debates whether guidance from neighbouring fields of law, specifically international humanitarian law (IHL), can be drawn to interpret the three eligibility clauses. Further literature review, reference to legal debates as well as reports of international organisations (IOs) and non-governmental organisations (NGOs) are essential to allow for a comprehensive analysis and put the current legal developments into context.

47 This book considers the hierarchy of the three pertinent fields of law regarding their scope of protection and aligned substantive rights. It does not understand these three fields of law as being in a hierarchical relationship, as such. Furthermore, it is beyond the scope of this book to analyse the relationship between the three fields of law in depth and their interaction is only referred to if essential in the conflict-context.

48 While the UNHCR takes the lead in refugee protection matters, human rights bodies have also engaged in the field when it comes to fundamental obligations, see United Nations Committee Against Torture, 'Question of Western Sahara Views of the Committee against Torture under Article 22, Concerning Communication No. 13/1993 submitted by Mr. Balabou Mutombo (Annual Report 1994)' (UN Doc. A/49/44, 1995), at 45. Human Rights Committee, 'General Comment No. 20: Article 7' (UN Doc. HRI\GEN\1\Rev.1, 1994), at 30. Similarly, Human Rights Committee, 'Views of the Human Rights Committee in respect of communication No. 469/1991, Charles Chitat Ng v. Canada, adopted on 5 November 1993, paras. 14.2 (Annual Report 1994, Vol. II)' (UN Doc. A/49/40, 1993), at 189.

its inclusion clause, the eligibility criteria for refugee protection of Article 1 A(2) are addressed: first and foremost, persecution, its nexus requirement and the discriminatory Convention grounds, which are relevant to distinguish between persons considered eligible for international protection in accordance with the 1951 Convention and those who are not.

The second chapter examines the relevant and evolving asylum law framework in the EU. Compared to developments in Africa and Latin America, the EU has established a new and harmonised form of complementary protection, one that still needs to be clarified in its application. Following the experiences of the Balkan conflicts of the mid-1990s, the EU set the goal of establishing a common asylum system with harmonised standards and procedures in 1999 and has since then communitarised asylum law. In the course of creating the CEAS, EU Member States established a complementary protection mechanism, based on the Qualification Directive (QD) (2004/83/EC) and the Recast Qualification Directive (2011/95/EU), namely the so-called subsidiary protection status. Following the transposition of the QD into national laws, subsidiary protection status has, however, been applied incoherently in EU Member States and their asylum and judicial systems, due to ambiguity in its terminology and scope of application. Only in the past few years has the CJEU reviewed those matters in an attempt to guide the Member States' implementation of Union law and to clarify the scope of the QD, its relation to refugee law and human rights law, as well as specific terms of its provisions.[49]

The field of European human rights is analysed in the third main chapter of this book using two separate approaches. The first part of the chapter examines the ECHR's principle of *non-refoulement* as it can be considered protection of last resort for those fleeing a conflict or a certain level of violence in their countries of origin. In the case that no primary or secondary protection status, i.e. refugee or subsidiary protection, is granted to the individuals concerned, human rights law delivers minimum protection from being forcibly returned to a country of origin. The second part of the chapter turns to the extraterritorial application of the ECHR and the principle of *non-refoulement.* In this analysis, the principle acts as first protection mechanisms for persons who are travelling to Europe but have not yet entered European territory. Recent jurisprudential developments are put in focus to determine the limitations of the EU's external immigration management and border controls.

49 Excluded from the scope of this book are contemporary considerations on the functioning of the CEAS, in particular the current malfunctions of the Dublin system. Burden-sharing and commitment to solidarity among the EU states is essential for the proper functioning of the system and indicative of its current failing. The distribution of asylum seekers and the allocation of responsibilities, however, is of no relevance for the interpretation of the eligibility criteria and the inclusion clause of Article 15 (c) (Recast) QD in the context of violence and conflict. While it will be decisive to revise the current EU migration policies, create a new mechanism of distribution and clarify the existing mechanism of burden-sharing, this topic is left for another examination.

References

Aranki, Dalia and Kalis, Olivia, 'Limited Legal Status for Refugees from Syria in Lebanon', 47 *Forced Migration Review* 17 (2011).

Asylum Information Database, 'Not there Yet: An NGO Perspective on Challenges to a Fair and Effective Common European Asylum System. Annual Report 2012/2013', 6 September 2013, available online at http://www.asylumineurope.org/sites/default/files/shadow-reports/not_there_yet_02102013.pdf (last visited 1 August 2018).

BAMF, 'Asylgeschäftsbericht', 2017, at 2, available online at http://www.bamf.de/SharedDocs/Anlagen/DE/Downloads/Infothek/Statistik/Asyl/201712-statistik-anlage-asyl-geschaeftsbericht.pdf (last visited 1 August 2018).

Bast, Jürgen, 'International Organization for Migration (IOM)' (Max Planck Encyclopedia of Public International Law, 2010).

Battjes, Hemme, *European Asylum law and International Law* (Martinus Nijhoff Publishers, 2006).

Betts, Alexander, 'Survival Migration: Conflicting Refugee Identities in Africa', in S. Kneebone, D. Stevens and L. Baldassar (eds.), *Refugee Protection and the Role of Law: Conflicting Identities* (Routledge, 2014).

Bitoulas, Alexandros, 'Asylum Applicants and First Instance Decisions on Asylum Applications: 2013', 24 March 2014, available online at http://ec.europa.eu/eurostat/documents/4168041/5948933/KS-QA-14-003-EN.PDF/3309ae42-431c-42d7-99a3-534ed5b93294 (last visited 1 August 2018).

Bundesamt für Migration und Flüchtlinge, 'Asylgeschäftsstatistik für den Monat Dezember 2015', 6 January 2016, available online at https://www.bamf.de/SharedDocs/Anlagen/DE/Downloads/Infothek/Statistik/Asyl/201512-statistik-anlage-asyl-geschaeftsbericht.pdf?__blob=publicationFile (last visited 1 August 2018).

Bundesamt für Migration und Flüchtlinge, 'Asylgeschäftsstatistik für den Monat April 2016', 9 May 2016, available online at https://www.bamf.de/SharedDocs/Anlagen/DE/Downloads/Infothek/Statistik/Asyl/201604-statistik-anlage-asyl-geschaeftsbericht.pdf?__blob=publicationFile (last visited 1 August 2018).

Cantor, David and Durieux, Jean-François (eds.), *Refuge from Inhumanity? War Refugees and International Humanitarian Law* (Brill, 2014).

Corkery, Allison, 'The Contribution of the UNHCR Executive Committee to the Development of International Refugee Law', 13 (1) *Australian International Law Journal* 97 (2006).

Directive 2011/95/EU of the European Parliament and of the Council of 13 December 2011 on standards for the qualification of third-country nationals or stateless persons as beneficiaries of international protection, for a uniform status for refugees or for persons eligible for subsidiary protection, and for the content of the protection granted (recast), 20 December 2011.

Durieux, Jean-François, 'Three Asylum Paradigms', 20 (2) *International Journal on Minority and Group Rights* 147 (2013).

European Council on Refugees and Exiles, 'Europe: Safe and Legal Access Channels. Ecre's Vision of Europe's Role in the Global Protection Regime' (Policy Paper 1), 2017.

European Legal Network on Asylum & European Council on Refugees and Exiles, 'Information Note on Syrian Asylum Seekers and Refugees in Europe', November 2013, available online at http://www.ecre.org/wp-content/uploads/2016/05/Information-Note-on-Syrian-Refugees-in-Europe-29112013-final_website.pdf (last visited 1 August 2018).

European Union Agency for Fundamental Rights, 'Legal Entry Channels to the EU for Persons in Need of International Protection: A Tool Box', 2015, available online at http://fra.europa.eu/sites/default/files/fra-focus_02-2015_legal-entry-to-the-eu.pdf (last visited 1 August 2018).

Eurostat, 'First Instance Decisions by Citizenship and Outcome, Selected Member States, 4th Quarter 2016', 16 March 2017, available online at http://ec.europa.eu/eurostat/statistics-explained/index.php/File:First_instance_decisions_by_citizenship_and_outcome,_selected_Member_States,_4th_quarter_2016.png (last visited 1 August 2018).

Fatima, Shaheed (ed.), *Using International Law in Domestic Courts* (Hart, 2005).

Fortin, Antonio, 'The Meaning of 'Protection' in the Refugee Definition', 12 (4) *International Journal of Refugee Law* 548 (2000).

Goodwin-Gill, Guy S., 'International Protection and Assistance for Refugees and the Displaced: Institutional Challenges and United Nations Reform' (Paper Presented at the Refugees Studies Centre Workshop, 2006).

Grahl-Madsen, Atle, 'Commentary of the Refugee Convention 1951 (Articles 2–11, 13–37)', October 1997, available online at http://www.refworld.org/docid/4785ee9d2.html (last visited 1 August 2018).

Howe, Tim, 'Refugee Protection and International Migration: Achievements, Challenges and Lessons Learned from UNHCR's 10-Point Plan Project', January 2012, available online at http://www.refworld.org/docid/4f2654362.html (last visited 1 August 2018).

Human Rights Committee, 'Views of the Human Rights Committee in Respect of Communication No. 469/1991, Charles Chitat Ng v. Canada, adopted on 5 November 1993, paras. 14.2 (Annual Report 1994, Vol. II)' (UN Doc. A/49/40, 1993).

Human Rights Committee, 'General Comment No. 20: Article 7' (UN Doc. HRI\GEN\1\Rev.1, 1994).

Informationsverbund Asyl und Migration, *Differential Treatment of Specific Nationalities in the Procedure* (2018), available online at http://www.asylumineurope.org/reports/country/germany/asylum-procedure/treatment-specific-nationalities (last visited 1 August 2018).

International Federation of Red Cross and Red Crescent Societies, *World Disasters Report 2012. Focus on Forced Migration and Displacement Urban Risk* (International Federation of Red Cross and Red Crescent Societies, 2012).

Juss, Satvinder and Harvey, Colin, 'Critical Reflections on Refugee Law', 20 (2) *International Journal on Minority and Group Rights* 143 (2013).

Karatani, Rieko, 'How History Separated Refugee and Migrant Regimes. In Search of Their Institutional Origins', 17 (3) *International Journal of Refugee Law* 517 (2005).

Kneebone, Susan (ed.), *Refugees, Asylum Seekers and the Rule of Law. Comparative Perspectives* (Cambridge University Press, 2009).

Kneebone, Susan, Stevens, Dallal and Baldassar, Loretta (eds.), *Refugee Protection and the Role of Law. Conflicting Identities* (Routledge, 2014).

Kugelmann, Dieter, 'Migration' (Max Planck Encyclopedia of Public International Law, 2009).

Legal Tribune Online, 'Weiterhin voller Flüchtlingsschutz für Syrer. VG Münster widerspricht OVG', 10 March 2017, available online at http://www.lto.de/recht/nachrichten/n/vg-muenster-urteil-14-a-2316-16-a-syrer-fluechtlingsstatus-widerspricht-ovg (last visited 1 August 2018).

Lord Bingham, 'Foreword', in S. Fatima (ed.), *Using International Law in Domestic Courts* (Hart, 2005).

McAdam, Jane, *Complementary Protection in International Refugee Law* (Oxford University Press, 2007).

OCHA, 'OCHA and Slow Onset Emergencies', 6 *OCHA Occassional Policy Briefing Series* (2011).

Ostrand, Nicole, 'The Syrian Refugee Crisis. A Comparison of Responses by Germany, Sweden, the United Kingdom, and the United States', 3 (3) *Journal on Migration and Human Security* 255 (2015).

O'Sullivan, Maria, 'The Intersection between the International, the Regional and the Domestic: Seeking Asylum in the UK', in S. Kneebone (ed.), *Refugees, Asylum Seekers and the Rule of Law: Comparative Perspectives* (Cambridge University Press, 2009).

Parliamentary Assembly of the Council of Europe, 'Environmentally Induced Migration and Displacement: A 21st Century Challenge' (Doc. 11785, 2008).

Phillips, Melissa and Starup, Kathrine, 'Protection Challenges of Mobility', 47 *Forced Migration Review* 27 (2011).

PRO ASYL, 'Neue Asylpraxis beim BAMF: Immer mehr Syrerinnen und Syrer kriegen „nur" subsidiären Schutz', 19 May 2016, available online at https://www.proasyl.de/news/neue-asylpraxis-beim-bamf-immer-mehr-syrerinnen-und-syrer-kriegen-nur-subsidiaeren-schutz/ (last visited 1 August 2018).

Shacknove, Andrew E., 'Who Is a Refugee?', 95 (2) *Ethics* 274 (1985).

Steiner, Niklaus, Gibney, Mark and Loescher, Gil (eds.), *Problems of Protection. The UNHCR, Refugees, and Human Rights* (Routledge, 2003).

Storey, Hugo, 'Armed Conflict in Asylum Law: The "War-Flaw"', 31 (2) *Refugee Survey Quarterly* 1 (2012).

Storey, Hugo, 'The "War Flaw" and Why it Matters', in D. Cantor and J.-F. Durieux (eds.), *Refuge from Inhumanity? War Refugees and International Humanitarian Law* (Brill, 2014).

UNHCR: Farrell and Schmitt, 'The Causes, Character and Conduct of Armed Conflict, and the Effects on Civilian Populations, 1990–2010' (UN Doc. PPLA/2012/03, 2012).

United Nations Committee Against Torture, 'Question of Western Sahara Views of the Committee against Torture under Article 22, Concerning Communication No. 13/1993 submitted by Mr. Balabou Mutombo (Annual Report 1994)' (UN Doc. A/49/44, 1995).

United Nations High Commissioner for Refugees, 'Statement by Mrs. Sadako Ogata, United Nations High Commissioner for Refugees, to the 54th Session of the United Nations Commission on Human Rights', 19 March 1998, available online at http://www.unhcr.org/3ae68fd48.html (last visited 1 August 2018).

United Nations High Commissioner for Refugees, 'Agenda for Protection', October 2003, available online at http://www.unhcr.org/protection/globalconsult/3e637b194/agenda-protection-third-edition.html (last visited 1 August 2018).

United Nations High Commissioner for Refugees, 'Refugee Protection and Mixed Migration: A 10-Point Plan of Action', January 2007, available online at http://www.refworld.org/docid/45b0c09b2.html (last visited 1 August 2018).

United Nations High Commissioner for Refugees, 'UNHCR's 10 Point Plan in Central America, Western Africa, Eastern Africa and Southern Asia - A Two Year Project', March 2008, available online at http://www.unhcr.org/4aa7a4bd9.pdf (last visited 1 August 2018).

United Nations High Commissioner for Refugees, 'Refugee protection and international migration in West Africa Statement by the Assistant High Commissioner – Protection, UNHCR Regional Conference on Refugee Protection and International Migration in

West Africa', 13 November 2008, available online at http://www.unhcr.org/en-au/admin/dipstatements/4937e7742/refugee-protection-international-migration-west-africa-statement-assistant.html (last visited 1 August 2018).

United Nations High Commissioner for Refugees, 'Summary Conclusions on International Protection of Persons Fleeing Armed Conflict and Other Situations of Violence. Roundtable 13 and 14 September 2012', 20 December 2012, available online at http://www.refworld.org/docid/50d32e5e2.html (last visited 1 August 2018).

United Nations High Commissioner for Refugees, 'UNHCR Chief Urges States to Maintain Open Access for Fleeing Syrians', 16 July 2013, available online at http://www.unhcr.org/51e55cf96.html (last visited 1 August 2018).

United Nations High Commissioner for Refugees, 'Ministerial Coordination Meeting of Major Host Countries for Syrian Refugees in Jordan', 4 May 2014, available online at http://www.unhcr.org/536652a39.html (last visited 1 August 2018).

United Nations High Commissioner for Refugees, 'Asylum Trends 2014. Level and Trends in Industrialized Countries', 26 March 2015, available online at http://www.unhcr.org/551128679.html (last visited 1 August 2018).

United Nations High Commissioner for Refugees, 'Wars in Syria and Iraq Drive Highest Asylum Numbers in 22 Years', 26 March 2015, available online at http://www.unhcr-centraleurope.org/en/news/2015/wars-in-syria-and-iraq-drive-highest-asylum-numbers-in-22-years.html (last visited 1 August 2018).

United Nations High Commissioner for Refugees, 'UNHCR Global Trends 2014: World at War', 18 June 2015, available online at http://www.unhcr.org/556725e69.pdf (last visited 1 August 2018).

United Nations High Commissioner for Refugees, 'Global Trends. Forced Displacement in 2015', 20 June 2016, available online at http://www.unhcr.org/statistics/unhcrstats/576408cd7/unhcr-global-trends-2015.html (last visited 1 August 2018).

United Nations High Commissioner for Refugees, 'UNHCR Syria Regional Refugee Response', 1 June 2017, available online at http://data.unhcr.org/syrianrefugees/regional.php (last visited 1 August 2018).

United Nations Security Council, 'Resolution 688' (UN Doc. S/RES/688, 1991).

United Nations Security Council, 'Resolution 1008' (UN Doc. S/RES/1008, 1995).

United Nations Security Council, 'Resolution 1199, The situation in Kosovo' (UN Doc. S/RES/1199, 1998).

Zetter, Roger, 'Protecting Forced Migrants. A State of the Art Report of Concepts, Challenges and Ways Forward' (Federal Commission on Migration, 2014).

Zolberg, Aristide R., Suhrke, Astri and Aguayo, Sergio, *Escape from Violence. Conflict and the Refugee Crisis in the Developing World* (Oxford University Press, 1992).

2 Refugee protection in the context of conflict and violence

The international legal framework for the protection of refugees, in its current form, developed after the Second World War. As a universal instrument, the 1951 Convention has been subsequently underpinned by the adoption of regional refugee instruments and the creation of various complementary protection mechanisms. Since extensive research has already been conducted concerning international refugee law and its protection regime,[1] the following analysis proceeds without a general overview of the field of refugee law and focuses specifically on the protection of persons fleeing violence and conflict.

Divergence in the application of the 1951 Convention indicates the existence of implementation gaps in the wider refugee protection regime in Europe and beyond. That has attracted and will continue to attract attention from researchers from various disciplines. However, before addressing implementation matters, clarity on the legal applicability of the respective instrument to the situation in question must be provided. If there is no legal basis for any implementation at all, then the focus must be shifted to protection offered by other legal instruments. Therefore, if the 1951 Convention is not applicable to conflict-induced displacement, implementation gaps are not an issue.

This analysis primarily examines the normative foundation as to whether the 1951 Convention is generally designed to cover and protect persons fleeing

1 The most prominent ones being, Goodwin-Gill, Guy S. and McAdam, Jane, *The Refugee in International Law* (3rd ed., Oxford University Press, 2007). Hathaway, James C. and Foster, Michelle, *The Law of Refugee Status* (2nd ed., Cambridge University Press, 2014). Betts, Alexander and Loescher, Gil (eds.), *Refugees in International Relations* (2010). Costello, Cathryn, *The Human Rights of Migrants and Refugees in European Law* (Oxford University Press, 2016). Feller, Erika, Türk, Volker and Nicholson, Frances (eds.), *Refugee Protection in International Law. UNHCR's Global Consultations on International Protection* (2003). Brownlie, Ian and Goodwin-Gill, Guy S. (eds.), *Basic Documents on Human Rights* (5th ed., 2006). Gammeltoft-Hansen, Thomas, *Access to Asylum: International Refugee Law and the Globalisation of Migration Control* (Cambridge University Press, 2011). Heijer, Maarten d., *Europe and Extraterritorial Asylum* (Hart, 2012). Kugelmann, Dieter, 'Refugees' (Max Planck Encyclopedia of Public International Law, 2010). Zimmermann, Andreas (ed.), *The 1951 Convention Relating to the Status of Refugees and its 1967 Protocol. A Commentary* (2011). Weis, Paul, *The Refugee Convention, 1951: The Travaux Préparatoires Analysed, with a Commentary by the Late Dr Paul Weis* (Cambridge University Press, 1995). Hailbronner, Kay and Thym, Daniel (eds.), *EU Immigration and Asylum Law. A Commentary* (2016).

situations of conflict. For this purpose, the chapter firstly introduces the broader field of protection, including the extended refugee definitions, to take comprehensive account of refugee and regional protection explicitly addressing flight from conflict and to highlight the centrality of the 1951 Convention. Secondly, the focus of the chapter shifts to the United Nations High Commissioner for Refugees (UNHCR). As the UN's designated organ for the protection of refugees mandated to oversee implementation, including the interpretation of the Convention, its interpretative approach to the Convention has greatly influenced treaty interpretation by (national) bodies as well as state practice. Following an elaboration of its mandate, particularly concerning the legal instruments, the changing policy of the Office is highlighted and examined on the basis of various output documents. Its prominent role in the interpretation and supervision of the Convention, however, only goes so far. Therefore, the main part of the chapter covers a detailed analysis of the 1951 Convention and its refugee definition in Article 1 A (2). Employing the traditional means of treaty interpretation and embedding it in state practice and scholarly literature, the question to be answered is whether the conflict context changes the application of the definition. Due to the existing literature on general refugee law and the special attention paid to conflict and violence, only the pertinent parts of the refugee definition that are relevant for conflict-induced status determination are analysed. In a last step, international refugee law is embedded in the EU asylum law framework, as the geographical scope of this analysis centres around persons fleeing to Europe to escape from conflict and violence.

2.1 An introduction to the 1951 Convention as the primary refugee protection instrument

The 1951 Convention has constituted the cornerstone of the international protection regime since its entry into force on 22 April 1954.[2] State parties have affirmed their commitment to the Convention in 1967:

> [w]e, representatives of States Parties to the 1951 Convention relating to the Status of Refugees and/or its 1967 Protocol […] [r]eaffirm […] that the 1951 Convention, as amended by the 1967 Protocol, has a central place in the international refugee protection regime […] Solemnly reaffirm our commitment to implement our obligations under the 1951 Convention and/ or its 1967 Protocol fully and effectively in accordance with the object and purpose of these instruments […],[3]

2 United Nations General Assembly, 'Report of the Forty-Fifth Session of the Executive Committee of the High Commissioner's Programme' (UN Doc. A/AC.96/839, 1994), at 19 (d).

3 United Nations High Commissioner for Refugees, *Declaration Reaffirming Principles of 1951 Refugee Convention Adopted* (2001), available online at http://www.unhcr.org/3c18e6054.html (last visited 1 August 2018), at preambular paragraph.

and in 2011:

> [w]e reaffirm that the 1951 Convention relating to the Status of Refugees and its 1967 Protocol are the foundation of the international refugee protection regime and have enduring value and relevance in the twenty-first century.[4]

The 1951 Convention provides the legal basis for the well-developed protection regime for refugees. The regime has a narrow personal scope of application, meaning that only a clearly defined and limited group of individuals falls within its ambit.[5] Its definition of 'refugee' demarcates between *de jure* refugee status, migrants and forced *de facto* refugees. Although it was created after the Second World War against a background of massive, post-war displacement flows, the application of the 1951 Convention to conflict-induced displacement had, for quite some time, been rejected and is still disputed – not only on political but also on legal grounds.[6] In the 1950s, when the Convention was adopted, it addressed more than one million persons displaced by the conflict caused by National Socialism and by the 1990s had garnered new addressees displaced by the dissolution of Communist states.[7] And yet, the Convention was designed to protect individuals persecuted in the context of the 1940s and did not include a group-based approach to displacement. The tension still remains. The political background then and today explains the restraints concerning the definition of a Convention refugee in the context of conflict. Given the unmatched numbers of conflict-induced displaced persons in recent years and no reasons to expect a significant decline in these numbers in the near future, the adequacy of the 1951 Convention in addressing contemporary challenges is again called into question.

Like any other international treaty, in order to maintain its legitimacy for contemporary and future developments, the application of the 1951 Convention requires a balancing exercise between the original interpretation of the treaty text and adaptation to changing realities. In this respect, caution should be exercised so as not to apply the Convention "in an improperly or overly restrictive manner (but based on) a purposive and dynamic interpretation".[8] In particular, the human rights law movement has paved the way for a more sensitive and

4 United Nations High Commissioner for Refugees, 'Ministerial Communiqué' (UN Doc. HCR/MINCOMMS/2011/6, 2011), at paragraph 2.

5 "In contrast to other destitute people the refugee is eligible for many forms of international assistance, including material relief, asylum, and permanent resettlement", Shacknove, Andrew E., 'Who Is a Refugee?', 95 *Ethics* (1985) 274, at 277.

6 Goodwin-Gill, Guy S. and McAdam, Jane, *supra* note 1, at 126.

7 Feller, Erika, 'The Evolution of the International Refugee Protection Regime', 5 *Washington University Journal of Law & Policy* (2001) 129, at 129.

8 *AC (Syria)*, [2011] NZIPT 800035, New Zealand: Immigration and Protection Tribunal (2011), at para. 62. And *Refugee Appeal No. 74665, RSSA per Haines QDC*, New Zealand: Refugee Status Appeals Authority (2004), at 56.

comprehensive interpretation which addresses contemporary challenges[9] beyond the traditional understanding of the treaty terminology. Prominent examples of such awareness that have been 'borrowed' from human rights law by refugee law include the role of non-state armed groups and actors as persecutors, sensitive interpretations of gender issues, sexual orientation or the discriminatory Convention ground of membership of a particular social group (MPSG).[10] An evolutive interpretation[11] is mostly linked to the treaty's object and purpose that is indicative of the states' commitment to "a programme of progressive development".[12] This evolutive interpretation, nonetheless, remains restricted and conditioned by the general rules of treaty interpretation as laid down in the Vienna Convention on the Law of Treaties (VCLT), Article 31 and in supplement Article 32 and yet is endorsed by it.[13] However, even evolutive treaty interpretation can only go so far and the terms of the Convention need thorough and careful interpretation.

Refugee law has been criticised explicitly for protection gaps concerning its applicability to current realities. "[T]he adaptation of protection norms and instruments has been insufficient to keep pace with the changing dynamics of forced displacement."[14] In this regard, one has to distinguish between a) normative protection gaps that result from the inapplicability of the Convention to certain groups of *de facto* refugees with a simultaneous absence of other protection instruments; and b) implementation gaps that result from the inadequate practical application of an otherwise pertinent instrument. Before taking a stand, it must be assessed whether the convention applies at all to conflict-induced

9 Nolte states in his work for the ILC in this regard that treaties can "change over time", "evolve according to the needs of the international community", however, there is always some form of tensions between "the requirements of stability and change in the law of treaties" in: Nolte, Georg, 'Treaties Over Time in Particular; Subsequent Agreement and Practice', in United Nations Organisation (ed.), *Report of the International Law Commission* (2008), at 365, para. 1f.

10 Fitzpatrick, Joan, 'Revitalizing the 1951 Convention', 9 *Harvard Human Rights Journal* (1996), at 230f.

11 See in a detailed analysis, Arato, Julian, 'Subsequent Practice and Evolutive Interpretation. Techniques of Treaty Interpretation over Time and Their Diverse Consequences', 9 *The Law & Practice of International Courts and Tribunals* (2010) 443.

12 Koskenniemi, Martti, 'Fragmentation of International Law: Difficulties Arising from the Diversification and Expansion of International Law, in: Report of the Study Group of the International Law Commission' (UN Doc. A/CN.4/L.682, 2006).

13 *Advisory Opinion: The Right to Information on Consular Assistance in the Framework of the Guarantees of the Due Process of Law*, OC-16/99, Inter-American Court of Human Rights (1999), at 114. "[E]volutive interpretation is consistent with the general rule of treaty interpretation established in the 1969 Vienna Convention", Rietiker, Daniel, 'The Principle of "Effectiveness" in the Recent Jurisprudence of the European Court of Human Rights. Its Different Dimensions and Its Consistency with Public International Law – No Need for the Concept of Treaty Sui Generis', 79 *Nordic Journal of International Law* (2010) 245, at 255.

14 Zetter, Roger, 'Protecting Forced Migrants. A State of the Art Report of Concepts, Challenges and Ways Forward' (Federal Commission on Migration, 2014), at 27. Cantor, David and Durieux, Jean-François, 'Introduction', in D. Cantor and J.-F. Durieux (eds.), *Refuge from In-humanity? War Refugees and International Humanitarian Law* (Brill, 2014), at 5.

displacement. Either the Convention explicitly rejects persons fleeing conflict from its scope of protection and from the *de jure* refugee status, or alternatively, one rather encounters implementation gaps, the result of misconceptions of the Convention and inconsistencies in its application by state parties.

2.2 The 1951 Convention and the regional extended instruments

The 1951 Convention is the primary universal instrument of refugee law, but since its adoption, additional regional refugee law instruments have been codified. Further, while the protection of persons fleeing conflict and situations of general violence is disputed under the 1951 Convention, the regional refugee conventions have, on paper, extended their scope. These instruments were developed some decades after the 1951 Convention in order to cover the specific and different characteristics of regional displacement in Africa, Latin America, Asia and the Arab states. They have incorporated risks stemming from indiscriminate and widespread situations of violence into their framework of refugee protection and, as such, go beyond the definition of refugee enshrined in the 1951 Convention. For this analysis, the normative characteristics of the regional instruments are of relevance and are displayed in the following. Nonetheless, a report of the actual practice of and politics behind the regional instruments is beyond the scope of this book.

The binding Organisation of African Unity (OAU) Refugee Convention entered into force in 1974. Article 1 encompasses both the 1951 refugee definition and an extended definition, unique to Africa.[15] Paragraph 2 adds:

> The term 'refugee' shall also apply to every person who, owing to external aggression, occupation, foreign domination or events seriously disturbing public order in either part or the whole of his country of origin or nationality, is compelled to leave his place of habitual residence in order to seek refuge in another place outside his country of origin or nationality.

The 1984 Cartagena Declaration is the second regional refugee instrument that extends protection explicitly to people fleeing generalised situations of violence. It is considered the regional response of Latin American states to the drafting and entry into force of the OAU Convention. Its refugee definition in conclusion III (3) states:

> [...] the definition or concept of a refugee to be recommended for use in the region is one which, in addition to containing the elements of the 1951 Convention and the 1967 Protocol, includes among refugees persons who

15 Doutum, M. H., 'Opening Statement at the OAU/UNHCR meeting of Government and Non-Government Technical Experts on the 30th Anniversary of the 1969 OAU Convention Governing the Specific Aspects of the Refugee Problem in Africa, 27–29 March, h.E. Ambassador Doutum' (Conakry, Guinea, UN Doc. CONF.P/OAU/30th/Report Annex IV), at 48.

> have fled their country because their lives, safety or freedom have been threatened by generalized violence, foreign aggression, internal conflicts, massive violation of human rights or other circumstances which have seriously disturbed public order.

Although the Cartagena Declaration is not a legally binding document, its refugee definition has extensively influenced or was incorporated into the national legislation of Latin American states, which, for the most part, previously did not have specific refugee regulations.[16] Due to its incorporation into some states' national laws, the extended refugee definition has become binding. It now provides the basis for status determination in some Latin American states, while remaining a non-binding proposal in others.[17]

Similar developments resulting in non-binding instruments can be traced to the Bangkok Principles on the Status and Treatment of Refugees, drafted by the Asian-African Legal Consultative Organization and the 1994 Arab Convention on Regulating Status of Refugees in the Arab Countries. Both contain extended definitions encompassing persons fleeing generalised situations of violence. Article 1 (2) of the Bangkok Principles covers:

> every person, who owing to external aggression, occupation, foreign domination or events seriously disturbing public order in either part of the whole of his country of origin or nationality, is compelled to leave his place of habitual residence in order to seek refuge in another place outside his country of origin or nationality,[18]

while the Arab Convention in Article 1 adds to the 1951 Convention definition a broad extension of the refugee, as follows:

> any person who unwillingly takes refuge in a country other than his country of origin or his habitual place of residence because of sustained aggression against, occupation and foreign domination of such country

16 Reed-Hurtado, Michael, *The Cartagena Declaration on Refugees and the Protection of People fleeing Armed Conflict and Other Situations of Violence in Latin America. Division of International Protection* (2013), available online at http://www.refworld.org/docid/51c801934.html (last visited 1 August 2018), at 4. *Brazil Declaration. A Framework for Cooperation and Regional Solidarity to Strengthen the International Protection of Refugees, Displaced and Stateless Persons in Latin America and the Caribbean* (2014), available online at http://www.refworld.org/docid/5487065b4.html (last visited 1 August 2018). United Nations High Commissioner for Refugees, 'The Refugee Situation in Latin America: Protection and Solutions Based on the Pragmatic Approach of the Cartagena Declaration on Refugees of 1984. Discussion Document UNHCR November 2004', 18 *International Journal of Refugee Law* (2006) 252.

17 Despite the incorporation practice, it has been reported that the "[d]eclaration has been seldom applied in practice, guidance on its interpretation is underdeveloped and national authorities rarely consult its provisions when providing international refugee protection", Reed-Hurtado, Michael, *supra* note 16, at 5.

18 Asian-African Legal Consultative Organization, 'Bangkok Principles on the Status and Treatment of Refugees ("Bangkok Principles")' (1966)

> or because of the occurrence of natural disasters or grave events resulting in major disruption of public order in the whole country or any part thereof.[19]

One can ask whether the creation of these regional extended refugee instruments hints at dissatisfaction with the 1951 Convention in the context of conflict, or were they simply intended as regional counterparts to supplement the universal instrument?[20] Generally, regional instruments are designed to accommodate special regional developments. Furthermore, they do not require such extensive universal negotiations and, as such, are often a more straightforward and suitable legal reaction to existing needs. The regional focus is highly welcomed by the UN.[21] For refugee status determination (RSD) and the procedural order in assessing such protection claims, it is, however, essential to establish a strict hierarchy among the existing legal bases. The non-binding regional instruments, due to their voluntary nature, do not challenge the primary role of the universal instrument or question procedural order in status determination. The binding OAU Convention and the national laws implementing the Cartagena Declaration, with their extended refugee definitions could, theoretically, endanger this primacy. However, the treaty itself, as well as its *travaux préparatoires*, directly addresses the relationship between the regional and the universal Refugee Convention, emphasising the primacy of the latter and the complementary character of the former. The OAU, in its preamble,

> [r]ecogniz[es] that the United Nations Convention of 28 July 1951, as modified by the Protocol of 31 January 1967, constitutes the basic and universal instrument relating to the status of refugees and reflects the deep concern of States for refugees and their desire to establish common standards for their treatment[22]

and underlines:

> that the efficiency of the measures recommended by the present Convention to solve the problem of refugees in Africa necessitates close and continuous collaboration between the Organization of African Unity and the Office of the United Nations High Commissioner for Refugees.[23]

19 The Arab Convention, adopted in 1994 by the League of Arab States, has still not been ratified.

20 See more on the discussion in UNHCR: Sharpe, 'The 1969 OAU Refugee Convention and the Protection of People fleeing Armed Conflict and Other Situations of Violence in the Context of Individual Refugee Status Determination' (UN Doc. PPLA/2013/01, 2013).

21 UN Charter, Chapter VIII on Regional Arrangements.

22 1969 OAU Convention, Preamble, para. 9.

23 1969 OAU Convention, Preamble, para. 11.

The OAU Council of Ministers emphasised, furthermore, their attempt to adapt a regional specific instrument and not a universal replacement: "[T]he African instrument should govern the specifically African aspects of the refugee problem and it should therefore be the effective regional complement [...]"[24]

Comparably, the Cartagena Declaration, in its preamble,[25] refers to the protection regime as established by the 1951 Convention and the 1967 Protocol, as well as the outstanding role of the UNHCR as the Office responsible for pursuing the protection of refugees in Latin America. The following conclusions of the Colloquium in part III firstly acknowledge the status of the 1951 Convention and the Protocol by calling all remaining countries to facilitate the application by adopting or revising their respective national laws and procedures and to harmonise those laws and procedures with the principles and criteria of the universal instrument.[26] Furthermore, they call upon Latin American countries to ensure the ratification of the instrument and/or to withdraw existing reservations so as not to limit its scope of application. Only then, following this confirmation of the position of the 1951 Convention and the 1967 Protocol and reflecting on the special characteristics of Latin American displacement, the Declaration encourages the signatories to reflect upon a broader, extended refugee definition.[27]

From both texts, as well as their drafting contexts, one can determine that the regional instruments were designed as complementary instruments to supplement, but not replace, the 1951 Convention. Their focus on persons fleeing generalised violence is therefore no indication that the 1951 Convention itself was considered inapplicable in the context of violence or conflict per se. Also, in this regard, the UNHCR's guidance for status determination holds that

> The criteria for refugee status in the 1951 Convention need to be interpreted in such a manner that individuals or groups of persons who meet these criteria are duly recognized and protected under that instrument. Only when an asylum-seeker is found not to meet the refugee criteria in the 1951 Convention should broader international protection criteria as contained in UNHCR's mandate and regional instruments be examined.[28]

The effectiveness of the regional extended refugee instruments and the implementation of the obligations is subject to criticism, as is the actual scope of

24 'Resolution on the Adoption of a Draft Convention on the Status of Refugees in Africa, Addis Ababa, 31 October - 4 November 1966' (CM/Res.88 (IVV), 1966), at preamble.

25 See Part II, paragraphs (a)-(p).

26 See Part III of the Cartagena Declaration, paragraphs 1, 2, 3, 8, 17.

27 See Part III, Conclusion I, II, III.

28 United Nations High Commissioner for Refugees, 'UNHCR Eligibility Guidelines for Assessing the International Protection Needs of Asylum-seekers from Afghanistan' (UN Doc. HCR/EG/AFG/13/01, 2013), at 7.

protection attached to the status.[29] Furthermore, displacement realities in Africa and Asia are distinct from those in Europe creating different drafting histories for the respective Conventions. Nonetheless, their codification of extended refugee definitions illustrates the legal differences with regard to the universal instrument and offers an overview and inventory of the existing various legal approaches to conflict-induced displacement.

The regional instruments and varying state practice of countries of origin, transit and host countries constitute the broader framework of refugee protection. Meanwhile, the context of conflict adds additional layers of complexity and uncertainty to the interpretation of the pertinent instruments. What they all have in common, however, is that the UNHCR plays a prominent role in their interpretation in particular and their application in general.

2.3 UNHCR – the mechanism of implementation and its position on persons fleeing conflict

The UNHCR is the designated UN organ with responsibility for refugee protection matters, both in terms of operations and legal oversight. Since its establishment, the Office has expanded both institutionally and in regards to its protection mandate.[30] This expansion is reflected in the Office's position towards persons fleeing conflict. When considering what influence the UNHCR can exert over states and their interpretation of the refugee law instruments, one firstly has to consider the legal basis for the UNHCR's authority to act.

The Statute of the Office enshrines the mandate of UNHCR as well as some of the obligations of states to cooperate. Additional obligations are contained in the UN Charter, the 1951 Convention itself and the other regional refugee instruments. In the following, firstly, the general mandate of the UNHCR, relevant for conflict-induced displacement, is laid out, as this is the legal basis of the Office's engagement in interpretative processes. Secondly, to establish a basis for the relationship between the UNHCR and states, the obligations to cooperate with the Office are analysed, in order to evaluate the influence that the UNHCR

29Sharpe, Marina, 'Engaging with Refugee Protection? The Organization of African Unity and African Union since 1963' (UNHCR Research Paper No 226, 2011). Rankin, Micah B., 'Extending the Limits or Narrowing Down the Scope? Deconstructing the OAU Refugee Definition Thirty Years on', 21 *South African Journal of Human Rights* (2005) 406, at 430f. Edwin Odhiambo-Abuya, E., 'Past Reflections, Future Insights: African Asylum Law and Policy in Historical Perspective', 19 *International Journal of Refugee Law* (2007) 51. Davies, Sara E., 'The Asian Rejection? International Refugee Law in Asia', 52 *Australian Journal of Politics & History* (2006) 562.

30 In the ECOSOC key document "A Study of Statelessness", the main elements of the later drafted 1951 Convention, which were taken over by pre-war predecessors, were carved out, including the assumption that the provision of status is not a standalone pillar of refugee protection: "*The conferment of a status is not sufficient in itself to regularize the standing of stateless persons and bring them into the orbit of law; they must also be linked to an independent organ* which would to some extent make up for the absence of national protection [...]", (emphasis added by the author) Chapter 2 (1), United Nations Economic and Social Council, 'A Study of Statelessness' (UN Doc. E/1112, E/1112/Add.1, 1949), at 56.

can exert over states, especially when interpreting the terms of the Convention. This evaluation provides clarity on the legal nature of UNHCR's output. Only then, the evolution of the UNHCR's position concerning persons fleeing conflict is brought into focus. While the Office has clearly included persons fleeing conflict under its operational umbrella, its legal assessment concerning conflict-induced displacement has changed over time. The UNHCR has made substantial revisions which are reflected in its different guidance documents, such as the Handbook, Notes on International Protection and the Eligibility Guidelines. The subsequent chapter, therefore, analyses the Office's legal and policy development concerning persons fleeing conflict under the 1951 Convention definition of refugee. In these documents, the (changing) position of the Office towards the application of the Convention for persons fleeing conflict is illustrated.

2.3.1 The nature of the UNHCR

The UNHCR is a subsidiary organ of the UN and was created to advance the goals set forth in the UN Charter. The humanitarian and non-political Office[31] has been established by a UN principal organ, the United Nations General Assembly (UNGA), in accordance with Articles 7 (2) and 22 of the UN Charter and generally remains under its principal's authority and control.[32] Its powers and authority in refugee protection derive from its own founding Statute, as adopted by the UNGA, as well as responsibilities acquired later. Although a subsidiary organ of the UN and despite the fact that the Secretary General retains competencies such as to ensure proper administration,[33] the UNHCR has considerable independence, including through its almost independent budget, which is mainly based on voluntary contributions, and its own working secretariat. The authority to negotiate and conclude international treaties directly with single or multiple states further illustrates its semi-autonomous character.[34]

31 Paragraph 2 of the UNHCR Statute.

32 UN Charter, Article 7 (1): "There are established as principal organs of the United Nations: a General Assembly, a Security Council, an Economic and Social Council, a Trusteeship Council, an International Court of Justice and a Secretariat. (2) Such subsidiary organs as may be found necessary may be established in accordance with the present Charter", Article 22 "The General Assembly may establish such subsidiary organs as it deems necessary for the performance of its functions." United Nations Organisation, *Official Records of the General Assembly, Ninth Session, Annexes, Agenda Item 67* (1954), available online at http://unbisnet.un.org:8080/ipac20/ipac.jsp?go_sort_limit.x=5&go_sort_limit.y=5&npp=50&ipp=20&spp=20&profile=bib&aspect=alpha&term=General+Assembly.+Official+Records.+Annexes&index=YTIAUAL&uindex=&oper=&session=J4871B85T9373.13437&menu=search&aspect=alpha&npp=50&ipp=20&spp=20&profile =bib&ri=1&source=%7E%21horizon&sort=3100053 (last visited 1 August 2018), at 13.

33 UNHCR Statute, para. 13, 15 (c), 17, 18, 21, 22.

34 Feller, Erika and Klug, Anja, 'Refugees, United Nations High Commissioner for (UNHCR)' (Max Planck Encyclopedia of Public International Law, 2013). In particular, as both the Statute, in para. 8 (a), as well as the Convention in Article 31 (1), assign the Office a role in the further evolvement of refugee law, see also Goodwin-Gill, Guy S., 'Refugee Identity and Protection's Fading Prospects', in F. Nicholson and P. M. Twomey (eds.), *Refugee Rights and Realities: Evolving International Concepts and Regimes* (Cambridge University Press, 1999), at 132.

2.3.2 UNHCR's protection mandate

The UNGA, as a principal organ of the UN, delegates the task of refugee protection to the UNHCR, its subsidiary organ established solely for this purpose. The Office's mandate and the resulting field of cooperation contains two main functions: to protect refugees and to promote sustainable solutions. Paragraph 1 of the UNHCR Statute enshrines these functions:

> the United Nations High Commissioner for Refugees, acting under the authority of the General Assembly, shall assume the function of providing international protection, under the auspices of the United Nations, to refugees who fall within the scope of the present Statute and of seeking permanent solutions for the problem of refugees.[35]

The mandate and focus of the Office have grown and expanded since its creation in the 1950s, adapting to the new challenges arising in refugee protection, concerning persons in need and expanding geographically. Furthermore, the protection mandate includes a variety of tasks. While the Office's first focus was on the resettlement of the Second World War refugees, the provision of material assistance in developing countries beyond Europe shaped the end of the 1950s and early 1960s. The UNGA has repeatedly authorised the UNHCR to establish various budgeting programmes, including emergency funds, and to lend its good offices to address situations arising in different countries, primarily following the decolonisation processes in Africa.[36] Since then, the UNHCR has further expanded, addressing newly erupting or stagnating wider displacement issues around the world, including those in Europe since the 1990s and the conflict in the former Yugoslavia as well as more recently.[37]

The Office tackles its protection mandate in a twofold manner, consisting of its operational functions and of doctrinal oversight over the pertinent legal framework. The core protection function encompasses tasks ranging from "ensuring the basic rights of refugees, and increasingly their physical safety and security"[38] and "securing their admission, asylum, and respect for basic human rights [...]",[39]

35 1950 UNHCR Statute, para. 6 A (II).

36 Feller, Erika and Klug, Anja, *supra* note 34.

37 *Ibid.* See more also United Nations High Commissioner for Refugees, *Partnership: An Operations Management Handbook for UNHCR's Partners* (2003), available online at http://spanish.careemergencytoolkit.org/Assets/Files/cae7a393-d68f-46c6-bc08-cad16ba8dc61.pdf (last visited 1 August 2018), at 5f.

38 United Nations General Assembly, 'Note on International Protection' (UN Doc. A/AC.96/930, 2000b), at para. 2. United Nations General Assembly, 'Note on International Protection' (UN Doc. A/AC.96/830, 1994a), at para. 12.

39 United Nations General Assembly, *supra* note 38, at para. 9. United Nations General Assembly, *supra* note 38, at para. 12.

to finding and providing for durable solutions.[40] Paragraph 8 of the UNHCR Statute lays out a non-exhaustive list of protection tasks, which reflect the UNHCR's primary responsibilities such as the promotion of refugee law treaties and special agreements, supervision and assistance in developing national laws, advancing durable solutions and assisting in their implementation.[41]

In contrast to other international organisations, the UNHCR is authorised to "promote the conclusion and ratification of international conventions for the protection of refugees", as listed firstly under paragraph 8 (a) of its Statute. As such, it has an overall role in the development of international refugee law.[42] The concrete design of this function is mirrored in the involvement of the Office in the drafting and conclusion of regional refugee treaties, amendment procedures, the interaction with courts and determining authorities, all of which are discussed further below.

Key terminology, such as "supervising the application of the Convention" in paragraph 8 (a), remains undetermined, which can lead to uncertainty around the given tasks of the Office. On the other hand, the open and future-orientated phrasing of Articles 8 and 9 are also the basis for any expanding role and activities taken on by the Office.[43] In particular, the UNHCR Executive Committee has prioritised and, according to protection needs, clarified tasks falling under

40 United Nations High Commissioner for Refugees, *Framework for Durable Solutions for Refugees and Persons of Concern* (2003), available online at http://www.refworld.org/docid/4124b6a04.html (last visited 1 August 2018). United Nations High Commissioner for Refugees, 'Finding Durable Solutions' (UNHCR GLOBAL APPEAL 2014–2015).

41 "8. The High Commissioner shall provide for the protection of refugees falling under the competence of his Office by:
- a Promoting the conclusion and ratification of international conventions for the protection of refugees, supervising their application and proposing amendments thereto;
- b Promoting through special agreements with governments the execution of any measures calculated to improve the situation of refugees and to reduce the number requiring protection;
- c Assisting governmental and private efforts to promote voluntary repatriation or assimilation within new national communities;
- d Promoting the admission of refugees, not excluding those in the most destitute categories, to the territories of States;
- e Endeavouring to obtain permission for refugees to transfer their assets and especially those necessary for their resettlement;
- f Obtaining from governments information concerning the number and conditions of refugees in their territories and the laws and regulations concerning them;
- g Keeping in close touch with the governments and inter-governmental organizations concerned;
- h Establishing contact in such manner as he may think best with private organizations dealing with refugee questions;
- i Facilitating the co-ordination of the efforts of private organizations concerned with the welfare of refugees." Paragraph 9 expands the list of tasks to include competences that are to be determined in the future (...).

42 Feller, Erika and Klug, Anja, *supra* note 34. UNHCR: ExCom, *Conclusion No. 51 (XXXIX) Promotion and Dissemination of Refugee Law* (1988) (last visited 1 August 2018). UNHCR: ExCom, *Conclusion No. 87 (L) - General* (1999) (last visited 1 August 2018).

43 "[F]rom the beginning the practice of the UNHCR has been to ignore the obscurities of para. 8 and to rely instead on the broad phrasing of the paragraph and the general tenor of the Statute

the Office's mandate.[44] The UNGA has furthermore expanded the Office's mandate with subsequent resolutions. One might therefore argue that the open phrasing of the Statute and its terms are also representative of the Office's role, being a tool of states on the one hand and an advocate for refugees and a surrogate for lacking state protection on the other. In regard to the legal and policy focus this chapter pursues, the supervisory functions[45] of the Office are of the greatest relevance for the interpretation of refugee law matters. Its supervisory role encompasses, most prominently, the interpretation of the 1951 Convention as well as monitoring and intervening in refugee protection. These tasks may be considered an interference with domestic legal and policy frameworks and are thus highly politicised.

2.3.2.1 UNHCR, the states and refugee law

A first indication of the UNHCR's influential position vis-à-vis states is found in the relationship between the UNHCR, the 1951 Convention and the Convention's state parties. In contrast to the auspices of the Office of the High Commissioner for Human Rights (OHCHR) which oversees the nine core human rights conventions, the UNHCR was established prior to the 1951 Convention. States became contracting parties to the Convention, consenting to work together with the already established refugee protection Office.[46] To bind states to cooperate with the UNHCR and ultimately follow its interpretation, it is necessary to identify and assess the value of clear legally binding provisions that entail a duty to cooperate.[47]

---

to support its contention that international protection should be interpreted broadly", Holborn, Louise W., *Refugees, a Problem Of Our Time* (Scarecrow Press, 1975), at 100.

44 Examples are, UNHCR: ExCom Standing Committee, *Overview of Regional Developments (October to December 1995)* (1996), available online at http://www.unhcr.org/3ae68d2c0.pdf (last visited 1 August 2018), at para. 2f. United Nations General Assembly, *supra* note 38, at paras. 10–29. UNHCR: ExCom, *Conclusion No. 29 (XXXIV) General* (1983), available online at http://www.refworld.org/pdfid/4b28bf1f2.pdf (last visited 1 August 2018), at paras. b and j. UNHCR: ExCom, *Conclusion No. 22 (XXXII) Protection of Asylum-Seekers in Situations of Large- Scale Influx* (1981), available online at http://www.refworld.org/pdfid/4b28bf1f2.pdf (last visited 1 August 2018), at para. III.

45 See more on the supervisory function in subchapter 2.3.2.2.

46 For a detailed analysis, Kälin, Walter, 'Supervising the 1951 Convention on the Status of Refugees: Article 35 and Beyond' (UNHCR Background paper commissioned for the 2nd Expert Roundtable in the context of the 50th anniversary of the 1951 Convention, 2001).

47 To exert its influence over the state parties, the UNHCR can fall back on state obligations arising from different legal sources, including those arising from international treaties, or bilateral agreements. In this regard, various agreements can be adopted including on transfer arrangements. United Nations High Commissioner for Refugees, *Guidance Note on Bilateral and/or Multilateral Transfer Arrangements of Asylum-Seekers* (2013), available online at http://www.refworld.org/pdfid/51af82794.pdf (last visited 1 August 2018). For examples of repatriation, see among others the United Nations High Commissioner for Refugees, Government of Pakistan & Government of Afghanistan, *Tripartite Repatriation Agreement between UNHCR and the Governments of Pakistan and Afghanistan* (2003), available online

2.3.2.1.1 THE DUTY TO COOPERATE BY VIRTUE OF THE UNHCR STATUTE AND THE 1951 CONVENTION

For the fulfilment of the functions of UNHCR, the Statute[48] contains the states' primary obligation to cooperate with the Office. UNGA Resolution 428 (V) adopting the UNHCR Statute on 14 December 1950, a formal expression of the UN member states' opinion, reflects the general obligation of states "to cooperate with the United Nations High Commissioner for Refugees in the performance of its functions".[49] Apart from this broad and general terminology, this duty is not elaborated further in the Statute.

More concrete, specific and binding state obligations to cooperate with UNHCR are enshrined in the pertinent and legally binding refugee treaties. The obligations of interest for this book are, however, not those between states, but those between states and the UNHCR, as these lay the foundations for the Office's influence in state implementation of the Convention. Of considerable interest is the preamble of the 1951 Convention, paragraph 6,

> the grant of asylum may place unduly heavy burden on certain countries, and that a satisfactory solution of a problem of which the United Nations has recognized the international scope and nature cannot therefore be achieved without international cooperation,

which, in relation to the obligation to cooperate, states:

> that the United Nation's High Commissioner for Refugees is charged with the task of supervising international conventions providing for the protection of refugees, and recognizing that the effective co-ordination of measures taken to deal with the problem will depend upon the co-operation of States with the High Commissioner.

Article 35 (1) of the 1951 Convention and, respectively, Article II (1) of the 1967 Protocol then codify the single primary obligation towards the UNHCR,

---

at http://www.refworld.org/docid/55e6a5324.html (last visited 1 August 2018). Agreements for resettlement operations, among others, the United Nations High Commissioner for Refugees, Government of Romania & International Organization for Migration, *Agreement between the Government of Romania and the Office of the United Nations High Commissioner for Refugees and the International Organization for Migration Regarding Temporary Evacuation to Romania of Persons in Urgent Need of International Protection and their Onward Resettlement* (2008), available online at http://www.refworld.org/docid/4a7c221c2.html (last visited 1 August 2018).

48 A general obligation to cooperate with the UN arises from the UN Charter itself. Concerning the obligation to cooperate and assist with specialised UN organs, see Karrenstein, Daniela, *Der Menschenrechtsrat der Vereinten Nationen* (Mohr Siebeck, 2011), at 69ff. Article 56 lays down this duty, Grahl-Madsen, Atle, *Commentary of the Refugee Convention 1951 (Articles 2–11, 13–37)* (1997), available online at http://www.refworld.org/docid/4785ee9d2.html (last visited 1 August 2018), at 252.

49 United Nations General Assembly, 'Resolution 428 (V)' (UN Doc. A/RES/428 (V), 1950),

which builds the legal basis of cooperation with and obligations owed by the state parties:

> the Contracting States undertake to co-operate within the Office of the United Nations High Commissioner for Refugees, or any other agency of the United Nations which may succeed it, in the exercise of its functions, and shall in particular facilitate its duty of supervising the application of the provisions of this Convention.

The obligation contains a broad and clear obligation to cooperate, albeit one that is openly phrased. The awareness of states and their willingness to codify very flexible and evolutive duties towards the UNHCR are demonstrated in the Convention's *travaux préparatoires*.[50] The original draft of Article 35 (1) contained the obligation "to facilitate the work of UNHCR", a phrase which was heavily debated upon, due to the weak phrasing and, relatedly, the weak obligation it would create.[51] The US delegation to the Conference of Plenipotentiaries introduced the version which was later codified[52] to "remove the hesitant tone" in the obligation and strengthen the states' obligation towards the UNHCR.[53] The Assistant High Commissioner for Protection at the Global Consultations Conference summed up that the Article consequently obliges states:

> (1) not to act in any way that might undermine the UNHCR's international protection function towards such people and (2) to cooperate fully with the UNHCR in discharging its international protection mandate, including monitoring and oversight responsibilities related to its supervisory role.[54]

With regard to the important aspect of expansion of the Office's protection mandate, one can state that the general obligation to cooperate with the UNHCR in

50 On the discussion surrounding the duty to cooperate with the future Office, see United Nations General Assembly, 'Conference of Plenipotentiaries on the Status of Refugees and Stateless Persons: Summary Record of the Twenty-fifth Meeting' (UN Doc. A/CONF.2/SR.25, 1951).

51 Draft Article 30, reprinted in Weis, Paul, *supra* note 1, at 355.

52 For a further discussion, see also United Nations General Assembly, 'Conference of Plenipotentiaries on the Status of Refugees and Stateless Persons: Summary Record of the Twenty-seventh Meeting' (UN Doc. A/CONF.2/SR.27, 1951), at 10–16. United Nations General Assembly, 'Conference of Plenipotentiaries on the Status of Refugees and Stateless Persons: Summary Record of the 2nd Meeting' (UN Doc. A/CONF.2/SR.2, 1951), at 17.

53 Weis, Paul, *supra* note 1, at 356.

54 Türk, Volker, 'The UNHCR's Role in Supervising International Protection Standards in the Context of its Mandate', in J. C. Simeon (ed.), *The UNHCR and the Supervision of International Refugee Law* (Cambridge University Press, 2013), 39, at 48. An affirmation of this role was given at the 2002 Declaration of State Parties, Ministerial Meeting of States Parties to the 1951 Convention and/or Its 1967 Protocol relating to the Status of Refugee, 'Declaration of States Parties to the 1951 Convention and or Its 1967 Protocol relating to the Status of Refugees' (UN Doc. HCR/MMSP/2001/09, 2002). UNHCR: ExCom, *Agenda for Protection* (2002), available online at http://www.unhcr.org/en-us/excom/standcom/3d12f1982/agenda-protection.html (last visited 1 August 2018), at para. 8f.

the light of Article 35 is codified in a broad manner and is not limited to specific tasks listed in the article. The reference to the UNHCR's functions – "in the exercise of its functions" – already gave way to a potentially changing role for the Office, which depends on the future protection needs identified. This sentence indicates that states were aware of the Office's strong role and the necessity to adapt to future changes in displacement realities. This changing role includes the potential for expanding obligations towards a broader set of beneficiaries, i.e. persons of concern to UNHCR who are nonetheless outside the group of Convention refugees. Both commentaries by Grahl-Madsen and Zimmermann/Mahler highlight that in order to enable UNHCR to fulfil its mandate, the duty to cooperate refers to the Office's function and its "persons of concern", "irrespective of the fact that their own obligations under the 1951 Convention and the 1967 Protocol are predicated on a categorical smaller group of beneficiaries".[55] The obligation codified in Article 35, therefore, goes beyond the narrow personal scope of the refugee definition enshrined in the 1951 Convention. As such and in regard to the specific focus of this book, it broadens both the obligation to cooperate with respect to the UNHCR's protection mandate, including persons fleeing conflict, and the obligations owed to a group or individuals identified as being of concern to the UNHCR but not the more exclusive group of Convention refugees.

However, generally, the obligations created are phrased broadly. They do not include specific aspects of cooperation or references to the role of the UNHCR concerning the interpretation of the Convention. As such, they must be evaluated as rather weak state obligations to cooperate; they themselves do not offer a specific basis for the binding interpretative aspirations of the UNHCR.

2.3.2.1.2 THE UNHCR AND THE REGION – CONSIDERING ITS ROLE FOR REGIONAL REFUGEE LAW INSTRUMENTS

The supervisory function of the Office is not limited to the 1951 Convention. The regional instruments contain similar obligations, as phrased in the preamble of the OAU Convention:

> [c]onvinced that the efficiency of the measures recommended by the present Convention to solve the problem of refugees in Africa necessitates close and continuous collaboration between the Organisation of African Unity and the Office of the United Nations High Commissioner for Refugees

and Article VIII:

> para. 1 Member States shall co-operate with the Office of the United Nations High Commissioner for Refugees.

55 Grahl-Madsen, Atle, *supra* note 48, at 254. And Zieck, Marjoleine, 'Art. 35/Art. II', in A. Zimmermann (ed.), *The 1951 Convention Relating to the Status of Refugees and its 1967 Protocol: A Commentary* (Oxford University Press, 2011), at 1492.

Paragraph II(e) of the Cartagena Declaration includes a comparable recommendation to cooperate and "[t]o support the work performed by the United Nations High Commissioner for Refugees (UNHCR) in Central America and to establish direct co-ordination machinery to facilitate the fulfilment of his mandate". This duty to cooperate is again phrased in an open manner, as it refers to the states' obligation to facilitate the Office's fulfilment of the mandate.[56]

2.3.2.2 The supervisory functions of the UNHCR

The interplay of the UNHCR, states and the pertinent refugee and asylum law treaties concerning the Office's supervisory role is rooted primarily in the Statute's paragraph 8, mostly subparagraphs (a), (b), (f) and (g).[57] The Statute in this regard corresponds to and elaborates on Articles in the pertinent refugee and asylum law treaties, particularly the aforementioned obligation of Article 35 (1) and (2).[58]

The UNHCR is tasked, most importantly, with promoting international refugee law, supervising its application and proposing further developments, and reporting on interactions or interventions with states. It may provide consultation on asylum applications and procedures, in which it is entitled to intervene and submit observations, obtain access to files and decisions[59] as well as to the applicants themselves; the latter activity is regulated either by domestic laws or administrative practice.[60] The influence that the UNHCR has exerted since the early days of its establishment includes these interventions in individual cases and specific country situations. This recognition of the UNHCR's specific role deviates from that of most human rights monitoring bodies. Establishing focus on individual cases had to be negotiated in the face of state resistance. Classically, human rights bodies function as expert committees and not as fora for state delegations. Further, refugee law does not create any institutionalised reporting or enforcement mechanisms. The UNHCR, in this regard, is a body *sui generis*. Its strong field presence allows the Office to observe and report on state performances and, in the Annual Note on International Protection, observed trends and concerns are presented to the Executive Committee by the

56 Reference to aligned duties for the EU instruments is given in the respective sections.

57 "a Promoting the conclusion and ratification of international conventions for the protection of refugees, supervising their application and proposing amendments thereto; [...]
b Promoting through special agreement with Governments the execution [...]
f Obtaining from Government the information concerning [...] the laws and regulations
g Keeping in close touch with Governments and inter-governmental organizations concerned."

58 Kälin, Walter, *supra* note 46, at 7.

59 UNHCR: ExCom Standing Committee, 'Progress Report on Informal Consultations on the Provision of International Protection to All Who Need It' (UN Doc. EC/47/SC/CRP.27, 1997), at para. 7.

60 Kälin, Walter, 'Supervising the 1951 Convention Relating to the Status of Refugees: Article 35 and beyond', in E. Feller, V. Türk and F. Nicholson (eds.), *Refugee Protection in International Law: UNHCR's Global Consultations on International Protection* (Cambridge University Press, 2003), 613, at 648f.

Office. Each state, in turn, is obliged to provide the Office with information and statistical data for its performance. While it is part of the UN with the Executive Committee as a governing Committee made up of states' representatives, the Office itself employs expert staff for refugee matters. Additionally, the overall objective of the Office is the protection of the refugee, acting primarily when states have failed to do so. As such, the Office does not act as an intergovernmental organisation, i.e. as a representation of states and their official positions, but as an advocate for refugees. "UNHCR does not have to be invited to become involved in protection matters [which renders] UNHCR's mandate distinct, even unique, within the international system."[61]

A major part of the Office's workload revolves around its legal consultative role. With considerable effort, which can be considered both as part of its consultative function but also under a broader advocacy title, the UNHCR advises states, i.e. governments, parliaments and determining authorities, on legislation.[62] This mostly takes the form of comments on draft or enacted legislation and their conformity with international standards.[63] Both individual states and the EU have acknowledged this function of the UNHCR legally in its asylum *acquis*. As an example, Recital 15 of the Qualification Directive (QD) stresses, with equal phrasing in Recital 22 of the Recast QD, the importance of consultations for providing valuable guidance when determining refugee status and procedures: "Consultations with the United Nations High Commissioner for Refugees may provide valuable guidance for Member States when determining refugee status according to Article 1 of the Geneva Convention." More often, the involvement goes further, including substantial involvement in asylum procedures or even the provision of RSD procedures in cooperation with or on behalf of the state.[64]

Another essential 'supervisory' tool of the UNHCR is its court intervention as a third-party *amicus curiae* ('friend of the court')[65]. Interventions and advisory opinions in asylum cases before national and regional courts are one of the primary instruments the UNHCR uses to provide, on the one hand, doc-

61 United Nations General Assembly, *supra* note 38, at para. 71.

62 For a detailed assessment of the guidance instruments, see Hathaway, James C., *The Rights of Refugees under International Law* (Cambridge University Press, 2005), at 113ff.

63 Kälin, Walter, 'Supervising the 1951 Convention Relating to the Status of Refugees: Article 35 and beyond', *supra* note 60, at 648f.

64 See below subchapter 2.3.3.3.

65 The ECtHR is one prominent example that entails a long-standing practice of third party interveners from state governments, international institutions, such as the UNHCR, the European Commission, OHCHR, Organisation for Security and Cooperation in Europe, Council of Europe Commissioner for Human Rights, national human rights institutions or NGOs. For some contemporary cases, see Strasbourg Observers, *Third Party Interventions before the ECtHR: A Rough Guide* (2015), available online at https://strasbourgobservers.com/2015/02/24/third-party-interventions-before-the-ecthr-a-rough-guide (last visited 1 August 2018). Schjatvet, Cecilie and Hestenes og Dramer & Co., 'The making of UNHCR's guidance and its implementation in the national jurisdiction of the United Kingdom, Norway and Sweden' (Research Report for the Norwegian Directorate of Immigration, 2010), at 18.

trinal advice to the courts, potentially to influence legal precedents established by national jurisprudence and, on the other hand, lead the interpretation and implementation of refugee law.[66] In contrast to, for instance, some regional human rights regimes that enforce human rights Conventions' obligations through judicial mechanisms, i.e. the European Court of Human Rights (ECtHR) and the African Court on Human and People's Rights, no comparable international refugee court exists. The dispute settlement procedure through the International Court of Justice (ICJ)[67] is not open to the UNHCR itself but requires a detour through a state party – which has not been done as yet.[68] Therefore, the commonly used judicial tool of the UNHCR to address systemic difficulties is by taking up individual protection cases as a friend of the court. While courts can and have disregarded the UNHCR's position on disputed matters, the Office can again address the same matter in a different court and in a different case. This strategic litigation stimulates the evolution of the interpretation of asylum law principles and makes use of those arguments and cases that underline the UNHCR's protection approach.[69]

The decision to intervene in asylum cases on the national or regional[70] level is taken against the background of the procedural laws of the court in question, its influence both on national (lower) courts and in transnational judicial dialogues[71] while taking into account the available resources within the UNHCR. Requests mostly enter through field offices and regional bureaux to the focal point within the Protection Policy and Legal Advice (PPLA) Section, commonly a senior legal advisor. These are based on internal guidelines,

66 With regard to the EU, the Asylum Procedures Directive (2005/85/EC) states that all EU Members shall permit the UNHCR to "present its view, in the exercise of its supervisory responsibilities under Article 35 of the Geneva Convention, to any competent authorities regarding individual applications for asylum at any stage of the procedure".

67 Article 38 1951 Convention: "Any dispute between Parties to this Convention relating to interpretation or application, which cannot be settled by other means, shall be referred to the International Court of Justice at the request of any one of the parties to the dispute."

68 Only through its primary organ, the General Assembly, the UNHCR could theoretically seek guidance of the ICJ by means of an Advisory Opinion, based on Article 65 Statute of the ICJ and Article 96 UN Charter.

69 "In the same way that domestic courts develop the understanding of the law within their jurisdiction, UNHCR can utilize the best understanding and analysis from all court hearings that deal with the 1951 Convention [...] international refugee law is developed through continual interaction between the courts and those arguing for the asylum seeker", Gilbert, Geoff, 'UNHCR and Courts. Amicus curiae ... sed curia amica est?', 28 *International Journal of Refugee Law* (2016) 623, at 628. Goodwin-Gill, Guy S., 'The Dynamic of International Refugee Law', 25 *International Journal of Refugee Law* (2013) 651, at 657.

70 The CJEU in this regard hampers the direct influence of the UNHCR in procedures based on Article 267 TFEU, as only EU Member States have the right of audience. UNHCR inclusion thus depends on the Member State court referring the preliminary ruling to include UNHCR in its reference.

71 Criteria are the procedural laws of the countries and whether they establish intervention procedures, whether judgments are precedent setting, whether the courts have a practice in referring to external guidance, whether the court's language is widely accessible, such as English.

including the provision of information on the process within the courts, information on the facts and legal questions and an assessment of the importance of the requested intervention and its objective.[72]

The Office regularly exercises its advisory or consultative role in refugee law matters. The more interventional tools of the Office, such as engaging in litigation, however, are much more difficult to implement and, more often than not are confronted with strong state reluctance.[73]

2.3.2.3 The UNHCR's legal and policy guidance

The evolution of the UNHCR's positions concerning the interpretation of the Convention, in particular, sometimes titled the 'UNHCR Doctrine',[74] is manifested not only through interventions in individual cases but more abstractly through the different documents the Office produces. These include documents requested and subsequently adopted by the Executive Committee as well as those produced by the UNHCR itself, such as the Handbook, Guidelines, Notes, and Statements. These different documents are introduced initially and subsequently examined as a mechanism to transport and advance the Office's interpretation of the 1951 Convention in the context of violence and conflict.

The Executive Committee's Conclusions[75] belong to the most influential type of document and mirror the development of the interpretation of refugee instruments and implementation practices around the globe. They are adopted by consensus of the Executive Committee, namely 98 states, most of which are state parties to the Convention and/or Protocol, and have considerable weight in "providing guidance and forging consensus on vital protection policies and practices".[76] With the Executive Committee as the global-intergovernmental forum and their negotiations presented formally as the Conclusions on International Protection, annexed to the High Commissioner's annual report and endorsed by the UNGA, the Conclusions play an important role in the development of

72 Information obtained at PPLA.

73 Kälin, Walter, *supra* note 46, at 7.

74 See for a detailed legal and historical analysis of the development of a UNHCR 'Doctrine' as well as its potential nature as a subsidiary source of international law under Article 38 ICJ Statute, which the author rejects, Lewis, Corinne, *UNHCR and International Refugee Law* (Routledge, 2012), at 60ff.

75 The Executive Committee Programme was established by ECOSOC in R1858 by Resolution 672 (XXV) following a request of the UNGA in Resolution 1166 (XII). It consists of representatives of UN member states and members of specialised agencies. Its Conclusions are adopted at its annual session in Geneva. United Nations General Assembly, 'Rules of Procedure of the Executive Committee of the High Commissioner's Programme' (UN Doc. A/AC.96/187/Rev.8, 2016).

76 The Executive Committee as of 2016 was constituted by 98 member states, 15 observer states, plus 25 other observers. For a list of Committee Members, stand annual session 2016, United Nations High Commissioner for Refugees, *UNHCR Executive Committee of the High Commissioner's Programme Composition for the Period October 2016 – October 2017* (2017), available online at http://www.unhcr.org/excom/scaf/5748082a4/list-members-observers-2016-2017.html (last visited 1 August 2018).

recognised standards. And, since they are adopted by consensus, the Conclusions mirror state practice in some key areas of protection and can be evidence of custom, or the creation of law.[77] The UNHCR plays a pivotal role in the preparation, drafting and direction of the Executive Committee Conclusions. Therefore, they can also be considered as reflecting the standard to which the UNHCR refers when assessing national performances in refugee protection by virtue of Article 35.[78]

Their political significance has been affirmed by the states themselves through their consensus conclusions. "[T]hey are the result of consensus resolutions of the Executive Committee by the representatives of states"[79] and by domestic courts,[80] "Conclusions of the Executive Committee of the UNHCR Programme [...], while not binding upon the Authority, are nonetheless of considerable persuasive authority",[81] and similarly:

> [...] in Article 35 of the Convention the signatory states undertake to cooperate with the [UNHCR] in the performance of its functions and, in particular, to facilitate the discharge of its duty of supervising the application of the Convention. *Accordingly, considerable weight should be given to recommendations of the Executive Committee of the High Commissioner's Program* on issues relating to refugee determination and protection [...].[82]

The Executive Committee's Conclusions, while representative of adopted protection standards, are not legally binding instruments as such. However, this does not render them irrelevant. In legal terms, the question arises whether they might be more than just documents carrying a strong *political* significance. As a reflection of agreed and shared will and practice of a group of states, broader than the actual Member States of the 1951 Convention and the 1967 Protocol, some have claimed that they now possess the character of refugee soft law.[83] The exact nature of soft law, a theoretical concept created by scholars, is still somewhat vague and debated upon, although prominent in some fields of public

77 UNHCR: ExCom, *Conclusion No. 81 (XLVII) General* (1997), available online at http://www.refworld.org/pdfid/4b28bf1f2.pdf (last visited 1 August 2018).

78 Lewis, Corinne, *supra* note 74, at 54.

79 Feller, Erika and Klug, Anja, *supra* note 34.

80 On the inclusion of national jurisprudence in UNHCR policy, Bailliet, Cecilia M., 'National Case Law as a Generator of International Refugee Law. Rectifying an Imbalance within the UNHCR Guidelines on International Protection' (European Society of International Law Conference Series, No. 7, 2014).

81 *Refugee Appeal No. 1/92 Re SA,* New Zealand: Refugee Status Appeals Authority (1992).

82 *Rahaman v. Minister of Citizenship and Immigration, per Evans JA*, 2002 ACWSJ Lexis 1026, Canada: Federal Court of Appeal (2002) (emphasis added by the author).

83 See for a detailed analysis of the Handbook as instrument of refugee soft law, Juss, Satvinder S., 'The UNHCR Handbook and the Interface between 'Soft Law' and 'Hard Law' in International Refugee Law', in S. S. Juss and C. Harvey (eds.), *Contemporary Issues in Refugee Law* (Edward Elgar, 2013).

international law.[84] Some commentators even consider refugee soft law as more influential in practice than the actual refugee law treaties.[85] This opinion seems, at least currently, far-fetched, in particular, due to the importance of the widely ratified, recognised and binding 1951 Convention.[86] They are "recommendations that rest on the consensus of states and thereby assume some authority that may be taken into account in legal proceedings, but whose breach does not constitute a violation of international law in the strict sense […]".[87] The Conclusions can, however, help to generate state practice and might equally be considered as evidence of an emerging custom in the field of customary international law.[88]

Executive Committee Conclusions are but one of several types of documents produced by the Office. The Handbook and Guidelines on International Protection are another major source of reference. In 1977, the Executive Committee itself explicitly requested more guidance for the state parties from the UNHCR:

> [R]equested the Office to consider the possibility of issuing – for the Guidance of Governments – a handbook relating to procedures and criteria for determining refugee status.[89]

84 Reflection of the debate see, Chinkin, Christine M., 'The Challenge of Soft Law. Development and Change in International Law', 38 *International and Comparative Law Quarterly* (1989) 850, at 850. Boyle, A. E., 'Some Reflections on the Relationship of Treaties and Soft Law', 48 *International and Comparative Law Quarterly* (1999) 901, at 902.

85 "Few of the innovations are codified in international law. The public face of international protection of refugees is still the 1951 Convention relating to the Status of Refugees, but by default", Newland, Kathleen, 'Refugee Protection and Assistance', in P. J. Simmons and C. d. Jonge Oudraat (eds.), *Managing Global Issues: Lessons Learned* (Carnegie Endowment for International Peace, 2001), 508, at 531. "[S]oft laws offer […] the inestimable advantage of being vague enough in formulation and non-binding enough in effect to find acceptance easily and pass without too much opposition. The process of practice and repetition […] then serves as basis for hard law." Alborzi, Mohammad R., *Evaluating the Effectiveness of International Refugee Law* (Brill, 2006), at 274. Garlick, Madeline, 'International Protection in Court. The Asylum Jurisprudence of the Court of Justice of the EU and UNHCR', 34 *Refugee Survey Quarterly* (2015) 107, at 113.

86 Schachter, Oscar, *International Law in Theory and Practice* (Martinus Nijhoff Publishers/Kluwer Academic Publishers, 1991), at 99.

87 Kälin, Walter, *How Hard is Soft Law? The Guiding Principles on Internal Displacement and the Need for a Normative Framework. Round Table Meeting, CUNY Graduate Center* (2001), available online at https://www.brookings.edu/wp-content/uploads/2016/06/20011219.pdf (last visited 1 August 2018), at 6.

88 The *North Sea Continental Shelf Cases (Federal Republic of Germany v. Denmark; Federal Republic of Germany v. Netherlands)*, [1969], International Court of Justice (1969), at 42. Corkery, Allison, 'The Contribution of the UNHCR Executive Committee to the Development of International Refugee Law', 13 *Australian International Law Journal* (2006) 97, at 98ff.

89 UNHCR: ExCom, *Conclusion No. 8 (XXVIII) Determination of Refugee Status* (1977), available online at http://www.refworld.org/pdfid/4b28bf1f2.pdf (last visited 1 August 2018), at para. (g).

Rather than the Office itself putting forward interpretations of the Convention, guidance was requested by the state parties, seeking guidance on the interpretation of refugee treaty law.[90] The result was the Handbook on Procedures and Guidelines (hereafter the Handbook), published in 1979, and its revision in 1992. The Handbook can be understood as a tool to ensure states' endorsement for doctrinal positions developed by the Office on the Convention definition criteria and the determination of refugee status.[91] Since its revised version was published in 1992, the Handbook has not been subject to change, except for updated annexes, in order to preserve its integrity.

In addition to the Handbook, states requested even further guidance. The Executive Committee required the UNHCR

> to produce complementary guidelines to its Handbook on Procedures and Criteria for Determining Refugee Status, drawing on applicable international legal standards, on State practice, on jurisprudence and using, as appropriate, the inputs from the debates in the Global Consultations' expert roundtable discussions.[92]

The Division of International Protection (DIP), as the responsible section of the UNHCR Headquarters, has followed this request. The Office considers these documents as output arising out of Article 35 of the Convention, thereby remaining within the realm of state parties' obligations.[93] For instance, the introduction to the Eligibility Guidelines reads:

> UNHCR issues its Eligibility Guidelines pursuant to its responsibility to promote the accurate interpretation and application of the above-mentioned refugee criteria as envisaged by Article 8 of its Statute, Article 35 of the 1951 Convention and Article II of its 1967 Protocol and based on the expertise it has developed over several years in eligibility and refugee status determination.[94]

90 Regarding the Handbook, "It is not clear what is 'law' here. [...] The manner in which the handbook was written, and at whose instance, and for what ends, forces us to ask: what is the nature of the 'rule', that is being put out by the UNHCR? Is it being followed? Should it be followed? The answer is wholly unclear", Juss, Satvinder S., *supra* note 83. Regarding the Handbook and ExCom Conclusions: "[...] it is, as it seems to me, neither necessary nor desirable that this House should attempts to interpret an instrument of this character which is of no binding force either in municipal or international law". On the general matter, Hathaway, James C., *supra* note 62, at 116.

91 See in this regard, Lewis, Corinne, *supra* note 74, at 68.

92 UNHCR: ExCom, *supra* note 54, at Part III, Goal 1 Point 6.

93 Schjatvet, Cecilie and Hestenes og Dramer & Co., *supra* note 65, at 16.

94 Among others, United Nations High Commissioner for Refugees, *UNHCR's Eligibility Guidelines for Assessing the International Protection Needs of Iraqi Asylum-seekers* (2009), available online at http://www.refworld.org/docid/49f569cf2.html (last visited 1 August 2018), at 2.

Different Guidance Notes or Background Notes are continuously published, starting with the first one in 1995 on Agents of Persecution, most of them concerning matters relating to the refugee definition and its evaluation.[95] The Global Consultations process of 2000–2002, which took place in close cooperation with experts from academia and practice, NGOs and other international and regional organisations, as well as states' representatives, was an extensive consultative process that initiated further publications by the DIP, clarifying particular interpretative issues, such as the scope of *non-refoulement* and the interpretation and requirements of internal flight alternatives (IFAs). The outcome of this 18-month, inter-state and inter-organisational process was the Agenda for Protection, endorsed by the Executive Committee and welcomed by the UNGA in 2002. Again, as a non-binding instrument, the Agenda reflects the broad consensus of states in cooperation with the Office on actions and agreed goals in refugee protection.[96]

Based on its formulated Agenda of Protection, the UNHCR publishes the Guidelines on International Protection to complement its Handbook, firstly on Gender-Related Persecution (No. 1) and Membership of a Particular Group (No. 2).[97] These guidelines do not assess specific factual situations but

95 Among others, United Nations High Commissioner for Refugees, *UNHCR Guidance Note on Refugee Claims Relating to Sexual Orientation and Gender Identity* (2008), available online at http://www.refworld.org/docid/48abd5660.html (last visited 1 August 2018). United Nations High Commissioner for Refugees, *UNHCR Note on the Interpretation of Article 1E of the 1951 Convention relating to the Status of Refugees* (2009), available online at http://www.refworld.org/docid/49c3a3d12.html (last visited 1 August 2018). United Nations High Commissioner for Refugees, *Guidance Note on Refugee Claims Relating to Female Genital Mutilation* (2009), available online at http://www.refworld.org/docid/4a0c28492.html (last visited 1 August 2018). United Nations High Commissioner for Refugees, *Guidance Note on Refugee Claims Relating to Victims of Organized Gangs* (2010), available online at http://www.refworld.org/docid/4bb21fa02.html (last visited 1 August 2018). United Nations High Commissioner for Refugees, *supra* note 47.

96 United Nations High Commissioner for Refugees, *Agenda for Protection* (2003), available online at http://www.unhcr.org/protection/globalconsult/3e637b194/agenda-protection-third-edition.html (last visited 1 August 2018), at 9.

97 United Nations High Commissioner for Refugees, 'Guidelines on International Protection No. 3: Cessation of Refugee Status under Article 1C(5) and (6) of the 1951 Convention relating to the Status of Refugees (the "Ceased Circumstances" Clauses)' (HCR/GIP/03/03, 2003). United Nations High Commissioner for Refugees, 'Guidelines on International Protection No. 4: "Internal Flight or Relocation Alternative" Within the Context of Article 1A(2) of the 1951 Convention and/or 1967 Protocol Relating to the Status of Refugees' (HCR/GIP/03/04, 2003). United Nations High Commissioner for Refugees, 'Guidelines on International Protection No. 5: Application of the Exclusion Clauses: Article 1F of the 1951 Convention relating to the Status of Refugees' (HCR/GIP/03/05, 2003). United Nations High Commissioner for Refugees, 'Guidelines on International Protection No. 6: Religion-Based Refugee Claims under Article 1A(2) of the 1951 Convention and/or the 1967 Protocol relating to the Status of Refugees' (HCR/GIP/04/06, 2004). United Nations High Commissioner for Refugees, 'Guidelines on International Protection No. 7: The Application of Article 1A(2) of the 1951 Convention and/or 1967 Protocol Relating to the Status of Refugees to Victims of Trafficking and Persons At Risk of Being Trafficked' (HCR/GIP/06/07, 2006). United Nations High Commissioner

exclusively analyse legal interpretative issues. Consultations take place within the UNHCR's relevant sections and units, however, the additional round of external consultations is even more important. The process of drafting involves a broad consultation process both within UNHCR and with leading external scholars, NGOs, the association of national refugee law judges, other UN Agencies such as UNICEF and OHCHR,[98] before finalisation.[99] While, in particular, the Guidelines on International Protection, according to the Assistant High Commissioner for Protection, have "[...] been preceded by an analysis of State practice and an examination of the applicable international legal framework",[100] the other documents could be regarded as simple products of UNHCR expert staff – highly qualified and knowledgeable, but not necessarily a representation of states' positions.

The Eligibility Guidelines are an example of such a product from the Office's expert staff. They encompass interpretations and applications of the refugee definition to a specific country situation and assessments on the legal and factual situation, as well as the wider human rights and human security situation in the country concerned. The overarching objective of the Eligibility Guidelines is to provide recommendations for states and UNHCR officials to handle status determination in accordance with the standards of the Convention and the broader refugee mandate of the Office. In contrast to the Guidelines on International Protection, however, the Eligibility Guidelines are not the result of extensive consultation processes among states and the Office. Rather, they "are researched strictly and are written based on factual evidence provided by UNHCR's global network of field offices and information from independent country specialists, researchers and other sources". They are commonly requested by the Office's staff, NGOs and sometimes courts such as the ECtHR to clarify country-specific considerations.[101]

---

for Refugees, 'Guidelines on International Protection No. 8: Child Asylum Claims under Articles 1(A)2 and 1(F) of the 1951 Convention and/or 1967 Protocol relating to the Status of Refugees' (HCR/GIP/09/08, 2009). United Nations High Commissioner for Refugees, 'Guidelines on International Protection No. 9: Claims to Refugee Status based on Sexual Orientation and/or Gender Identity within the context of Article 1A(2) of the 1951 Convention and/or its 1967 Protocol relating to the Status of Refugees' (HCR/GIP/12/01, 2012). United Nations High Commissioner for Refugees, 'Guidelines on International Protection No. 10: Claims to Refugee Status related to Military Service within the context of Article 1A (2) of the 1951 Convention and/or the 1967 Protocol relating to the Status of Refugees' (UN Doc. HCR/GIP/13/10/Corr. 1, 2013). United Nations General Assembly, 'Guidelines on International Protection No. 11: Prima Facie Recognition of Refugee Status' (HCR/GIP/15/11, 2015).

98 Schjatvet, Cecilie and Hestenes og Dramer & Co., *supra* note 65, at 25.

99 *Id.*, at 24.

100 Türk, Volker, 'Introductory Note to UNHCR Guidelines on International Protection', 15 *International Journal of Refugee Law* (2003) 303, at 303.

101 Schjatvet, Cecilie and Hestenes og Dramer & Co., *supra* note 65, at 35.

As states are not necessarily involved in the development of the Eligibility Criteria, they react to their publication in different ways.[102] One very critical reaction was demonstrated by Eriteria to the UNHCR Eligibility Guidelines on Eritrea of 2009, which stated that the Criteria

> epitomize sloppy, cut-and-paste, desk 'research', characterized as they were, by wholesale regurgitation of prevalent, negative literature on Eritrea from biased and politically motivated entities" and stating that
>
> "the UNHCR is guilty of a breach of trust to the host nation. Common sense, normative decency and agreed ground rules dictate that the UNHCR communicate its findings, however unsavory, to the host nation. The UNHCR is also duty-bound to request policy clarifications from the host nation instead of second-guessing them and/or seeking third party interpretation.[103]

This negative reaction again reflects the inherent tensions of the UNHCR's position between states and refugees, between an intergovernmental Office following states' commands and an Office created to represent and protect individuals against states that either persecute their own citizens or are unable to protect them. Furthermore, the documents have a rather double-edged nature, as, on the one hand, they are supposed to represent a balanced perspective on state practices and state assessments concerning the 1951 Convention and yet, on the other hand, they also contain interpretative assessments created by the UNHCR itself which do not necessarily coincide with practices of contracting parties.[104] They often reflect the tensions between protection-orientated broad interpretations of treaty terminology, pursued by the Office, and the – often more restrictive – immigration policy-orientated states' approaches and practices. Additionally, the variety of instruments, as reflected above, can be criticised for creating uncertainties, especially when considering the differences in both their content and legal quality.

102 Another example of this acknowledged role of the Office are the Country of Origin Information (COI) provided by UNHCR, which are explicitly listed by the Asylum Procedures Directive as important source, Article 8 (2) (b) "precise and up-to-date information is obtained from various sources such as the United Nations High Commissioner for Refugees (UNHCR)". Council Directive 2005/85/EC of 1 December 2005 on Minimum Standards on Procedures in Member States for Granting and Withdrawing Refugee Status, 2 January 2006. United Nations High Commissioner for Refugees, *UNHCR Eligibility Guidelines for Assessing the International Protection Needs of Asylum-Seekers from Afghanistan* (2009), available online at http://www.refworld.org/docid/4a6477ef2.html (last visited 1 August 2018), at 4.

103 Eritrea: Ministry of Foreign Affairs, *UNHCR Eligibility Guidelines: Factual Findings or Recycled Defamation?* (2015), available online at http://www.shabait.com/news/local-news/20954-unhcr-eligibility-guidelines-factual-findings-or-recycled-defamation (last visited 1 August 2018).

104 In theory, rather than in practice, the guidance documents published by the Office elaborate on legal concepts and offer ways for precise legal argumentation. They should not be part of an adversarial process, as argued by Schjatvet, Cecilie and Hestenes og Dramer & Co., *supra* note 65, at 101f.

Despite this criticism, as a result of the authority provided by Article 35 of the 1951 Convention and, as explicitly requested by the Executive Committee seeking guidance on the interpretation of the Convention, these documents are not to be disregarded. They are, of course, not legally binding as such. Nonetheless, their normative value is strong. This has been reaffirmed by the constant use of these documents, the best practical example of which is shown in asylum court decisions that held, among others,[105] "having regard to Article 35(1) of the Convention, it seems to me that such Guidelines should be accorded considerable weight",[106] and they are an "important source of law (though it does not have the force of law itself)".[107] In these judgements, it becomes apparent that UNHCR documents possess influential political value, reflecting the Office's interpretation of the Convention with regard to conflict-induced displacement and are even considered a conceptual foundation for law despite not being formally binding. The reference to "source of law" in this context must be understood as an intellectual, normative foundation for binding laws and not in the sense of formal, primary sources of law.

2.3.3 The protection mandate concerning persons fleeing conflict – the expanding personal scope

The expanding role of the Office relating to persons fleeing conflict and violence is reflected in the ever-increasing number of authorities that the UNGA has referred to the UNHCR on numerous occasions. Explicitly excluded, on the other hand, from the Office's protection were and are Palestinian refugees, whose protection was conferred upon the United Nations Relief and Work Agency for Palestine Refugees in the Near East (UNRWA). Their specific protection claims are excluded here. In the early days, broadening tasks allocated to the UNHCR concerned internal functions, e.g. the budget or its geographical application areas. But the UNGA has also continuously expanded the UNHCR's mandate concerning its protection beneficiaries. This expansion of protection responsibilities *ratione personae* goes beyond the 1951 Convention's limited definition of refugee, explicitly bringing persons fleeing situations of conflict and violence within its ambit.

105 Lord Lloyd of Berwick in: *Horvath v. Secretary of State for the Home Department,* [2000] UKHL 37, United Kingdom: House of Lords (2000). Lord Hoffmann in: *Islam (A.P.) v. Secretary of State for the Home Department; R v. Immigration Appeal Tribunal and Another, Ex Parte Shah (A.P.)*, United Kingdom: House of Lords (1999). Here the 1985 Executive Committee Conclusion No. 39 "Refugees, Women and International Protection" were quoted in approval.

106 *R v. Uxbridge Magistrates Court & Another ex Parte Adimi R v. Crown Prosecution Service ex Parte Sorani R v. Secretary of State for Home Department ex Parte Sorani R v. Secretary of State for Home Department and Another ex Parte Kaziu*, [1999] EWHC Admin 765, United Kingdom: High Court (Divisional Court) (1999).

107 *T v. Secretary of State for the Home Department*, [1996] 2 All ER 865, United Kingdom: House of Lords (1996).

2.3.3.1 The UNHCR's legal and policy development – documents of declaratory nature

The UNHCR's competence *ratione personae*, in its current form, deviates from the 1951 Convention's narrow definition of a refugee and thereby from the original scope of responsibilities conferred upon it by the state parties. The so-called persons of concern to the UNHCR nowadays include, among others internally displaced persons, resettled and returned individuals, persons in refugee-like situations and others.[108]

The original mandate concerning the provision of international protection for refugees and assistance in finding durable solutions covered only *de jure* refugees, as defined in the 1951 Convention and comparably in the 1950 Statute, paragraph 6 A (ii):

> Any person who, as a result of events occurring before 1 January 1951 and owing to well-founded fear of being persecuted for reasons of race, religion, nationality or political opinion, is outside the country of his nationality and is unable or, owing to such fear or for reasons other than personal convenience, is unwilling to avail himself of the protection of that country; or who, not having a nationality and being outside the country of his former habitual residence, is unable or, owing to such fear or for reasons other than personal convenience, is unwilling to return to it,

and paragraph 6b,

> Any other person who is outside the country of his nationality, or if he has no nationality, the country of his former habitual residence, because he has or had a well-founded fear of persecution by reason of his race, religion, nationality or political opinion and is unable or, because of such fear, is unwilling to avail himself of the protection of the government of the country of his nationality, or, if he has no nationality, to return to the country of his former habitual residence.[109]

The expansion of the Office's mandate was not achieved by amending the statutory refugee definition contained in the UNHCR Statute, 1951 Convention and its 1967 Protocol. Rather, the UNHCR Statute was supplemented and its scope

108 United Nations High Commissioner for Refugees, *Ensuring Protection for Persons of Concern 2010-2011. UNHCR Global Appeal* (2011), available online at http://www.unhcr.org/4b040a429.pdf (last visited 1 August 2018). United Nations High Commissioner for Refugees, *Who We Help* (2017), available online at http://www.unhcr.org/who-we-help.html (last visited 1 August 2018). United Nations High Commissioner for Refugees, 'Report of the sixty-sixth meeting of the Standing Committee (21–23 June 2016)' (UN Doc. A/AC.96/1162, 2016).

109 *Id.*, at para. 6b. Kneebone, Susan, Stevens, Dallal and Baldassar, Loretta (eds.), *Refugee Protection and the Role of Law. Conflicting Identities* (2014).

regularly broadened by subsequent UNGA and Economic and Social Council (ECOSOC) resolutions[110] which entrusted the UNHCR with protecting and assisting particular groups of people whose circumstances had not necessarily met the refugee definition in the Statute or the 1951 Convention and its 1967 Protocol. This competence to protect a broader range of beneficiaries is linked to the openly phrased and forward-looking paragraph 9 of the UNHCR Statute:

> The High Commissioner shall engage in such additional activities, including repatriation and resettlement, as the General Assembly may determine, within the limits of the resources placed at his disposal.

Examples for this course of action can be found, among others, in Resolution 1673 (XVI) of 1961 referring to the broadened personal scope of the Office's responsibility with reference to "refugees for whom [the High Commissioner] lends his good offices"[111] or with reference to man-made disasters in 1967, 2294 (XXII), similarly emphasised by ECOSOC Resolution 2011 (LXI) of 1976 concerning, "refugees and displaced persons, victims of man-made disasters".[112]

The Conclusions of the Executive Committee have considered the link between the refugee regime and forced displacement by conflict and violence on numerous occasions.[113] In 1996, Committee raised the issue of forced displacement due to armed violence and conflict, emphasising that

> the underlying causes of large-scale involuntary population displacements are complex and interrelated and encompass gross violations of human rights, including in armed conflict, poverty and economic disruption, political conflicts, ethnic and inter-communal tensions and environmental degradation, and that there is a need for the international community to address these causes in a concerted and holistic manner.[114] (No. 80 XLVII, 1996)

110 They can be considered binding resolutions of the UNGA. While the UNGA normally only adopts non-binding resolutions, those addressing internal organisational matters, in contrast, are legally binding. For a detailed analysis, see Öberg, Marko D., 'The Legal Effects of Resolutions of the UN Security Council and General Assembly in the Jurisprudence of the ICJ', 16 *European Journal of International Law* (2005) 879.

111 United Nations General Assembly, 'Resolution 1672 (XVI). Refugees from Algeria in Morocco and Tunisia Refugees from Algeria in Morocco and Tunisia' (UN Doc. A/RES/1672(XVI), 1961).

112 The expansion and recommendation to take action concerning for instance IDPs must be considered controversial. IDPs remain under the sovereignty of their state. While the UNHCR can be mandated to their protection, it is still within the respective state's sovereign decision to allow or to deny the Office access. In this regard, the expanding protection mandate *ratione personae* by UNGA Resolutions differs from the original protection mandate provided by the Statute in reflection of the 1951 Convention.

113 Türk, Volker and Dowd, Rebecca, 'Protection Gaps', in E. Fiddian-Qasmiyeh, G. Loescher, K. Long and N. Sigona (eds.), *The Oxford Handbook of Refugee and Forced Migration Studies* (Oxford University Press, 2014), at 281.

114 UNHCR: ExCom, *Conclusion No. 80 (XLVII) Comprehensive and Regional Approaches within a Protection Framework* (1996), available online at http://www.refworld.org/pdfid/4b28bf1f2.pdf (last visited 1 August 2018).

Also, on several occasions, the Executive Committee Conclusions acknowledged the specifics of conflict and refugeehood concerning different thematic points, such as root causes, procedures or cooperation with host communities. Conclusion No. 74 (XLV) of 1994

> (k) [n]otes that a large number of those persons in need of international protection have been forced to flee or to remain outside their countries of origin as a result of danger to their life or freedom owing to situations of conflict.

In the 1994 Executive Committee Conclusion No. 75 (XLV), the Committee

> (i) [c]alls on the Governments concerned to ensure safe and timely humanitarian access to persons in need of protection and assistance, including the internally displaced and victims of armed conflict, as well as refugees within their territories [...]

The thematic focus of forced displacement resulting from conflict and violence has been equally addressed in some of the Notes on International Protection. They indicate how the Office positions itself and views its mandate in relation to international protection for people fleeing conflict and violence. The 1994 Note on International Protection addresses the extended personal scope of the Office's responsibilities with regards to conflicts:

> With respect to the mandate of UNHCR, successive General Assembly resolutions have had the effect of extending the High Commissioner's competence to refugees fleeing armed conflict. [...] In accordance with these resolutions, and with the strong support of the Executive Committee and of the international community as a whole, it has been the regular and consistent policy and practice of UNHCR to provide international protection, mobilize humanitarian assistance and seek solutions for refugees from armed conflicts as well as those fleeing persecution.[115]

It was further emphasised that "[i]n several regions new refugees have been forced to flee armed conflict, generalized violence and grave human rights abuses in their countries of origin"[116] and "[p]rotection included ensuring that the special needs of refugee women, particularly victims of violence [...] are met"[117]. While often the more general relation between conflict and displacement is drawn, the Office has itself also underlined the concrete link to the interpretation of the

115 United Nations General Assembly, *supra* note 38, at para. 8, 10–11, 31–32.
116 *Id.*, at para. 3.
117 *Id.*, at para. 12.

1951 Convention. In 1995, the Note on International Protection in Mass Influx Situations emphasises the following:

> It is recalled that in many situations, persons fleeing conflict may also be fleeing a well-founded fear of persecution for Convention reasons. This is the case, for example, when a segment of the population is targeted by government or non-government forces due to their ethnic, religious or political affiliation [...] Steps towards strengthening the international protection required by all persons fleeing conflict must take this into account to avoid diminishing the protection to which refugees are entitled.[118]

In 1998, the Note addresses conflict as a cause of refugee flow and clearly emphasises the interrelationship between conflict-induced displacement and the 1951 Convention. The same argumentation would be upheld later during treaty interpretation, referring to the fact that persons displaced by conflict can also fulfil the inclusion criteria for refugeehood under the Convention. The Office's decision to include conflict-related claims in their interpretation of the convention is already indicative of its openness. Hostilities and conflict, in general, and means and methods employed by the belligerent can very well be treated as persecutory acts in the refugee law sense:

> [T]he root causes of refugee displacement are inextricably linked to conflict, persecution and the denial of human rights. These causes are not mutually exclusive. Persons displaced by war or conflict can legitimately fear persecution. War may well be the very instrument of persecution, the method chosen by the persecutors - whether part of the state apparatus or not - to repress or eliminate entire groups of people because of their ethnicity or other affiliations.[119]

On the declaratory level and particularly with regard to the Office's mandate, one can observe the continued recognition of conflict as a root cause of displacement as well as an acknowledgement of the responsibilities of the UNHCR towards persons fleeing such conflict. This link was confirmed by both the Office and state parties on an abstract level. More interesting than a general acknowledgement of conflict-induced displacement and its role in the UNHCR's operational mandate, is, however, the legal interpretation of the 1951 Convention in the context of violence and conflict. The legal and policy guidance documents of the Office itself can offer more concrete insights into the legal interpretation and application of the Convention to persons fleeing conflict.

118 United Nations General Assembly, 'Note on International Protection: International Protection in Mass Influx' (UN Doc. A/AC.96/850, 1995), at para. 11.

119 United Nations General Assembly, 'Note on International Protection' (UN Doc. A/AC.96/898, 1998), at para. 4.

2.3.3.2 The UNHCR's legal and policy development – documents of interpretative nature

The importance of conflict-induced displacement is mirrored in very recent developments in the work of the Office and DIP. The UNHCR has prepared the new Guidelines on Conflict and Violence, which were only finalised at the end of 2016. These guidelines are one comprehensive document that aims to clarify and promote the Office's legal position on the 1951 Convention and individuals fleeing conflicts in their countries of origin. The timing of the adoption of such a document again indicates that the necessity of guidance and clarification in this context has been acknowledged. With conflict-induced displacement at its peak, the UNHCR issued these guidelines at a time in which European states have increasingly reverted back to granting less substantial forms of protection than refugee status for those asylum seekers fleeing major conflict, such as in Syria, or started to return persons to countries partly affected, such as Afghanistan. In this time, additional legal certainty for when and how to apply the Convention and its regional supplements comes at a right time.

In order to trace the evolution of the UNHCR's position on conflict-induced displacement, the 1979 Handbook, as the major interpretative instrument of the UNHCR, provides a key starting point. The significance of the handbook explains why its paragraph concerning persons fleeing conflict has so strongly shaped and mirrored the Office's early position on that matter:

> Persons compelled to leave their country of origin as a result of international or national armed conflicts *are not normally considered refugees under the 1951 Convention or 1967 Protocol.* They do, however, have the protection provided for in other international instruments, e.g. the Geneva Conventions of 1949 on the Protection of War Victims and the 1977 Protocol additional to the Geneva Conventions of 1949 relating to the protection of Victims of International Armed Conflicts.[120]

The Handbook paragraph is ambiguous in its interpretation, to say the least, but it was used to reject the assumption that people fleeing conflict were protected by the 1951 Convention: "[…] they are not normally considered refugees under the 1951 Convention"; this general assumption has stuck for a long time. The same position is emphasised in the discussion note, issued 2 April 1992, addressing the "Protection of persons of concern to UNHCR who fall outside of the 1951 Convention: a discussion note." The discussion note emphasised "the ever-increasing number of persons in many regions of the world [who] are forced

120 United Nations High Commissioner for Refugees, *Handbook on Procedures and Criteria for Determining Refugee Status under the 1951 Convention and the 1967 Protocol Relating to the Status of Refugees. UN Doc. HCR/IP/4/Eng/REV.1 Reedited* (1992/UNHCR 1979), available online at http://www.unhcr.org/4d93528a9.pdf (last visited 1 August 2018), at para. 164 (emphasis added by the author).

to flee their country as a result of generalised situations of violence threatening their safety or freedom."[121] The title itself reflects the general assumption that their protection lies outside of obligations enshrined in the 1951 Convention when their flight is brought about by conflict.

The Note and terminology, if read carefully, does not really promote a rejection of conflict-induced refugees as such, but simply argues that if persons flee generalised violence without the fear of, or actually suffering persecutory harm based on a Convention ground, they are not covered by the instrument. This argument is still supported today. However, at that time, it was used as argument to support the rejection of conflict-induced asylum applications. This rejection is further supported by the fact that the Note understands the decision to grant any protection for persons fleeing conflict as lying within states' discretion:

> There are clearly inherent ambiguities in a situation where refugees meeting broader regional definitions, but outside the relevant regions, are considered to be of international concern and are receiving international protection and assistance on a mandatory basis from the international community, but on a discretionary basis from individual States.[122]

The distinction between discretion and obligation reflects the assumption of non-applicability of the Convention in this context.

The UNHCR's departure from that position can be traced through several of its subsequent guidance documents. The UNHCR main legal section within the DIP, PPLA, has pursued further research in the intersection of refugee law with neighbouring fields of law, while also addressing the challenges pertaining to conflict.

Within the DIP/PPLA, Notes on varying thematic matters have been published since 1995 on issues arising, among others, during the aforementioned Global Consultation Process. The "Interpretative Guidance on Article 1 A (2)" issued in 2001 is one important example that includes a paragraph shedding light on the Office's understanding of the application of the Convention and its refugee definition to people fleeing conflict. The Office expressed a new openness towards protection claims,[123] stating that, if sufficient harm can be shown, plus a link to a Convention ground, persons fleeing from countries in conflict could be protected by the Convention.[124] Here, it becomes clear that the treaty

121 United Nations High Commissioner for Refugees, *Protection of Persons of Concern to UNHCR Who Fall Outside the 1951 Convention: A Discussion Note. UN Doc. EC/1992/SCP/CRP.5* (1992), available online at http://www.unhcr.org/3ae68cc518.html (last visited 1 August 2018).

122 *Ibid.*

123 On the shift in approaches to protection claims, Symes, Mark and Jorro, Peter, *Asylum Law and Practice* (Bloomsbury Professional, 2003), at 114.

124 United Nations High Commissioner for Refugees, *Interpreting Article 1 of the 1951 Convention Relating to the Status of Refugees* (2001), available online at http://www.refworld.org/docid/3b20a3914.html (last visited 1 August 2018), at para. 21f.

is applicable, provided that the violence arising in conflict is generated by discrimination, in accordance with the 1951 criteria:

> It should be recalled that the Convention was drafted in the aftermath of World War II, at least in part as a means of protecting victims of persecution in that war. Where conflicts are rooted in ethnic, religious or political differences which specifically victimise those fleeing, as is so often the case today, persons fleeing such conflicts would qualify as 1951 Convention refugees.[125]

In this guidance document, the Office, on the other hand, correctly stresses that, if persons flee from the indiscriminate violence of hostilities alone, their protection must be based on other instruments:

> [...] it is equally recognised that there are persons who flee the indiscriminate effects of violence associated with conflict with no element of persecution. Such persons might not meet the Convention definition, but may still require international protection on other grounds.[126]

The country-specific Eligibility Guidelines produced within the DIP are another instrument of the Office that clarify positions concerning protection claims. They include examples of the expansion of the Office's mandate, covering different groups, including persons fitting the extended regional refugee definitions – namely persons fleeing conflict, generalised situations of violence or other events seriously disturbing public order:

> The High Commissioner's core mandate covers refugees, that is all persons outside their country of origin for reasons of feared persecution, conflict, generalized violence, or other circumstances that gave seriously disturbed public order and who, as a result, require international protection,

or, as expressed in a court submission: "In light of this evolution, UNHCR considers that serious (including indiscriminate) threats to life, physical integrity or freedom resulting from generalised violence or events seriously disturbing public order are valid reasons for international protection under its mandate."[127]

125 *Id.*, at paras. 21f.

126 *Id.*, at para. 22.

127 United Nations High Commissioner for Refugees, *Note on the Mandate of the High Commissioner for Refugees and His Office* (2013), available online at http://www.refworld.org/docid/5268c9474.html (last visited 1 August 2018), at 3. United Nations High Commissioner for Refugees, 'UNHCR intervention before the Court of Appeal of England and Wales in the case of MM (Iran) v. Secretary of State for the Home Department' (UN Doc. C5/2009/2479, 2010), at 10.

Eligibility Guidelines analysed for their treatment of conflict situations mirror the general position that:

> *Persons fleeing their country or origin in situations of armed conflict may have a well-founded fear of persecution based on one or more of the 1951 Convention grounds.* This is particularly relevant where, as in Afghanistan, the internal armed conflict is rooted in religious, ethnic and/or political disputes [...] *When examining the link to a 1951 Convention ground in the claims of persons who are fleeing a situation of armed conflict, there is no requirement that the individual be known to, and sought personally by the agent(s) of persecution. Whole communities may risk or suffer persecution* [...][128]

The Eligibility Guidelines for Afghanistan are of interest, as they include individual aspects of the interpretation of conflict-related claims. The DIP's attempt to emphasise the issue of indiscriminate violence in the document significantly slowed down the drafting process of the 2009 Eligibility Guidelines.[129] The updated Guidelines for Afghanistan of 2013 more specifically analyse the various threats arising in conflict, as well as their inclusion in the specific refugee instruments.

> Afghanistan continues to be affected by a non-international armed conflict. Individuals fleeing harm in the context of this conflict may meet the criteria for refugee status as contained in Article 1 (A)(2) of the 1951 Convention. For this to be the case, there must be a reasonable possibility that the individual would experience serious harm amounting to persecution for reasons related to the grounds set out in Article 1 (A)(2).[130]

The assessment for asylum-seekers from Iraq is similarly phrased:

> Given the widespread human rights violations against individuals with specific profiles in many parts of Iraq it can be expected that *many asylum-seekers from Iraq, including those originating from areas where a situation of generalized violence or events seriously disturbing public order exists at the moment of adjudication of their claims, will be eligible for refugee protection* under the 1951 Convention. [...] Only when an asylum seeker is found not to meet the refugee criteria in the 1951 Convention, should complementary or subsidiary forms of protection be examined.[131]

128 United Nations High Commissioner for Refugees, *supra* note 102, at 40 (emphasis added by the author).

129 Schjatvet, Cecilie and Hestenes og Dramer & Co., *supra* note 65, at 40.

130 United Nations High Commissioner for Refugees, *supra* note 28, at 5.

131 United Nations High Commissioner for Refugees, 'UNHCR Eligibility Guidelines for Assessing the International Protection Needs of Asylum-Seekers from Iraq' (UN Doc. HCR/EG/IRQ/12/03, 2012), at 44 (emphasis added by the author).

Beyond that, the DIP has conducted further legal research on the matter. The new Guidelines on International Protection concerning conflict and violence No. 12, adopted by the end of 2016, are expected to clarify the Office's standing specifically concerning the protection of persons fleeing conflict. These new Guidelines complement the Handbook through their provision of interpretative guidance for governments, legal practitioners, decision-makers and the judiciary, as well as UNHCR staff. The guidelines aim at providing clarity on the doctrinal position of the UNHCR in relation to the main legal instruments and their applicability in conflict contexts.

The guidelines explicitly refer to paragraph 164 of the Handbook and elaborate that "[t]he phrase 'persons compelled to leave their country of origin as a result of international or national armed conflicts are not normally considered refugees under the 1951 Convention or 1967 Protocol' contained in paragraph 164 of the UNHCR Handbook needs to be understood as limited to situations where there is no causal link between a person's well-founded fear of being persecuted and a 1951 Convention ground."[132] The definition of the refugee per 1951 Convention is key in the debate concerning the application of the 1951 Convention to conflicts and the protection of those colloquially known as 'war refugees'. The major question that we must pose is whether, while legally interpreting the treaty's definition of a refugee, one can also find legal grounds to reject its application to persons fleeing conflict.

The preparations for the Guidelines took different forms. Roundtable meetings in collaboration with academic experts and organisations working in the area were organised and held. The roundtable in Arusha in 2011 concerned the complementarities between international refugee law, international criminal and human rights law.[133] Equally, the Geneva Meeting of 2004 on the Civilian and Humanitarian Character of Asylum addressed questions relating to protection for people fleeing conflict, taking into account both the inclusive and exclusive aspects of the refugee definition.[134] The output of other roundtables on related issues, such as temporary protection, held in San Remo in 2013, has flowed into the constitution and clarification of the Office's standing. The current developments in Europe that followed the establishment of the Common

132 United Nations High Commissioner for Refugees, 'Guidelines on International Protection No. 12: Claims for refugee status related to situations of armed conflict and violence under Article 1A(2) of the 1951 Convention and/or 1967 Protocol relating to the Status of Refugees and the regional refugee definitions' (UN Doc. HCR/GIP/16/12, 2016), at 5.

133 United Nations High Commissioner for Refugees, *Expert Meeting on Complementarities between International Refugee Law, International Criminal Law and International Human Rights Law. Summary Conclusions* (2011), available online at http://www.unhcr.org/4e16d0a59.html (last visited 1 August 2018).

134 See more United Nations High Commissioner for Refugees, *Expert Meetings* (2014), available online at http://www.unhcr.org/3e5f78bc4.html (last visited 1 August 2018). UNHCR: Jaquemet, 'Under What Circumstances Can a Person Who Has Taken an Active Part in the Hostilities of an International or a Non-International Armed Conflict Become an Asylum Seeker?' (UN Doc. PPLA/2004/01, 2004).

European Asylum System (CEAS), particularly the status of subsidiary protection under the QD, have promoted extensive research on the implementation of the respective instrument in the EU Member States. "Safe at Last?",[135] an extensive study from 2011, is a product of this process and concerns the transposition and implementation of the QD, specifically Article 15 (c) in chosen national case studies.

The "Roundtable on international protection of persons fleeing armed conflict and other situations of violence" was held on 13–14 September 2012 at the University of Cape Town. For that occasion, five background papers were commissioned by the DIP, more specifically the PPLA, to form a first research-based assessment of the background, legal challenges and developments. Farell and Schmitt addressed "The Causes, Character and Conduct of Armed Conflict, and the Effects on Civilian Populations", Holzer, the "1951 Refugee Convention and the Protection of People fleeing Armed Conflict and other Situations of Violence" and Oosterveld focused on "Women and Girls Fleeing Conflict and Generalized Violence". Following the Roundtable debate, two additional background papers were written to include research on the regional expanded refugee definition, considering the "1969 OAU Convention and the Protection of People fleeing Armed Conflict" by Sharpe and the "Cartagena Declaration on Refugees and the Protection of People fleeing Armed Conflict and Other situations of Violence in Latin America" by Reed-Hurtado, both published in 2013. The Summary Conclusion of the roundtable not only mirrors the issues debated but give further indications on the developing position of the UNHCR in this context. These two later background papers follow the expert roundtable on the interpretation of the extended refugee definition contained in the 1984 Cartagena Declaration on Refugees, which was held in Montevideo in October 2013.

These five background papers commissioned by the UNHCR, together with three new studies on subsidiary protection in the EU by Garlick, the extended inter-relation of the OAU, and the 1951 refugee definition by Rutinwa, and the special focus on children and armed conflict by Brett/Brett/Rashed, were published in a new edited volume by the UNHCR in 2017.[136] This process was envisaged to end the uncertainty of the Office's position stemming from the interpretation surrounding the handbook's phrasing on the general inapplicability of the Convention to persons fleeing violence and conflict.

The documents reflect the UNHCR's changing position and its focus on conflict-induced displacement under the 1951 Convention. Despite the evolution of its doctrinal position and adding to the complexity of conflict-induced

135 United Nations High Commissioner for Refugees, *Safe at Last? Law and Practice in Selected EU Member States with Respect to Asylum-Seekers Fleeing Indiscriminate Violence* (2011), available online at http://www.unhcr.org/protection/operations/4e2d7f029/safe-law-practice-selected-eu-member-states-respect-asylum-seekers-fleeing.html (last visited 1 August 2018).

136 United Nations High Commissioner for Refugees, *supra* note 132.

displacement and protection claims, the framework now faces a threefold dilemma: the 1951 Convention activates refugee protection for a very small and exclusive group of persons. 1) Traditionally, the UNHCR and states have, in the majority of cases, not afforded refugee status to persons fleeing conflict. 2) Now, however, the UNHCR has changed its interpretative position and acknowledged that persons fleeing conflict can also fall under the 1951 Convention. State practice in this regard, as seen below, is highly ambivalent. 3) Finally, the UNHCR's protection mandate goes beyond the protection of Convention refugees and covers explicitly those fleeing situations of generalised violence. This divide between, on the one hand, the acknowledged persons of concern within the UNHCR's mandate – including those fleeing conflict and violence – and the obligations of states towards refugees, as defined by the 1951 Convention, creates a legal protection gap.

This issue is reflected upon in the Note on International Protection of 1991:

> *Looking forward, there is a need for States on their own and in concert, as well as for UNHCR, to apply themselves actively to the progressive development of both the law and existing international machinery so that the response capability of the international community is reinforced to meet the new complexities of today's population movements. The 1951 Convention reflects the classical approach* to the protection of refugees, which conceptualizes a refugee as an individual victim of persecution and assumes implicitly that the main obligations to refugees are those of asylum States. Refugees so defined are, however, only one part of modern movements of persons in search of asylum. *Refugees in the broader sense, meaning persons fleeing generalized violence*, external aggression, internal conflict, massive violation of human rights and other phenomena seriously disturbing public order are *also a significant part.*[137]

The change in the UNHCR's assessment of persons fleeing conflict situations and their claims under the 1951 Convention is of particular practical relevance, not only in the Office's task as supervisor of the Convention but also in its operational function when involved in status determination processes.

2.3.3.3 The UNHCR's application of the extended definition of its mandate

The process of RSD is the formal and declaratory recognition of the protection status. The contemporary reality is that often the "UNHCR acts as the gatekeeper."[138] RSD is, on the one hand, only a declaratory acknowledgement

137 United Nations General Assembly, 'Note on International Protection' (UN Doc. A/AC.96/777, 1991), at para. 4.

138 Kagan, Michael, 'The Beleaguered Gatekeeper: Protection Challenges Posed by UNHCR Refugee Status Determination' (Scholarly Works. Paper 636, 2006), at 3.

of a person's refugee status, while, on the other hand, it is still the legal and administrative process by which primarily states, or the UNHCR, determine whether the person is eligible for international protection. Through this procedure, the state or the UNHCR grants him or her access to either the state or the UNHCR protection scheme.[139] Usually, it is the state's obligation and prerogative to conduct these RSD proceedings and the state's decision-making authority makes the final decision. Due to the unwillingness or inability of a number of states, the UNHCR has, however, taken a major role in RSD worldwide, both as a surrogate in countries where the government does not have a state RSD system in place and as a supporting agent for countries struggling with the process. As of 2013,[140] the UNHCR has been conducting RSD, including reception and registration, in 50 countries and assists in another 20 countries jointly or in parallel with the respective government.[141] "UNHCR has the single largest RSD system in the world and UNHCR's RSD operations are larger than Germany and the United States combined the two single largest State RSD systems."[142]

RSD has become one of the Office's core protection functions[143] which the UNHCR is mandated to conduct due to its "special status within the UN [to] possess the degree of independence and the prestige which would seem to be required for the effective performance of his functions".[144] UNGA Resolution 428 (V) calls on governments to cooperate with the Office in the fulfilment of its functions, explicitly referring to eight tasks, including the following:

> 2(b) [e]ntering into special agreements with the High Commissioner for the execution of measures calculated to improve the situation of refugees and to reduce the number requiring protection; 2(c) Admitting refugees to their territories not excluding those in the most destitute categories.[145]

139 See United Nations High Commissioner for Refugees, *Refugee Status Determination*, available online at http://www.unhcr.org/uk/refugee-status-determination.html (last visited 1 August 2018).

140 No official newer dates available.

141 United Nations High Commissioner for Refugees, *Refugee Status Determination*, available online at http://www.unhcr.org/pages/4a16b1d06.html (last visited 1 August 2018).

142 Simeon, James C., 'Excluding Refugee and Asylum Applicants Under the UNHCR's Statute or Mandate' (Paper presented at the "Undesirable and Unreturnable? Policy Challenges Around Excluded Asylum Seekers and other Migrants Suspected of Serious Criminality Who Cannot be Removed" Preliminary Workshop, 27 March 2015, Centre for International Criminal Justice, Faculty of Law, VU University Amsterdam, The Netherlands, 2015), at 21.

143 United Nations High Commissioner for Refugees, *Procedural Standards for Refugee Status Determination Under UNHCR's Mandate* (2003), available online at http://www.refworld.org/docid/42d66dd84.html (last visited 1 August 2018), at 1.

144 United Nations General Assembly, 'Refugees and Stateless Persons: Report of the Secretary-General' (UN Doc. A/C.3/527, 1949), at para. 11.

145 United Nations General Assembly, *supra* note 49.

Meanwhile, paragraph 2 provides the basis on which the Office and states adopt specific agreements including those concerning common or individual RSD proceedings.

While the obligation to cooperate, as discussed above, is legally binding upon states, the decision to allow the UNHCR to support or take over a state's determination processes rests with the state alone. The UNHCR in this regard has no legal means to enforce entry into a state's territories. The excessive demands on national authorities, however, work in the UNHCR's favour and have often simplified the UNHCR's standing towards a failing government. While the latter still holds the sovereign and final decision-making power to determine status, the state's position is politically weakened if it lacks sufficient capacity to conduct the process and depends on the Office's support. However, putting in place the UNHCR's RSD operations brings about discrepancies in both operations and practice among states: the granting of a legal protection status means that the beneficiary enjoys access to the respective state's protection and asylum system as well as a bundle of rights flowing from that status. When the UNHCR processes claims, the Office determines whether the person is eligible for international protection or not. However, that determination does not necessarily allow access to the state protection system.[146] In this regard, the state is not obliged to follow the UNHCR's assessment, but is free to create its own evaluation, taking into account the UNHCR's guidance among others, such as reports by international and national NGOs, human rights institutions or by the state's own embassies. While the UNHCR can "recognize refugees under its mandate" and thus include them within its protection mandate, the Office cannot grant a domestic or regional legal asylum status, as "territorial asylum can only be provided by States".[147]

These different routes to international protection hamper the consistent and uniform administration of protection status. The parallel competencies have caused concern and criticism in the international community and in academia. UNHCR's RSD

> poses serious protection challenges because it is founded on a basic contradiction. On the one hand, government action is essential for effective refugee protection. On the other hand, UNHCR RSD is premised on at least partial government failure. Therefore UNHCR activities are an ambiguous

146 Simeon, while underlining the importance of the contribution of UNHCR, cautions additionally that the UNHCR bases its RSD on administrative structures, which, also due to the confidentiality and privacy principles upheld strongly by the Office, lack transparency. In this regard, it performs completely differently from the highly structured asylum architectures in states. For a critical assessment, see Simeon, James C., *supra* note 142, at 23.

147 United Nations High Commissioner for Refugees, *Statistical Yearbook 2003* (2005), available online at http://www.unhcr.org/statistics/country/42aff7e84/unhcr-statistical-yearbook-2003.html (last visited 1 August 2018), at Chapter 3, Asylum and Refugee Status Adjudication, p. 38.

> function in providing assistance and assisting governments in providing assistance but primarily responsibility lies with the governments.[148] UNHCR steps in to determine refugee status only when governments prove unwilling or unable to do so.[149]

The consequences of status recognition by both states and the UNHCR are usually that either a) the recognition of the UNHCR is acknowledged by the state as the basis of its determination and no independent interrogation is conducted; or b) it is included in the state's assessment, in particular, in the absence of any reasons to disregard it; or finally (c) states do not take UNHCR recognition into account at all.

In 2014, an asylum judgement from a national court addressed the issue of a state's non-recognition of the UNHCR's assessment of refugee status. In *I.A. v The Secretary of State for the Home Department*, the UK Supreme Court decided on the status of a Kurdish applicant who had already been recognised by the UNHCR as a refugee. He had claimed that the Iraqi government would not provide any assistance to UNHCR refugees and therefore moved onward to Turkey, where he was again recognised as a refugee by the UNHCR. After three years, he left for the UK.[150] The UK Supreme Court, therefore, assessed the weight given to the prior UNHCR recognition by the second assessing state, namely the UK. Although the Court ultimately dismissed the appeal, it held that the national decision-making authorities needed to pay close attention to the UNHCR's grant of refugee status before arriving at a different conclusion. And, referring to the special supervisory role of the UNHCR under the Convention, the judges considered the role of the UNHCR as influential, although of simple evidentiary value in a status determination process:

> It is accepted by all that, despite the expertise and experience in dealing with refugees which UNHCR enjoys and despite the responsibilities with which it is charged, *its decisions as to refugee status do not oblige countries to accede to applications for asylum by those who have been accorded that status by UNHCR*. This is frankly accepted by UNHCR itself. Importantly, it is not only accepted, it is positively asserted by UNHCR that states have an independent, autonomous responsibility under the 1951 Convention and the 1967 Protocol to determine a person's refugee status when that is claimed.

148 United Nations General Assembly, 'Office of the United Nations High Commissioner for Refugees: Resolution adopted by the General Assembly' (UN Doc. A/RES/57/187, 2003), at para 7f.: "[B]earing in mind that the protection of refugees is primarily the responsibility of States, whose full and effective cooperation, action and political resolve are required to enable the Office of the High Commissioner to fulfil its mandated functions."

149 Kagan, Michael, 'The Beleaguered Gatekeeper. Protection Challenges Posed by UNHCR Refugee Status Determination', 18 *International Journal of Refugee Law* (2006) 1, at 4.

150 *I.A. v. The Secretary of State for the Home Department*, [2014] UKSC 6, United Kingdom: Supreme Court (2014), at 4f.

> That duty cannot be relinquished to UNHCR. These considerations provide the setting for the examination of the role that a UNHCR decision on refugee status should play in the assessment by a country of a claim to asylum the Extra Division considered that ***a decision of the UNHCR on refugee status would constitute an important "piece of evidence" in the decision maker's evaluation*** of the claim for asylum.[151]

Similarly, the case of prior recognition by another state in *Secretary of State for the Home Department v. KK (Congo)* of 2005 assessed that the UNHCR's position concerning the validity of certain claims is not binding, but is still a highly significant starting point for the state's analysis:

> [T]***he earlier grant of asylum is not binding, but*** it is the appropriate starting point for the consideration of the claim; ***the grant is a very significant matter.*** There should be some certainty and stability in the position of refugees. The adjudicator must consider whether there are the most clear and substantial grounds for coming to a different conclusion.[152]

In one of its written court interventions, the UNHCR promotes a practical approach in regard to its own standing in states' determination processes and supports deviations only when 'cogent reasons' can be given:

> A state decision-maker cannot disregard UNHCR's recognition of refugee status in evaluating the individual's claim unless there are cogent reasons for doing so. A state decision-maker may, after an examination of all the evidence available to him or her arrive at a decision regarding an applicant's eligibility for refugee status different from the UNHCR recognition where there are cogent reasons for doing so.[153]

Clearly, the interplay between states' and the UNHCR's RSD processes is not without difficulties. The matter is further aggravated when one considers that the UNHCR and the states, depending on their asylum laws, work on the basis of different protection bases. The 2003 Procedural Standards for Refugee Status Determination under the UNHCR's Mandate, in conjunction with its guidelines on procedural aspects of the determination procedure, form the basis of

151 *Id.*, at paras. 28f. (emphasis added by the author), para. 28 and 29. Similar: "It is accepted that a prior recognition of 'mandate refugee status' does not bind a State to recognise as a refugee the person who has benefited from that earlier recognition. However, it is submitted that in determining the asylum claim of a person whose refugee status has been recognised by UNHCR, the UK decision-maker must give that prior recognition considerable weight and must seriously take it into account when determining the risk and assessing credibility." United Nations High Commissioner for Refugees, *supra* note 127, at para. 14.

152 *KK (Recognition elsewhere as refugee), per Ouseley*, [2005] UKIAT 00054, United Kingdom: Immigration Appeal Tribunal (2005), at para. 18 (emphasis added by the author).

153 *I.A. v. The Secretary of State for the Home Department, supra* note 150, at para. 45.

the Office's RSD work.[154] This is not only to provide international protection to *de jure* Convention refugees but the UNHCR's approach to status determination also derives from its mandate, which encompasses the extended refugee definition[155]:

> Persons who are outside their country of origin because of a threat of serious and indiscriminate harm arising from a situation of generalized (...) may also be recognized under as refugees under the broader international protection criteria where applicable. Such broader criteria are reflected in regional human rights instruments and from part of UNHCR's extended mandate.[156]

As a result of this tension, persons fleeing conflict and violence can be caught in the divide between, on the one hand, a state's recognition under the restrictive definition of refugee within the 1951 Convention and, on the other, the UNHCR's recognition based on the extended definition under the Office's mandate:

> [I]t is possible to envisage circumstances in which UNCHR's mandate would be triggered but a state may be justified in concluding that the 1951 Convention is inapplicable. A pertinent illustration is the position of civilians outside of the 1951 Convention refugee definition. However, the clear danger to life and limb from a situation of armed conflict may well bring such persons within the scope of UNHCR's mandate for refugees.[157]

For these cases, states are less likely to be willing to adopt the view of a UNHCR determination. The practical effects of these existing legal uncertainties for the interpretation of the 1951 Convention and persons fleeing conflict highlight, once again, the need for legal clarification.

154 In 1999, a study on the UNHCR's RSD procedures by Michael Alexander revealed inadequate procedural safeguards and assessed that UNHCR status determination was not up to date with human rights and administrative law developments, including no written reasons for rejection provided, withholding of medical reports, negative creditability decisions reached without specific reasons. The UNHCR addresses the issue in a follow up "Procedural standards for refugee status determination under UNHCR's mandate" of 2005. Alexander, Michael, 'Refugee Status Determination Conducted by UNHCR', 11 *International Journal of Refugee Law* (1999) 251, at 255. Kagan, Michael, 'Assessment of Refugee Status Determination Procedure at UNHCR's Cairo Office 2001–2002' (American University of Cairo. Forced Migration and Refugee Studies Working Paper No 1, 2002), at 37.

155 Simeon, James C., *supra* note 142, at 9.

156 United Nations High Commissioner for Refugees, 'Interim Eligibility Guidelines for Assessing the International Protection Needs of Asylum-Seekers from Côte d'Ivoire' (UN Doc. HCR/EG/CIV/12/01, 2012), at 32.

157 UNHCR: Mandal, 'Protection Mechanisms Outside of the 1951 Convention ("Complementary Protection")' (UN Doc. PPLA/2005/02, 2005), at para. 24.

2.4 Interpreting the 1951 Convention criteria of a conflict-displaced refugee

Mass displacement is often the result of the outbreak or aggravation of violent conflicts, or of secondary movements arising from a protracted conflict situation. The number of asylum seekers generated in these situations of generalised violence intensifies pressure on transit and destination countries. Considerations of the capacity of states to cope with and handle the numbers of people fleeing conflict and violence worldwide, as well as their competing obligations towards their own citizens, are brought forward to explain both states' reluctance to apply and misconceptions of the meaning of the 1951 Convention in this context. Such misconceptions are commonly based on a) the nature of the conflict and b) the identification and the use of the pertinent legal instrument and, hence, the correct protection status.

> Problems may arise not only from the way in which the law is perceived but also from the inability of those responsible for the refugee status determination to duly recognize and reflect the political, ethnic and other such dimensions of civil wars and other large-scale conflicts.[158]

Legal premises on the applicability of the Convention to conflict situations were and are brought forward, separately or cumulatively, that demand a rejection of the application in total or alter the interpretation of the Convention's eligibility criteria.

To follow the examination, the next chapter focuses on the 1951 Convention as a whole and the respective elements of its refugee definition that merit particular discussion in the context of conflict and violence. Due to the volume of literature and research on general refugee protection and the 1951 Convention, this chapter does not offer a general interpretation of the refugee definition first before applying it to the case of persons fleeing conflict. On the contrary, the conflict lens guides the interpretation and is the starting point for this chapter's interpretative efforts. For this reason, the chapter does not conduct a broad interpretation of the refugee definition, as has been already provided by existing commentaries, but focuses on the question whether the refugee definition expresses a premise concerning its application during times of peace or of conflict.

2.4.1 Interpreting the Convention and its application in and for times of conflict

Before going into the single elements of Article 1 A (2), the 1951 Convention should be considered as a whole. The primary question to be answered is whether the treaty impedes its application to persons fleeing conflict. The

158 Nykänen, Eeva, *Fragmented State Power and Forced Migration* (Martinus Nijhoff Publishers, 2012), at 5.

following analysis takes two approaches to answering the question posed. First, it examines whether the treaty as a whole applies in times of conflict.

Some commentators have claimed that the 1951 Convention is generally not applicable to people fleeing situations of conflict.[159] Even the UNHCR, in its 1979 Guiding Handbook, had adopted the already discussed position that persons fleeing conflict were excluded from the Convention's definition of refugee. Historically, states and their decision-making authorities have tended to apply this overly restrictive definition when faced with a mass influx of asylum seekers fleeing situations of conflict.

> Persons compelled to leave their country of origin as a result of international or national armed conflicts are not normally considered refugees under the 1951 Convention or 1967 Protocol. They do, however, have the protection provided for in other international instruments, e.g. the Geneva Conventions of 1949 on the Protection of War Victims and the 1977 Protocol additional to the Geneva Conventions of 1949 relating to the protection of Victims of International Armed Conflicts.[160]

The UNHCR's blunt recognition that persons leaving their country due to a conflict are typically not considered Convention refugees, together with its reference to the International Humanitarian Law (IHL) cornerstone treaties, would appear to transfer responsibility for protection to the framework of the laws of armed conflict and thereby away from international refugee law.[161] This approach to the protection of persons fleeing conflict can be titled "the exceptionality approach".[162] Proponents of this approach have, however, blurred the legal arguments for the application of refugee law and IHL. They assume that IHL rather than the 1951 Convention is applicable during times of armed conflict.

To address the question of applicability of the treaty as a whole, interpretative principles derived from the VCLT and the ordinary meaning of the 1951 Convention's terms in their context are chosen as a starting point. The 1951 Convention does not contain its own explicit terminology concerning the context of its application. Further, it does not contain any Articles encompassing a limitation or expansion to its application, either during times of peace or of conflict. Therefore, it is clearly not restricted by the factual relationships of its state parties or the international community more generally. One can set up a

159 Storey, Hugo, 'Armed Conflict in Asylum Law: The "War-Flaw"', 31 *Refugee Survey Quarterly* (2012) 1, at 4.

160 United Nations High Commissioner for Refugees, *supra* note 120, at para. 164f.

161 German determining authorities came to a similar conclusion by arguing that only states could be persecutors in the 1951 Convention's sense and when states lost control over their territory during internal armed conflict, there could be no persecution in the 1951 Convention's sense during such conflict. See here the discussion in Markard, Nora, *Kriegsflüchtlinge* (Mohr Siebeck, 2012), at 127f.

162 Storey, Hugo, *supra* note 159, at 4.

first strong argument that the treaty itself is silent on the matter because it was not considered to be of essence for its application.

The broader public international law framework offers a helpful reference point from which one can seek further guidance concerning the application of treaties in the context of conflict. Therefore, the aforementioned argument shall be supported secondly by turning to the Draft Articles on the Effects of Armed Conflicts on Treaties[163] as an indicative and supportive reference for this assumption. Turning to the object and purpose of the treaty as a means of interpretation, its proximity to the human rights law framework is another argument in support of its applicability. For this reason, the argument shall be supported thirdly by the broader development of complementarity between the laws of peace and the laws of armed conflict.

The legal understanding of the effect of conflict on treaties has been a debated issue in general public international law. The traditional view, upheld for most of the 19th century and supported by consistent state practice, was that clearly war *ipso facto* terminates treaty obligations (between the belligerent parties).[164] Treaties belonging to the realm of time of peace would terminate and be displaced by those stemming from the laws of war. It was either one or the other, but not both. This view on a mutually exclusive relationship of the laws of peace and the laws of war has since changed.[165] Nonetheless, the VCLT, as a major source of guidance in the field of treaty interpretation, is silent on the effects of armed conflict on treaties, other than by Article 73:

> [t]he provisions of the present convention shall not prejudge any question that may arise in regard to a treaty from a succession of States or from the international responsibilities if a State or from the outbreak of hostilities between states.

During the drafting of the VCLT, this point caused concern among states.[166] The International Law Commission (ILC), avoided further debate on the matter, as the legal effects of war were still greatly debated and would cause too many complications for the adoption.[167] The VCLT does, however, contain general rules on the continuity of treaties and their termination or suspension. These include the most fundamental principle of *pacta*

163 International Law Commission, 'Draft Articles on the Effects of Armed Conflict on Treaties, with Commentaries, adopted by the ILC, 63rd session, submitted to the UNGA' (A/66/10, Yearbook of the International Law Commission, 2011, Vol. II, Part Two, 2011), at para. 100.

164 Prescott, M., 'How War Affects Treaties Between Belligerents: A Case Study of the Gulf War', 7 *Emory International Law Review* (1993), at 197.

165 Schäfer, Bernhard, *Zum Verhältnis Menschenrechte und humanitäres Völkerrecht* (Universitätsverlag Potsdam, 2006), at 12.

166 Rosenne, Shabtai, *The Law of Treaties* (Sijthoff, 1970), at 372.

167 United Nations Organisation, *Yearbook of the International Law Commission 1966 Vol. II* (UN Doc. A/CN.4/Ser.A/1966/Add.1, 1967), at para. 29.

sunt servanda – treaties are binding and must be performed in good faith.[168] Grounds for termination include, among others, the passing of an expiration date, denunciation by virtue of Article 54 VCLT, material breach by one of the parties resulting in the right of the other(s) to terminate in accordance with Article 60, norm conflict with a peremptory norm of international law, as per Article 53, or as laid down in Article 62, a fundamental change in the circumstances (*rebus sic stantibus* doctrine).

Uncertainty of the legal consequences of conflict on treaties led to discontent and further development on the matter. The ILC was mandated in 1947 to codify and develop international law,[169] its successes evident in the codification of major multilateral treaties such as the VCLT or the United Nations Convention on the Law of the Sea (UNCLOS). However, not all preparatory Draft Articles have evolved into multilateral treaties.[170] With a silent VCLT, for the issue at stake, codification attempts conducted by the ILC that resulted so far in the Draft Articles on the Effects of Armed Conflicts on Treaties are a prominent point of reference here. In 1986, the International Law Institute made an effort to draft a Resolution concerning the outbreak of hostilities and its effects on treaties. This included the general assumption that the outbreak of conflict as such would not automatically terminate a treaty.[171] In 2004, the ILC inserted this debate in its programme and, in 2011, the Commission finally adopted 18 specific draft articles on the effect of armed conflict on treaties.[172] They were transmitted to the UNGA,[173] which accepted the articles in resolution 66/99 on 9 December 2011, with the goal of inviting comments and revising the matter at the end of 2014. The process was delayed and a similar call was made in Resolution 69/125 of 10 December 2014, when the Secretary General was again requested to invite comments by governments and put the item "Effects of armed conflicts on treaties" on the agenda of its 72nd session.[174]

The draft articles are a legally non-binding document and, although written in a form comparable to a treaty, are not a source of international law itself.

168 VCLT, Art. 26.

169 By virtue of article 13 (1) (a), the UNGA established the ILC by resolution 174 (II) in 21 November 1947, with the original Statute annexed to the resolution. It stated in Article 1 that the ILC is responsible for the "promotion of the progressive development of international law and its codification". More on the work of the ILC, United Nations Organisation, *The Work of the International Law Commission* (8th ed., United Nations, 2012).

170 One prominent example are the Draft Articles on State Responsibility, Caron, David D., 'The ILC Articles on State Responsibility: The Paradoxical Relationship between Form and Authority', 96 *American Journal of International Law* (2002) 857, at 858.

171 International Law Commission, 'The Effects of Armed Conflicts on Treaties' (61 II Yearbook of the Institute for International Law 199, 1986), at Article 3 and its commentary.

172 United Nations General Assembly, 'Report of the International Law Commission' (UN Doc. A/66/10, 2011), at 176.

173 Based on Articles 22 and 23 of the ILC Statute.

174 International Law Commission, *Analytical Guide to the Work of the International Law Commission* (2016), available online at http://legal.un.org/ilc/guide/1_10.shtml (last visited 1 August 2018).

In reference to Article 38 (1) of the ICJ Statute, they qualify as a subsidiary means of interpretation, similar to the writings of qualified publicists, although with a high standing, given that they were written by a representative group of experts.[175] Nonetheless, when their constitutive elements of pertinent state practice and opinio juris can be identified, ILC Draft Articles as drafted in co-operation with states can evolve to become binding norms of customary international law. As yet, however, the Draft Articles on the Effect of Conflict have not achieved this legal quality.[176]

Article 1 of the Draft Articles addresses the scope as "apply[ing] to the effects of armed conflict on the relations between states under a treaty", thereby also covering states which are not parties to the armed conflict.[177] It is Article 3 that reaffirms the central principle of continuity and stability in public international law: "The existence of an armed conflict does not ipso facto terminate or suspend the operation of treaties."[178] Of further interest for the analysis of the 1951 Convention is Article 4, which underlines that when the treaty itself creates a rule (which the 1951 Convention does not) the rule of this treaty prevails.[179] Article 5 provides further guidance: When the treaty itself does not give a clear indication, the regular rules of treaty interpretation shall be used to establish whether the treaty in question is susceptible to termination, withdrawal or suspension in the event of an armed conflict. The nature of the treaty, by virtue of Article 6 (a), in particular its subject matter, object, purpose, content and the number of parties to the treaty, are factors shaping its interpretation. Article 7 then provides an indicative list of treaties of which the subject matter implies a continuation. This list annexed to the Draft Articles also contains treaties for the protection of human rights under point (f).

Applying this argumentation to the 1951 Convention and its object and purpose,[180] it is clear that, while not a human rights law treaty per se, it fulfils human rights related protection, contains human rights language and has always

175 International Law Commission, 'Survey of International Law in Relation to the Work of Codification of the International Law Commission' (UN Doc. A/CN.4/Rev.1, 1949), at 15f. "Most probably their authority would be considerably higher", Brownlie, Ian, *Principles of Public International Law* (3rd ed., Clarendon Press, 1979), at 26. Caron, David D., *supra* note 170, at 867.

176 The customary nature of the ILC Draft Articles on State Responsibility is a prominent example of developing customary law. See, among others, the assessment of the representative from Germany that international and German courts have referred to the Articles as legally binding statements of customary international law, United Nations General Assembly, 'Summary Record of the 15th Committee' (UN Doc. A/C.6/65/SE.15, 2010), at 3.

177 Draft Articles on the Effects of Armed Conflict on Treaties, with Commentaries, adopted by the ILC, 63rd session, submitted to the UNGA, at 2.

178 See Commentaries and Acknowledgement in jurisprudence, International Law Commission, *supra* note 163, at 5ff.

179 "Where a treaty itself contains provisions on its operation in situations of armed conflict, those provisions shall apply."

180 An extended reference to the use of object and purpose of a treaty as a means of interpretation in the context of the 1951 convention, Hathaway, James C., *supra* note 62, at 55.

been an extended part of the human rights law framework.[181] Already, the preamble of the 1951 Convention[182] links refugee protection to the protection of human rights and positions the treaty as an integral part into the broader human rights law framework.[183] The overall goal of the 1951 Convention is the protection of persons who seek international protection explicitly because their human rights have been violated or are under threat.[184] The UNHCR, Executive Committee and legal scholarship have also elaborated on this proximity.[185]

After accepting the close relationship between human rights and refugee law, the debate about the separation of the laws of peace and the laws of armed conflict can be used as an additional point of reference. In particular, the evolution of a majority view on the complementarity of human rights law and humanitarian law supports this position, as has been promoted by the treaty-based monitoring bodies, the UNGA and the ICJ.[186] In particular, the ICJ has emphasised

181 United Nations High Commissioner for Refugees, *supra* note 124, at 1f.

182 The VCLT acknowledges the preamble as a source of the object and purpose of the instrument, Article 31 (2).

183 In particular, paragraphs 1 and 2 "CONSIDERING that the Charter of the United Nations and the Universal Declaration of Human Rights approved on 10 December 1948 by the General Assembly have affirmed the principle that human beings shall enjoy fundamental rights and freedoms without discrimination; CONSIDERING that the United Nations has, on various occasions, manifested its profound concern for refugees and endeavoured to assure refugees the widest possible exercise of these fundamental rights and freedoms", Preamble of the 1951 Convention.

184 *Id.*, at 2.

185 United Nations General Assembly, *supra* note 119. UNHCR: ExCom, *supra* note 114, at para. e; UNHCR: ExCom, *supra* note 77, at para. h; UNHCR: ExCom, *Conclusion No. 82 (XLVIII) Safeguarding Asylum* (1997), available online at http://www.refworld.org/pdfid/4b28bf1f2.pdf (last visited 1 August 2018), at para. d (vi); UNHCR: ExCom, *Conclusion No. 85 (XLIX) International Protection* (1998), available online at http://www.refworld.org/pdfid/4b28bf1f2.pdf (last visited 1 August 2018), at paras. f-m. Chetail, Vincent, 'Armed Conflict and Forced Migration: A Systemic Approach to International Humanitarian Law, Refugee Law and Human Rights Law', in A. Clapham and P. Gaeta (eds.), *The Oxford Handbook of International Law in Armed Conflict* (Oxford University Press, 2014), 700. Durieux, Jean-Francois, 'Of War, Flows, Laws and Flaws. A Reply to Hugo Storey', 31 *Refugee Survey Quarterly* (2012) 161, at 165f.

186 Human Rights Committee, 'General Comment No. 31: The nature of the general legal obligation imposed on States Parties to the Covenant' (UN Doc. CCPR/C/21/Rev.1/Add.13, 2004), at 101. "While in respect of certain Covenant rights, more specific rules of international humanitarian law may be specially relevant for the purpose of the interpretation of the Covenant rights, both spheres of law are complementary, not mutually exclusive" and additionally, *Loizidou v. Turkey*, App. No. 15318/89, European Court of Human Rights (1995). *Bámaca Velásquez Case (Petition No. 11.129)*, Series C No. 70 (2000), Inter-American Court of Human Rights (2000). United Nations Security Council, 'Resolution 237' (UN Doc. S/RES/237, 1967), at para. 2. United Nations General Assembly, 'Resolution 2675 (XXV), Basic Principles for the Protection of Civilian Populations in Armed Conflicts' (UN Doc. A/RES/2675, 1970). For legal scholarship, see Heintze, Hans-Joachim, 'Theorien zum Verhältnis von Menschenrechten und humanitärem Völkerrecht', 24 *Humanitäres Völkerrecht - Informationsschriften* (2011) 4. Kolb, Robert, 'Human Rights and Humanitarian Law' (Max Planck Encyclopedia of Public International Law, 2013).

the parallel application of both IHL and human rights law in prominent cases: "[m]ore generally, the Court considers that the protection offered by human rights conventions does not cease in case of armed conflict, save through the effect of provisions for derogation."[187]

Furthermore, in contrast to IHL, which creates obligations for the state and non-state parties to the conflict, including on the protection of civilians, refugee protection concerns protection in transit or host countries. And, in contrast to human rights law treaties that have traditionally created obligations for the state in relation to its citizens, the 1951 Convention does not trigger obligations for state parties which have violated or failed to prevent the violation of its citizens' human rights. The 1951 Convention creates obligations for states other than the one of the refugee's citizenship to take responsibility for the citizens in question following their flight.[188] The application of the Convention to the country in conflict is irrelevant for the assessment of protection claims in host countries.

With the overall object and purpose of the 1951 Convention itself and through its close alignment with the human rights law framework, one can undoubtedly argue that the 1951 Convention is not susceptible to termination in the event of an outbreak of hostilities. This argument is bolstered by the general rule of continuity, the lack of a pertinent clause in the treaty itself and the object and purpose of the Convention. The termination of the treaty would severely impede the protection of refugees against serious violations of their rights. Additionally, the assumption that IHL does not suppress the application of treaties of the law of peace, particularly human rights treaties, supports the finding that the 1951 Convention remains applicable even after the outbreak of conflict.

One further historical argument can be drawn from the historical setting in which the 1951 Convention came into being – the Second World War and its resulting massive displacement. Although the Convention at first contained a geographical and temporal limitation, it was nonetheless created to address the consequences of the massive displacement of persons fleeing conflict and violence. Parts of the *travaux preparatoires*[189] point to a comparable debate that already took place in 1951. At first glance, it appears to contradict the indifference of the 1951 Convention towards conflict or peace. The International Committee of the Red Cross (ICRC), at the Conference of Plenipotentiaries on the Status of Refugees and Stateless Persons on 26 November of 1951, submitted a proposal to broaden the original personal scope of the Convention. Their

187 *Legal Consequences of the Construction of a Wall in the Occupied Palestinian Territory. Advisory Opinion,* International Court of Justice (2004), at para. 106. Confirmed in *Armed Activities on the Territory of the Congo (Democratic Republic of the Congo v. Uganda)*, International Court of Justice (2005), at para. 216. *Legality of the Threat or Use of Nuclear Weapons. Advisory Opinion*, International Court of Justice (1996), at para. 25.

188 Zimmermann, Andreas and Mahler, Claudia, 'Article 1 A, para. 2 1951 Convention', in A. Zimmermann (ed.), *The 1951 Convention Relating to the Status of Refugees and its 1967 Protocol: A Commentary* (Oxford University Press, 2011), at 348.

189 A lengthy overview is given in the Commentary by *id.*, at 308ff.

proposal stated that the scope should include "[e]very person forced by grave events to seek refuge outside his country of origin".[190] This proposal comes close to the extended regional refugee definition adopted later, which offered protection for those fleeing generalised situations of violence or other events seriously disturbing public order. This proposal was, however, rejected by the delegations. The delegate representative from Israel assessed that the definition of refugee contained in Article 1 A. (2) "did not refer to natural disasters [...] [n]or did the text cover all man-made events. There was no provision, for example, for refugees fleeing from hostilities, unless they were in fact covered by Article 1 of the Convention"[191] and the US delegation cautioned against writing a "blank check"[192] in the light of unclear future developments. The statement mirrors the reluctance of state parties to apply the Convention in the event of mass disasters. Despite this reluctance, the *travaux preparatoires* do not contain explicit references to any complete rejection of an application of the treaty as such in times of conflict or to persons fleeing conflict, as long as they fit the eligibility criteria as beneficiaries of protection.

Various strong legal arguments lead to the conclusion that the Convention as such is definitely applicable, starting firstly with the absence of any explicit clause that denies the applicability of the treaty in times of conflict. Also, the broad protection-orientated object and purpose of the treaty do not allow for any other reading. Both arguments are further supported by broader public international law developments concerning, firstly, the effects of conflict on treaties and, secondly, the nowadays widely acknowledged assumption of complementarity[193] of the laws of peace and armed conflict. Finally, the context of war in the country of origin and potential application of IHL in that geographical sphere has no bearing on the application of the 1951 Convention in the refugee's host country. Therefore, this analysis holds that the treaty itself does not impede its application in times of conflict. On a theoretical note, this interpretation does not necessarily mean that one should adopt the so-called normalcy-approach,[194] which assumes that, as a consequence, most or even all conflict-related protection claims fall under the scope of the 1951 Convention. Rather, the Convention must be

190 International Committee on the Red Cross, 'Aide Memoire on the Refugee Question. Statement submitted by the International Committee on the Red Cross' (UN Doc. A/CONF./NGO.2, 1951).

191 United Nations General Assembly, 'Conference of Plenipotentiaries on the Status of Refugees and Stateless Persons, Summary Record of the Twenty-Second Meeting' (UN Doc. A/CONF.2/SR.22, 1951), at 6.

192 Ad Hoc Committee on Refugees and Stateless Persons, 'First Session: Summary Record of the Third Meeting' (UN Doc. E/AC.32/SR.3, 1950), at para. 37.

193 "[B]oth spheres of law are complementary, not mutually exclusive", Human Rights Committee, *supra* note 186, at 11. "Though separate and non-overlapping, are nonetheless complementary" and "[l]egally speaking, this relationship may be characterized by mutual complementarity and also by the lex specialis principle", Fleck, Dieter (ed.), *The Handbook of International Humanitarian Law* (2nd ed., 2008), at 74f.

194 See in detail Storey, Hugo, *supra* note 159, at 9ff.

assessed in detail and solely with regard to the criteria of its definition of refugee in order to identify the legally correct interpretation and application in the context of violence and conflict.

2.4.2 The refugee definition of Article 1 A (2) and persons fleeing conflict

The second major part of the analysis now turns to the definition of the Convention refugee in Article 1 A (2) in the context of violence and conflict. The refugee definition has generated lasting controversies on the application of the international refugee law regime to constantly escalating challenges, as "virtually every word of the core phrase of the refugee definition has been subject to interpretative dispute."[195] The question posed in this book is whether the refugee definition itself rejects its application to persons fleeing conflict and violence. The analysis does not start with a general interpretation of the elements of the 1951 Convention, but solely addresses their interpretation in the conflict context.

The whole definition of a Convention refugee, in the light of Article 1 (A), while rather long when one takes all the elements of the definition into account, i.e. the inclusion, the exclusion and the cessation clauses, does not make any textual reference to times of peace, times of armed conflict, conflict, violence, or any other synonym for unrest or distress. This shall be considered again as the first strong argument that the refugee definition *per se* does not preclude its application to persons fleeing countries in conflict and violence. When focusing on the inclusion clause containing the eligibility criteria, it becomes clear that the Article, at least by virtue of its word choice, is indifferent towards the contextual situation in which the refugee protection claim is generated. To provide clarity on a potential implicit interpretation, the elements of the refugee definition are carefully examined, criterion by criterion.[196]

For the specific application within the CEAS, one has to take into account that the QD and the Recast QD provide the legal basis for the incorporation of a refugee protection status in accordance with the 1951 Convention.[197] The transposed definition of a refugee, while stated as being in accordance with

195 Steinbock, Daniel, 'The Refugee Definition as a Law: Issues of Interpretation', in F. Nicholson and P. M. Twomey (eds.), *Refugee Rights and Realities: Evolving International Concepts and Regimes* (Cambridge University Press, 1999), at 14.

196 In this regard, the elements of the refugee definition are not interpreted according to the VCLT in general but only in reference to their sensitivity towards situations of conflict.

197 Prior to that, the Council of the EU adopted in 1996 a Joint Position on the Harmonized Application of the Definition of the Term "Refugee", Council of the European Union, 'Joint Position of 4 March 1996 defined by the Council on the basis of Article K.3 of the Treaty on European Union on the harmonized application of the definition of the term 'refugee' in Article 1 of the Geneva Convention of 28 July 1951 relating to the status of refugees. OJ 1996 L 63' (1996), at 2.

the 1951 Convention, does contain differences to the definition contained in the universal instrument. Most importantly, the scope *ratione personae* is considerably limited, as the (Recast) QD only covers third country nationals and stateless persons, but not every individual. This limitation clearly contradicts the 1951 Convention's phrasing of 'any person' irrespective of its country of origin. A further difference can be found in the regulations concerning exclusion from protection under Article 12 QD and the respective Article 1 (D), (E) and (F) of the Convention.[198] Otherwise, and specifically with regard to the focus of this book, the EU definition, contained in the (Recast) QD, reproduces the refugee definition of Article 1 A (2) and the eligibility criteria, examined in the following.[199]

The 1951 Convention defines in Article 1 A,

> [f]or the purposes of the present Convention, the term 'refugee' shall apply to any person who: [...] (2). As a result of events occurring before 1 January 1951 and owing to well-founded fear of being persecuted for reasons of race, religion, nationality, membership of a particular social group or political opinion, is outside the country of his nationality and is unable or, owing to such fear is unwilling to avail himself of the protection of that country; or who, not having a nationality and being outside the country of his former habitual residence as a result of such events, is unable or, owing to such fear is willing to return to it.

2.4.2.1 Back to the basic criteria – a well-founded fear of persecution

First in line when assessing the defining terminology of Article 1 A (2) for persons fleeing conflict is the criterion of the 'well-founded fear of persecution'. The well-founded nature of the fear is considered firstly, concerning the assumption that the risk of persecution during conflict should be elevated, in comparison to the risk assessed during times of peace. Secondly, it is discussed whether the term persecution itself presupposes its occurrence during conflict or peacetime.

2.4.2.1.1 THE WELL-FOUNDED NATURE OF FEAR

The well-founded nature of fear is one new element that distinguishes the persecutory criterion of the 1951 Convention from previous or older refugee treaties, which had all listed distinct groups of persons as being worthy of protection.[200]

198 Hailbronner, Kay and Thym, Daniel, *supra* note 1, at 1122f.

199 Zimmermann, Andreas and Mahler, Claudia, *supra* note 188, at 321.

200 Examples of treaties that codify protection based on distinct and predefined groups of beneficiaries are the 1928 Arrangement on Russian and Armenian Refugees, the 1933 Convention Relating to the International Status of Refugees applying to Russian, Armenian, Turkish, Assyrian, and Assyro-Chaldean Refugees, the 1938 Convention concerning the Status of Refugees coming from Germany.

The 1951 Convention no longer codifies such a specific reference or list of beneficiaries of its protection, but has replaced it with abstract criteria. These are intended to enable the determining state authorities to assess the protection claim on an individual basis.

Of general importance is the fact that refugee protection includes a forward-looking, preventive momentum and does not follow a solely reactive protection principle. The wording of the criterion of a well-founded fear already demonstrates that past persecution is not the only option to substantiate a protection claim. The fear of persecution expresses the openness of the criterion, which includes the risk of persecution that has not taken place, but is likely to happen in the future. The broader context of the 1951 Convention can be used to support this argument, especially its cornerstone obligation of *non-refoulement* in Article 33, which also suggests that a future-orientated risk assessment is required: "No contracting state shall expel or return ('refouler') a refugee [...] to the territories of countries where his life or freedom *would* be threatened."[201] The object and purpose of the Convention to broadly protect individuals from being returned to countries where they are vulnerable to persecution additionally supports the reading that protection not only from past persecution but also from probable *future* persecution is covered. As such, past persecution can be a strong indicator for such a well-founded nature of fear; it is, however, not a necessary precondition. This interpretation is also given by the UNHCR, emphasising that a "forward-looking expectation of risk"[202] is the basis for a claim, which is constituted when the person has demonstrated "to a reasonable degree" that a continued stay in his or her country of origin would have been intolerable.[203] It is only decisive whether, at the time the protection claim is assessed, reasonable grounds for fear exist.[204]

The phrase 'well-founded fear of persecution' not only reveals that both past and future persecution are covered, it is, furthermore, the basis for a debate that has arisen over the subjective and/or objective dimensions of the criterion.

The wording can be construed as encompassing a combination of two conditions: one relates to fear, a subjective feeling of "emotion of pain or uneasiness caused by the sense of impending danger".[205] The necessity to validate this fear with its "well-founded nature" could demonstrate that some objective

201 Article 33 (1) 1951 Convention (emphasis added by the author).

202 See United Nations General Assembly, *supra* note 118, at para. 197.

203 United Nations High Commissioner for Refugees, *supra* note 120, at para. 42.

204 UNHCR's Position United Nations High Commissioner for Refugees, *Note on Burden and Standard of Proof in Refugee Claims* (1998), available online at http://www.refworld.org/docid/3ae6b3338.html (last visited 1 August 2018). Examples of case law addressing the well-founded nature of fear, among others: *Immigration and Naturalization Service v. Cardoza-Fonseca U.S. Supreme Court, I.N.S. v. Cardoza-Fonseca, 67 U.S. 407 (1987)*, 480 U.S. 421 (1987), United States: Supreme Court (1987), at 453. *Mileva v. Canada (Minister of Employment and Immigration)*, [1991] 3 F.C. 398 (C.A.), Canada: Federal Court (1991), at 404.

205 Oxford English Dictionary, *fear, n.1* (2017), available online at http://www.oed.com/view/Entry/68773?rskey=LFJr1E&result=1 (last visited 1 August 2018).

reasons supporting this subjective feeling of an individual are required. The UNHCR has repeatedly included this combination of subjective and objective elements.[206] The Office emphasises the notion that the individual's predicament, rather than the objective circumstances in his or her country of origin, are in focus. That means the determining authority should be sensitive to an applicant's background, his or her personal characteristics and sensitivities.[207] The latter, objective element, would then support the claimant's credibility, as his or her statement cannot "be considered in the abstract, and must be viewed in the context of the relevant background situation. A knowledge of conditions in the applicant's country of origin – while not a primary objective – [are] an important element".[208]

While the general necessity to validate a subjective feeling of fear with more objective criteria of well-founded grounds for this fear is comprehensible, especially in the light of the refugee framework's exclusionary nature, a combined subjective-objective assessment would create misleading status determination results. The Zimmermann commentary underlines that

> [t]he risk-oriented focus of the 1951 Convention does not suggest that states should distinguish between applicants finding themselves in the very same situation depending on how they perceive their situation. Such would be the case, however if status determination decisions would on the one hand positively identify applicants who show their fear easily and thus grant them refugee status, while on the other hand disadvantaging persons who are not ready to give subjective evidence of trepidation.[209]

The distinction between persons showing their individual feeling, in contrast to those keeping back their feelings while objectively in the same situation, including facing the same expectations of persecution, does not reflect the object and purpose of the Convention.[210] And already, Grahl-Madsen in the Convention's first commentary stated that "every person claiming [...] to be a refugee has 'fear' ('well-founded' or otherwise) of being persecuted [...] irrespective of whether he jitters at the very thought of his return to his home country, is prepared to brave all hazards, or is simply apathetic or even unconscious of the

206 See for a divergent minority view on the subjective element, Hathaway, James C. and Hicks, William S., 'Is There a Subjective Element in the Refugee Convention's Requirement of 'well-founded fear'?', 26 *Michigan Journal of International Law* (2005) 505.

207 United Nations High Commissioner for Refugees, *supra* note 120, at para. 40. "[S]ince psychological reactions of different individuals may not be the same in identical situations. One person may have strong political or religious convictions, the disregard of which would make life intolerable; another may have no such strong convictions. One person may make an impulsive decision to escape, another may carefully plan his departure."

208 *Id.*, at para. 12.

209 Zimmermann, Andreas and Mahler, Claudia, *supra* note 188, at 338. Similarly and in more detail on the discussion, Hathaway, James C. and Hicks, William S., *supra* note 206.

210 Zimmermann, Andreas and Mahler, Claudia, *supra* note 188, at 338.

possible dangers."[211] When one interprets the wording of the Convention, the text strongly supports an objective risk assessment. The Oxford English Dictionary defines fear as "a particular apprehension of some future evil".[212] If one takes this definition as the basis, fear only concerns an expectation of danger and not an individual sentiment of trepidation. As such, the understanding also supports an objective assessment of the subjective element.

Interestingly, it is not the debate over the inclusion or rejection of a subjective element that has become highly disputed in the context of conflict, but the objective assessment of the risk that persons claim to be faced with during conflict in their country of origin. The background situation of generalised conflict and its assessment have raised far more challenges in status determination than the individual and subjective risk assessment of the individual asylum seeker.

2.4.2.1.2 IN REJECTION OF A DIFFERENT ASSESSMENT OF RISK IN TIMES OF CONFLICT

The risk assessment of a claimant is conducted by taking into account the different aspects of the individual's situation[213] against the background of the general situation in her country of origin. Other elements play into the assessment, such as issues of the claimant's credibility, as well as documentary, medical or expert evidence provided, which will not be addressed here in more detail. For conflict-related claims, the assessment of the context of conflict itself and its consequences for the substantiation of a refugee claim must be put in focus.

The wording, context, object and purpose of Article 1 A (2) do not describe or refer to any specific background circumstances in the country of origin, i.e. armed conflict, sporadic violent incidents or peace, as influencing the occurrence of the required persecutory acts. The treaty itself gives only the necessary criteria to determine if a person is considered a refugee in the Convention's sense. The number of persons affected and the relation of one claimant to other claimants are not criteria for eligibility. That has not prevented state practice from limiting the recognition of claims from persons fleeing conflict, although jurisprudence in this regard is far from consistent.[214] This limitation has prominently been achieved through an interpretative change in the assessment of risk and the employment of an aggravated, differentiated-risk. This is known as the 'differential-risk approach'.

211 Grahl-Madsen, Atle, *supra* note 48, at 174.

212 Zimmermann, Andreas and Mahler, Claudia, *supra* note 188, at 338.

213 United Nations High Commissioner for Refugees, *UNHCR's Eligibility Guidelines for Assessing the International Protection Needs of Afghan Asylum-Seekers* (2007), available online at http://www.unhcr.org/refworld/docid/477ce70a2.html (last visited 1 August 2018).

214 The issue of a differentiated risk has not only been addressed with regard to the 1951 Convention but similarly on 15 Recast QD and subsidiary protection as well as regarding Article 3 ECHR which is discussed in the respective chapters below.

At the centre of this debate is the risk an individual faces within a wider situation of generalised violence, i.e. the issue of individualisation and the alleged necessity of clearly identifying individuals who have been 'singled out' from the mass of other people affected by conflict and violence: "[I]t encompasses the idea that there must be a purposeful discrimination against the persecuted persons for the definition to apply."[215] One can distinguish between two trends in the jurisprudence regarding the specific risk requirement in times of conflict:[216] at one end of the spectrum the restrictive differential-risk approach and, on the other, the 'non-comparative approach'.[217]

The *Adan* decision of the UK House of Lords in 1999 is one clear example of the application of the differential-risk approach: in the assessment of claims from Somalia, the bench required evidence of a risk "over and above the normal effects of warfare".[218] The judges argued that, in the light of the violence in Somalia and its widespread nature, to substantiate a refugee claim, a different and higher level of individualised threat than in times of peace must be presented. The House of Lords opined that "those in power change from time to time so that the persecutors become the persecuted"[219] and "all sections of society in northern Somalia are equally at risk so long as the civil war continues."[220] In their debate, the fact of danger for all parts of society leads to the rejection of asylum claims, due to a lack of a differentiated or heightened risk of persecution in the context of violence. "[W]here a state of civil war exists, it is not enough for an asylum-seeker to show that he would be at risk if he were returned to his country. He must be able to show [...] a differential impact."[221]

In other US and UK case law, the courts have argued, using comparable lexicon, that applicants needed "to show fear of persecution for Convention grounds over and above the risk to life and liberty inherent in the civil war",[222] "[t]o succeed in his claim that he has a well-founded fear of persecution, [the claimant] must demonstrate that his fear of being singled out for persecution is subjectively genuine and that there is objective evidence to justify his fear",[223]

215 Kälin, Walter, 'Refugees and Civil Wars: Only a Matter of Interpretation?', 3 *International Journal of Refugee Law* (1991) 435, at 438.

216 Markard, Nora, *supra* note 161, at 127. Storey, Hugo and Wallace, Rebecca, 'War and Peace in Refugee Law Jurisprudence', 95 *The American Journal of International Law* (2001) 349, at 349ff. Zimmermann, Andreas and Mahler, Claudia, *supra* note 188, at 316.

217 See further Markard, Nora, *supra* note 161, at 137.

218 *Adan v. Secretary of State for the Home Department, per Lord Slynn of Hadley*, [1998] UKHL 15, United Kingdom: House of Lords (1998).

219 *Id.*, at 302.

220 *Id.*, at 312.

221 *Id.*, at 325.

222 *Id.* The UKIAT subsequently applied the requirement of a higher risk in *NM and Others (Lone Women - Ashraf) Somalia v. Secretary of State for the Home Department*, CG [2005] UKIAT 00076, United Kingdom: Asylum and Immigration Tribunal / Immigration Appellate Authority (2005), at paras. 118 and 135.

223 *Wackowski v. Immigration and Naturalization Service*, 1999 U.S. App. LEXIS 26590, United States: Court of Appeals, Seventh Circuit (1999).

and "persecution by the guerrillas was also shared by his neighbours; he was not singled out."[224] As a broad consequence, claims arising from conflict situations were rejected where the claimant could not provide sufficient evidence to satisfy the court that his or her risk was more aggravated than that of fellow citizens: "There is no indication that [the claimant] faces a danger of persecution that is appreciably different from that faced by the hundreds of thousands of others."[225] The argumentation buttressing the differential-risk approach is that, even if there is evidence of harm amounting to persecution by on one or more Convention grounds, such harm is not enough to trigger refugee protection if it occurs during ongoing hostilities widely affecting the civilian population. In a general situation of violence, an *aggravated* risk is considered necessary to substantiate a protection claim.

What has come to be known as the 'non-comparative approach'[226] diverges considerably from the approach presented above. Based on the wording of the Convention, it emphasises a regular application of the Convention, irrespective of context: "[I]t is important to keep firmly in mind the wording of the Convention definition. The definition makes no reference to any different approach being adopted where the persecution exists in the context of civil war."[227]

The Federal Court of Canada in its leading *Vahe Salibian* judgement employs this approach:

> In sum, while modern refugee law is concerned to recognize the protection needs of particular claimants, the best evidence that an individual faces a serious chance of persecution is usually the treatment afforded similarly situated persons in the country of origin. *In the context of claims derived from situations of generalized oppression, therefore, the issue is not whether the claimant is more at risk than anyone else in her country, but rather whether the broadly based harassment or abuse is sufficiently serious to substantiate a claim to refugee status.*[228]

Here, the court even used the situational context as an indicator to further substantiate the claim rather than use it to demand a higher risk.

This non-comparative test was reiterated in *Ali, Shayasta-Ameer*, as the proper test to assess refugee status in the context of civil war. In reference to the

224 *Julio Cesar Quevedo; Megdy Perez De Quevedo v. John Ashcroft, Attorney General*, No. 02-2227, United States: Court of Appeals, First Circuit (2003), at 44.

225 *Patel v. Immigration and Naturalization Service*, US App. Lexis 30517, United States: Court of Appeals, Ninth Circuit (1999), at 5.

226 See also in detail the comparison of Storey, Hugo and Wallace, Rebecca, *supra* note 216, at 349ff.

227 *Minister for Immigration and Multicultural Affairs v. Abdi*, [1999] FCA 299; 162 ALR 105, Australia: Federal Court (1999), at para. 37f.

228 *Vahe Salibian v. Canada (Minister of Employment and Immigration), per Décary, JA*, [1990] 3 F.C. 250 (C.A.), Canada: Federal Court (1990), at 259 (emphasis added by the author). Hathaway, James C., *The Law of Refugee Status* (Butterworths, 1991), at 97.

UNHCR Guidelines on Civilian Non-combatants Fearing Persecution in Civil War Situations, the bench held:

> The non-comparative approach to the assessment of a claim is the approach advocated in these Guidelines. [...] *The issue is not a comparison between the claimant's risk and the risk faced by other individuals or groups at risk for a Convention reason, but whether the claimant's risk is a risk of sufficiently serious harm and is linked to a Convention reason as opposed to the general, indiscriminate consequences of civil war.* A claimant should not be labelled as a "general victim" of civil war without full analysis of her personal circumstances and that of any group to which she may belong. Using a non-comparative approach results in a focusing of attention on whether the claimant's fear of persecution is by reason of a Convention ground.[229]

Equally, in *Bolonos Hernandes*:

> Not once have we considered a specific threat against a petitioner insufficient because it reflected a general level of violence [...] It should be obvious that the significance of a specific threat to an individual's life or freedom is not lessened by the fact that the individual resides in a country where the lives and freedoms of a large number of persons are threatened.[230]

The UNHCR now takes a neutral stance to the number of claims and relations between claimants: "The fact that all members of the community are equally affected does not in any way undermine the legitimacy of any particular individual claim."[231] A personalised risk of persecution can be "shared by many other individuals"[232] and the number of people whose rights are potentially violated does not invalidate or undermine an individual's refugee claim:

> A proper interpretation of Article 1, it is not relevant how large or indeed how small the affected group may be. *Whole communities may risk or suffer persecution for Convention reasons, and the fact that all members of the community are equally affected does not in any way undermine the legitimacy of*

229 *Ali, Shaysta-Ameer v. Canada (Minister of Employment and Immigration), Décary, Stone, Strayer*, (F.C.A., no. A-772-96), Canada: Federal Court of Appeal (1999) (emphasis added by the author).

230 *Bolanos-Hernandez v. Immigration and Naturalization Service*, 767 F.2.d, United States: Court of Appeals, Ninth Circuit (1984), at 1285.

231 United Nations High Commissioner for Refugees, *UNHCR's Eligibility Guidelines for Assessing the International Protection Needs of Iraqi Asylum-seekers* (2007), available online at http://www.refworld.org/docid/46deb05557.html (last visited 1 August 2018), at 129.

232 *Prophete v. Canada*, 2009 FCA 31, Canada: Federal Court (2009), at para. 18.

> ***any particular individual claim. On the contrary, such facts should facilitate recognition***, as the sociological process of marginalisation that such stigmatisation engenders is a powerful archetype of persecution.[233]

Also in this regard, the new Guidelines No. 12 on Conflict and Violence stress that "[…] the impact of a situation of armed conflict and violence on an entire community, or on civilians more generally, strengthens rather than weakens the well-founded nature of the fear of being persecuted of a particular individual."[234]

Legally, the risk assessment for cases in which huge numbers of individuals are affected still remains something to be carried out on an individual or case-by-case basis. However, for reasons of practicality in status determination, it has, on some occasions, been usual practice to grant a group-based *prima facie* status.[235] Concerning the wording of the 1951 Convention, it remains that Article 1 A (2) does not balance the claims of individuals against each other. The conflict as the context in which a claim is made can constitute the grounds for various acts of harm of different levels and natures and the product of different motivations. Refugee law, as codified in the universal instrument, does not pose the question whether one person is more at risk than others; rather, it asks whether the harm he or she fears or endures is sufficiently serious and caused by one of the factors laid out in the Convention itself.[236] A different risk assessment for peacetime persecution must therefore be rejected as adding an additional criterion of eligibility which is not justified by reference to the treaty text.

2.4.2.1.3 AT THE HEART OF REFUGEEHOOD – PERSECUTION

Persecution is morally and legally at the heart of the distinction between refugees and migrants. The term has been subject to considerable debate and change since the treaty's entry into force. Changes have included interpretative shifts and adaptation to altering circumstances in forced displacement realities. The necessity of potentially adapting and applying the term flexibly was already foreseen, as for this exact reason, this central term was left undefined in the 1951 Convention. The drafters of the Convention, according to its first commentary, "capitulated before the inventiveness of humanity to think up new ways

233 United Nations High Commissioner for Refugees, *supra* note 124, at para. 21 (emphasis added by the author). Kälin, Walter, *Refugees and Civil Wars: Only a Matter of Interpretation?, supra* note 215, at para. 1. *Minister for Immigration and Multicultural Affairs v. Haji Ibrahim*, [2000] HCA 55, Australia: High Court (2000).

234 United Nations High Commissioner for Refugees, *supra* note 132, at 6.

235 See for more, Albert, Matthew, 'Prima facie determination of refugee status. An overview and its legal foundation. Refugee Studies Centre, University of Oxford, Working Paper Series No. 55' (2010).

236 Hathaway, James C. and Foster, Michelle, *supra* note 1, at 181.

of persecuting fellow men".[237] For that reason, the term was not exhaustively defined in a way that set its legal parameters in a binding manner. However, its scope can be deduced from legal interpretation.

2.4.2.1.3.1 The ordinary meaning From its Latin origin 'persequi', the ordinary meaning of the term 'persecution' means to pursue "with hostile intent".[238] The Oxford English Dictionary defines it as "[t]he action of persecuting with enmity and malignity; especially the infliction of death, torture or penalties for adhering to a religious belief or an opinion as such, with a view to the repression or extirpation of it"[239] and "[t]o chase, hunt, or pursue with intent to capture, injure, or kill".[240] That alone does not clarify which persecutory acts are covered by the Convention and which are not, or at what level of violence or threat of violence a refugee claim can be constituted. Of most importance is that the wording does not limit persecution to only arising in certain contexts, whether war or peace.

2.4.2.1.3.2 The systemic interpretation – persecution in context By way of systemic interpretation, the context of Article 1 A (2) could offer clarification. The 1951 Convention itself has been used as a first point of reference on the design of persecution, for instance by referring to the principle of *non-refoulement* in Article 33. This reference could indicate that persecution encompasses any "threat to life or freedom", as any return to a country where the individual would be at such risk is prohibited. However, since *non-refoulement* is merely a negative obligation and offers only a minimal standard of protection, this reference is not of much help in interpreting a major element of the *positive* protection obligation.[241] What, then, does the broader context tell us? While the Preamble of the Convention refers explicitly to both the UN Charter and the Universal Declaration of Human Rights of 1948, it only includes that previous international (human rights) agreements relating to the status of refugees shall be revised and consolidated.[242]

Common practice in the predecessor instruments of refugee protection, as established by the League of Nations, cannot be consulted when determining the meaning of the term 'persecution'. This is because they followed a different approach, in which the establishment of persecution in a refugee claim was not conducted as a central test. In fact, both the 1933 League of Nations Conventions relating to the Status of Refugees and the 1938 Convention concerning

237 Grahl-Madsen, Atle, *supra* note 48, at 193.
238 Oxford English Dictionary, *Persecution, n.* (2017), available online at http://www.oed.com/view/Entry/141431?redirectedFrom=persecution (last visited 1 August 2018).
239 Simpson, John A. (ed.), *The Oxford English Dictionary, Vol. XI* (2nd ed., 1989), at 591f.
240 Oxford English Dictionary, *Persecute, v.* (2017), available online at http://www.oed.com/view/Entry/141429?redirectedFrom=persecute (last visited 1 August 2018).
241 Zimmermann, Andreas and Mahler, Claudia, *supra* note 188, at 346.
242 1951 Convention, preambular paragraph 1.

the Status of Refugees Coming from Germany defined refugees as persons of a specific origin without the protection of their country of nationality; reference to any reasons for flight were not given.[243] No further guidance on the term can be drawn from these instruments. The establishment of the International Refugee Organisation, the UNHCR's predecessor and its Constitution, for the first time in the body of asylum law, included the abstract test of 'persecution' in its Article 26, but still following a detailed list of groups that would qualify as refugees. Also, this inclusion came without a definition, as did the decisions taken by the Ad Hoc Committee on Statelessness and Related Problems when preparing the draft for the new Refugee Convention.[244] Lengthy discussions took place on either the traditional approach, which would include, as previously, groups eligible for refugee protection due to membership of a particular group lacking national protection, or a second approach, namely a more general definition without reference to a specific origin.[245] However, also here, the term 'persecution' was not further defined in detail, which was later underlined at the Conference of Plenipotentiaries by the Israeli delegate: "Of the three factors governing the definition of the term 'refugee', practically no attention had been paid to the substantive requirements for qualification as a refugee […]"[246]

The refugee law context of Article 1 A (2) is thus not suitable for advancing the interpretation of the term 'persecution'.

2.4.2.1.3.3 The object and purpose The Convention's main purpose is to consolidate the state's obligations to grant international protection to those who have fled (or are in fear of) persecution and to refrain from returning them to countries where they are at risk of being persecuted.

Neither the wording, nor the context of the Convention indicate that persecution can only arise during times of peace, or that conduct and acts committed during or as part of hostilities are beyond the scope of persecution. The object and purpose of the Convention, particularly as an instrument of the Post-Second World War international legal order, equally do not require on overly restrictive interpretation of the term. A situation of conflict in the country of origin would not run counter to the protection purpose, but rather would enhance an asylum-seeker's claim to protection.

A pivotal question is whether the context of the conflict changes the nature of persecution. During an armed conflict, violations of the rules of IHL can

243 Fripp, Eric, 'International Humanitarian Law and the Interpretation of 'Persecution' in Article 1A(2) CSR51', 26 *International Journal of Refugee Law* (2014) 382, at 387. Zimmermann, Andreas and Mahler, Claudia, *supra* note 188, at 270.

244 IRO Constitution Article 26, para. 3: "persecution, or fear, based on reasonable ground of persecution because of race, religion, nationality or political opinions". Groups specifically listed were among others, victims of the Nazi or fascist regimes, Spanish Republicans and other victims of the Falangist regime in Spain, Annex 1, p 1, s A, paras. 1–4.

245 Debates of Ad Hoc Committee on Refugees and Stateless Persons, *supra* note 192, at 3.

246 United Nations General Assembly, *supra* note 191, Mr. Robinson (Israel).

simplify the decision of the persecutory or non-persecutory nature of certain acts.[247] Serious violations of IHL constitute war crimes.[248] That their level of harm amounts to persecution is indisputable. More interesting is whether acts committed by lawful combatants during conflict, justified under IHL, can nevertheless constitute persecution in the refugee law sense. The ordinary understanding of the term 'persecution' refers to harm conducted with a hostile intention. One can, therefore, argue that, for instance, civilians harmed as collateral damage during an attack on a legitimate target are not persecuted in the required refugee law sense. However, if the consequences of an otherwise legitimate act under IHL exceed the necessary level of violence, this could render the harm caused persecutory. In this scenario, the IHL criterion of proportionality would be the decisive factor in determining persecutory acts. But, on the other hand, IHL and refugee law are two distinct fields of law and the targeting decisions of the former cannot be the decisive criterion to establish protection claims in the latter. The IHL criterion of proportionality could, in exceptional cases, be indicative of a hidden persecutory act, in which civilians suffer direct attack rather than excessive collateral damage. This could amount to persecution in the refugee law sense. In conclusion, however, one must state that IHL considerations, in the majority of cases, cannot simply be carried over to refugee determination claims, as both assessments follow different criteria and purposes. The refugee status claim thus requires a proper assessment in accordance with the standards of its own field of law.

The 1951 Convention establishes a close link with the broader human rights framework. The Convention's preamble refers to the UN Charter and the Universal Declaration of Human Rights, holding that "the principle that human beings shall enjoy fundamental rights and freedoms without discrimination" is to be upheld.[249] The reference indicates that persecution is constituted by the violation of human rights. This reference, including in the preamble, to human rights law is broad and does not refer to specific human rights that should be protected. This would point to the inclusion of those rights protected in the Universal Declaration and the subsequent major human rights law treaties, such as the nine deriving from the UN, as there is no indication that only qualified rights count. On the other hand, one has to keep in mind that the 1951 Convention as an instrument does not provide substitute protection for all the rights a person normally holds in his or her country of origin. This supports the argument that not all violations of human rights can amount to persecution in

247 Holzer, Vanessa, 'The Relevance of the 1951 Refugee Convention for the Protection of Individuals Forced to Flee Armed Conflicts', in J. Hertwig (ed.), *Global Risks: Constructing World order through Law, Politics and Economics* (P. Lang, 2010), 95, at 104ff. Zimmermann, Andreas and Mahler, Claudia, *supra* note 188, at 371, 319–320. Markard, Nora, *supra* note 161, at 158ff.

248 Rule 156 Customary IHL, ICC Statute, Article 8, ICTY Statute, Article 1, ICTR Statute, Article 1, Statute of the Special Court for Sierra Leone, Article 1(1).

249 Preamble, para. 1.

the sense of the 1951 Convention. The object and purpose of the Convention in relation to the human rights framework has inspired scholars to embark on a further attempt at definition.[250]

The Recast QD, as transposed to the EU asylum scheme, provides more clarification on the term persecution. The (Recast) QD's emphasis lies on serious violations of basic human rights, in particular rights from which no derogation under the ECtHR is allowed. Article 9 Recast QD holds:

> 1. In order to be regarded as an act of persecution within the meaning of Article 1(A) of the Geneva Convention, an act must:
>
> (a) be sufficiently serious by its nature or repetition as to constitute a severe violation of basic human rights, in particular the rights from which derogation cannot be made under Article 15 (2) of the European Convention for the Protection of Human Rights and Fundamental Freedoms; or
>
> (b) be an accumulation of various measures, including violations of human rights which is sufficiently severe as to affect an individual in a similar manner as mentioned in point (a).

If the (Recast) QD did not encompass the phrasing 'in particular', there would be a strong presumption that *only* violations of the most fundamental, non-derogable rights can constitute persecution. In turn, this wording equally stresses that the most basic non-derogable rights are listed as examples, but not as exclusive grounds for persecution.[251]

The object and purpose of the Convention do not give more direction concerning the exact definition of the term. It was, however, always intended to leave the term itself open to subsequent interpretation, as the various potential types of persecution could have not been foreseen in the 1950s. For the assessment of acts amounting to persecution that take place during a conflict, short of a limiting definition of the term, different broadening interpretations are reflected in the subsequent interpretative practice of the Convention.

250 One comprehensive attempt to define the term, offered by Hathaway and Foster, is the "sustained or systemic violation of basic human rights demonstrative of a failure of state protection in relation to one of the core entitlements recognized by the international community". Hathaway, James C. and Foster, Michelle, *supra* note 1, at 204. Hathaway, James C., *supra* note 228, at 104f. This understanding was acknowledged in national courts, among others, *Horvath v. Secretary of State for the Home Department, supra* note 105, at 495F, 501C, 512F and 517D. Kirby J in *Minister for Immigration and Multicultural Affairs v. Khawar,* 187 ALR 574; [2002] HCA 14, Australia: High Court (2002), at para. 111. Goodwin-Gill and McAdam turn their focus on the violation or threat of life or physical freedom, although if violations of other rights take place in a severe form, these could also result in persecution, Goodwin-Gill, Guy S. and McAdam, Jane, *supra* note 1, at 208f. The approach by Zimmermann and Mahler renders human dignity their central point of assessment that is "unbearable and prevent this person from living life without fear due to his or her political conviction or other inalienable aspects, depriving the individual of being recognized as an equal part of society", Zimmermann, Andreas and Mahler, Claudia, *supra* note 188, at 347.

251 Hailbronner, Kay and Thym, Daniel, *supra* note 1, at 1169ff.

2.4.2.1.3.4 Subsequent interpretative practice During conflict, persecution does not change its nature, but it can take on different forms and characteristics. The openness of the terminology employed calls for an open mind concerning potential forms of persecution. The conflict context adds different layers of vulnerabilities through the means employed, the general degenerating situation and the varying effects it has on different people. The UNHCR regularly publishes examples of conflict-specific occurrences of persecutory acts. The Office uses these country-specific guidelines to present the different forms that persecution can and has taken, including during conflict. The Eligibility Guidelines for Assessing the International Protection Needs for Asylum Seekers from certain countries are a means to raise awareness, specifically in the determining RSD authorities. They can be considered as the UNHCR's practical implementation guide based on its legal interpretation of the Convention in one specific context. They also advance the list of witnessed forms of persecutory acts. While the Office, to some extent, uses a particular country or conflict-specific focus in order to clarify interpretative issues, the national context is always just one facet of the characterisation of a conflict. The wholesale application of these forms of persecution to other conflicts is not possible. The variety of means and methods of persecution and different shapes of violence makes it important to remain adaptable to the changing circumstances of ongoing and future conflict and not to restrict understandings of persecution.

One example of the UNHCR's approach to assessment is provided by the Eligibility Guidelines for International Protection Needs for Asylum Seekers from Afghanistan,[252] which address specific forms of persecution arising on the road to conflict:

> Human Rights and other consequences of exposure to conflict-related violence may amount to persecution within Article 1 (A)(2) of the 1951 Convention, either independently or cumulatively. In the context of Afghanistan, relevant factors in assessing the human rights violations or other serious harm that would be reasonably possible for an individual fleeing the conflict include *(i) the control over civilian populations by anti-government elements (AGEs), including through the imposition of parallel justice structures and the meting out of illegal punishments, as well as by means of threats and intimidation of civilians, restrictions on freedom of movement, and the use of extortion and illegal taxation; (ii) forced recruitment; (iii) the impact of violence and insecurity on the humanitarian situation as manifested by food insecurity, poverty and the destruction of livelihoods* [...].[253]

252 Other specifics of persecution in conflict situations can be deduced from the eligibility guidelines for asylum seekers from Somalia (2010), Eritrea (2011), Ivory Coast (2012), Iraq (2012) and Sri Lanka (2012).

253 United Nations High Commissioner for Refugees, *supra* note 28, at 7 (emphasis added by the author).

These guidelines provide examples to increase the sensitivity for the broad nature of the term persecution in various past and contemporary contexts.

The practice of refugee protection and status determination, since the Convention's entry into force, has changed, not least because of the broader and continuously advancing human rights law framework. Developments in the latter have almost always had a direct influence on the interpretation of the term 'persecution'. This influence, in methodological terms, is exerted through an interpretation of the object and purpose of the 1951 Convention and its reference to human rights law.

Of importance for the application of the term 'persecution' in the conflict context are two developments that have found their way into the 1951 Convention refugee definition via its human rights-adapted object and purpose. On the one hand, there is heightened sensitivity towards vulnerable groups and the different effects of violence. On the other hand, cumulative violations of socio-economic rights are increasingly recognised as amounting to a level of harm comparable to that of violations of civil and political rights. National courts have not so far presented one picture of common state practice in this regard. However, there is evidence of a progressive interpretation in line with both human rights developments and the UNHCR's guidelines.

Turning to the awareness of special vulnerabilities, the notion of persecution was not only kept open with regard to what conduct constitutes it. If directed at younger people, conduct that would otherwise fail to establish persecution, such as lighter forms of ill-treatment or separation from family members, might indeed amount to persecution.[254] For women or the elderly, perpetrators might choose different forms of ill-treatment than for young or middle-aged men. Even aside from the identifiable, alleged vulnerabilities of specific groups, for one individual, some forms of harm are more cruel than for others. This has been taken on by the UNHCR in its various guidelines, arguing for the inclusion of differences in "the psychological make-up" and personal circumstances of the individual affected.[255] When assessing whether certain conduct amounts to persecution, the claimant's profile, experience, age, and gender must be taken into consideration. This assessment has been adapted in scholarly debates and to some extent in national judicial practice. One prominent example that arises in the context of conflict is gender-sensitivity.

Gender-sensitive status determination and assessments of persecution have taken a leading position in this human rights-guided conceptualisation of persecution. The 1951 Convention and its 1967 Protocol address neither sex nor gender as a category relevant for legal status or eligibility. However, it has been shown that "women refugees often experience persecution differently from

254 See Brett, Rachel A., Brett, Margaret and Rashed, Haifa, 'Children Fleeing Conflict: Age and the Interpretation and Application of the 1951 Refugee Convention', in V. Türk, A. Edwards and C. W. Wouters (eds.), *In Flight from Conflict and Violence: UNHCR's Consultations on Refugee Status and Other Forms of International Protection* (Cambridge University Press, 2017).

255 United Nations High Commissioner for Refugees, *supra* note 120, at para. 52.

men", and sensitivity towards gender differences is a necessary element of an effective asylum system.[256] The impact of disaster and conflict on women and girls heavily depends on their status prior to the events leading to displacement[257]:

> [T]he additional layer of pre-existing exclusions and discrimination that typify women's status in many societies has an additional and compounding effect on the waging of and experiences that follow from war in conflicted societies.[258]

Even looking at one very classical fact of sexual violence and rape, the obstacles that arise for female asylum applicants due to interpretative disagreements over the 1951 Convention still persist. Although one can generally observe a recognition of the special nature of rape in a conflict situation, transferring it to asylum application has been a major challenge. On the one hand, rape victims, like victims of torture, are often reluctant to address the issue in their testimonies. On the other hand, the act itself has for quite some time been solely addressed as one type of ordinary crime, not related to the context of conflict or understood as engaging the 1951 Convention.

In the case of *Najjemba v. UK*, raping the applicant was considered as a personal sexual crime, characterised by "simple and dreadful loss", however not related to persecution.[259] It was similarly phrased in the case of *RE B (FC)* House of Lords decision, a decision that was criticised by Baroness Hale of Richmond for not recognising that "the persecution of Mrs. B was expressed in a different way from the persecution of her husband and sons" through rape and that was a strategy of war."[260] In the case of *NS (Afghanistan)* the court equally denied the asylum request as it found that the rape had been committed because "the assailant found her attractive, and therefore that attack was a purely personal one, and no more than a common crime".[261] On appeal, however, the Immigration Appeal Tribunal overthrew the argumentation and final assessment, stating the "finding was not based on the evidence"[262] and "to take as a wife, by force,

256 Haines, Rodger, 'Gender-Related Persecution', in E. Feller, V. Türk and F. Nicholson (eds.), *Refugee Protection in International Law: UNHCR's Global Consultations on International Protection* (Cambridge University Press, 2003), at 329.

257 Gardam, Judith G. and Jarvis, Michelle J., *Women, Armed Conflict and International Law* (Kluwer Law International, 2001), at 21.

258 Ní Aoláin, Fionnuala, Haynes, Dina F. and Cahn, Naomi R., *On the Frontlines* (Oxford University Press, 2011), at 46.

259 *Najjemba v. Secretary of State for Home Department*, [2002] EWCA Civ 1082, United Kingdom: Court of Appeal (England and Wales) (2002), at para. 9.

260 *In re B (FC) (Appellant) (2002). Regina v. Special Adjudicator, Ex parte Hoxha (FC)*, [2005] UKHL 19, United Kingdom: House of Lords (2005), at para. 30.

261 *NS (Social Group - Women - Forced Marriage) Afghanistan v. Secretary of State for the Home Department*, CG [2004] UKIAT 00328, United Kingdom: Asylum and Immigration Tribunal / Immigration Appellate Authority (2004), at para. 16.

262 *Ibid.*

the wife of one's enemy, after first imprisoning him, is not an uncommon act in the course of war or other conflict, such as an act of aggression against the enemy."[263]

More recent case law shows the slow change in interpreting specific ill-treatment as amounting to persecution, in the case of rape from a realisation of a private lust to a conflict related act amounting to persecution, an interpretation that is strongly supported by scholars such as Oosterveld[264] or Macklin:

> [R]ape [is considered] as an integral and tactical part of the arsenal of weapons deployed to brutalise, dehumanise, and humiliate women and demoralise their kin and community.[265]

While some types of gender-related ill-treatment can more easily be identified, in other conduct, the special gender component might not be so apparent. The UNHCR Guidelines on International Protection address this issue explicitly and one can observe the increasing recognition even in subsequently developed and binding regional instruments. Also, forms of forcible recruitment of women and children for forced prostitution or sexual exploitation and specific types of harm against women have been addressed as persecutory acts, such as forced marriages, forced abortion as well as forced sterilisation, or local practices such as bride burning. From this example, one can see a direct link between the broader human rights law development as well as the recognition of particularly the UNHCR's role in the interpretation of refugee law.[266]

The second transfer of human rights developments to refugee law matters concerns the increasing recognition of socio-economic rights violations as cumulatively amounting to persecution. The protection purpose of the Convention again opens the door for this broadening interpretation that not only single acts of ill-treatment can severely violate the most basic rights of the persons concerned. Also, cumulative effects of harm below the threshold can constitute persecution in the refugee law sense. The UNHCR Handbook states that these acts could, for instance, include different forms of discrimination, combined with "other adverse factors (e.g. general atmosphere of insecurity in the country of origin) [...] can reasonably justify a claim to well-founded fear of persecution".[267] Various domestic courts reflect this interpretation as examples of state practice in the interpretation of the term:

263 *Id.*, at para. 101.

264 UNHCR: Oosterveld, 'Women and Girls Fleeing Conflict: Gender and the Interpretation and Application of the 1951 Refugee Convention, UNHCR Legal and Protection Research Series. UN Doc. PPLA/2012/06' (2012), at 24.

265 Macklin, Audrey, 'Refugee Women and the Imperative of Categories', 17 *Human Rights Quarterly* (1995) 213, at 226.

266 European Parliament, 'Directorate General for Internal Policies', *Gender Related Asylum Claims in Europe* (EUR-OP, 2012), at 11 and 16.

267 United Nations High Commissioner for Refugees, *supra* note 120, at para. 53.

> Hence, whilst there will always be heavy factual obstacles in the way of a finding that socio-economic circumstances can constitute persecution, there is no reason of principle why a claim of this kind cannot succeed.[268]

The inclusion is of great importance for claims and arguments concerning, *inter alia*, the eligibility for people fleeing climate-related risks or those in severe medical conditions.[269] It equally allows for an accumulation of harm arising through the socio-economic shortcomings that characterise situations of conflict. While the evolution follows a legal theoretical consistency, one cannot expect that states in their determination practices will follow this interpretation to provide protection for persons fleeing solely socio-economic harm in the near future and the current political climate.

2.4.2.2 Persecuted? Why? Constituting the nexus to the Convention grounds

The 1951 Convention is considered a very exclusive instrument that stands at the centre of the divide between refugee law and the broader field of migration. That exclusivity that the Convention awards the refugee is not simply based on his or her victimhood. Persecution or fear of persecution is only one element. The Convention is only concerned with those acts that are linked to exclusive reasons. They were perpetrated 'for reason of'. The causal link criterion, or the so-called nexus criterion, binds the persecutory acts to the five discriminatory grounds of the Convention, namely race, religion, nationality, MPSG and political opinion.[270]

The assumption of the inapplicability of the 1951 Convention to conflict-induced flight is commonly linked to a certain assessment of contemporary conflict dynamics and contemporary warfare – one that can be heavily contested. By way of example, the Syrian conflict has yielded detailed reports to the contrary.[271] The conventional assumption is that violence arising during conflict is generalised and indiscriminate in its effects on the civilian population. This assessment is mainly based on the

268 *AM & AM (Armed Conflict: Risk Categories) Somalia v. Secretary of State for the Home Department*, [2008] UKAIT 00091, United Kingdom: Asylum and Immigration Tribunal / Immigration Appellate Authority (2009), at 79.

269 See for these arguments Myrstad, Finn and Kolmannskog, Vikram, 'Environmental Displacement in European Asylum Law', 11 *European Journal of Migration and Law* (2009) 313. McAdam, Jane, *Climate Change, Forced Migration, and International Law* (Oxford University Press, 2012). And the landmark judgments in the European context in this regard, *D v. The United Kingdom*, App. No. 30240/96, European Court of Human Rights (1997). *M.S.S. v. Belgium and Greece*, App. No. 30696/09, European Court of Human Rights (2011). *N. v. The United Kingdom*, App. No. 26565/05, European Court of Human Rights (2008).

270 Zimmermann, Andreas and Mahler, Claudia, *supra* note 188, at 372.

271 Human Rights Council, 'Report of the Independent International Commission of Inquiry on the Syrian Arab Republic, 31st session, Advance Edited Version' (UN Doc. A/HRC/31/68, 2016).

premise that hostilities take place among combatants and parties to the conflict and the civilian population is negatively affected as collateral damage. This would be true if IHL was constantly and correctly applied by all parties to the conflict. This would be true if the civilian population or parts of the civilian population were not dragged in intentionally through direct attacks, used as human shields, by means of starvation or siege.[272] If this assessment were true, the attacks resulting in harm for civilians could be considered random violence on a larger scale, lacking a specific targeting, or singling-out aspect. Consequently, such an assessment then precludes the application of the 1951 Convention. Being a victim of harm, even if it amounts to persecution in a refugee law sense, is not sufficient to establish refugeehood. The nexus element of the refugee definition demands a targeted action for one or more of the exclusively listed reasons for persecution. Random collateral damage occurring during a targeted attack on hostile combatants does not fulfil this link. However, the assessment fails to take into account the factual situation in contemporary conflicts.

Conflicts are of a different nature, fought between different actors and for a variety of motives. This book can therefore not take on any generalised assumptions on contemporary conflicts. Violence can be based on economic or purely criminal motives. Violence can also be the result of indiscriminate attacks. In those two scenarios, they would not be linked to a discriminatory Convention ground and would not trigger claims for international protection. While the general assumption of violence in conflict situations against civilians often presumes it to be widespread and random, possibly following the motto: the larger the scale, the more indiscriminate it becomes, this assumption is equally often wrong. The underlying causes of conflict then become relevant for refugee law. When classical tensions along political, religious or ethical lines are present, violence can equally be more targeted and more individualised and in this case, it can activate 1951 Convention protection:

> Recognizing that the underlying causes of large-scale involuntary population displacement are complex and interrelated and encompass gross violations of human rights, including in armed conflict, poverty and economic disruption, political conflicts, ethic and inter-communal tensions and environmental degradation, and that there is a need for the international community to address these causes in a concerted and holistic manner [...].[273]

Opponents of the application of the 1951 Convention to conflict have referenced the usage of certain types of weapons as supporting their argument. Certain types of weapons would indicate randomisation in targeting decisions due to their

272 Reports of the use of the illegal means and methods of warfare are confirmed by various sources in contemporary conflicts including the one taking place in Syria, for instance Pinheiro, Paulo, *Presentation: The Use of Barrel Bombs and Indiscriminate Bombardment in Syria* (2015), available online at http://www.ohchr.org/Documents/HRBodies/HRCouncil/CoISyria/CoISyriaIndiscriminateBombardment12032015.pdf (last visited 1 August 2018).

273 UNHCR: ExCom, *supra* note 114.

widespread effects.[274] Suicide bombers, landmines, cluster munition, classical chemical or biological weapons, remnants of weapons, cyberattacks or IEDs are all means or methods of warfare that have a clear indiscriminate character; their effects are not limited to solely negatively affect hostile combatants. And, even though specific international treaties explicitly prohibit most of these, and/or their deployment is prohibited by fundamental regulations of IHL, examples of their use in contemporary conflicts are numerous. While these tactics or weapons can kill, injure or destroy whole neighbourhoods indiscriminately, their deployment does not need to be equally indiscriminate and untargeted.[275] This assumption is based on the doubtful rationale that the parties to the conflict do not use weapons with widespread effects against numerous civilians. But armed attacks have often proven to be more discriminating than apparent at first glance.[276]

Studies concerning the on-going Syrian conflict have reported seemingly general dangers of on-going conflicts but, if analysed deeper, it is shown that these attacks follow specific motivations and targeting decisions and they were not necessarily random but often based on a multi-causality of reasons, including violence against particular social, ethical or religious groups, which brings these acts within the realm of the Convention.[277]

One prominent example of potentially persecutory acts that are committed during situations of generalised violence is to target parts of the population mostly living in specific geographic regions or neighbourhoods that are associated with or belong to a specific political party, movement, religious, or ethnic group.[278] Being attacked for association with religious, political, social, ethical, or national reasons does fall into the classical scope of the 1951 Convention and activates refugee protection – even if broader geographical areas are targeted. The UNHCR asserts in this regard,

274 See for this reason the prohibitions of certain weapons under IHL.

275 "This has further strengthened the dangerous perception of a link between some ethnicities and/or religions and political allegiances. Consequently, indiscriminate attacks on areas held by an opposing warring party are increasingly likely to affect specific religious or ethnic communities." Human Rights Council, 'Report of the Independent International Commission of Inquiry on the Syrian Arab Republic' (UN Doc. A/HRC/30/48, 2015), at para. 135.

276 UNHCR: Farrell and Schmitt, 'The Causes, Character and Conduct of Armed Conflict, and the Effects on Civilian Populations, 1990–2010' (UN Doc. PPLA/2012/03, 2012), at 3.

277 Markard, Nora, *supra* note 161, at 285. Holzer, Vanessa, *supra* note 247, at 23. "No doubt, as a practical matter in such situations, the Tribunal will often find it difficult to determine whether the feared persecution is 'for reasons' specified in the Convention or for military or economic reasons or other reasons." *Minister for Immigration and Multicultural Affairs v. Haji Ibrahim, supra* note 233, at para. 66.

278 United Nations High Commissioner for Refugees, 'International Protection Considerations with Regard to People Fleeing the Syrian Arab Republic, Update IV' (HCR/PC/SYR/01, 2015c). United Nations High Commissioner for Refugees, *International Protection Considerations with Regard to People Fleeing the Syrian Arab Republic, Update III* (2014b), available online at http://www.refworld.org/docid/544e446d4.html (last visited 1 August 2018). United Nations High Commissioner for Refugees, *International Protection Considerations with Regard to People Fleeing the Syrian Arab Republic, Update II* (2013a), available online at http://www.refworld.org/docid/5265184f4.html (last visited 1 August 2018), at 8.

> [M]any ordinary civilians may be at risk of harm from bombs, shelling, suicide attacks, and improvised explosive devices. [...] [T]hese methods of violence may be used against targets or in areas where civilians of specific ethnic or political profiles predominantly reside or gather, and for this reason, may be linked to a 1951 Convention ground.[279]

2.4.2.3 *One exhaustive list of Convention grounds*

The complexity of violence that arises in times of conflict aggravates the identification of flight causes as these can be concealed, can overlap or cannot be identified simply due the level of violence and the chaos of conflict. However, violence in a conflict is seldom a means to itself, carried out without reasons. Despite their complexity, their protracted nature, and often seemingly unlimited and untargeted violence, conflicts follow underlying rationales and motivations. Violence is not as random as one might think, but is more often intentionally deployed, for reasons overlapping with the 1951 Convention grounds.[280] The complexity of identifying and determining 'a' cause disregards the complexity and interconnectedness of situations, in particular in a conflict setting. This multi-causality hinders RSD, although the Convention does not state anywhere that one distinct reason is to be identified as the basis for status determination. Trends in state practice supported by the UNHCR and the majority of legal scholars have taken on the position that one or more Convention grounds must be identifiable as a contributing cause for persecution, but not necessarily as the decisive one:[281] "[I]t is immaterial whether the persecution arises from any single one of these reasons or from a combination of two or more of them."[282]

Both the commentaries to the 1951 Convention and the pertinent scholarly literature provide extensive interpretations of each Convention criterion. For this reason, the discussion in this book addresses the Convention grounds solely in regard to their relevance for flight from conflict. A traditional general interpretation of the treaty terms in this context is not necessary. The Convention grounds' wording (race, religion, nationality, MPSG and political opinion) and the context of Article 1 A (2) is not explicitly linked to the conflict context, as previously discussed. Therefore, these steps in the treaty interpretation

279 United Nations High Commissioner for Refugees, 'UNHCR Eligibility Guidelines for Assessing the International Protection Needs of Asylum-Seekers from Sri Lanka' (UN Doc. HCR/EG/LKA/12/04, 2012), at 32.

280 The 1951 Convention grounds are reflected in Article 10 (Recast) QD. Commission Proposal concerning grounds for persecution: Council doc. 12199/02, at 14.

281 Lambert, Hélène, 'Causation in International Protection from Armed Conflict', in D. Cantor and J.-F. Durieux (eds.), *Refuge from Inhumanity? War Refugees and International Humanitarian Law* (Brill, 2014), at 6. For the development of that practice, Hathaway, James C. and Foster, Michelle, 'The Causal Connection ("Nexus") to a Convention Ground. Discussion Paper No. 3 Advanced Refugee Law Workshop International Association of Refugee Law Judges Auckland, New Zealand, October 2002', 15 *International Journal of Refugee Law* (2003) 461.

282 United Nations High Commissioner for Refugees, *supra* note 120, at para. 66.

process are omitted when they do not provide more clarity concerning the conflict context. The object and purpose can offer some indications concerning the scope of the Convention grounds and are therefore referred to when necessary. Otherwise, pertinent practice in the interpretation of a Convention ground in the conflict context is elaborated upon in order to further clarify the application of the treaty.

2.4.2.3.1 RACE

'Race' is a long-standing and frequently identified reason for conflict and violence in Europe and beyond. The ordinary understanding and its object and purpose, as represented also by interrelations with human rights treaties, such as the 1965 Convention on the Elimination of All Forms of Racial Discrimination, UN Resolutions and human rights monitoring bodies, confirm a broad interpretation of the term 'race'.[283] A broad understanding of discrimination based on race, colour, descent, or national or ethnic origin is also the common interpretation in the refugee law context.[284]

In various conflict contexts, the Convention ground of 'race' has been identified as a main or compounding basis for violence and resulting protection claims of a conflict. Examples of these can be found in Somalia, where various risk categories were identified, most commonly a combination of imputed political opinion linked to racial or religious grounds. These encompassed for instance individuals perceived as supporting the Transitional Federal Government (TFG), allegedly favouring certain clans, specifically the Darod/Majerteen,[285] the Ethiopian National Defence Forces (ENDF), intervening in the conflict in support of the TFG or the African Mission in Somalia (AMISOM).[286] The Eligibility Guidelines equally identify different members of a minority (particularly outcast-clans) as being at higher risk in Southern and central Somalia.[287] The Eligibility Guidelines for Iraq are another example in which specific groups were identified in central and southern Iraq as being vulnerable to persecution on the basis of their ethnicity. These covered, in particular, Turkmen and Shabak.[288] The conflict in Eritrea caused members of "minority ethnic groups [to be] perceived

283 Article 2, 7 UDHR, Article 2, 20. 26, 27 ICCPR, Article 14 ECHR, Article 18 ACHPR, Article 30 CERD, Lerner, Natan, *The UN Convention on the Elimination of All Forms of Racial Discrimination* (Brill, 2014), at 42. United Nations High Commissioner for Refugees, *supra* note 120, at 16. *Ali (M.M.H.) and Others v. Secretary of State for the Home Department,* [1978] Imm AR 126, United Kingdom: High Court (England and Wales) (1978).

284 Detailed in the commentary of Hailbronner, Kay and Thym, Daniel, *supra* note 1, at 1185f. It is in this broad understanding also transposed in Article 10 (1) (a) Recast QD.

285 United Nations High Commissioner for Refugees, 'UNHCR Eligibility Guidelines for Assessing the International Protection Needs of Asylum-Seekers from Somalia' (UN Doc. HCR/EG/SOM/10/1, 2010), at 3.

286 *Id.*, at 11.

287 *Id.*, at 16.

288 United Nations High Commissioner for Refugees, *supra* note 131, at 33.

as historically sympathetic to Ethiopia, particularly the Kunama", and therefore prone to persecution.[289] While these groups can be used as examples, the identification of such racial grounds for persecution is unique in every setting and cannot be generalised.

2.4.2.3.2 RELIGION

Religion or religious beliefs constitute another prominent and recognised motive of violence between states, groups and individuals. A definition of the Convention ground of 'religion' is not contained in the refugee law framework but draws from the broader evolution of human rights law, as highlighted by treaties and resolutions. It is commonly understood as holding or not holding "any form of theistic, non-theistic or atheistic belief".[290] Persecution based on religion encompasses "[p]ersons who do not wish to profess any religion, refuses to take up a particular religion or do not wish to comply with all or part of the rites and customs relating to religion".[291]

In recent conflicts, claims have based on religious beliefs often overlap or intersect with the grounds of nationality, race and political opinion. Both state and non-state actors have imposed a certain religious habitus in territories under their control, giving rise to a number of successful asylum claims on the basis of discrimination on the grounds of religion.[292] In the enduring conflict in Afghanistan, this often affects persons perceived as contravening Sharia law, including persons accused of blasphemy, converts from Islam and members of minority religious groups.[293] As another group with an aggravated risk of persecution, individuals perceived as contravening the Taliban's interpretation of islamic principles, norms and values are identified by the UNHCR as being at an aggravated risk of persecution.[294] In Iraq, several Sunni and Shia groups residing in particular areas of the country, as well as religious minorities such as Christians, Sabaen-Mandaeans, Yazidis, Baha'is, Kaka'I and Jews, have been identified for the same reasons.[295]

289 United Nations High Commissioner for Refugees, 'UNHCR Eligibility Guidelines for Assessing the International Protection Needs of Asylum-Seekers from Eritrea' (UN Doc. HCR/EG/ERT/11/01_Rev.1, 2011), at 32.

290 United Nations High Commissioner for Refugees, 'Guidelines on International Protection No. 6: Religion-Based Refugee Claims under Article 1A(2) of the 1951 Convention and/or the 1967 Protocol relating to the Status of Refugees' (UN Doc. HCR/GIP/04/06, 2004), at 3, 5.

291 European Commission, 'Proposal for a Council Directive on minimum standards for the qualification and status of third country nationals and stateless persons as refugees or as persons who otherwise need international protection. COM(2001)510 final' (2001), at 21.

292 See *Refugee Appeal No. 76457*, New Zealand: Refugee Status Appeals Authority (2010). *Refugee Appeal No. 75879*, New Zealand: Refugee Status Appeals Authority (2007).

293 United Nations High Commissioner for Refugees, *supra* note 28, at 49.

294 United Nations High Commissioner for Refugees, *supra* note 102, at 47.

295 United Nations High Commissioner for Refugees, *supra* note 131, at 24ff.

2.4.2.3.3 NATIONALITY

Nationality in the 1951 Convention's context is again understood broadly as including origin and membership of particular ethnic, religious, cultural, and linguistic communities. It therefore goes beyond the legal term, which links nationality primarily to citizenship.[296] Persecution based on nationality can, contrary to the more prominent case, also include the persecution of a majority group by a dominant minority.[297] Examples of such interlinkage with the previously discussed grounds are equally common during times of conflict and have been referenced in protection claims, for instance from Tamils in Sri Lanka.[298] The example of the Ivory Coast and the politicisation of Ivorian nationality in the 1990s shows that individuals have been persecuted on the grounds of nationality and ethnicity, closely linked, triggering intercommunity clashes.[299]

2.4.2.3.4 MEMBERSHIP OF A PARTICULAR SOCIAL GROUP

The MPSG ground is again a strong reflection of the interconnectedness of the different fields of law in general and their treaties in particular.[300] As such, the refugee law's discriminatory ground of MPSG has gained extensively from the steady evolution of human rights law.[301]

> Membership of a particular social group may be at the root of persecution because there is no confidence in the group's loyalty to the government or because the political outlook, antecedents or economic activity of its members, or the very existence of the social group as such, is held to be an obstacle to the Government's policies.[302]

Persecution of a group itself cannot, according to the logic of the 1951 Convention, be sufficient to render a group of persons a 'particular social group' in the Convention sense, otherwise the two separate parts of the definition, namely a) persecution and b) grounds for persecution, would merge, contrary to the wording of

296 G. Goodwill-Gill, The Refugee, at 45, UNHCR Handbook at 97, Zimmermann/Mahler, at 387ff.

297 Goodwin-Gill, Guy S. and McAdam, Jane, *supra* note 1, at 73.

298 Refugee *Appeal No. 76006*, New Zealand: Refugee Status Appeals Authority (2007). *Refugee Appeal No. 76199*, New Zealand: Refugee Status Appeals Authority (2008). *Judgment of 10 July 1989*, 2 BvR 502/86; 2 BvR 961/86; 2 BvR 1000/86, Germany: Federal Constitutional Court (1989).

299 See more in United Nations High Commissioner for Refugees, *supra* note 156, at 18.

300 Aleinikoff, Alexander, 'Protected Characteristics and Social Perceptions: An Analysis of the Meaning of 'membership of a particular social group'', in E. Feller, V. Türk and F. Nicholson (eds.), *Refugee Protection in International Law: UNHCR's Global Consultations on International Protection* (Cambridge University Press, 2003), 263, at 264f.

301 Among others, Article 2 UDHR, Article 2 ICESCR, Article 2 and 26 ICCPR.

302 United Nations High Commissioner for Refugees, *supra* note 120, at para. 78.

the definition.[303] For this reason, one must identify grounds other than persecution to define and separate distinct social groups from the population.

The terminology itself does not give any further indication on what constitutes a social group. Jurisprudence from national courts has made reference to interpretative practice of human rights bodies, developing two distinct approaches to the constitution of such a social group: a) the 'protected characteristics approach' on the one hand and b) the 'social perceptions approach' on the other. The first approach dates back to the Canadian Supreme Court's decision in *Canada (Attorney-General) v. Ward*, which based identification on the "Internal factors" of a group, namely their innate, unchangeable and shared characteristics.[304] *Applicant A. v. Minister of Immigration and Ethnic Affairs*, on the other hand, approached the ground in reliance on the social perception that a social group shares a "common attribute and a societal perception that they stand apart" and that "[t]he existence of such a group depends in most, perhaps all, cases on external perceptions of the group."[305] The group, as it is generally assessed, need not be homogenous, of a particular size, measurable by a specific number of people, and not all its members need be at risk of persecution.[306]

The debate over which approach to apply in this regard was actively pursued at the UNHCR Global Consultation process of 2001 and was subject to discussion between the states' delegations. In some cases, the group in question is identifiable by both approaches, as groups targeted on the basis of a common unchangeable characteristic are often also perceived as a distinct group. In contrast, groups perceived by society as such, but which do not share immutable characteristics would for instance be specific professions or members of a certain social class. Against this background, the UNHCR has endorsed a reconciliation, based on which:

> a particular social group is a group of persons who share a common characteristic other than their risk of being persecuted, or who are perceived as a group by society. The characteristics will often be one which is innate, unchangeable, or which is otherwise fundamental to identify, conscience or the exercise of one's human rights.[307]

The determination of refugee protection claims stemming from claimants from conflict-riven countries have necessitated the consideration of distinct professions as specific social groups for the purpose of status determination. Depending

303 United Nations High Commissioner for Refugees, 'Guidelines on International Protection No. 2: "Membership of a Particular Social Group" Within the Context of Article 1A(2) of the 1951 Convention and/or its 1967 Protocol Relating to the Status of Refugees' (UN Doc. HCR/GIP/02/02, 2002), at 1.

304 *Canada (Attorney General) v. Ward*, [1993] 2 S.C.R. 689; (1993) DLR (4th) 1, Canada: Supreme Court (1993), at para 33f.

305 *A and Another v. Minister for Immigration and Ethnic Affairs and Another*, HCA 4; (1997) 190 CLR 225; (1997) 142 ALR 331, Australia: High Court (1997), at para. 264ff.

306 *United Nations High Commissioner for Refugees, supra note 303, at 18.*

307 *Id.*, at 3.

on the nature of the conflict and the underlying motives of its parties, certain professions, such as medicine, academia, journalism and teachers, are targeted explicitly.[308] For example, reports of government officials describing attacks of armed groups particularly on teachers, academics and medical personnel as an "effort [...] to 'empty' Iraq of its elite"[309] have been relied upon in claims made by individuals who had fled from that country. However, when reviewing the exercise of a profession in the light of the established practice of identifying social groups in the 1951 Convention sense, not all professions can be addressed under this Convention ground. The ground would therefore require that disassociation from the profession is tantamount to a violation of one's basic rights.[310] Otherwise, different Convention grounds might be more suitable for evaluating the respective claim.

In the context of mass, conflict-induced displacement, an interesting question is whether civilians can generally constitute a distinct particular social group. This would essentially open the door for refugee claims from everyone who is not a combatant from a country in conflict. To substantiate these claims, civilians would need to fulfil the recognised interpretation of a social group within the meaning of the Convention. The protected characteristics approach requires the identification of an innate, unchangeable and shared characteristic of the group, which is perceived to be fundamental to human dignity and human rights and cannot be required to change.[311] Being a civilian is not an innate and unchangeable characteristic. There is, however, one type of civilian that shows that it can be an innate characteristic of one's personal identity: deserters or draft resisters. They refrain from changing their civilian status due to their most fundamental beliefs. However, in this case, civilians as a broad group do not constitute a specific social group for the purpose of the Convention, but rather the group of draft resisters or deserters.[312]

The second option is to identify civilians as a particular social group according to the social perception approach. This more external approach presupposes that the group is viewed by society as a group. Civilians constitute 'society', hence the prevalent majority group of reference, while combatants, at least in the

308 See for discussion of case law among others, Aleinikoff, Alexander, *supra* note 300. Carter, Edward L. and Clark, Brad, 'Membership in a Particular Social Group: International journalists and U.S. Asylum Law', 12 *Communication Law and Policy* (2007) 279.

309 AKnews, *Assassination of lecturers continues in Mosul. Recited in UNHCR, Eligibility Guidelines for Assessing the International Protection Needs of Asylum-Seekers from Iraq* (2011), available online at http://www.refworld.org/pdfid/4fc77d522.pdf (last visited 1 August 2018). United Nations High Commissioner for Refugees, *supra* note 131, at 20.

310 United Nations High Commissioner for Refugees, *supra* note 95, at para. 39.

311 Aleinikoff, Alexander, *supra* note 300, at 294ff. Hruschka, Constantin and Löhr, Tillmann, 'Das Konventionsmerkmal „Zugehörigkeit zu einer bestimmten sozialen Gruppe" und seine Anwendung in Deutschland' *Neue Zeitschrift für Verwaltungsrecht* (2009) 205, at 207. United Nations High Commissioner for Refugees, *supra* note 303, at para. 7.

312 United Nations High Commissioner for Refugees, *UNHCR's Position on Certain Types of Draft Evasion* (1991), available online at http://www.refworld.org/docid/4a54bc1f0.html (last visited 1 August 2018).

traditional IHL and quantitative sense, constitute a minority.[313] The increase in non-international armed conflicts (NIACs) and the rise in the phenomenon of direct participation in hostilities by 'farmers by day and fighters by night' render identification as civilians in the social group sense even more difficult. One can conclude that, under both approaches, the characterisation of civilians as a particular social group cannot be supported.

In Afghanistan, for instance, boys and men of fighting age who live in a part of the country controlled by a non-state actor and who are at risk of being forcefully recruited, were identified as potential refugees based on MPSG.[314] Protection claims from women are another disputed example. The 1951 Convention does not list women as a social group *per se*. In previous and ongoing conflicts, the Convention ground of MPSG was frequently employed in regard to women and children, often in combination with specific profiles. Special characteristics attached to activate the MPSG grounds are commonly the (potential) victimhood to harmful traditional practices such as female genital mutilation, child marriage, or trafficking or bonded labour.[315] The approaches to addressing women under the context of social group, however, vary widely between different states. In some states, courts have recognised the claims of women from certain countries, such as Somalia, as constituting a particular social group.[316] In other cases, being a woman alone was not regarded as sufficient and additional differentiating elements were supplemented: Iraqi widows of former Baath Party members,[317] Somali Ashraf women with children,[318] Somali women with children but without clan or family protection.[319] Examining the argumentation of the respective tribunals, one can see that their assessments vary: Somali women were considered in *HM* to be a particular social group because they were women and, as such, suffered discrimination.[320] On the other hand, the analysis in *HH and others* engaged a more narrow reading, addressing not the overall living conditions of Somali women, but their position in existing clan relations. The bench

313 Holzer, Vanessa, *supra* note 247, at 33.

314 United Nations High Commissioner for Refugees, *supra* note 28, at 41.

315 United Nations High Commissioner for Refugees, *supra* note 289, at 30f. United Nations High Commissioner for Refugees, 'UNHCR Eligibility Guidelines for Assessing the International Protection Needs of Asylum-Seekers from Afghanistan' (UN Doc. HCR/EG/AFG/16/02, 2016), at 62ff.

316 United Nations High Commissioner for Refugees, *supra* note 285, at 18.

317 *NA. v. The United Kingdom*, App. No. 25904/07, European Court of Human Rights (2008), at 93, 97.

318 *HH (Somalia) & Others v. Secretary of State for the Home Department*, [2010] EWCA Civ 426, United Kingdom: Court of Appeal (2010), at 369.

319 *AMM and Others (conflict; humanitarian crisis; returnees; FGM) Somalia v. Secretary of State for the Home Department*, CG [2011] UKUT 00445 (IAC), United Kingdom: Upper Tribunal (Immigration and Asylum Chamber) (2011), at 631.

320 *HM (Somali Women - Particular Social Group) Somalia v. Secretary of State for the Home Department*, [2005] UKIAT 00040, United Kingdom: Asylum and Immigration Tribunal / Immigration Appellate Authority (2005), at 35.

stressed in this decision that being a woman in a war-torn country "is not a sufficient differentiator".[321]

The discrimination ground of MPSG has increasingly covered other "individuals who believe in, or are perceived to believe in values and standards at odds with the social mores of the society in which they live".[322] This does not solely apply, for instance, to women failing to comply with certain societal gender customs, but equally for lesbian, gay, bisexual, transgender and intersexual (LGBTI)[323] individuals, whose claims are increasingly considered by adjudicators under this Convention ground.[324]

2.4.2.3.5 POLITICAL OPINION

The inclusion of 'political opinion' as a Convention ground mirrors the traditional focus of the Convention and its state-centric approach. The political activist opposing a fascist regime has long been at the heart of the common understanding of what constitutes a textbook Convention refugee.[325] Political opposition and political opinion seldom take directly comparable forms. The 1951 Convention itself does not further elaborate on how political opinion is constituted or identified. The wording chosen by the 1951 Convention drafters, 'political opinion', clearly implies that political opinion does not need to be expressed. It refers explicitly to opinion and not specific or non-specific political acts. Therefore, it can also equally encompass refusals to express a certain opinion. In the QD, this broad conceptualisation is reflected in the wording:

> [T]he concept of political opinion shall, in particular, include the holding of an opinion, thought or belief on a matter related to the potential actors of persecution mentioned in Article 6 and to their policies or methods, whether or not that opinion, thought or belief has been acted upon by the applicant.[326]

The practical interpretation and identification of this Convention ground can be found, *inter alia*, in contemporary conflicts. A range of types of individuals with an aggravated risk of being persecuted due to their political opinion have been identified by the UNHCR when providing an overview and assessment of a

321 *HH (Somalia) & Others v. Secretary of State for the Home Department, supra* note 318, at para. 15.

322 UNHCR: ExCom, *Conclusion No. 39 (XXXVI) Refugee Women and International Protection* (1985), available online at http://www.refworld.org/pdfid/4b28bf1f2.pdf (last visited 1 August 2018), at (k).

323 Lesbian, Gay, Bisexual, Transgender and Intersexual.

324 *X, Y, Z v. Minister voor Immigratie en Asiel,* C-199/12 to C-201/12, Court of Justice of the European Union (2013). In 2013, the CJEU prominently acknowledged in its judgment that homosexual applicants for asylum can constitute a particular social group who may be persecuted on account of their sexual orientation under the QD (in reference to the provisions of the 1951 Convention).

325 Goodwin-Gill, Guy S. and McAdam, Jane, *supra* note 1, at 87.

326 Recast QD, Article 10 (e).

specific conflict in relation to arising protection claims. These include, very generally, the respective supporter or opponent of parties to conflicts, something that most conflicts have in common. Further individuals are identified, such as individuals associated with authorities, i.e. government officials and employees, former members of the Security forces, members of political parties or certain tribes or communities associated with a political party or their opposition, more generally persons affiliated with foreign governments, NGOs or companies.[327] The involvement of these is highly dependent on underlying conflict dynamics. Civil society actors, opponents of Islamists or individuals belonging to a clan engaged in a blood feud were identified as vulnerable in Somalia[328]; for Sri Lanka persons who had witnessed human rights abuses were added as additionally vulnerable to persecution.[329] The UNHCR Protection Consideration for Persons fleeing Syria identifies types of individuals who are commonly identifiable as being at risk of persecution for their political opinions in most conflicts, i.e. persons opposing the government, persons opposing the opposition or more specifically, persons opposing the various hostile parties involved. In this specific case, it encompasses persons opposing the Islamic State (IS) in the territory under its *de facto* control; persons opposing the military wing of the Syrian affiliate of the PKK; the Yekîneyên Parastina Gel (YPG)/Partiya Yekîtiya Demokrat (PYD); and persons opposing Shari'a law in general in territories under the control of extremist groups or specific minority groups. It furthermore includes more general risk types such as certain professionals, particularly journalists and other media professionals, doctors and other health professionals, human rights defenders, humanitarian workers, artists and businessmen.[330] More recent events have illustrated that (former) members of the armed forces and military command hierarchy can also become a distinct target group, for instance during or following a coup.

These examples stemming from conflict countries mostly reflect the realities of a combination of various risk and overlapping Convention grounds. The weight of the UNHCR when identifying these risk groups is of significance and is often reflected in national jurisprudence. Examples can be chosen from the recent asylum claims of persons fleeing Syria. For instance, one Syrian asylum seeker had applied for refugee protection in Spain. She claimed that she had been interrogated and beaten after participating in a demonstration and had conducted humanitarian aid in Homs before leaving Syria for Lebanon and later Spain, due to her fear of persecution. Her appeal was launched in the Spanish Supreme Court

327 See in detail, United Nations High Commissioner for Refugees, *supra* note 131, at 14ff.

328 United Nations High Commissioner for Refugees, *supra* note 285, at 22ff.

329 United Nations High Commissioner for Refugees, *supra* note 279, at 32f.

330 United Nations High Commissioner for Refugees, *supra* note 278, at 25. Concerning a Pharmacist, *M.A.A. v. Office of Immigration and Nationality,* 6.K.31830/2013/6, Hungary: Administrative and Labour Court of Budapest (2013). *No. 103921,* CCE, arrêt n°103921, Belgium: Council for Alien Law Litigation (2013). *S.A. v Office of Immigration and Nationality,* 3.K.31404/2013/4, Hungary: Administrative and Labour Court of Budapest (2013). *A und B (Syrien) v. Staatssekretariat für Migration,* D-5779/2013, Switzerland: Federal Administrative Court (2015).

against the determination of subsidiary protection status. The Court overturned the prior status determination, basing its argument mainly on the error of the lower court in not taking the UNHCR's reports into consideration. These reports had included the claimant's membership of a particular religious group as a significant risk factor for persecution in Syria. Further reports by a Spanish NGO had provided further support for her claims based on persecution for political activities as well as her familial ties to the Free Army.[331]

A Slovenian case in which the Supreme Court rejected the claimant's appeal, upholding the decision taken by the Ministry of the Interior to grant subsidiary protection status, similarly reflects this combination of risk factors in conflict and the value of reports and guidance delivered by the UNHCR and prominent NGOs analysing the specific situation in Syria. This claimant had fled Syria because he had refused to take part in the conflict, arguing that it most likely included committing crimes against the civilian population, which potentially amounted to war crimes or crimes against humanity. Reportedly, soldiers who had refused to follow orders had been incarcerated, tortured or even executed. In this context, given that the claimant was a Kurd and was therefore a member of a group considered to oppose the Syrian regime, the Supreme Court held that he faced a considerable danger of persecution if he returned to Syria as a political opponent and evader of compulsory military service.[332] Similar combinations were recognised in cases concerning members of minority groups whose claims were substantiated by the linked grounds of holding a specific or imputed political opinion.[333]

2.4.2.3.6 IMPUTATION OF CONVENTION GROUNDS

In contemporary conflicts and resulting refugee claims, the imputation of a certain opinion, role or position towards the conflict plays a major role. This

331 STS 5211/2015, Spain: Supreme Court, Chamber for Contentious-Administrative proceedings, Section III (2015), at 5.

332 I Up 47/2015, Slovenia: Supreme Court of the Republic of Slovenia (2015). Background information on the situation of Kurds, the general conflict and situation of compulsory military services and consequences of draft evasion or desertion were among others taken from the United Nations High Commissioner for Refugees, *supra* note 97. Amnesty International, *Amnesty Report 2012. Syrien* (2012), available online at https://www.amnesty.de/jahresbericht/2012/syrien (last visited 1 August 2018). United Nations High Commissioner for Refugees, *Independent International Commission of Inquiry on the Syrian Arab Republic*, available online at http://www.ohchr.org/EN/HRBodies/HRC/IICISyria/Pages/IndependentInternationalCommission.aspx (last visited 1 August 2018). United Kingdom: Home Office, *Operational Guidance Note: Syria* (2014), available online at http://www.refworld.org/docid/530b11374.html (last visited 1 August 2018). Concerning journalists, *Judgment of 03 March 2006,* 21 K 1464/02.A, Germany: Administrative Court Düsseldorf (2006).

333 See for instance, on the minority group of the Maktoumeen, UM 1802-07, Sweden: Migration Court of Appeal (2008). Concerning Kurd applicants, *Refugee Appeal No. 76094*, New Zealand: Refugee Status Appeals Authority (2008). *Refugee Appeal No. 75779,* New Zealand: Refugee Status Appeals Authority (2006). *Judgment of 22 May 2006*, 9A 326/05 MD, Germany: Administrative Court Magdeburg (2006).

imputation is a stance of the claimant perceived by persecutor, state or non-state actor alike, and must not coincide with the individual's actual state of mind or opinion. While the wording and context of the Convention does not refer to imputation or association, it is evident that the motivation of the persecutor is the relevant link and not whether the victim of persecution is indeed connected to one or more of the Convention grounds. To consider and assess the imputation of Convention grounds, the fact that political opinions often form the basis for refugee claims highlights the necessity of understanding the conflict and the objectives and beliefs of the conflict parties involved. Retaliation based on an imputed political opinion of alleged supporters of foreign states or regime-opposing groups has been a major basis for claims. In Syria, it has become evident that whole neighbourhoods are considered to be linked to either one of the conflict parties, often due to their religious or ethnical backgrounds, or as victims of forced support for conflict parties.[334]

The UN Inquiry Commission on Syria addresses this link between seemingly indiscriminate violence and underlying motivations:

> As communities and groups are, or feel, threatened, they have retreated into areas where they believe themselves to be more protected. This has further strengthened the dangerous perception of a link between some ethnicities and/or religions and political allegiances. Consequently, indiscriminate attacks on areas held by an opposing warring party are increasingly likely to affect specific religious or ethnic communities.[335]

And the UNHCR addressed these realities with regard to refugee protection:

> For many civilians who have fled Syria, the nexus to a 1951 Convention ground will lie in the direct or indirect, real or perceived association with one of the parties the conflict [...] Syrians or habitual residents of Syria who have fled may, for example be at risk of persecution for reason of an imputed political opinion because of who controls the neighbourhood or village where they used to live, or because they belong to a religious or ethnic minority that is associated or perceived to be associated with a particular party to the conflict.[336]

There are many of these *sur place* cases, in which the courts acknowledged that the claim of asylum abroad is considered an act of opposition to the regime and therefore either granted refugee status directly or overturned prior determinations

334 Tax, Blanche, 'Refugee by Association', 47 *Forced Migration Review* (2014) 26. United Nations High Commissioner for Refugees, *supra* note 278, at 8.

335 Human Rights Council, *supra* note 275, at para. 135.

336 United Nations High Commissioner for Refugees, *supra* note 278, at para. 14. United Nations High Commissioner for Refugees, *supra* note 278, at 10. United Nations High Commissioner for Refugees, *supra* note 278, at 12.

of subsidiary protection.[337] Against the historical development of the Convention in the aftermath of the Second World War, the basic understanding of refugee protection concerns people who had a well-founded fear of, or were subjected to persecution in their country of origin and, for this reason, became eligible for refugee protection. In contrast, "a person becomes a refugee 'sur place' due to circumstances arising in his country of origin during his absence."[338] The Convention in this regard does not turn a blind eye to other potential chronological events, which has proven most relevant concerning cases of people fleeing conflict. People who left their country of origin or habitual residence prior to the outbreak of conflict were not yet subjected to persecution in the conventional sense, or serious harm resulting from the conflict. That being said, a well-founded fear of persecution on their return can render them refugees, even when they had left their country voluntarily. Their refugee claim is constituted either through the changing factual circumstances in the country of origin, the outbreak of conflict, a regime change, or by changes in the individual's circumstances, as based on Article 1 A (2) – being outside of the country – and Article 1 C (4).[339] IOs and NGOs have observed that in particular after flight, the imputed closeness to opposition groups in exile is commonly the basis for a well-founded fear of persecution in case of return to the country of origin. Even if the asylum seeker has not actively participated in political activities after leaving the country, the Syrian regime, as one example, has developed a practice of considering every illegal departure and the application for asylum as a hostile act.[340]

Similar assessments have been made concerning prior conflicts. In the Zimbabwean context, the UK Supreme Court illustrated in *RT (Zimbabwe)* that flight from countries could be a sign of opposition: "The idea that 'if you are not with us, you are against us' pervades the thinking of dictators. From their perspective, there is no real difference between neutrality and opposition."[341] And:

> [t]he status of deemed political opponent, whether it is the product of imputation of political opposition or merely the arbitrary decision of those testing the degree of conviction or fervour with which support for Zanu-PF

337 G.T [2013] Attica Regional Asylum Office 95/000186182, Greece: Asylum Service, Attica Regional Asylum Office (2013) Case number 755, background information taken into consideration in these decisions stem among others from the reports of the Council of Europe, annual Amnesty International Reports on Syria, Human Rights Watch information on Syria, Kurdwatch or the European Center for Kurdish Studies and again the position of other immigration boards and general asylum policies from Canada, Australia, the US, and the UK.

338 United Nations High Commissioner for Refugees, *supra* note 120, at para. 95.

339 Zimmermann, Andreas and Mahler, Claudia, *supra* note 188.

340 German courts have considered these claims at length and widely recognised their *sur place* refugee claims even if the claimants had not been involved in political activities explicitly opposing the regime. Illegal flight and applying for asylum abroad are already grounds for a well-founded fear due to reported retaliations by the regime for returnees, examples in *Judgment of 08 July 2016*, 1 K 1922/16.TR, Germany: Administrative Court Trier (2016).

341 *RT (Zimbabwe) and Others v. Secretary of State for the Home Department*, [2012] UKSC 38, United Kingdom: Supreme Court (2012), at para. 44.

> is expressed, is the gateway to persecution [...] That is why the emphasis must be not on the disposition of the individual liable to be the victim of persecution but on the mind of the persecutor.[342]

The UNHCR, supported by the Human Rights Committee,[343] has addressed the imputation of certain opinions and beliefs concerning traditional gender roles and therefore stressed in its Guidelines on Gender-Related Persecution:

> Political opinion [...] would also include non-conformist behaviour which leads the persecutor to impute a political opinion to him or her. In this sense, there is not as such an inherently political or an inherently non-political activity, but the context of the case should determine its nature.[344]

Article 10 (2) Recast QD states explicitly how the Convention is to be interpreted as a matter of regional EU practice in relation to the imputation of Convention grounds:

> [w]hen assessing if an applicant has a well-founded fear of being persecuted it is immaterial whether the applicant actually possesses the racial, religious, national, social or political characteristic which attracts the persecution, provided that such a characteristic is attributed to the applicant by the actor of persecution.

2.4.2.4 The actors of persecution

"[I]t is to his own government that the individual will look for his most basic needs. At the same time, it is from his own government that an individual often most needs protection",[345] Higgins opined twenty years ago. While the authorities of the state were the traditional actors of persecution, changing patterns of persecution throughout the last decades have illustrated the need for adaptation. Next to state actors of persecution, non-state actors, particularly non-state conflict parties, have evolved as serious persecutors in a refugee law sense. International refugee law in this regard has followed a broader public international law development that was prominently triggered by human rights law bringing violations by non-state actors inside its ambit. This has resulted in further expansion: IHL has strengthened the obligations of non-state conflict

342 *Id.*, at para. 75.

343 This position is reflected in Human Rights Committee, 'General Comment No. 34: Freedom of Opinion and Expression' (UN Doc. CCPR/C/GC/34, 2011), at para. 9.

344 United Nations High Commissioner for Refugees, 'Guidelines on International Protection No. 1: Gender-Related Persecution Within the Context of Article 1A(2) of the 1951 Convention and/or its 1967 Protocol Relating to the Status of Refugees' (UN Doc. HCR/GIP/02/01, 2002), at para. 32.

345 Higgins, Rosalyn, *Problems and Process* (Clarendon Press; Oxford University Press, 1995), at 95.

parties[346] and international criminal law (ICL) has developed the concept of criminal responsibility for all individuals. Furthermore, due diligence obligations and state complicity for the human rights violations of non-state actors have been developed.[347] This very decisive adaptation of traditional refugee law interpretation to the factual changes in refugees' realities is still of great relevance to today's application to situations of conflict, particularly in the light of the high number of internal conflicts.

The 1951 Convention itself does not make any explicit reference to the source of persecution, but the refugee definition includes that the refugee is unwilling or unable to avail himself of the protection of the state. The traditional nature of treaties, as mirrored in general public international law, concerned the conduct of states. For the 1951 Convention, this could mean that it concerned acts of state culpability and state protection obligations. A lack of state protection equally amounts to persecution in the sense of the 1951 Convention, if the state is targeting, for instance, a particular part of the population through negligence or intent.[348] In these cases, either the persecutory conduct or the unwillingness or inability of the state to accord protection must illustrate the necessary link to one of the Convention grounds.[349] The nature of such state culpability in the commission of persecution can vary from a) direct conduct by state agents, to b) acts condoned by the state or c) acts tolerated by the state.[350] The customary rules of state responsibility,[351] as ascertained by the ILC Draft Articles on the Responsibility of States for Internationally Wrongful Acts, give guidance on the general matters of attribution to the state. These do not need to be further elaborated upon in this context.

Experience has shown that non-state actors can commit persecutory acts, without any necessary involvement of the state. The broader topic concerning the role of non-state actors and refugee protection arises both in times of peace as well as in times of conflict. Still, persecution by non-state actors can increasingly occur during times of NIAC. If one applies the Convention restrictively as covering only persecution committed by state agents or state involvement, a vast number

346 See prominently Article 1 (1) AP II to the 1949 Geneva Conventions codifying obligations under IHL also for the non-state party to the non-international armed conflict.

347 Wagner, Markus, 'Non-State Actors' (Max Planck Encyclopedia of Public International Law, 2013). Alston, Philip (ed.), *Non-state Actors and Human Rights* (2011). Clapham, Andrew (ed.), *Human Rights and Non-state Actors* (2013). On migration-related matters, see Fitzpatrick, Joan, 'Human Rights and Forced Displacement: Converging Standards', in A. F. Bayefsky and J. Fitzpatrick (eds.), *Human Rights and Forced Displacement* (Martinus Nijhoff Publishers, 2001), at 7ff.

348 Ad Hoc Committee on Refugees and Stateless Persons, 'Report of the Ad Hoc Committee on Statelessness and Related Persons' (UN Doc. E/1618, E/AC.35/5, 1950), at para. 39.

349 Zimmermann, Andreas and Mahler, Claudia, *supra* note 188, at 374.

350 Hathaway, James C., *supra* note 228, at 129.

351 *Application of the Convention on the Prevention and Punishment of the Crime of Genocide (Bosnia and Herzegovina v. Serbia and Montenegro),* International Court of Justice (2007), at para. 385.

of claims committed during internal conflicts would be disregarded.[352] Nevertheless, in the 1990s, states widely denied protection for people fleeing areas affected by internal conflict or severe violence by non-state armed groups, as shown for instance by the low percentage of Algerians recognised as Convention refugees.[353] A similar position can be deduced from the early, non-binding EU Council Joint Position of 1995, an eligibility assessment for the 1951 Convention protection which suggested that non-state violence should be excluded.[354] This understanding of the state as the sole relevant driver of persecution must be rejected.

While the general focus of international law at the time of drafting the Convention was one of state centricity, neither the wording nor the Convention's context indicates that persecution by non-state actors is excluded from the treaty's scope. Its object and purpose of protection for individuals fearing or having experienced persecution does not offer a starting point for such an interpretation, but rather the contrary. The interrelation between state and non-state actors in relation to persecution has led scholars to debate on the matter. The general approach to non-state actors as sources of persecution or serious harm is divided into what is considered a) the 'accountability theory' on the one hand and b) the 'protection theory' on the other. The accountability theory entails the assumption that state involvement is a necessary precondition of non-state actor persecution. Among others, it is reflected in German asylum law, which has historically only acknowledged individuals or non-state groups as actors of persecution if their acts were attributable to the state.[355]

This argumentation poses a severe obstacle to ensuring protection for persons fleeing conflict, because it links the granting of refugee protection to the existence of a functioning (albeit persecutory) state system. In situations where the state has no effective authority or is unable to function as an actor of protection, refugee status would not be granted at all.[356] The lack of effective authority is present, however, in failing or failed states, including those involved in conflicts. This is the case in states with strong non-state actors exercise authority or when the state is under the occupation of foreign armed forces. However, given that

352 Fitzpatrick, Joan, 'Human Rights and Forced Displacement: Converging Standards', *supra* note 347, at 5. Goodwin-Gill, Guy S., *The Refugee in International Law* (2nd ed., Clarendon Press, 1996), at 70ff.

353 Sandra Lavenex, 'France: International Norms, European Integration and State Discretion', in Joanne van Selm (ed.), *Kosovo's Refugees in the European Union* (Pinter, 2000).

354 European Council on Refugees and Exiles, *Recommendations on the Treatment of Algerian Refugees and Asylum Seekers in Europe* (1995), available online at http://www.refworld.org/publisher,ECRE,,DZA,3ae6a6618,0.html (last visited 1 August 2018). Council of the European Union, *Joint Position of 4 March 1996 defined by the Council on the basis of Article K.3 of the Treaty on European Union on the harmonized application of the definition of the term 'refugee' in Article 1 of the Geneva Convention of 28 July 1951 relating to the status of refugees, supra* note 197.

355 *Judgment of 02 August 1983*, 9 C 818/81, Germany: Federal Administrative Court (1983), at 744.

356 *Id.*, at 744f.

the Convention establishes a duty of foreign states to take over protection and is not further concerned with any questions of attribution, this attribution theory lacks any basis in the 1951 Convention framework.

By contrast, a number of other states follow the 'protection theory' in their asylum practice. This holds that the acts of non-state actors amount to persecution if the state is unwilling or unable to provide protection. The ability of the state itself to function and exert control is irrelevant.[357] With the inception of the CEAS and its various legal instruments, the EU clearly positioned itself in favour of the protection theory. Non-state actors are explicitly listed as actors of persecution in the (Recast) QD. On 4 March 1996, the Joint position adopted by the Council of the EU on a harmonised application of the definition of the term 'refugee' in Article 1 of the 1951 Convention recognised non-state actors as agents of persecution in the Geneva Convention's terms.[358] Heading *5.2. Persecution by third parties* is explicitly considered as being within the scope of the Convention and again, taken up in *paragraph 6 on civil war and other internal or generalized armed conflict*, the EU underlines that persecution in this context

> may stem either from the legal authorities or third parties encouraged or tolerated by them, or from de facto authorities in control of part of the territory within which the state cannot afford its nationals protection.[359]

The (Recast) QD has clarified the recognition of non-state actors as actors of persecution in its explicit incorporation contained in Article 6:

> Actors of persecution or serious harm include: (a) the State; (b) parties or organisations controlling the State or a substantial part of the territory of the State; (c) non-State actors, if it can be demonstrated that the actors mentioned in points (a) and (b), including international organisations, are unable or unwilling to provide protection against persecution or serious harm as defined in Article 7.

The Recast QD addresses both actors of persecution and serious harm and actors of protection under a general provision, thereby merging the regulations concerning the actors of persecution both from refugee protection and subsidiary protection.[360]

357 Battjes, Hemme, *European Asylum Law and International Law* (Martinus Nijhoff Publishers, 2006), at 245.

358 Council of the European Union, *Joint Position of 4 March 1996 defined by the Council on the basis of Article K.3 of the Treaty on European Union on the harmonized application of the definition of the term 'refugee' in Article 1 of the Geneva Convention of 28 July 1951 relating to the status of refugees, supra* note 197.

359 Chetail, Vincent and Bauloz, Céline, *Research Handbook on International Law and Migration* (Edward Elgar, 2014), at 486f.

360 See further, Chetail, *id.*, at 485.

2.4.2.5 *The actors of protection*

The Convention refugee definition is built on two limbs – one concerning persecution and the other concerning the provision of protection. The traditional state centricity of the 1951 Convention is reflected in different pillars of refugee protection. The protection from persecution is one area in which the role of the state has a prominent position, as it is traditionally the state, its law enforcement and social services that assume protection tasks.

The Convention itself is silent on the matter of non-state actors of protection. While harm can be a result of state and non-state actors alike, the responsibility to provide public services, infrastructure, security and so on is borne solely by states.[361] In particular, the broader context of Article 1 A (2) concerns the relationship between a (potential or former) refugee towards his or her state of nationality or habitual residence. Article 1 A (2) itself refers to the availability of protection from the country of nationality or habitual residence. The cessation clause of Article 1 C encompasses the cessation of refugee protection if the refugee re-avails him or herself of the protection of his or her country of nationality. Article 1 E excludes claims from persons recognised in their country of residence as "having the rights and obligations which are attached to the possession of the nationality of that country". All these Articles emphasise the protection as understood in relation to protection by the state, including with regard to traditional forms of state protection – those attached to the possession of nationality.

Practice, however, shows that, increasingly, non-state actors take on refugee protection, such as international organisations, organs of the UN, NGOs, or even corporations. As addressed above, refugee law has acknowledged the role of non-state actors of persecution in situations where the state is unwilling or unable to provide protection from harm. There has been growing attention for the question of whether non-state actors are also valid agents of protection in this context. Since the (Recast) QD provides further examination, the issue is again highlighted in the counterpart subchapter for the EU asylum regime.[362]

2.4.2.6 *The concept of an IFA in the 1951 Convention*

Refugee protection is not only conditional upon the fulfilment of refugee eligibility criteria. Even if the claimant meets all of the criteria discussed above, refugee protection is not granted in cases where the claimant could have fled persecution by escaping to other parts of her or his own country. The existence of an IFA[363] marks the distinction between refugees and internally displaced persons. While, with regards to the former, it is acknowledged, through refugee law but also through pertinent

361 O'Sullivan, Maria, 'Acting the Part: Can Non-State Entities Provide Protection Under International Refugee Law?', 24 *International Journal of Refugee Law* (2012) 85, at 89.

362 In the EU, the (Recast) QD has considered actors of protection both with regard to refugees and subsidiary protection in one common scheme in more detail.

363 Other terms used are internal protection alternative or internal relocation alternative.

human rights law, that foreign states have specific protection obligations, IDPs are clearly not under a foreign state's legal responsibility. They are considered to be under the *de jure* sovereign protection of their home state – even when this might not be factually true.[364] Refugee status in itself is a construct of a temporary nature, premised on the assumption that people fleeing their country want to return as soon as possible. Refugee status itself foresees cessation clauses to end the protection status by a foreign state as soon as individuals can return to their countries of origin without fear. A similar notion constitutes the basis for an IFA. Before leaving a country of origin and before responsibilities of foreign states are triggered, internal flight options should be assessed, both practically and legally.

Article 1 A (2) itself does not explicitly address the existence of an IFA as precluding refugee protection. Nonetheless, the Article encompasses the already considered phrasing that a refugee is unwilling or unable to avail him- or herself of the protection of the country. This in turn can be interpreted as an implicit prerequisite of the absence of internal protection in the country. What constitutes an IFA and under which conditions can one expect people to become internally displaced rather than to cross the border and apply for asylum? The UNHCR Handbook stresses:

> The fear of being persecuted need not always extend to the whole territory of the refugee's country of nationality. Thus in ethnic clashes or in cases of grave disturbances involving civil war conditions, persecution of a specific ethnic or national group may occur in only one part of the country. In such situations, a person will not be excluded from refugee status merely because he could have sought refuge in another part of the same country, if under all the circumstances it would not have been reasonable to expect him to do so.[365]

The UNHCR has promoted a twofold test on the existence of a relocation alternative within the country, including an a) relevance and b) reasonableness part.

The relevance analysis addresses four sub-questions: firstly, whether the area of relocation is practically, safely and legally accessible. Physical dangers, including remnants of war or forms of harassment or exploitation are grounds for rejecting an IFA already at this stage of analysis. Secondly, one has to consider whether the actor of persecution is the state or a non-state actor. States are presumed to act throughout the country, which means having both *de jure* and *de facto* control over their territory. If they are the feared persecutors, there is a presumption that an internal flight or relocation alternative is not available.[366]

364 In contrast to the refugee law framework, other areas of displacement, such as the field of internal displacement, is mostly regulated by soft law such as the Guiding Principles on Internal Displacement. Also, the UNHCR covers their protection under its broader mandate of persons of concern to the Office.

365 United Nations High Commissioner for Refugees, *supra* note 120, at para. 91.

366 United Nations High Commissioner for Refugees, 'Guidelines on International Protection: Internal Flight or Relocation Alternative' within the Context of Article 1 A (2) of the 1951 Convention and/or 1967 Protocol relating to the Status of Refugees' (UN Doc. HCR/GIP/03/04, 2003), at 3.

In the case that non-state actors of persecution are feared, it must be determined whether the persecutors have access to the given area and are likely to pursue the claimant there. Thirdly, the state's ability or willingness to protect against harm needs to be assessed.

> In situations where the proposed internal flight or relocation alternative is under the control of an armed group and/or State-like entity, careful examination must be made of the durability of the situation there and the ability of the controlling entity to provide protection and stability.[367]

Fourthly, and to end the relevance analysis, the determining authorities are obliged to inquire whether exposure to the risk of being persecuted might arise upon relocation.

Following the relevant analysis, the second part of the assessment, namely the reasonableness analysis, should answer the question whether the claimant could also be expected to live a normal life in a different area of his or her country of origin[368] or whether relocation amounts to undue hardship. The assessment includes taking into account:

> factors such as health, age, sex, health, disability, family situation and relationships, social or other vulnerabilities, ethnic, cultural or religious considerations, political and social links and compatibility, language abilities, educational, professional and work background and opportunities, and any past persecution and its psychological effects [...].[369]

Within the EU, Article 8 Recast QD addresses the existence of an IFA but only as one of interpretative support.[370] The existence of an IFA, as Article 1 A (2)'s wording implies, is not a standalone criterion in the assessment of a refugee claim. Its relevance in status determination is considered ambiguously and implemented inconsistently, as the determination of an IFA is always an easy tool to reduce the numbers of otherwise *prima facie* legitimate protection claims.

2.5 Intermediate conclusion on the 1951 Convention and persons fleeing conflict and violence

The application of the 1951 Convention to persons fleeing conflict is heavily debated both legally and politically. The complementary regional refugee protection regimes codified some decades later to accommodate the regional specifics of displacement in Africa or Asia encompass extended refugee definitions which cover situations of generalised violence. The 1951 Convention, albeit adopted

367 *Id.*, at para. 27.
368 *Id.*, at paras. 6f.
369 *Id.*, at para. 25.
370 The IFA, as an internal protection alternative common for both refugee and subsidiary protection, is assessed in more detail under chapter 3.4.5.

after the Second World War, has not been used as an instrument to cover whole groups of persons but addresses each person individually. This, however, does not *ipso facto* deny its application to such situations of mass displacement. Since future codification processes are not realistically envisaged at this point, the 1951 Convention remains the most important refugee law treaty. Therefore, the pertinent question that was posed in this chapter was whether there are doctrinal obstacles to the application of the Convention and specifically Article 1 (A) (2) in the context of conflict and mass displacement.

The first part of the chapter turned towards the position of the UNHCR as a major actor in the supervision and interpretation of the Convention. The Office has a strong position in the broad field of refugee protection within the international community, also due to its influential operational role in assisting states. Its legal role in regard to the 1951 Convention and its interpretation is more controversial, in particular when deviating from states' interpretations and applications of the Convention. Throughout the last years, the Office has further developed its conflict-sensitive interpretation of the Convention. To evaluate whether and how the interpretation of the Office influences states and their positions, it was necessary to determine the role and nature of the Office and the legal value of its interpretative guidance documents.

On the one hand, the UNHCR is a UN subsidiary organ, with the Executive Committee constituted by state representatives directing the Office. On the other hand, the Office as such has considerable commonalities with an independent expert body, advocating for the sake of its beneficiaries, in this case, refugees lacking state protection. This torn nature is mirrored in the sometimes vague terminology of the constituting documents, which give leeway for expanding, independent and discretionary actions of the Office, while simultaneously providing only a vague legal basis for the Office's influence towards states' practices.

The start of the analysis was the examination of the cooperation obligation of states towards the UNHCR which stems from different legal sources, including, the UN Charter and, more specifically, from the Office's Statute, the 1951 Convention and its regional counterparts. The Statute, subsequent UNGA Resolutions and the refugee law instruments shape the UNHCR's supervisory role, which includes its role in the interpretation of the Convention. Further, it sets them alongside the obligations of states to cooperate in the fulfilment of its functions. And yet, the cooperation obligations are abstract and do not specifically refer to the UNHCR's interpretative work. They cannot be the basis for arguing that states need to adhere to any of the Office's guidance as such. Nonetheless, the sustained use of Executive Committee Conclusions, the UNHCR's Handbook and Guidelines as pertinent standards by determining authorities and asylum jurisprudence reflects their value, their important role in the field of refugee protection and also the recognition of states – in political terms. While legally non-binding, their political value is therefore not to be disregarded or underestimated.

After evaluating the role of the Office, its legal basis and the nature of its guidance documents, the analysis turned to the evolution of the UNHCR's position on conflict-induced protection claims. A problematic element in this regard, and potentially an additional ground for inconsistencies in national determination practices, is the change in the Office's position. While the first edition of its Handbook contains almost a general rejection of conflict-related claims under the 1951 Convention, its subsequent interpretative practice changed, lately culminating in the new 2016 Guidelines on International Protection No. 12. The applicability of the 1951 Convention to situations of conflict is generally confirmed in these Guidelines and refugee protection for persons fleeing conflict and violence is made solely dependent on a positive assessment of the eligibility criteria of Article 1 A (2).

The second part of the chapter turned towards the legal interpretation of the Convention's definition, as contained in the Convention itself. The 1951 Convention is an international treaty that was adopted nearly 70 years ago and challenges to its application are based on legal uncertainty in interpretation as well as practical obstacles to its application. The context of its application is constantly changing, and "it would be an error to construe the definition so as to ignore the changing circumstances of the world in which the Convention now operates."[371] One of these changes is increasing conflict-induced displacement and the mixed movements from areas and countries experiencing violence. "One particular problem [...] is the often automatic denial of refugee status to persons who happen to come from a civil war situation, often on the grounds that even excessively cruel treatment is merely the inevitable by-product of generalized violence."[372]

What is obvious is that, with increasing political pressure, states very much retain their sovereign powers to take final decisions in both asylum status determination and immigration matters. In this regard, "[i]t is sometimes argued that the 1951 Convention does not provide a suitable legal framework for addressing present-day refugee problems as these often occur in the context of war and conflict."[373] Yet, since new codification processes in the protection sense are not realistically foreseeable, the interpretation of the Convention within its legal boundaries is the only accessible means to address contemporary challenges and therefore, a treaty interpretation analysis was conducted in the second part of the chapter.

The first part of the analysis examined the applicability of the treaty as a whole in conflict contexts, by reference to the general development of public international law and to the Draft Articles on the Effects of Armed Conflict more specifically. All of these supported a positive answer to the question posed, underlining the general applicability of the treaty as a whole to situations of conflict. The second part examined the single pertinent criteria of the Convention definition for their interpretation in the context of conflict and violence. A major issue in assessing conflict-related protection claims revolves around determination of the risk faced

371 *A v. Minister for Immigration & Ethnic Affairs*, (1997) 190 CLR 225, Australia: High Court (1997), at para. 227.

372 United Nations General Assembly, 'International Protection' (UN Doc. A/AC.96/75, 1990), at 16.

373 *Manuel Diaz Arteaga v. Immigration and Naturalization Service*, 836 F.2d 1227, United States: Court of Appeals, Ninth Circuit (1988), at 1232.

during situations of violence and conflict. While accepting that conflict, as such, neither rules out nor suffices to activate refugee status, determining authorities and courts use restrictive interpretative practices, such as the 'differentiated risk' approach to reject claims.[374] This approach requires claimants to have a risk, over and above the risk faced by others affected by the conflict or violent setting, in order to support their protection application. However, as rightfully emphasised in subsequent case law employing the non-comparative approach, "it is [...] difficult to see the basis on which a super-added requirement of 'greater-risk', 'differential risk' or 'risk over and above that arising from clan warfare' can be derived as a criterion for the application of the Convention definition [...]."[375] Such an additional risk and the comparison other persons affected lacks basis in the individual assessment according to the refugee criteria codified in the 1951 Convention.

Reference to means and methods of warfare and widespread indiscriminate violence are equally often used to deny application of the Convention. Here, opponents argue that the lack of targeted persecution, as envisaged by the Convention grounds, required the rejection of such claims.[376] The conflict in Syria is a useful example which has shown that generalised violence is often misjudged as random and indiscriminate, while it is often anything but. It is just as often rooted in political, religious or ethnical cleavages that can trigger the engagement of the 1951 Convention. The complexity of conflict both obscures the motives to flee and to persecute or otherwise maltreat, thereby leaving decision-makers with the uncertain tasks as to which instrument to apply and which status to grant. For this reason, legal certainty in the interpretation of the existing instruments is essential. The refugee definition of Article 1 A (2) is applicable in the same way it is applicable during times of peace. Its criteria still distinguish between those persecuted for specific reasons and those who are not. These have, however, remained the same since 1951 and must be applied accordingly and independently of the context in which the discriminatory persecution occurs.

On the contrary, if the harm caused by the conflict is unrelated to the discriminatory grounds of the 1951 Convention, the treaty is not applicable and refugee status in accordance with the universal instrument must be denied. In such a case, one needs to identify a regional extended refugee instrument or subsidiary protection as basis for protection.

References

'Brazil Declaration. A Framework for Cooperation and Regional Solidarity to Strengthen the International Protection of Refugees, Displaced and Stateless Persons in Latin America and the Caribbean', 3 December 2014, available online at http://www.refworld.org/docid/5487065b4.html (last visited 1 August 2018).

374 *Adan v. Secretary of State for the Home Department, per Lord Slynn of Hadley, supra* note 218, at 311. (Lord Lloyd of Berwick).

375 *Minister for Immigration and Multicultural Affairs v. Abdi, supra* note 227.

376 United Nations High Commissioner for Refugees, *supra* note 124, at para. 20.

Ad Hoc Committee on Refugees and Stateless Persons, 'First Session: Summary Record of the Third Meeting' (UN Doc. E/AC.32/SR.3, 1950).

Ad Hoc Committee on Refugees and Stateless Persons, 'Report of the Ad Hoc Committee on Statelessness and Related Persons' (UN Doc. E/1618, E/AC.35/5, 1950).

AKnews, 'Assassination of lecturers continues in Mosul. Recited in UNHCR, Eligibility Guidelines for Assessing the International Protection Needs of Asylum-Seekers from Iraq', 10 September 2011, available online at http://www.refworld.org/pdfid/4fc77d522.pdf (last visited 1 August 2018).

Albert, Matthew, 'Prima Facie Determination of Refugee Status. An Overview and its Legal Foundation. Refugee Studies Centre, University of Oxford, Working Paper Series No. 55' (2010).

Alborzi, Mohammad R., *Evaluating the Effectiveness of International Refugee Law. The Protection of Iraqi Refugees* (Brill, 2006).

Aleinikoff, Alexander, 'Protected Characteristics and Social Perceptions: An Analysis of the Meaning of 'Membership of a Particular Social Group'', in E. Feller, V. Türk and F. Nicholson (eds.), *Protection in International Law: UNHCR's Global Consultations on International Protection* (Cambridge University Press, 2003).

Alexander, Michael, 'Refugee Status Determination Conducted by UNHCR', 11 (2) *International Journal of Refugee Law* 251 (1999).

Alston, Philip (ed.), *Non-state Actors and Human Rights* (Oxford University Press, 2011).

Amnesty International, 'Amnesty Report 2012. Syrien', 9 May 2012, available online at https://www.amnesty.de/jahresbericht/2012/syrien (last visited 1 August 2018).

Arato, Julian, 'Subsequent Practice and Evolutive Interpretation. Techniques of Treaty Interpretation over Time and Their Diverse Consequences', 9 (3) *The Law & Practice of International Courts and Tribunals* 443 (2010).

Asian-African Legal Consultative Organization, 'Bangkok Principles on the Status and Treatment of Refugees ("Bangkok Principles")' (1966).

Minister for Immigration and Multicultural Affairs v. Abdi, [1999] FCA 299; 162 ALR 105, Australia: Federal Court (1999).

A and Another v. Minister for Immigration and Ethnic Affairs and Another, HCA 4; (1997) 190 CLR 225; (1997) 142 ALR 331, Australia: High Court (1997).

A v. Minister for Immigration & Ethnic Affairs, (1997) 190 CLR 225, Australia: High Court (1997).

Minister for Immigration and Multicultural Affairs v. Haji Ibrahim, [2000] HCA 55, Australia: High Court (2000).

Minister for Immigration and Multicultural Affairs v. Khawar, 187 ALR 574; [2002] HCA 14, Australia: High Court (2002).

Bailliet, Cecilia M., 'National Case Law as a Generator of International Refugee Law. Rectifying an Imbalance within the UNHCR Guidelines on International Protection' (European Society of International Law Conference Series, No. 7, 2014).

Battjes, Hemme, *European Asylum Law and International Law* (Martinus Nijhoff Publishers, 2006).

Bayefsky, Anne F. and Fitzpatrick, Joan (eds.), *Human Rights and Forced Displacement* (Martinus Nijhoff Publishers, 2001).

Belgium: Council for Alien Law Litigation, *No. 103921*, CCE, arrêt n°103921 (2013).

Betts, Alexander and Loescher, Gil (eds.), *Refugees in International Relations* (Oxford University Press, 2010).

Boyle, A. E., 'Some Reflections on the Relationship of Treaties and Soft Law', 48 (4) *International and Comparative Law Quarterly* 901 (1999).

Brett, Rachel A., Brett, Margaret and Rashed, Haifa, 'Children Fleeing Conflict: Age and the Interpretation and Application of the 1951 Refugee Convention', in V. Türk, A. Edwards and C. W. Wouters (eds.), *In Flight from Conflict and Violence: Unhcr's Consultations on Refugee Status and Other Forms of International Protection* (Cambridge University Press, 2017).

Brownlie, Ian, *Principles of Public International Law* (3rd ed.: Clarendon Press, 1979).

Brownlie, Ian and Goodwin-Gill, Guy S. (eds.), *Basic Documents on Human Rights* (5th ed.: Oxford University Press, 2006).

Canada: Federal Court, *Vahe Salibian v. Canada (Minister of Employment and Immigration), per Décary, JA*, [1990] 3 F.C. 250 (C.A.) (1990).

Canada: Federal Court, *Mileva v. Canada (Minister of Employment and Immigration)*, [1991] 3 F.C. 398 (C.A.)(1991).

Canada: Federal Court, *Prophete v. Canada*, 2009 FCA 31 (2009).

Canada: Federal Court of Appeal, *Ali, Shaysta-Ameer v. Canada (Minister of Employment and Immigration), Décary, Stone, Strayer*, (F.C.A., no. A-772-96) (1999).

Canada: Federal Court of Appeal, *Rahaman v. Minister of Citizenship and Immigration, per Evans JA*, 2002 ACWSJ Lexis 1026 (2002).

Canada: Supreme Court, *Canada (Attorney General) v. Ward*, [1993] 2 S.C.R. 689; (1993) DLR (4th) 1 (1993).

Cantor, David and Durieux, Jean-François, 'Introduction', in D. Cantor and J.-F. Durieux (eds.), *Refuge from Inhumanity? War Refugees and International Humanitarian Law* (Brill, 2014).

Cantor, David and Durieux, Jean-François (eds.), *Refuge from Inhumanity? War Refugees and International Humanitarian Law* (Brill, 2014).

Caron, David D., 'The ILC Articles on State Responsibility: The Paradoxical Relationship between Form and Authority', 96 (4) *American Journal of International Law* 857 (2002).

Carter, Edward L. and Clark, Brad, 'Membership in a Particular Social Group: International Journalists and U.S. Asylum Law', 12 (3) *Communication Law and Policy* 279 (2007).

Chetail, Vincent, 'Armed Conflict and Forced Migration: A Systemic Approach to International Humanitarian Law, Refugee Law and Human Rights Law', in A. Clapham and P. Gaeta (eds.), *The Oxford Handbook of International Law in Armed Conflict* (Oxford University Press, 2014).

Chetail, Vincent and Bauloz, Céline, *Research Handbook on International Law and Migration* (Edward Elgar, 2014).

Chinkin, Christine M., 'The Challenge of Soft Law. Development and Change in International Law', 38 (4) *International and Comparative Law Quarterly* 850 (1989).

Clapham, Andrew (ed.), *Human Rights and Non-state Actors* (Edward Elgar, 2013).

Clapham, Andrew and Gaeta, Paola (eds.), *The Oxford Handbook of International Law in Armed Conflict* (Oxford University Press, 2014).

Corkery, Allison, 'The Contribution of the UNHCR Executive Committee to the Development of International Refugee Law', 13 (1) *Australian International Law Journal* 97 (2006).

Costello, Cathryn, *The Human Rights of Migrants and Refugees in European Law* (Oxford University Press, 2016).

Council of the European Union, 'Joint Position of 4 March 1996 defined by the Council on the basis of Article K.3 of the Treaty on European Union on the harmonized application of the definition of the term 'refugee' in Article 1 of the Geneva Convention of 28 July 1951 relating to the status of refugees. OJ 1996 L 63' (1996).

Council Directive 2005/85/EC of 1 December 2005 on Minimum Standards on Procedures in Member States for Granting and Withdrawing Refugee Status, 2 January 2006.

Court of Justice of the European Union, *X, Y, Z v. Minister voor Immigratie en Asiel*, C-199/12 to C-201/12, (2013).

Davies, Sara E., 'The Asian Rejection? International Refugee Law in Asia', 52 (4) *Australian Journal of Politics & History* 562 (2006).

Doutum, M. H., 'Opening Statement at the OAU/UNHCR Meeting of Government and Non-Government Technical Experts on the 30th Anniversary of the 1969 OAU Convention Governing the Specific Aspects of the Refugee Problem in Africa, 27–29 March, h.E. Ambassador Doutum' (Conakry, Guinea, UN Doc. CONF.P/OAU /30th/Report Annex IV).

Durieux, Jean-Francois, 'Of War, Flows, Laws and Flaws. A Reply to Hugo Storey', 31 (3) *Refugee Survey Quarterly* 161 (2012).

Edwin Odhiambo-Abuya, E., 'Past Reflections, Future Insights: African Asylum Law and Policy in Historical Perspective', 19 (1) *International Journal of Refugee Law* 51 (2007).

Eritrea: Ministry of Foreign Affairs, 'UNHCR Eligibility Guidelines: Factual Findings or Recycled Defamation?', 17 December 2015, available online at http://www.shabait.com/news/local-news/20954-unhcr-eligibility-guidelines-factual-findings-or-recycled-defamation (last visited 1 August 2018).

European Commission, 'Proposal for a Council Directive on Minimum Standards for the Qualification and Status of Third Country Nationals and Stateless Persons as Refugees or As Persons Who Otherwise Need International Protection. COM(2001)510 final' (2001).

European Council on Refugees and Exiles, 'Recommendations on the Treatment of Algerian Refugees and Asylum Seekers in Europe', 1 June 1995, available online at http://www.refworld.org/publisher, ECRE, DZA, 3ae6a6618,0.html (last visited 1 August 2018).

European Court of Human Rights, *Loizidou v. Turkey*, App. No. 15318/89 (1995).

European Court of Human Rights, *D v. The United Kingdom*, App. No. 30240/96 (1997).

European Court of Human Rights, *N. v. The United Kingdom*, App. No. 26565/05 (2008).

European Court of Human Rights, *NA. v. The United Kingdom*, App. No. 25904/07 (2008).

European Court of Human Rights, *M.S.S. v. Belgium and Greece*, App. No. 30696/09 (2011).

European Parliament, Directorate General for Internal Policies, *Gender Related Asylum Claims in Europe. A Comparative Analysis of Law, Policies and Practice Focusing on Women in Nine EU Member States: France, Belgium, Hungary, Italy, Malta, Romania, Spain, Sweden and the United Kingdom: Study* (EUR-OP, 2012).

Feller, Erika, 'The Evolution of the International Refugee Protection Regime', 5 *Washington University Journal of Law & Policy* 129 (2001).

Feller, Erika and Klug, Anja, 'Refugees, United Nations High Commissioner for (UNHCR)' (Max Planck Encyclopedia of Public International Law, 2013).

Feller, Erika, Türk, Volker and Nicholson, Frances (eds.), *Refugee Protection in International Law. UNHCR's Global Consultations on International Protection* (Cambridge University Press, 2003).

Fiddian-Qasmiyeh, Elena *et al. (eds.), The Oxford Handbook of Refugee and Forced Migration Studies* (Oxford University Press, 2014).

Fitzpatrick, Joan, 'Revitalizing the 1951 Convention', 9 *Harvard Human Rights Journal* (1996).

Fitzpatrick, Joan, 'Human Rights and Forced Displacement: Converging Standards', in A. F. Bayefsky and J. Fitzpatrick (eds.), *Human Rights and Forced Displacement* (Martinus Nijhoff Publishers, 2001).

Fleck, Dieter (ed.), *The Handbook of International Humanitarian Law* (2nd ed.: Oxford University Press, 2008).

Fripp, Eric, 'International Humanitarian Law and the Interpretation of 'Persecution' in Article 1A(2) CSR51', 26 (3) *International Journal of Refugee Law* 382 (2014).

Gammeltoft-Hansen, Thomas, *Access to Asylum: International Refugee Law and the Globalisation of Migration Control* (Cambridge University Press, 2011).

Gardam, Judith G. and Jarvis, Michelle J., *Women, Armed Conflict and International Law* (Kluwer Law International, 2001).

Garlick, Madeline, 'International Protection in Court. The Asylum Jurisprudence of the Court of Justice of the EU and UNHCR', 34 (1) *Refugee Survey Quarterly* 107 (2015).

Germany: Administrative Court Düsseldorf, *Judgment of 03 March 2006*, 21 K 1464/02.A (2006).

Germany: Administrative Court Magdeburg, *Judgment of 22 May 2006*, 9A 326/05 MD (2006).

Germany: Administrative Court Trier, *Judgment of 08 July 2016*, 1 K 1922/16.TR (2016).

Germany: Federal Administrative Court, *Judgment of 02 August 1983*, 9 C 818/81 (1983).

Germany: Federal Constitutional Court, *Judgment of 10 July 1989*, 2 BvR 502/86; 2 BvR 961/86; 2 BvR 1000/86 (1989).

Gilbert, Geoff, 'UNHCR and Courts. Amicus curiae ... sed curia amica est?', 28 (4) *International Journal of Refugee Law* 623 (2016).

Goodwin-Gill, Guy S., *The Refugee in International Law* (2nd ed.: Clarendon Press, 1996).

Goodwin-Gill, Guy S., 'Refugee Identity and Protection's Fading Prospects', in F. Nicholson and P. M. Twomey (eds.), *Refugee Rights and Realities: Evolving International Concepts and Regimes* (Cambridge University Press, 1999).

Goodwin-Gill, Guy S., 'The Dynamic of International Refugee Law', 25 (4) *International Journal of Refugee Law* 651 (2013).

Goodwin-Gill, Guy S. and McAdam, Jane, *The Refugee in International Law* (3rd ed.: Oxford University Press, 2007).

Grahl-Madsen, Atle, 'Commentary of the Refugee Convention 1951 (Articles 2–11, 13–37)', October 1997, available online at http://www.refworld.org/docid/4785ee9d2.html (last visited 1 August 2018).

G.T [2013] Attica Regional Asylum Office 95/000186182, Greece: Asylum Service, Attica Regional Asylum Office (2013) Case number 755.

Hailbronner, Kay and Thym, Daniel (eds.), *EU Immigration and Asylum Law. A Commentary* (Beck/Hart/Nomos, 2016).

Haines, Rodger, 'Gender-related Persecution', in E. Feller, V. Türk and F. Nicholson (eds.), *Refugee Protection in International Law: Unhcr's Global Consultations on International Protection* (Cambridge University Press, 2003).

Hathaway, James C., *The Law of Refugee Status* (Butterworths, 1991).

Hathaway, James C., *The Rights of Refugees Under International Law* (Cambridge University Press, 2005).

Hathaway, James C. and Foster, Michelle, 'The Causal Connection ("Nexus") to a Convention Ground. Discussion Paper No. 3 Advanced Refugee Law Workshop International Association of Refugee Law Judges Auckland, New Zealand, October 2002', 15 (3) *International Journal of Refugee Law* 461 (2003).

Hathaway, James C. and Foster, Michelle, *The Law of Refugee Status* (2nd ed.: Cambridge University Press, 2014).

Hathaway, James C. and Hicks, William S., 'Is there a Subjective Element in the Refugee Convention's Requirement of 'well-founded fear'?', 26 (2) *Michigan Journal of International Law* 505 (2005).

Heijer, Maarten d., *Europe and Extraterritorial Asylum* (Hart, 2012).

Heintze, Hans-Joachim, 'Theorien zum Verhältnis von Menschenrechten und humanitärem Völkerrecht', 24 (1) *Humanitäres Völkerrecht - Informationsschriften* 4 (2011).

Hertwig, Jana (ed.), *Global Risks. Constructing World Order through Law, Politics and Economics* (P. Lang, 2010).

Higgins, Rosalyn, *Problems and Process. International Law and How We Use it* (Clarendon Press; Oxford University Press, 1995).

Holborn, Louise W., *Refugees, a Problem of Our Time. The Work of the United Nations High Commissioner for Refugees, 1951–1972* (Scarecrow Press, 1975).

Holzer, Vanessa, 'The Relevance of the 1951 Refugee Convention for the Protection of Individuals Forced to Flee Armed Conflicts', in J. Hertwig (ed.), *Global Risks: Constructing World Order through Law, Politics and Economics* (P. Lang, 2010).

Hruschka, Constantin and Löhr, Tillmann, 'Das Konventionsmerkmal "Zugehörigkeit zu einer bestimmten sozialen Gruppe" und seine Anwendung in Deutschland' (4) *Neue Zeitschrift für Verwaltungsrecht* 205 (2009).

Human Rights Committee, 'General Comment No. 31: The Nature of the General Legal Obligation Imposed on States Parties to the Covenant' (UN Doc. CCPR/C/21/Rev.1/Add.13, 2004).

Human Rights Committee, 'General Comment No. 34: Freedom of Opinion and Expression' (UN Doc. CCPR/C/GC/34, 2011).

Human Rights Council, 'Report of the Independent International Commission of Inquiry on the Syrian Arab Republic' (UN Doc. A/HRC/30/48, 2015).

Human Rights Council, 'Report of the Independent International Commission of Inquiry on the Syrian Arab Republic, 31st session, Advance Edited Version' (UN Doc. A/HRC/31/68, 2016).

Hungary: Administrative and Labour Court of Budapest, *S.A. v Office of Immigration and Nationality*, 3.K.31404/2013/4 (2013).

Hungary: Administrative and Labour Court of Budapest, *M.A.A. v. Office of Immigration and Nationality*, 6.K.31830/2013/6 (2013).

Inter-American Court of Human Rights, *Advisory Opinion: The Right to Information on Consular Assistance in the Framework of the Guarantees of the Due Process of Law*, OC-16/99 (1999).

Inter-American Court of Human Rights, *Bámaca Velásquez Case (Petition No. 11.129)*, Series C No. 70 (2000).

International Committee on the Red Cross, 'Aide Memoire on the Refugee Question. Statement Submitted by the International Committee on the Red Cross' (UN Doc. A/CONF./NGO.2, 1951).

International Court of Justice, *North Sea Continental Shelf Cases (Federal Republic of Germany v. Denmark; Federal Republic of Germany v. Netherlands)*, (1969).

International Court of Justice, *Legality of the Threat or Use of Nuclear Weapons. Advisory Opinion* (1996).

International Court of Justice, *Legal Consequences of the Construction of a Wall in the Occupied Palestinian Territory. Advisory Opinion* (2004).

International Court of Justice, *Armed Activities on the Territory of the Congo (Democratic Republic of the Congo v. Uganda)* (2005).

International Court of Justice, *Application of the Convention on the Prevention and Punishment of the Crime of Genocide (Bosnia and Herzegovina v. Serbia and Montenegro)* (2007).

International Law Commission, 'Survey of International Law in Relation to the Work of Codification of the International Law Commission' (UN Doc. A/CN.4/Rev.1, 1949).

International Law Commission, 'The Effects of Armed Conflicts on Treaties' (61 II Yearbook of the Institute for International Law 199, 1986).

International Law Commission, 'Draft Articles on the Effects of Armed Conflict on Treaties, with Commentaries, adopted by the ILC, 63rd session, submitted to the UNGA' (A/66/10, Yearbook of the International Law Commission, 2011, Vol. II, Part Two, 2011).

International Law Commission, 'Analytical Guide to the Work of the International Law Commission', 19 September 2016, available online at http://legal.un.org/ilc/guide/1_10.shtml (last visited 1 August 2018).

Joanne van Selm (ed.), *Kosovo's Refugees in the European Union* (Pinter, 2000).

Juss, Satvinder S., 'The UNHCR Handbook and the Interface between 'Soft Law' and 'Hard Law' in International Refugee Law', in S. S. Juss and C. Harvey (eds.), *Contemporary Issues in Refugee Law* (Edward Elgar, 2013).

Juss, Satvinder S. and Harvey, Colin (eds.), *Contemporary Issues in Refugee Law* (Edward Elgar, 2013).

Kagan, Michael, 'Assessment of Refugee Status Determination Procedure at UNHCR's Cairo Office 2001-2002' (American University of Cairo. Forced Migration and Refugee Studies Working Paper No 1, 2002).

Kagan, Michael, 'The Beleaguered Gatekeeper. Protection Challenges Posed by UNHCR Refugee Status Determination', 18 (1) *International Journal of Refugee Law* 1 (2006).

Kagan, Michael, 'The Beleaguered Gatekeeper: Protection Challenges Posed by UNHCR Refugee Status Determination' (Scholarly Works. Paper 636, 2006).

Kälin, Walter, 'Refugees and Civil Wars: Only a Matter of Interpretation?', 3 *International Journal of Refugee Law* 435 (1991).

Kälin, Walter, 'Supervising the 1951 Convention on the Status of Refugees: Article 35 and Beyond' (UNHCR Background paper commissioned for the 2nd Expert Roundtable in the context of the 50th anniversary of the 1951 Convention, 2001).

Kälin, Walter, 'How Hard is Soft Law? The Guiding Principles on Internal Displacement and the Need for a Normative Framework. Round Table Meeting, CUNY Graduate Center', 19 December 2001, available online at https://www.brookings.edu/wp-content/uploads/2016/06/20011219.pdf (last visited 1 August 2018).

Kälin, Walter, 'Supervising the 1951 Convention Relating to the Status of Refugees: Article 35 and beyond', in E. Feller, V. Türk and F. Nicholson (eds.), *Refugee Protection in International Law: Unhcr's Global Consultations on International Protection* (Cambridge University Press, 2003).

Karrenstein, Daniela, *Der Menschenrechtsrat der Vereinten Nationen* (Mohr Siebeck, 2011).
Kneebone, Susan, Stevens, Dallal and Baldassar, Loretta (eds.), *Refugee Protection and the Role of Law. Conflicting Identities* (Routledge, 2014).
Kolb, Robert, 'Human Rights and Humanitarian Law' (Max Planck Encyclopedia of Public International Law, 2013).
Koskenniemi, Martti, 'Fragmentation of International Law: Difficulties Arising from the Diversification and Expansion of International Law, in: Report of the Study Group of the International Law Commission' (UN Doc. A/CN.4/L.682, 2006).
Kugelmann, Dieter, 'Refugees' (Max Planck Encyclopedia of Public International Law, 2010).
Lambert, Hélène, 'Causation in International Protection from Armed Conflict', in D. Cantor and J.-F. Durieux (eds.), *Refuge from Inhumanity? War Refugees and International Humanitarian Law* (Brill, 2014).
Lerner, Natan, *The UN Convention on the Elimination of All Forms of Racial Discrimination* (Brill, 2014).
Lewis, Corinne, *UNHCR and International Refugee Law. From Treaties to Innovation* (Routledge, 2012).
Macklin, Audrey, 'Refugee Women and the Imperative of Categories', 17 (2) *Human Rights Quarterly* 213 (1995).
Markard, Nora, *Kriegsflüchtlinge. Gewalt gegen Zivilpersonen in bewaffneten Konflikten als Herausforderung für das Flüchtlingsrecht und den subsidiären Schutz* (Mohr Siebeck, 2012).
McAdam, Jane, *Climate Change, Forced Migration, and International Law* (Oxford University Press, 2012).
Ministerial Meeting of States Parties to the 1951 Convention and/or Its 1967 Protocol relating to the Status of Refugee, 'Declaration of States Parties to the 1951 Convention and or Its 1967 Protocol relating to the Status of Refugees' (UN Doc. HCR/MMSP/2001/09, 2002).
Myrstad, Finn and Kolmannskog, Vikram, 'Environmental Displacement in European Asylum Law', 11 (4) *European Journal of Migration and Law* 313 (2009).
AC (Syria), [2011] NZIPT 800035, New Zealand: Immigration and Protection Tribunal (2011).
Refugee Appeal No. 1/92 Re SA, New Zealand: Refugee Status Appeals Authority (1992).
Refugee Appeal No. 74665, RSSA per Haines QDC, New Zealand: Refugee Status Appeals Authority (2004).
New Zealand: Refugee Status Appeals Authority, *Refugee Appeal No. 75779* (2006).
New Zealand: Refugee Status Appeals Authority, *Refugee Appeal No. 75879*, New Zealand: Refugee Status Appeals Authority (2007).
New Zealand: Refugee Status Appeals Authority, *Refugee Appeal No. 76006* (2007).
New Zealand: Refugee Status Appeals Authority, *Refugee Appeal No. 76094* (2008).
New Zealand: Refugee Status Appeals Authority, *Refugee Appeal No. 76199* (2008).
New Zealand: Refugee Status Appeals Authority, *Refugee Appeal No. 76457* (2010).
Newland, Kathleen, 'Refugee Protection and Assistance', in P. J. Simmons and C. d. Jonge Oudraat (eds.), *Managing Global Issues: Lessons Learned* (Carnegie Endowment for International Peace, 2001).
Ní Aoláin, Fionnuala, Haynes, Dina F. and Cahn, Naomi R., *On the Frontlines. Gender, War, and the Post-Conflict Process* (Oxford University Press, 2011).
Nicholson, Frances and Twomey, Patrick M. (eds.), *Refugee Rights and Realities. Evolving International Concepts and Regimes* (Cambridge University Press, 1999).

Nolte, Georg, 'Treaties Over Time in Particular; Subsequent Agreement and Practice', in United Nations Organisation (ed.), *Report of the International Law Commission* (2008).

Nykänen, Eeva, *Fragmented State Power and Forced Migration. A Study on Non-State Actors in Refugee Law* (Martinus Nijhoff Publishers, 2012).

'Resolution on the Adoption of a Draft Convention on the Status of Refugees in Africa, Addis Ababa, 31 October -4 November 1966' (CM/Res.88 (IVV), 1966).

Öberg, Marko D., 'The Legal Effects of Resolutions of the UN Security Council and General Assembly in the Jurisprudence of the ICJ', 16 (5) *European Journal of International Law* 879 (2005).

O'Sullivan, Maria, 'Acting the Part: Can Non-State Entities Provide Protection Under International Refugee Law?', 24 (1) *International Journal of Refugee Law* 85 (2012).

Oxford English Dictionary, 'fear, n.1', 2017, available online at http://www.oed.com/view/Entry/68773?rskey=LFJr1E&result=1 (last visited 1 August 2018).

Oxford English Dictionary, 'persecute, v.', 2017, available online at http://www.oed.com/view/Entry/141429?redirectedFrom=persecute (last visited 1 August 2018).

Oxford English Dictionary, 'persecution, n.', 2017, available online at http://www.oed.com/view/Entry/141431?redirectedFrom=persecution (last visited 1 August 2018).

Pinheiro, Paulo, 'Presentation: The Use of Barrel Bombs and Indiscriminate Bombardment in Syria', 12 March 2015, available online at http://www.ohchr.org/Documents/HRBodies/HRCouncil/CoISyria/CoISyriaIndiscriminateBombardment12032015.pdf (last visited 1 August 2018).

Prescott, M., 'How War Affects Treaties Between Belligerents: A Case Study of the Gulf War', 7 *Emory International Law Review* (1993).

Rankin, Micah B., 'Extending the Limits or Narrowing Down the Scope? Deconstructing the OAU Refugee Definition Thirty Years On', 21 *South African Journal of Human Rights* 406 (2005).

Reed-Hurtado, Michael, 'The Cartagena Declaration on Refugees and the Protection of People Fleeing Armed Conflict and Other Situations of Violence in Latin America. Division of International Protection', June 2013, available online at http://www.refworld.org/docid/51c801934.html (last visited 1 August 2018).

Rietiker, Daniel, 'The Principle of "Effectiveness" in the Recent Jurisprudence of the European Court of Human Rights. Its Different Dimensions and Its Consistency with Public International Law – No Need for the Concept of Treaty Sui Generis', 79 (2) *Nordic Journal of International Law* 245 (2010).

Rosenne, Shabtai, *The Law of Treaties. A Guide to the Legislative History of the Vienna Convention* (Sijthoff, 1970).

Sandra Lavenex, 'France: International Norms, European Integration and State Discretion', in Joanne van Selm (ed.), *Kosovo's Refugees in the European Union* (Pinter, 2000).

Schachter, Oscar, *International Law in Theory and Practice* (Martinus Nijhoff Publishers/Kluwer Academic Publishers, 1991).

Schäfer, Bernhard, *Zum Verhältnis Menschenrechte und humanitäres Völkerrecht. Zugleich ein Beitrag zur exterritorialen Geltung von Menschenrechtsverträgen* (Universitätsverlag Potsdam, 2006).

Schjatvet, Cecilie and Hestenes og Dramer & Co., 'The Making of UNHCR'S Guidance and its Implementation in the National Jurisdiction of the United Kingdom, Norway and Sweden' (Research Report for the Norwegian Directorate of Immigration, 2010).

Shacknove, Andrew E., 'Who Is a Refugee?', 95 (2) *Ethics* 274 (1985).
Sharpe, Marina, 'Engaging with Refugee Protection? The Organization of African Unity and African Union since 1963' (UNHCR Research Paper No 226, 2011).
Simeon, James C. (ed.), *The UNHCR and the Supervision of International Refugee Law* (Cambridge University Press, 2013).
Simeon, James C., 'Excluding Refugee and Asylum Applicants Under the UNHCR's Statute or Mandate' (Paper presented at the "Undesirable and Unreturnable? Policy Challenges Around Excluded Asylum Seekers and other Migrants Suspected of Serious Criminality Who Cannot be Removed" Preliminary Workshop, 27 March 2015, Centre for International Criminal Justice, Faculty of Law, VU University Amsterdam, The Netherlands, 2015).
Simmons, P. J. and Jonge Oudraat, Chantal d. (eds.), *Managing Global Issues. Lessons Learned* (Carnegie Endowment for International Peace, 2001).
Simpson, John A. (ed.), *The Oxford English Dictionary, Vol. XI* (2nd ed.: Clarendon Press, 1989).
Slovenia: Supreme Court of the Republic of Slovenia, I Up 47/2015 (2015).
Spain: Supreme Court, Chamber for Contentious-Administrative proceedings, STS 5211/2015, Section III (2015).
Steinbock, Daniel, 'The Refugee Definition as a Law: Issues of Interpretation', in F. Nicholson and P. M. Twomey (eds.), *Refugee Rights and Realities: Evolving International Concepts and Regimes* (Cambridge University Press, 1999).
Storey, Hugo, 'Armed Conflict in Asylum Law: The "War-Flaw"', 31 (2) *Refugee Survey Quarterly* 1 (2012).
Storey, Hugo and Wallace, Rebecca, 'War and Peace in Refugee Law Jurisprudence', 95 (2) *The American Journal of International Law* 349 (2001).
Strasbourg Observers, 'Third Party Interventions before the ECtHR: A Rough Guide', 24 February 2015, available online at https://strasbourgobservers.com/2015/02/24/third-party-interventions-before-the-ecthr-a-rough-guide (last visited 1 August 2018).
UM 1802-07, Sweden: Migration Court of Appeal (2008).
A und B (Syrien) v. Staatssekretariat für Migration, D-5779/2013, Switzerland: Federal Administrative Court (2015).
Symes, Mark and Jorro, Peter, *Asylum Law and Practice* (Bloomsbury Professional, 2003).
Tax, Blanche, 'Refugee by Association', 47 *Forced Migration Review* 26 (2014).
Türk, Volker, 'Introductory Note to UNHCR Guidelines on International Protection', 15 (2) *International Journal of Refugee Law* 303 (2003).
Türk, Volker, 'The UNHCR's Role in Supervising International Protection Standards in the Context of its Mandate', in J. C. Simeon (ed.), *The UNHCR and the Supervision of International Refugee Law* (Cambridge University Press, 2013).
Türk, Volker and Dowd, Rebecca, 'Protection Gaps', in E. Fiddian-Qasmiyeh, G. Loescher, K. Long and N. Sigona (eds.), *The Oxford Handbook of Refugee and Forced Migration Studies* (Oxford University Press, 2014).
Türk, Volker, Edwards, Alice and Wouters, C. W. (eds.), *In Flight from Conflict and Violence. UNHCR's Consultations on Refugee Status and other Forms of International Protection* (Cambridge University Press, 2017).
UNHCR: ExCom, 'Conclusion No. 8 (XXVIII) Determination of Refugee Status', 1977, available online at http://www.refworld.org/pdfid/4b28bf1f2.pdf (last visited 1 August 2018).

UNHCR: ExCom, 'Conclusion No. 22 (XXXII) Protection of Asylum-Seekers in Situations of Large- Scale Influx', 1981, available online at http://www.refworld.org/pdfid/4b28bf1f2.pdf (last visited 1 August 2018).
UNHCR: ExCom, 'Conclusion No. 29 (XXXIV) General', 1983, available online at http://www.refworld.org/pdfid/4b28bf1f2.pdf (last visited 1 August 2018).
UNHCR: ExCom, 'Conclusion No. 39 (XXXVI) Refugee Women and International Protection', 1985, available online at http://www.refworld.org/pdfid/4b28bf1f2.pdf (last visited 1 August 2018).
UNHCR: ExCom, 'Conclusion No. 51 (XXXIX) Promotion and Dissemination of Refugee Law', 1988 (last visited 1 August 2018).
UNHCR: ExCom, 'Conclusion No. 80 (XLVII) Comprehensive and Regional Approaches within a Protection Framework', 11 October 1996, available online at http://www.refworld.org/pdfid/4b28bf1f2.pdf (last visited 1 August 2018).
UNHCR: ExCom, 'Conclusion No. 81 (XLVII) General', 1997, available online at http://www.refworld.org/pdfid/4b28bf1f2.pdf (last visited 1 August 2018).
UNHCR: ExCom, 'Conclusion No. 82 (XLVIII) Safeguarding Asylum', 1997, available online at http://www.refworld.org/pdfid/4b28bf1f2.pdf (last visited 1 August 2018).
UNHCR: ExCom, 'Conclusion No. 85 (XLIX) International Protection', 1998, available online at http://www.refworld.org/pdfid/4b28bf1f2.pdf (last visited 1 August 2018).
UNHCR: ExCom, 'Conclusion No. 87 (L) - General', 1999 (last visited 1 August 2018).
UNHCR: ExCom, 'Agenda for Protection', 26 June 2002, available online at http://www.unhcr.org/en-us/excom/standcom/3d12f1982/agenda-protection.html (last visited 1 August 2018).
UNHCR: ExCom Standing Committee, 'Overview of Regional Developments (October to December 1995)', 4 January 1996, available online at http://www.unhcr.org/3ae68d2c0.pdf (last visited 1 August 2018).
UNHCR: ExCom Standing Committee, 'Progress Report on Informal Consultations on the Provision of International Protection to All Who Need It' (UN Doc. EC/47/SC/CRP.27, 1997).
UNHCR: Farrell and Schmitt, 'The Causes, Character and Conduct of Armed Conflict, and the Effects on Civilian Populations, 1990–2010' (UN Doc. PPLA/2012/03, 2012).
UNHCR: Jaquemet, 'Under What Circumstances Can a Person Who Has Taken an Active Part in the Hostilities of an International or a Non-International Armed Conflict Become an Asylum Seeker?' (UN Doc. PPLA/2004/01, 2004).
UNHCR: Mandal, 'Protection Mechanisms Outside of the 1951 Convention ("Complementary Protection")' (UN Doc. PPLA/2005/02, 2005).
UNHCR: Oosterveld, 'Women and Girls Fleeing Conflict: Gender and the Interpretation and Application of the 1951 Refugee Convention, UNHCR Legal and Protection Research Series. UN Doc. PPLA/2012/06' (2012).
UNHCR: Sharpe, 'The 1969 OAU Refugee Convention and the Protection of People fleeing Armed Conflict and Other Situations of Violence in the Context of Individual Refugee Status Determination' (UN Doc. PPLA/2013/01, 2013).
United Kingdom: Asylum and Immigration Tribunal / Immigration Appellate Authority, *NS (Social Group - Women - Forced Marriage) Afghanistan v. Secretary of State for the Home Department*, CG [2004] UKIAT 00328 (2004).

United Kingdom: Asylum and Immigration Tribunal / Immigration Appellate Authority, *HM (Somali Women - Particular Social Group) Somalia v. Secretary of State for the Home Department*, [2005] UKIAT 00040 (2005).

United Kingdom: Asylum and Immigration Tribunal / Immigration Appellate Authority, *NM and Others (Lone Women - Ashraf) Somalia v. Secretary of State for the Home Department*, CG [2005] UKIAT 00076 (2005).

United Kingdom: Asylum and Immigration Tribunal / Immigration Appellate Authority, *AM & AM (Armed Conflict: Risk Categories) Somalia v. Secretary of State for the Home Department*, [2008] UKAIT 00091 (2009).

United Kingdom: Court of Appeal, *HH (Somalia) & Others v. Secretary of State for the Home Department*, [2010] EWCA Civ 426 (2010).

United Kingdom: Court of Appeal (England and Wales), *Najjemba v. Secretary of State for Home Department*, [2002] EWCA Civ 1082 (2002).

United Kingdom: High Court (Divisional Court), *R v. Uxbridge Magistrates Court & Another ex Parte Adimi R v. Crown Prosecution Service ex Parte Sorani R v. Secretary of State for Home Department ex Parte Sorani R v. Secretary of State for Home Department and Another ex Parte Kaziu*, [1999] EWHC Admin 765 (1999).

United Kingdom: High Court (England and Wales), *Ali (M.M.H.) and Others v. Secretary of State for the Home Department*, [1978] Imm AR 126 (1978).

United Kingdom: Home Office, 'Operational Guidance Note: Syria', 21 February 2014, available online at http://www.refworld.org/docid/530b11374.html (last visited 1 August 2018).

United Kingdom: House of Lords, *T v. Secretary of State for the Home Department*, [1996] 2 All ER 865 (1996).

United Kingdom: House of Lords, *Adan v. Secretary of State for the Home Department, per Lord Slynn of Hadley*, [1998] UKHL 15 (1998).

United Kingdom: House of Lords, *Islam (A.P.) v. Secretary of State for the Home Department; R v. Immigration Appeal Tribunal and Another, Ex Parte Shah (A.P.)* (1999).

United Kingdom: House of Lords, *Horvath v. Secretary of State for the Home Department*, [2000] UKHL 37 (2000).

United Kingdom: House of Lords, *In re B (FC) (Appellant) (2002). Regina v. Special Adjudicator, Ex parte Hoxha (FC)*, [2005] UKHL 19 (2005).

United Kingdom: Immigration Appeal Tribunal, *KK (Recognition elsewhere as refugee), per Ouseley*, [2005] UKIAT 00054 (2005).

United Kingdom: Supreme Court, *RT (Zimbabwe) and Others v. Secretary of State for the Home Department*, [2012] UKSC 38 (2012).

United Kingdom: Supreme Court, *I.A. v. The Secretary of State for the Home Department*, [2014] UKSC 6 (2014).

United Kingdom: Upper Tribunal (Immigration and Asylum Chamber), *AMM and others (conflict; humanitarian crisis; returnees; FGM) Somalia v. Secretary of State for the Home Department*, CG [2011] UKUT 00445 (IAC) (2011).

United Nations Economic and Social Council, 'A Study of Statelessness' (UN Doc. E/1112, E/1112/Add.1, 1949).

United Nations General Assembly, 'Refugees and Stateless Persons: Report of the Secretary-General' (UN Doc. A/C.3/527, 1949).

United Nations General Assembly, 'Resolution 428 (V)' (UN Doc. A/RES/428 (V), 1950).

United Nations General Assembly, 'Conference of Plenipotentiaries on the Status of Refugees and Stateless Persons: Summary Record of the 2nd Meeting' (UN Doc. A/CONF.2/SR.2, 1951).

United Nations General Assembly, 'Conference of Plenipotentiaries on the Status of Refugees and Stateless Persons, Summary Record of the Twenty-Second Meeting' (UN Doc. A/CONF.2/SR.22, 1951).

United Nations General Assembly, 'Conference of Plenipotentiaries on the Status of Refugees and Stateless Persons: Summary Record of the Twenty-fifth Meeting' (UN Doc. A/CONF.2/SR.25, 1951).

United Nations General Assembly, 'Conference of Plenipotentiaries on the Status of Refugees and Stateless Persons: Summary Record of the Twenty-seventh Meeting' (UN Doc. A/CONF.2/SR.27, 1951).

United Nations General Assembly, 'Resolution 1672 (XVI). Refugees from Algeria in Morocco and Tunisia Refugees from Algeria in Morocco and Tunisia' (UN Doc. A/RES/1672(XVI), 1961).

United Nations General Assembly, 'Resolution 2675 (XXV), Basic Principles for the Protection of Civilian Populations in Armed Conflicts' (UN Doc. A/RES/2675, 1970).

United Nations General Assembly, 'International Protection' (UN Doc. A/AC.96/75, 1990).

United Nations General Assembly, 'Note on International Protection' (UN Doc. A/AC.96/777, 1991).

United Nations General Assembly, 'Note on International Protection' (UN Doc. A/AC.96/830, 1994).

United Nations General Assembly, 'Report of the Forty-Fifth Session of the Executive Committee of the High Commissioner's Programme' (UN Doc. A/AC.96/839, 1994).

United Nations General Assembly, 'Note on International Protection: International Protection in Mass Influx' (UN Doc. A/AC.96/850, 1995).

United Nations General Assembly, 'Note on International Protection' (UN Doc. A/AC.96/898, 1998).

United Nations General Assembly, 'Note on International Protection' (UN Doc. A/AC.96/930, 2000).

United Nations General Assembly, 'Office of the United Nations High Commissioner for Refugees: Resolution adopted by the General Assembly' (UN Doc. A/RES/57/187, 2003).

United Nations General Assembly, 'Report of the International Law Commission' (UN Doc. A/63/10, 2008).

United Nations General Assembly, 'Summary Record of the 15th Committee' (UN Doc. A/C.6/65/SE.15, 2010).

United Nations General Assembly, 'Report of the International Law Commission' (UN Doc. A/66/10, 2011).

United Nations General Assembly, 'Guidelines on International Protection No. 11: Prima Facie Recognition of Refugee Status' (HCR/GIP/15/11, 2015).

United Nations General Assembly, 'Rules of Procedure of the Executive Committee of the High Commissioner's Programme' (UN Doc. A/AC.96/187/Rev.8, 2016).

United Nations High Commissioner for Refugees, 'Finding Durable Solutions' (UNHCR GLOBAL APPEAL 2014–2015).

United Nations High Commissioner for Refugees, 'Independent International Commission of Inquiry on the Syrian Arab Republic', available online at http://www.ohchr.

org/EN/HRBodies/HRC/IICISyria/Pages/IndependentInternationalCommission.aspx (last visited 1 August 2018).
United Nations High Commissioner for Refugees, 'Refugee Status Determination', available online at http://www.unhcr.org/uk/refugee-status-determination.html (last visited 1 August 2018).
United Nations High Commissioner for Refugees, 'Refugee Status Determination', available online at http://www.unhcr.org/pages/4a16b1d06.html (last visited 1 August 2018).
United Nations High Commissioner for Refugees, 'UNHCR's Position on Certain Types of Draft Evasion', January 1991, available online at http://www.refworld.org/docid/4a54bc1f0.html (last visited 1 August 2018).
United Nations High Commissioner for Refugees, 'Handbook on Procedures and Criteria for Determining Refugee Status under the 1951 Convention and the 1967 Protocol relating to the Status of Refugees. UN Doc. HCR/IP/4/Eng/REV.1 Reedited', January 1992/UNHCR 1979, available online at http://www.unhcr.org/4d93528a9.pdf (last visited 1 August 2018).
United Nations High Commissioner for Refugees, 'Protection of persons of concern to UNHCR who fall outside the 1951 Convention: a discussion note. UN Doc. EC/1992/SCP/CRP.5', 2 April 1992, available online at http://www.unhcr.org/3ae68cc518.html (last visited 1 August 2018).
United Nations High Commissioner for Refugees, 'Note on Burden and Standard of Proof in Refugee Claims', 16 December 1998, available online at http://www.refworld.org/docid/3ae6b3338.html (last visited 1 August 2018).
United Nations High Commissioner for Refugees, 'Interpreting Article 1 of the 1951 Convention Relating to the Status of Refugees', April 2001, available online at http://www.refworld.org/docid/3b20a3914.html (last visited 1 August 2018).
United Nations High Commissioner for Refugees, 'Declaration reaffirming principles of 1951 Refugee Convention adopted', 13 December 2001, available online at http://www.unhcr.org/3c18e6054.html (last visited 1 August 2018).
United Nations High Commissioner for Refugees, 'Guidelines on International Protection No. 1: Gender-Related Persecution Within the Context of Article 1A(2) of the 1951 Convention and/or its 1967 Protocol Relating to the Status of Refugees' (UN Doc. HCR/GIP/02/01, 2002).
United Nations High Commissioner for Refugees, 'Guidelines on International Protection No. 2: "Membership of a Particular Social Group" Within the Context of Article 1A(2) of the 1951 Convention and/or its 1967 Protocol Relating to the Status of Refugees' (UN Doc. HCR/GIP/02/02, 2002).
United Nations High Commissioner for Refugees, 'Partnership: An Operations Management Handbook for UNHCR's Partners', February 2003, available online at http://spanish.careemergencytoolkit.org/Assets/Files/cae7a393-d68f-46c6-bc08-cad16ba8dc61.pdf (last visited 1 August 2018).
United Nations High Commissioner for Refugees, 'Guidelines on International Protection No. 3: Cessation of Refugee Status under Article 1C(5) and (6) of the 1951 Convention relating to the Status of Refugees (the "Ceased Circumstances" Clauses)' (HCR/GIP/03/03, 2003).
United Nations High Commissioner for Refugees, 'Framework for Durable Solutions for Refugees and Persons of Concern', May 2003, available online at http://www.refworld.org/docid/4124b6a04.html (last visited 1 August 2018).

United Nations High Commissioner for Refugees, 'Guidelines on International Protection No. 4: "Internal Flight or Relocation Alternative" Within the Context of Article 1A(2) of the 1951 Convention and/or 1967 Protocol Relating to the Status of Refugees' (HCR/GIP/03/04, 2003).

United Nations High Commissioner for Refugees, 'Guidelines on International Protection: Internal Flight or Relocation Alternative' Within the Context of Article 1 A (2) of the 1951 Convention and/or 1967 Protocol relating to the Status of Refugees' (UN Doc. HCR/GIP/03/04, 2003).

United Nations High Commissioner for Refugees, 'Guidelines on International Protection No. 5: Application of the Exclusion Clauses: Article 1F of the 1951 Convention relating to the Status of Refugees' (HCR/GIP/03/05, 2003).

United Nations High Commissioner for Refugees, 'Agenda for Protection', October 2003, available online at http://www.unhcr.org/protection/globalconsult/3e637b194/agenda-protection-third-edition.html (last visited 1 August 2018).

United Nations High Commissioner for Refugees, 'Procedural Standards for Refugee Status Determination Under UNHCR's Mandate', 20 November 2003, available online at http://www.refworld.org/docid/42d66dd84.html (last visited 1 August 2018).

United Nations High Commissioner for Refugees, 'Guidelines on International Protection No. 6: Religion-Based Refugee Claims under Article 1A(2) of the 1951 Convention and/or the 1967 Protocol Relating to the Status of Refugees' (UN Doc. HCR/GIP/04/06, 2004).

United Nations High Commissioner for Refugees, 'Guidelines on International Protection No. 6: Religion-Based Refugee Claims under Article 1A(2) of the 1951 Convention and/or the 1967 Protocol Relating to the Status of Refugees' (HCR/GIP/04/06, 2004).

United Nations High Commissioner for Refugees, 'Statistical Yearbook 2003', 2005, available online at http://www.unhcr.org/statistics/country/42aff7e84/unhcr-statistical-yearbook-2003.html (last visited 1 August 2018).

United Nations High Commissioner for Refugees, 'The Refugee Situation in Latin America: Protection and Solutions Based on the Pragmatic Approach of the Cartagena Declaration on Refugees of 1984. Discussion Document UNHCR November 2004', 18 (1) *International Journal of Refugee Law* 252 (2006).

United Nations High Commissioner for Refugees, 'Guidelines on International Protection No. 7: The Application of Article 1A(2) of the 1951 Convention and/or 1967 Protocol Relating to the Status of Refugees to Victims of Trafficking and Persons At Risk of Being Trafficked' (HCR/GIP/06/07, 2006).

United Nations High Commissioner for Refugees, 'UNHCR's Eligibility Guidelines for Assessing the International Protection Needs of Iraqi Asylum-seekers', August 2007, available online at http://www.refworld.org/docid/46deb05557.html (last visited 1 August 2018).

United Nations High Commissioner for Refugees, 'UNHCR's Eligibility Guidelines for Assessing the International Protection Needs of Afghan Asylum-Seekers', 31 December 2007, available online at http://www.unhcr.org/refworld/docid/477ce70a2.html (last visited 1 August 2018).

United Nations High Commissioner for Refugees, 'UNHCR Guidance Note on Refugee Claims Relating to Sexual Orientation and Gender Identity', 21 November 2008, available online at http://www.refworld.org/docid/48abd5660.html (last visited 1 August 2018).

United Nations High Commissioner for Refugees, 'UNHCR Note on the Interpretation of Article 1E of the 1951 Convention Relating to the Status of Refugees', March 2009, available online at http://www.refworld.org/docid/49c3a3d12.html (last visited 1 August 2018).

United Nations High Commissioner for Refugees, 'UNHCR's Eligibility Guidelines for Assessing the International Protection Needs of Iraqi Asylum-seekers', April 2009, available online at http://www.refworld.org/docid/49f569cf2.html (last visited 1 August 2018).

United Nations High Commissioner for Refugees, 'Guidance Note on Refugee Claims relating to Female Genital Mutilation', May 2009, available online at http://www.refworld.org/docid/4a0c28492.html (last visited 1 August 2018).

United Nations High Commissioner for Refugees, 'UNHCR Eligibility Guidelines for Assessing the International Protection Needs of Asylum-Seekers from Afghanistan', July 2009, available online at http://www.refworld.org/docid/4a6477ef2.html (last visited 1 August 2018).

United Nations High Commissioner for Refugees, 'Guidelines on International Protection No. 8: Child Asylum Claims under Articles 1(A)2 and 1(F) of the 1951 Convention and/or 1967 Protocol relating to the Status of Refugees' (HCR/GIP/09/08, 2009).

United Nations High Commissioner for Refugees, 'Guidance Note on Refugee Claims Relating to Victims of Organized Gangs', 31 March 2010, available online at http://www.refworld.org/docid/4bb21fa02.html (last visited 1 August 2018).

United Nations High Commissioner for Refugees, 'UNHCR Eligibility Guidelines for Assessing the International Protection Needs of Asylum-Seekers from Somalia' (UN Doc. HCR/EG/SOM/10/1, 2010).

United Nations High Commissioner for Refugees, 'UNHCR Intervention before the Court of Appeal of England and Wales in the Case of MM (Iran) v. Secretary of State for the Home Department' (UN Doc. C5/2009/2479, 2010).

United Nations High Commissioner for Refugees, 'Ensuring Protection for Persons of Concern 2010-2011. UNHCR Global Appeal', 2011, available online at http://www.unhcr.org/4b040a429.pdf (last visited 1 August 2018).

United Nations High Commissioner for Refugees, 'Expert Meeting on Complementarities between International Refugee Law, International Criminal Law and International Human Rights Law. Summary Conclusions', 11 April 2011, available online at http://www.unhcr.org/4e16d0a59.html (last visited 1 August 2018).

United Nations High Commissioner for Refugees, 'UNHCR Eligibility Guidelines for Assessing the International Protection Needs of Asylum-Seekers from Eritrea' (UN Doc. HCR/EG/ERT/11/01_Rev.1, 2011).

United Nations High Commissioner for Refugees, 'Safe at Last? Law and Practice in Selected EU Member States with Respect to Asylum-Seekers Fleeing Indiscriminate Violence', July 2011, available online at http://www.unhcr.org/protection/operations/4e2d7f029/safe-law-practice-selected-eu-member-states-respect-asylum-seekers-fleeing.html (last visited 1 August 2018).

United Nations High Commissioner for Refugees, 'Ministerial Communiqué' (UN Doc. HCR/MINCOMMS/2011/6, 2011).

United Nations High Commissioner for Refugees, 'UNHCR Eligibility Guidelines for Assessing the International Protection Needs of Asylum-Seekers from Iraq' (UN Doc. HCR/EG/IRQ/12/03, 2012).

United Nations High Commissioner for Refugees, 'Interim Eligibility Guidelines for Assessing the International Protection Needs of Asylum-Seekers from Côte d'Ivoire' (UN Doc. HCR/EG/CIV/12/01, 2012).
United Nations High Commissioner for Refugees, 'Guidelines on International Protection No. 9: Claims to Refugee Status based on Sexual Orientation and/or Gender Identity within the context of Article 1A(2) of the 1951 Convention and/or its 1967 Protocol relating to the Status of Refugees' (HCR/GIP/12/01, 2012).
United Nations High Commissioner for Refugees, 'UNHCR Eligibility Guidelines for Assessing the International Protection Needs of Asylum-Seekers from Sri Lanka' (UN Doc. HCR/EG/LKA/12/04, 2012).
United Nations High Commissioner for Refugees, 'International Protection Considerations with Regard to People Fleeing the Syrian Arab Republic, Update II', 22 October 2013, available online at http://www.refworld.org/docid/5265184f4.html (last visited 1 August 2018).
United Nations High Commissioner for Refugees, 'Guidance Note on Bilateral and/or Multilateral Transfer Arrangements of Asylum-seekers', May 2013, available online at http://www.refworld.org/pdfid/51af82794.pdf (last visited 1 August 2018).
United Nations High Commissioner for Refugees, 'UNHCR Eligibility Guidelines for Assessing the International Protection Needs of Asylum-seekers from Afghanistan' (UN Doc. HCR/EG/AFG/13/01, 2013).
United Nations High Commissioner for Refugees, 'Note on the Mandate of the High Commissioner for Refugees and his Office', October 2013, available online at http://www.refworld.org/docid/5268c9474.html (last visited 1 August 2018).
United Nations High Commissioner for Refugees, 'Guidelines on International Protection No. 10: Claims to Refugee Status related to Military Service within the context of Article 1A (2) of the 1951 Convention and/or the 1967 Protocol Relating to the Status of Refugees' (UN Doc. HCR/GIP/13/10/Corr. 1, 2013).
United Nations High Commissioner for Refugees, 'Expert Meetings', 19 February 2014, available online at http://www.unhcr.org/3e5f78bc4.html (last visited 1 August 2018).
United Nations High Commissioner for Refugees, 'International Protection Considerations with Regard to People Fleeing the Syrian Arab Republic, Update III', 27 October 2014, available online at http://www.refworld.org/docid/544e446d4.html (last visited 1 August 2018).
United Nations High Commissioner for Refugees, 'International Protection Considerations with Regard to People Fleeing the Syrian Arab Republic, Update IV' (HCR/PC/SYR/01, 2015).
United Nations High Commissioner for Refugees, 'UNHCR Eligibility Guidelines for Assessing the International Protection Needs of Asylum-Seekers from Afghanistan' (UN Doc. HCR/EG/AFG/16/02, 2016).
United Nations High Commissioner for Refugees, 'Report of the Sixty-sixth Meeting of the Standing Committee (21–23 June 2016)' (UN Doc. A/AC.96/1162, 2016).
United Nations High Commissioner for Refugees, 'Guidelines on International Protection No. 12: Claims for Refugee Status Related to Situations of Armed Conflict and Violence under Article 1A(2) of the 1951 Convention and/or 1967 Protocol Relating to the Status of Refugees and the Regional Refugee Definitions' (UN Doc. HCR/GIP/16/12, 2016).

United Nations High Commissioner for Refugees, 'Who We Help', 2017, available online at http://www.unhcr.org/who-we-help.html (last visited 1 August 2018).

United Nations High Commissioner for Refugees, 'UNHCR Executive Committee of the High Commissioner's Programme Composition for the period October 2016 – October 2017', 20 April 2017, available online at http://www.unhcr.org/excom/scaf/5748082a4/list-members-observers-2016-2017.html (last visited 1 August 2018).

United Nations High Commissioner for Refugees, Government of Pakistan & Government of Afghanistan, 'Tripartite Repatriation Agreement between UNHCR and the governments of Pakistan and Afghanistan', 17 March 2003, available online at http://www.refworld.org/docid/55e6a5324.html (last visited 1 August 2018).

United Nations High Commissioner for Refugees, Government of Romania & International Organization for Migration, 'Agreement between the Government of Romania and the Office of the United Nations High Commissioner for Refugees and the International Organization for Migration Regarding Temporary Evacuation to Romania of Persons in Urgent Need of International Protection and their Onward Resettlement', 8 May 2008, available online at http://www.refworld.org/docid/4a7c221c2.html (last visited 1 August 2018).

United Nations Organisation, 'Official Records of the General Assembly, Ninth Session, Annexes, Agenda Item 67', 21 September 1954, available online at http://unbisnet.un.org:8080/ipac20/ipac.jsp?go_sort_limit.x=5&go_sort_limit.y=5&npp=50&ipp=20&spp=20&profile=bib&aspect=alpha&term=General+Assembly.+Official+Records.+Annexes&index=YTIAUAL&uindex=&oper=&session=-J4871B85T9373.13437&menu=search&aspect=alpha&npp=50&ipp=20&spp=20&profile=bib&ri=1&source=%7E%21horizon&sort=3100053 (last visited 1 August 2018).

United Nations Organisation, *Yearbook of the International Law Commission 1966 Vol. II* (UN Doc. A/CN.4/Ser.A/1966/Add.1, 1967).

United Nations Organisation, *The Work of the International Law Commission. Vol. I* (8th ed.: United Nations, 2012).

United Nations Security Council, 'Resolution 237' (UN Doc. S/RES/237, 1967).

Julio Cesar Quevedo; Megdy Perez De Quevedo v. John Ashcroft, Attorney General, No. 02-2227, United States: Court of Appeals, First Circuit (2003).

United States: Court of Appeals, Ninth Circuit, *Bolanos-Hernandez v. Immigration and Naturalization Service*, 767 F.2.d (1984).

United States: Court of Appeals, Ninth Circuit, *Manuel Diaz Arteaga v. Immigration and Naturalization Service*, 836 F.2d 1227 (1988).

United States: Court of Appeals, Ninth Circuit, *Patel v. Immigration and Naturalization Service*, US App. Lexis 30517 (1999).

United States: Court of Appeals, Seventh Circuit, *Wackowski v. Immigration and Naturalization Service*, 1999 U.S. App. LEXIS 26590 (1999).

United States: Supreme Court, *Immigration and Naturalization Service v. Cardoza-Fonseca U.S. Supreme Court, I.N.S. v. Cardoza-Fonseca, 67 U.S. 407 (1987)*, 480 U.S. 421 (1987).

Wagner, Markus, 'Non-State Actors' (Max Planck Encyclopedia of Public International Law, 2013).

Weis, Paul, *The Refugee Convention, 1951: The Travaux Préparatoires Analysed, with a Commentary by the Late Dr Paul Weis* (Cambridge University Press, 1995).

Zetter, Roger, 'Protecting Forced Migrants. A State of the Art Report of Concepts, Challenges and Ways Forward' (Federal Commission on Migration, 2014).
Zieck, Marjoleine, 'Art. 35/Art. II', in A. Zimmermann (ed.), *The 1951 Convention Relating to the Status of Refugees and its 1967 Protocol: A Commentary* (Oxford University Press, 2011).
Zimmermann, Andreas (ed.), *The 1951 Convention Relating to the Status of Refugees and its 1967 Protocol. A Commentary* (Oxford University Press, 2011).
Zimmermann, Andreas and Mahler, Claudia, 'Article 1 A, para. 2 1951 Convention', in A. Zimmermann (ed.), *The 1951 Convention Relating to the Status of Refugees and its 1967 Protocol: A Commentary* (Oxford University Press, 2011).

3 European Union asylum law and persons fleeing conflict and violence

The 1951 Convention is the sole universal instrument of protection. Additional protection is, however, generated at the regional level. Since the establishment of the European Economic Community (EEC), complementary protection schemes supplementing the 1951 Convention differed widely among the EU Member States. This changed with the development of the Common European Asylum System (CEAS) in 1999. The creation of the CEAS encompassed the adoption of a common tool that covers forced migration beyond the Convention. The subsidiary protection status in EU asylum law forms one specific type of complementary protection and finds its legal basis in the (Recast) Qualification Directive (QD), a secondary Union law instrument. Comparable to the extended refugee law instruments already discussed under section 2.2 and in contrast to the wording of the 1951 Convention, the (Recast) QD explicitly refers to flight from conflict as an eligibility criterion for its status. In this regard, and at first sight, it follows a different approach to violence and conflict than that which focuses on discriminatory persecution. Nonetheless, the determination of the nature of the conflict and the violence therein remains a path with stumbling blocks.

Against the background of the EU's open internal borders and freedom of movement regime, the development of the common complementary protection status aims at harmonising asylum schemes and diminishing national variations.[1] However, the disparities concerning the application of either refugee

1 Looking at some figures from earlier years of the application of the (Recast) QD of 2011, the 28 Member States of the EU registered 398,925 asylum claims in 2013, a 32 per cent increase compared to 2012 (301,000). How do these figures relate to the granting of status? Numbers from that time report that 15.1% of the first instance decisions on asylum in Europe were granting refugee status, while 13.8% were granting subsidiary protection (10.8% in 2012). The proportional dissemination of refugee and subsidiary protection status varies greatly within the different EU Member States. While Sweden granted subsidiary protection in 35% of its decisions, the Netherlands 22.2%, Italy 22.0%, other countries such as the UK (0.3%), Greece (1.3%) or France (2.5%) only rarely consider subsidiary protection as an applicable status. Bundesamt für Migration und Flüchtlinge, *Das Bundesamt in Zahlen 2013. Asyl, Migration und Integration* (2014), available online at http://www.bamf.de/SharedDocs/Anlagen/DE/Publikationen/Broschueren/bundesamt-in-zahlen-2013.pdf?__blob=publicationFile (last visited 1 August 2018). For more

or subsidiary protection status constitute one quantifiable observation concerning the practical implementation of the asylum statuses. The different recognition practices of states regarding people fleeing from the same countries of origin provide even more evidence of the lack of uniform practices in applying the (Recast) QD.[2] And, despite the explicit reference to the conflict context of protection claims, the interpretation of the (Recast) QD and its application to ongoing conflicts have proven difficult. Clear legal interpretation on terminology and scope is still missing. The divergence in status allocation and the grant of attached substantive rights, however, render a clear and consistent interpretation of its terms and scope indispensable.

This chapter analyses the terms of the (Recast) QD and its subsidiary protection status.[3] The institutional architecture of the EU, with the Court of Justice of the European Union (CJEU) as final arbiter of the interpretation of EU primary and secondary legislation, offers unique support in the interpretation of the pertinent instrument and its disputed provisions. The CJEU has on two occasions been requested to deliver binding interpretations on the terms of the QD and therewith the determination of subsidiary protection status for persons fleeing conflict – these were the landmark cases of *Elgafaji* in 2009, followed in 2014 by the case of *Diakité*. However, the court held that not every conflict would attract the protection of the (Recast) QD. A certain threshold of conflict is the necessary precondition. Various domestic courts struggle with this threshold question. International Humanitarian Law (IHL) could be a point of reference in the interpretation process, as it contains threshold assessments and therefore concretisations on the classification of conflicts. However, it is a different field of international law, and it has developed differently and followed different goals and objectives. It needs to be assessed whether reference to IHL is irrelevant or whether one can indeed draw guidance from it for the interpretation of the (Recast) QD.

The following chapter, after providing an overview on the Union asylum scheme and the pertinent instruments for conflict-induced displacement,

statistics see Eurostat, *Asylum Applicants 2013* (2014), available online at http://ec.europa.eu/eurostat/documents/4168041/5948933/KS-QA-14-003-EN.PDF/3309ae42-431c-42d7-99a3-534ed5b93294 (last visited 1 August 2018).

2 "[S]triking disparities appeared in the research. For example, with regards to the Iraqi applicants, during the first quarter of 2007, the percentage recognized as refugees in Germany at first instance was 16, 3% and those qualifying for subsidiary protection 1.1%. In Sweden, 73,2% of Iraqi application were granted subsidiary protection at first instance in the first quarter of 2007 and 1.7% were recognized as refugees. [...] It must be a matter of deep concern to the European Union that the practice with regards to one group varies so greatly across just the five Member states studied." United Nations High Commissioner for Refugees, *Asylum in the European Union. A Study of the Implementation of the Qualification Directive* (2007), available online at http://www.refworld.org/docid/473050632.html (last visited 1 August 2018), at 13.

3 The focus of the chapter is on the inclusion clause and the eligibility criteria for subsidiary protection status. The broader EU asylum scheme, in particular the determination and allocation of procedural responsibilities of single EU states under the Dublin system, is not analysed in this context as it does not give further assistance in the interpretation of Article 15 (c) QD.

analyses the eligibility criteria for subsidiary protection in detail. Recourse to national jurisprudential practice is chosen to illustrate the wide divergence in the interpretative practices of the national courts and determining authorities when authoritative guidance is missing. It does not aim at providing a comprehensive overview of domestic practices in their transposition of the (Recast) QD. The judgements of the CJEU on the QD, on the other hand, provide this binding interpretation and are therefore the main focus of this chapter.

3.1 The historical development of a CEAS

The EU, with its distinct legal architecture, offers a specific regional approach to asylum law and asylum policies. Firstly, with the establishment of the EEC in 1985, a communication and consultation procedure on migration was implemented, allowing for the possibility to exchange information and develop common mechanisms concerning non-EU labour migration.[4] In its early days, however, the willingness to transfer immigration matters to the European level was rather weak. One early legal dispute between the EU and its Member States highlights the tensions inherent in attempts to harmonise and to restrict national sovereignty regarding migration matters. Following the implementation of the communication and consultation procedure, Germany, France, Denmark, the Netherlands and the UK brought an action against the Commission on the basis of Article 173 Treaty Establishing the European Economic Community (ECCT), for exceeding its competencies and infringing upon the domaine réservé of the Member States.[5] The European Court of Justice (ECJ), predecessor to the CJEU, gave its judgement in this case, acknowledging generally, on the one hand, the Commission's incentive to gather information relating to the labour force within the ECC. On the other hand, the ECJ rejected the Commission's attempt to gather information on third country nationals as beyond its authority.[6] That judgement reflects the understanding of the division of power at that time. The Member States themselves had exclusive jurisdiction on matters of asylum and migration, while the evolving supranational body complemented their objectives but was not yet an independent player in that field.

Since then, what is now known as the EU has acquired significant competences in this field; previously national authority and prerogatives were transferred from the national to the supranational level, which has led to an

4 Commission Directive 85/381/EEC of 14 December 1984 amending Annexes I and II to Council Directive 66/401/EEC on the marketing of fodder plant seed, 14 December 1984.

5 European Union, *The History of the European Union: 1980–1989, Official European Union Site*, available online at https://europa.eu/european-union/about-eu/history/1980-1989_en (last visited 1 August 2018). Fullerton, Maryellen, 'A Tale of Two Decades: War Refugees and Asylum Policies in the European Union', 10 *Washington University Global Studies Law Review* (2011) 87, at 90.

6 *Federal Republic of Germany and Others v. Commission of the European Communities*, C-281/85, Court of Justice of the European Union (1987).

"astounding burst of EU law-making regarding asylum policy".[7] Already in 1957, Article 63 of the Treaty of Rome, formally the Treaty Establishing the European Community, in paragraphs 1 and 2, set out the original legal basis for the adoption of secondary asylum legislation. The subsequent development and evolution of the EU treaties restructured the institutionalised power arrangements. The treaties of Maastricht and Amsterdam advanced the creation of a common European approach to asylum and migration as a counterpart to the abolition of internal border controls and the implementation of a zone of free movement. The Maastricht Treaty of 1992 still contained the Union's asylum policy within the so-called third pillar of 'Justice and Home Affairs', which meant that asylum was still subject to intergovernmental decision-making between the EU Member States. The 1997 Amsterdam Treaty then established the requirement to harmonise asylum, immigration and visa policies as part of the creation of one single market inside the Union.[8] The goal, as laid down in Articles 1 and 2 of the Treaty of Amsterdam, was to create one "area of Freedom, Security and Justice"[9] with the

> freedom to live in a law-abiding environment in the knowledge that public authorities are using everything in their individual and collective power (nationally, at the level of the Union and beyond) to combat and contain those who seek to deny or abuse that freedom.[10]

In this context, the transfer of asylum and immigration matters from the renamed intergovernmental third pillar on 'Police and Judicial Co-operation in Criminal Matters' to the first pillar of the European Communities brought the whole area of policy into the competence of the supranational European institutions.

The Member States explicitly expressed the idea to create one 'CEAS' in Tampere in 1999.[11] This date marked the final departure from the traditional

7 Fullerton, Maryellen, *supra* note 5, at 92.

8 Christian Kaunert and Sarah Leonard, 'The European Union Asylum Policy after the Treaty of Lisbon and the Stockholm Programme: Towards Supranational Governance in a Common Area of Protection', 31 *Refugee Survey Quarterly* (2012) 1, at 9ff.

9 Treaty of Amsterdam, Article 1 and 2.

10 European Council, 'Action Plan on How to Best Implement the Provisions of the Amsterdam Treaty Establishing an Area of Freedom, Security and Justice, Part II. A' (1999/C 19/01, 1998), at para. 6.

11 European Parliament, *Presidency Conclusions, Tampere European Council 15 and 16 October 1999. Towards a Union of Freedom, Security and Justice: The Tampere Milestones* (1999), available online at http://www.europarl.europa.eu/summits/tam_en.htm (last visited 1 August 2018), at para. 14. "[T]his System should include, in the short term, a clear and workable determination of the State responsible for the examination of an asylum application, common standards for a fair and efficient asylum procedure, common minimum conditions of reception of asylum seekers, and the approximation of rules on the recognition and content of the refugee status. It should also be completed with measures on subsidiary forms of protection offering an appropriate status to any person in need of such protection."

preservation of national sovereign prerogatives in asylum and migration matters. The first proposal for a new Community directive on a harmonised asylum policy in September 2001 then set out the goal to design one single space of protection for refugees and people in need of international protection:

> In the longer term, Community rules should lead to a common asylum procedure and a uniform status for those who are granted asylum valid throughout the union.[12]

Since then, the Union has shaped and expanded this field through various EU legal instruments in several phases. First-generation instruments provided the structure for the new asylum *acquis*, most importantly the QD, the Dublin Regulation 10/02/03, the Reception Conditions Directive 27/01/03, the Asylum Procedures Directive 01/12/05 and the EURODAC Regulation on data collection, adopted between 2000 and 2005. Further secondary legislation enacted in the first phase includes the Temporary Protection Directive 20/70/01, Long-Term Residence Directive of 2003, Family Reunification Directive of 2003 and the Returns Directive of 2008. These harmonising instruments encouraged Member States to adopt wider protection standards in their domestic frameworks but obliged them to implement minimum common standards set out at the EU level:

> Member States may introduce or retain more favourable standards for determining who qualifies as a refugee or as a person eligible for subsidiary protection, and for determining the content of international protection, in so far as those standards are compatible.[13]

The Treaty on the Functioning of the European Union (TFEU) entered into force in December 2009 and marked a subsequent phase in the completion of the CEAS. Articles 77 and 78 TFEU provided the basis for the second phase of asylum and immigration and the recast instruments.[14] Article 67 (2) TFEU lays down the competence to "frame a common policy on asylum, immigration and external border controls". In the so-called 'The Hague Programme', the Commission was tasked with evaluating the first-phase instruments and submitting second-phase instruments by the end of 2010. However, in the light of the continuous lack of harmonisation of national asylum systems and following the EU Policy Plan on Asylum of June 2008 and the European Pact on Immigration and Asylum of October 2008, the second-phase instruments were supposed to raise protection standards and advance uniformity in the

12 *Id.*, at para. 15.

13 Article 3 QD. See also Recital 14 and *Mohamed M'Bodj v. État belge: Opinion of Advocate General*, Case C-542/13, Court of Justice of the European Union (2014).

14 The Dublin II Directive of 2003, the Recast QD of 2011, the Recast Eurodac Directive of 2013, the Recast Dublin III regulation of 2013, the Recast RCD of 2013 and the Recast APD of 2013.

implementation of the legal instruments.[15] The focus in the second phase was that the lack of common conditions across national systems conflicted with the principle of providing equal access to protection throughout the EU territory. Against this background, the second-phase instruments were supposed to provide a remedy.[16] The subsequent 'Stockholm Programme' of 2010 carved out several areas that were to be prioritised until the end of 2014 and highlighted lessons learned from the previous programmes.[17] The new, post-2014 multi-annual programme in the area of justice and home affairs is considered to have followed the 'less is more' approach. Since legal practice needs a considerable amount of time to adjust to the fast changes of the last 15–20 years, the focus of the post-Stockholm era lies on the evaluation and improvement of the instruments in place.[18]

3.2 Union law instruments and the protection of persons fleeing conflict and violence

The protection of persons fleeing conflict and violence has been on the EU's agenda for nearly two decades and has led to the adoption of two different legal instruments as a basis for protection claims – one that has so far theoretically fulfilled this objective and another that has evolved into the major protection instrument. Yet, obstacles in interpretation and implementation remain.

15 The transition from the former 'minimum standards approach' to the 'uniform status and common procedures approach' is as such not included in the instruments, as emphasised by *Judgment of 17 June 2014*, BVerwG 10 C 7.13, Germany: Federal Administrative Court (2014), at para. 29. European Council, 'The Hague Programme: Strengthening Freedom, Security and Justice in the European Union' (2005/C 53/01, OJ C 53/1, 2004), at 3.

16 European Commission, 'Communication from the Commission to the European Parliament, the Council, the European Economic and Social Committee and the Committee of Region, Policy Plan on Asylum. An Integrated Approach to Protection Across the EU' (COM(2008)360 final, 2008), at 3.

17 Migration Policy Institute, *The European Union's Stockholm Program: Less Ambition on Immigration and Asylum, But More Detailed Plans* (2010), available online at http://www.migrationpolicy.org/article/european-unions-stockholm-program-less-ambition-immigration-and-asylum-more-detailed-plans (last visited 1 August 2018).

18 European Parliamentary Research Service Blog, *Justice and Home Affairs after the Stockholm Programme* (2014), available online at https://epthinktank.eu/2014/06/25/justice-and-home-affairs-after-the-stockholm-programme/ (last visited 1 August 2018). The focus is on transposition and implementation of the second phase measures constituting the CEAS. However, the Commission does have some concrete suggestions for further instruments: the mutual recognition of asylum decisions, rules on the transfer of protection, relocation of beneficiaries of international protection (which would necessarily entail rules on the transfer of protection), joint processing of asylum applications, and a more orderly arrival of persons needing protection, by means of protected entry procedures and possibly the joint processing of protection claims outside the EU (without affecting the right to claim asylum within the Member States' territories), Peers, Steve, *Analysis. The Next Multi-year EU Justice and Home Affairs Programme Views of the Commission and the Member States* (2014), available online at http://www.statewatch.org/analyses/no-238-new-jha-programme.pdf (last visited 1 August 2018), at 2.

3.2.1 Pertinent EU instruments – the irrelevance of the Temporary Protection Directive

The Temporary Protection Directive (TPD), adopted in 2001, was the EU's first conflict-sensitive asylum instrument and was drafted as the legal response to the Bosnian and Kosovan wars of the 1990s.[19] Two years after the conflict in Kosovo, the TPD was negotiated to respond to mass arrivals at the borders of the EU, despite the fact that varying degrees of the burden were being felt by different EU Member States.[20] The TPD was designed, according to Article 1,

> [...] to establish minimum standards for giving temporary protection in the event of a mass influx of displaced persons from third countries who are unable to return to their country of origin and to promote a balance of effort between Member States in receiving and bearing the consequences of receiving such persons.

Beneficiaries of temporary protection include, according to the definition in Article 2 (c), third country nationals or stateless persons who may be eligible for refugee protection through Article 1 A (2) 1951 of the Convention, but also other international or national protection instruments, such as

> (i) persons who have fled areas of armed conflict and endemic violence;
> (ii) persons at serious risk of, or who have been the victims of, systematic or generalised violations of their human rights.

Member States are obliged under Article 4 TPD to provide for residence permits of one year with a possible six-month extension and finally, under exceptional circumstances, for one other year. In parallel to the residence permits, Articles 13 and 14 provide for access to basic welfare and health care, as well as to housing and education opportunities for minors under 18 years. Freedom of movement within the EU territory is, however, not permitted. The TPD also constitutes a voluntary burden-sharing mechanism based on a country's assessment of its own capacity in receiving persons in need of protection.[21] As such, it supports the general commitment to solidarity among the Member States. Claimants can be transferred between the Member States depending on their capacity, as well as from third countries to an EU Member State, provided the consent of the person affected is given.[22]

19 For an extensive discussion of its drafting history and material scope, see Hailbronner, Kay and Thym, Daniel (eds.), *EU Immigration and Asylum Law. A Commentary* (2016), at 803ff.

20 UNHCR statistics stipulate that Germany, for instance, received around 60% of the Bosnian applicants. See, for more information, Sandra Lavenex, 'France: International Norms, European Integration and State Discretion', in Joanne van Selm (ed.), *Kosovo's Refugees in the European Union* (Pinter, 2000), at 229. Ramet, Sabrina P., 'War in the Balkans', 71 *Foreign Affairs* (1992).

21 Based on Article 25 (1) TPD.

22 Based on Article 26 (1) TPD.

The Directive only applies in situations of mass influx into the EU territory, which explicitly includes displacement as a result of conflict, under the above-referenced paragraphs (i) and (ii). While theoretically there is no doubt that the Directive is legally applicable to conflict cases, a political obstacle hinders the application of the instrument in practice. Prior to activation, the Council of Europe has to determine the existence of a situation of mass influx and, at the end, the termination of the situation of protection.[23] To engage the Directive, the Council must adopt this decision with a qualified majority of votes, which renders the application of the instrument dependent on a highly political decision.[24]

This political activation of a legal instrument has led to its complete ineffectiveness in practice. So far, the TPD has never even been engaged. Situations of massive influx of people, such as those witnessed in Malta, Greece or Italy, following the Arab Spring, or the conflicts in Syria and Iraq, all highlight the inadequacy of this procedure, as the Council did not, even once, react under the TPD to counter the situation.[25] And, while the political predicaments are an obstacle to the activation of this specific legal instrument, one can equally question whether its protection standards would in any case undermine another suitable protection mechanism. When considering status determination from a hierarchical perspective, it is essential to adhere to the primacy of the 1951 Convention, before examining the application of instruments providing lower protection standards. The proliferation of different legal instruments for congruent or at least comparable situations increases uncertainty concerning the appropriate protection status and the substantive rights attached. This would specifically be the case for conflict-induced displacement. Subsidiary protection status is already, to some extent, perceived as countering and undermining refugee protection status.[26] The TPD would go one step further and potentially lead to the disengagement of not only the 1951 Convention but also the (Recast) QD, in favour of short-term solutions to protection.

23 Article 6 TPD.

24 Article 5 (1) TPD.

25 Donadio, Rachel, 'Italy Lashes Out at European Union Over Immigrants' (New York Times, 2011).

26 Costello, Cathryn, *The Human Rights of Migrants and Refugees in European Law* (Oxford University Press, 2016), at 199. Chetail, Vincent and Bauloz, Céline, *Research Handbook on International Law and Migration* (Edward Elgar, 2014), at 555f. United Nations High Commissioner for Refugees, 'Submission by the Office of the United Nations High Commissioner for Refugees in the case of S.A. v. Section for Asylum, Ministry of Interior of the Former Yugoslav Republic of Macedonia' (2010), at para. 3.2., at 5. Fiddian-Qasmiyeh, Elena *et al. (eds.)*, *The Oxford Handbook of Refugee and Forced Migration Studies* (2014), at 209. McAdam, Jane, *Complementary Protection in International Refugee Law* (Oxford University Press, 2007), at 61. Vedsted-Hansen, Jens, 'Complementary or Subsidiary Protection? Offering an Appropriate Status without Undermining Refugee Protection' (UNHCR Working Paper No. 52, 2002).

3.2.2 Pertinent EU instruments – the relevance of the (Recast) QD and its subsidiary protection status

The (Recast) QD is, firstly, the legal basis for the implementation of the Union's *de jure* refugee status in accordance with the 1951 Convention and, secondly, the instrument which creates one common status of complementary protection for certain kinds of forced migrants.[27] In comparison to the TPD, the (Recast) QD is designed to address individual claims and grant individual protection to non-Europeans who are otherwise not eligible for protection under the 1951 Convention.[28] It was not intended "as a radical overhaul of protection", but rather as a harmonising codification of the existing and observed state practice of complementary protection.[29]

The subsidiary protection status was designed to function as a complementary mechanism, paralleling but not questioning the primacy of the 1951 Convention[30]: "It is clear from the above that the subsidiary protection provided by Directive 2004/83 is complementary and additional to the protection of refugees enshrined in the Geneva Convention",[31] which is also affirmed in recital 33 of the Recast QD, referring to its status as "complementary and additional to the refugee protection enshrined in the Geneva Convention". This assessment is, furthermore, reflected in relevant case law. In its HN judgement of May 2014, the CJEU reaffirmed that:

> the use of the term 'subsidiary' and the wording of Article 2 (e) of Directive 2004/83, 2 (f) of the recast QD indicate that subsidiary protection status is intended for third country nationals who do not qualify for refugee status. Moreover, it is apparent [...] subsidiary protection must serve to complement and add to the protection of refugees enshrined in the Geneva Convention through the identification of persons genuinely in need of international protection and though such persons being offered an appropriate status (Case C-285/12 Diakité EU:C:2014:39, paragraph 33). It is clear from the above that subsidiary protection provided by Directive 2004/83 is complementary and additional to the protection of refugees enshrined in the Geneva Convention.[32]

27 Jakulevičienė, Lyra, 'Is There a Need for an Extension of Subsidiary Protection in the European Union Qualification Directive?', 2 *Jurisprudencjia* (2010) 215, at 216.

28 European Commission, 'Proposal for a Council Directive on Minimum Standards for the Qualification and Status of Third Country Nationals and Stateless Persons as Refugees or as Persons Who Otherwise Need International Protection. COM(2001)510 final' (2001).

29 Tsourdi, Evangelia, 'What Protection for Persons Fleeing Indiscriminate Violence? The Impact of the European Courts on the EU Subsidiary Protection Regime', in D. Cantor and J.-F. Durieux (eds.), *Refuge from Inhumanity? War Refugees and International Humanitarian Law* (Brill, 2014), 270, at 272.

30 United Nations High Commissioner for Refugees, 'Ministerial Communiqué' (UN Doc. HCR/MINCOMMS/2011/6, 2011).

31 *H. N. v. Minister for Justice, Equality and Law Reform, Ireland, Attorney General*, C-604/12, Court of Justice of the European Union (2014), at para. 32.

32 *Id.*, at paras. 29–32.

The Recast Asylum Procedures Directive of 2013, addressing the broader procedural obligations of asylum application processes, also emphasises that "[w]hen examining applications for international protection, the determining authority shall first determine whether the applicants qualify as refugees and, if not, determine whether the applicants are eligible for subsidiary protection."[33] This clearly reflects the hierarchy of the instruments and respective statuses – including in procedural status determination order – with the 1951 Convention being the primary instrument to the supplementing (Recast) QD.

Prior to the adoption of the QD, countries relied on national protection instruments or discretionary decisions not to expel asylum applicants, but there was no common, overarching framework to address forced migration outside the 1951 Convention. France, for instance, when faced with people fleeing the civil war in Algeria, broadly granted territorial asylum, as the majority was not considered to be covered by the 1951 Convention protection status.[34] The UK similarly had an operational enforcement manual in place that stressed that "enforcement measures should not be taken against nationals who originated from countries which are currently active war zones."[35] These complementary forms of protection derived from the nation states' discretion and had various titles such as temporary protection, humanitarian asylum, *de facto* refugees status or contingent refugees status.[36] These different approaches, however, led to a "patchwork of legal arrangements [in which] flexibility trumped coherence".[37]

The EU Directive 2004/83/EC, the QD, and its Recast 2011/95/EC, for the first time established a unique complementary protection status under Union law. As a legislative act under the EU's first pillar, the QD was drafted to extend a harmonised minimum standard of EU-wide protection and thereby replace a complicated web of deviating domestic legislation. With the QD, the EU set forth an instrument to conflate existing national practices to create not only a common approach, but also a status that was supposed to include a majority of the different types of non-Convention forced migrants under a single framework: beneficiaries of subsidiary protection. Article 1 states:

> [T]he purpose of this Directive is to lay down standards for the qualification of third-country nationals or stateless persons as beneficiaries of international protection, for a uniform status for refugees or for persons eligible for subsidiary protection, and for the content of the protection-granted.

33 Recast APD, Art. 10 (2).

34 Lambert, Hélène and Farrell, Theo, 'The Changing Character of Armed Conflict and the Implications for Refugee Protection Jurisprudence', 22 *International Journal of Refugee Law* (2010) 237, at 239.

35 *Secretary of State for the Home Department v. HH (Iraq)*, [2009] EWCA Civ 727, United Kingdom: Court of Appeal (England and Wales) (2009), at Lord Justice Sedley, para. 1.

36 In the European Union, see McAdam, Jane, 'The European Union Qualification Directive. The Creation of a Subsidiary Protection Regime', 17 *International Journal of Refugee Law* (2005) 461, at 463f.

37 Fullerton, Maryellen, *supra* note 5, at 121.

The QD and Recast QD do not offer a definition of subsidiary protection, but establish criteria to identify beneficiaries of this protection status. Third country nationals and stateless persons, not qualifying as Convention refugees, are eligible under Article 2 (f)[38] and (g)[39] if they face a real risk of suffering serious harm in case of return to their country of origin or former habitual residence. The concept of serious harm, enshrined as a counterpart to persecution, is the quintessential concept that legitimises the claim for international protection.[40] Serious harm is defined in Article 15 (Recast) QD as:

a the death penalty or execution,
b torture or inhumane and degrading treatment or punishment of the applicant in the country of origin,
c serious threat to a civilian's life by reason of indiscriminate violence in situations of international or internal armed conflict.

The (Recast) QD followed the goal set out in Article 78 (19) TFEU to "offer [...] an appropriate status to any third country national requiring international protection". This creation of an additional protection status constitutes a paradigm shift in the legal framework.[41] The (Recast) QD provides for more than just the negative obligation of *non-refoulement*, but evolves into a concept entailing positive obligations for forced migrants other than the exclusive Convention refugee. In terms of substance, the (Recast) QD commonly enshrines rights and duties of both Convention refugees and beneficiaries of subsidiary protection. Albeit with some national divergences in substantive rights, three-year residence permits are normally obtained by traditional refugees, while beneficiaries of subsidiary protection are eligible for one-year, renewable residence permits. While refugees have access to travel documents, employment, social welfare and education, following Articles 25 (1), 26 (1), 28 (1) and 27, beneficiaries of subsidiary protection generally have a right to work, however, the discretion of Member States limits their access in accordance with national labour market situations.[42]

38 Article 2 (f) and (g) "'person eligible for subsidiary protection' means a third- country national or a stateless person who does not qualify as a refugee but in respect of whom substantial grounds have been shown for believing that the person concerned, if returned to his or her country of origin, or in the case of a stateless person, to his or her country of former habitual residence, would face a real risk of suffering serious harm as defined in Article 15, and to whom Article 17 (1) and (2) does not apply, and is unable, or, owing to such risk, unwilling to avail himself or herself of the protection of that country", Recast QD.

39 Article 2 (g) "'subsidiary protection status' means the recognition by a Member State of a third-country national or a stateless person as a person eligible for subsidiary protection", Recast QD.

40 Nicolosi, Salvatore F., 'Disconnecting Humanitarian Law from EU Subsidiary Protection. A Hypothesis of Defragmentation of International Law', 29 *Leiden Journal of International Law* (2016) 463, at 467.

41 Francois Durieux, Quote given at ERA Conference, ERA, 2014, Trier.

42 Article 26 (3).

The respective state can put limitations to provide for only core welfare benefits (Article 29 (2)) providing beneficiaries with an entitlement to travel documents in the case of serious humanitarian reasons that require them to travel.[43] Since the codification of the QD, countries had continued to align the substantive rights attached to refugee and subsidiary protection, respectively. This practice has, however, been halted due to the political caution regarding increasing numbers of applications, derivative applications, family reunification processes and attached substantial services.

The adoption and transposition of the subsidiary protection status, as well as its legal basis, the (Recast) QD, have been subject to sound criticism – concerning its relationship to the 1951 Convention, its terminology and interpretation and its substantive rights.[44] Subsidiary protection has been described as a "very dynamic and young concept that still needs to be invented largely" and as a "novel that needs to be reflected".[45] Others have opposed the ambiguity more strongly and consider the vagueness of its terminology "poorly drafted"[46] and in a "convoluted language of political compromise"[47] and as leading to a decline in its protection powers.[48] The observed inconsistencies and criticism make it essential to analyse the provisions in detail.

3.2.3 Renewal and improvement? The Qualification Directive and the Recast Qualification Directive

The original QD was part of the first phase of asylum instruments. On 21 October 2009, the Commission proposed an amendment to the QD in conjunction with the revision of the Asylum Procedures Directive. The different practices in rejecting or approving the status of applicants from the same country of origin were contradicting the incentive of providing equal access to protection, as highlighted in Recital 6 QD. The explicit goal was to limit the secondary

43 Article 24 (2). See for more on the issue, McAdam, Jane, *supra* note 26.

44 Costello, Cathryn, *supra* note 26, at 200. Gil-Bazo, María-Teresa, 'Refugee Status and Subsidiary Protection under EC Law: The Qualification Directive and the Right to Be Granted Asylum', in A. Baldaccini, E. Guild and H. Toner (eds.), *Whose Freedom, Security and Justice? EU Immigration and Asylum Law and Policy* (Hart, 2007), at 243ff. Spijkerboer, Thomas, 'Subsidiarity in Asylum Law. The Personal Scope of International Protection', in D. Bouteillet-Paquet and K. Hailbronner (eds.), *Subsidiary Protection of Refugees in the European Union: Complementing the Geneva Convention?* (Bruylant, 2002), 19, at 28f. McAdam, Jane, *The European Union Qualification Directive, supra* note 36, at 467f.

45 Francois Durieux, Quote given at ERA Conference, ERA, 2014, Trier.

46 Lord Justice Sedley in *QD (Iraq) v. Secretary of State for the Home Department; AH (Iraq) v. Secretary of State for the Home Department,* [2009] EWCA Civ 620, United Kingdom: Court of Appeal (England and Wales) (2009), at para. 19.

47 UNHCR, Statement by Volker Türk, requoted from Bauloz, Céline, 'The (Mis)Use of International Humanitarian Law under Article 15(C) of the EU Qualification Directive', in D. Cantor and J.-F. Durieux (eds.), *Refuge from Inhumanity? War Refugees and International Humanitarian Law* (Brill, 2014), at 247.

48 McAdam, Jane, *The European Union Qualification Directive, supra* note 36, at 498f.

movement of people seeking refuge in the EU, where this was caused by the differences in status allocation practices of the EU Member States.[49] The recast instrument was expected to provide a higher degree of harmonisation and improve substantive as well as procedural protection standards.[50] Following the adoption of the amendment in the EU Parliament and Council, the Recast Directive was approved and published on 13 December 2011 with a transposition deadline of 21 December 2013.[51]

The Recast QD contains nine chapters, addressing (I) general provisions including definitions and the more favourable standards clause, (II) assessment of applications for international protection; (III) Qualification for refugee status, (IV) refugee status detailing the granting of such status but also the criteria for revoking, ending or refusing to renew it, (V) qualification for subsidiary protection, (VI) subsidiary protection status detailing the granting of such status but also the criteria for revoking, ending or refusing to renew it, (VII) content of international protection laying down the rights and benefits to be granted to refugees and beneficiaries of subsidiary protection, (VIII) administrative cooperation and (IX) final provisions. Comparing the first-and second-phase instruments against the goal of greater harmonisation and strengthening of protection standards, one can identify alterations in the Recast QD.

The amendment procedure was heavily based on assessments and reports drafted by the United Nations High Commissioner for Refugees (UNHCR), academic networks such as Odysseus and NGOs such as ECRE concerning the past and current state of transposition practices of the 2004 QD.[52] The UNHCR, when commenting on the draft, had also stipulated the necessity to

> spell out in greater detail the legal concepts in the existing provisions recognize existing state practice, and strive to streamline the application of the protection criteria.[53]

49 Recital 13 Recast QD.

50 European Commission, 'Report from the Commission to the European Parliament and the Council On the Application of Directive 2004/83/EC of 29 April 2004 on Minimum Standards for the Qualification and Status of Third Country Nationals or Stateless Persons as Refugees or as Persons who Otherwise Need International Protection and the Content of the Protection' (COM(2010)314 final, 2010), at 3.

51 Exceptions are Denmark, Ireland and UK, which opted out of the Recast.

52 See, United Nations High Commissioner for Refugees, *UNHCR comments on the European Commission's proposal for a Directive of the European Parliament and of the Council on minimum standards for the qualification and status of third country nationals or stateless persons as beneficiaries of international protection and the content of the protection granted (COM(2009)551, 21 October 2009)* (2010), available online at http://www.refworld.org/docid/4c503db52.html (last visited 1 August 2018). European Council on Refugees and Exiles, *Comments from the European Council on Refugees and Exiles on the European Commission Proposal to Recast the Qualification Directive* (2010), available online at http://www.ecre.org/wp-content/uploads/2016/07/ECRE-Comments-on-the-Commission-Proposal-to-Recast-the-Qualification-Directive_March-2010.pdf (last visited 1 August 2018).

53 United Nations High Commissioner for Refugees, *supra* note 2, at 13.

Changes were made with regard to certain legal concepts addressed in the Recast QD, in particular concerning actors of persecution, internal protection and the membership of a particular social group. Further changes concern family unification. The Recast QD now contains an enlarged definition of family, which encompasses not only spouses or unmarried partners but also the guardians of unmarried minors applying for asylum and unaccompanied minors. The status of subsidiary protection was further approximated with the status of refugee protection with regard to access to employment and health care, education opportunities and vocational training. Differences, however, still remain concerning residence permits. While beneficiaries of subsidiary protection are usually eligible for one-year permits, subsequently followed by a renewal of at least two years, Convention refugees are granted three-year permits at the outset.[54] Furthermore, while the status was further aligned in the Recast QD, the alignment is not included in all pertinent instruments of the asylum *acquis*. The Family Reunification Directive, for instance, does not apply to persons receiving subsidiary protection.[55]

Most importantly, and despite the criticism[56] concerning the original QD relating to protection from violence and conflict, the recast process did not address changes to the status criteria or further interpretation of the disputed Article 15 (c), an omission which is itself reflected in the Recast QD. This decision was made, regardless of the fact that the European Commission's proposal in 2009 stressed the "need for clarification".[57] The CJEU then considered the interpretation of the QD and its single elements to provide more clarity.

3.3 Adjudicating asylum law on the supranational level – the role of the CJEU and subsidiary protection

The interpretation of the (Recast) QD and more broadly the CEAS has generated great ambiguity within the European asylum framework and in its interaction with neighbouring fields of law, particularly international refugee law, European human rights law and IHL. The CJEU is the main actor delivering authoritative guidance on the interpretation of the legal instrument and its jurisprudence is therefore put into focus here.

54 European Council on Refugees and Exiles, *Asylum on the Clock? Duration and Review of International Protection Status in Europe* (2016), available online at http://www.ecre.org/wp-content/uploads/2016/07/AIDA-Briefing-Asylum-on-the-Clock-duration-and-review-of-international-protection-status-in-Europe_-June-2016.pdf (last visited 1 August 2018).

55 Council Directive 2003/86/EC of 22 September 2003 on the Right to Family Reunification, 3 October 2003.

56 Simeon, James C. (ed.), *Critical Issues in International Refugee Law. Strategies toward Interpretive Harmony* (2010), at 77ff. United Nations High Commissioner for Refugees, *supra* note 52. McAdam, Jane, *The European Union Qualification Directive, supra* note 36.

57 European Commission, 'Proposal for a Directive of the European Parliament and of the Council on minimum standards for the qualification and status of third country nationals or stateless persons as beneficiaries of international protection and the content of the protection granted' (COM(2009)551 final, 2009/0164 (COD), 2009), at 5.

The general basis for the CJEU's interpretation of EU asylum law lies in Article 267 TFEU, formerly 68 TEU, constituting its jurisdiction to give preliminary rulings "(a) on the interpretation of the Treaties; (b) and the validity and interpretation of acts of the institutions, bodies, offices or agencies of the Union". According to the Article, in the case of uncertainty about the meaning or scope of EU legislation, the CJEU *may* be requested by a Member State's court or tribunal to give a ruling "if it considers that a decision on the question is necessary to enable it to give judgment". By contrast, when interpretative questions arise in national courts of last instance, these courts *shall* request a preliminary ruling.

Preliminary rulings on the interpretation of EU primary or secondary legislation, as discussed below on Article 15 (c), are framed as questions, but they do not need to follow a specific format, and the CJEU is free to reconsider the scope of the question referred to it. Concerning non-EU legislation, the CJEU generally has no jurisdiction to directly interpret treaties to which the EU as a collective whole is not a party, even though EU Member States may be, but on an individual basis. However, if international law provisions are incorporated into EU primary or secondary legislation, the CJEU can exercise jurisdiction, based on the doctrine of *renvoi*, upon which it relied, among others, in its *Bolbol*[58] and *El Kott* judgements.[59] A request from a national court can be initiated by either one of the parties or by the national court itself and has the effect of staying the national proceedings until the preliminary ruling is delivered. The referred CJEU judgement will provide an interpretation of the respective provisions in question, but it will not apply it to the merits of the national case.

The CJEU has dealt with various aspects of the QD by way of preliminary ruling. The two primary judgements, *Elgafaji* of 2009 and *Diakté* of 2014, concerning the interpretation of subsidiary protection in the EU, are analysed in more detail below, as they directly link to conflict-induced displacement and the constitution of conflict under asylum law. Apart from matters more specifically addressing the conflict context, various ambiguities of the QD have been clarified in recent years: *Abdullah and Others*[60] of 2 March 2010 concerned the cessation clause contained in Article 11 (1) (e) specifically for situations marked

58 "It is apparent from recitals 3, 16 and 17 in the preamble to the Directive that the Geneva Convention constitutes the cornerstone of the international legal regime for the protection of refugees and that the provisions of the Directive for determining who qualifies for refugee status and the content thereof were adopted to guide the competent authorities of the Member States in the application of that convention on the basis of common concepts and criteria (see *Aydin Salahadin Abdulla, Kamil Hasan, Ahmed Adem, Hamrin Mosa Rashi, Dier Jamal v. Bundesrepublik Deutschland,* C-175/08, C-176/08, C-178/08 and C-179/08, Court of Justice of the European Union (2010), at para. 52.)", *Bolbol v. Bevándorlási és Állampolgársági Hivatal,* C-31/09, Court of Justice of the European Union (2010), at para. 37.

59 *Mostafa Abed El Karem El Kott and Others v. Bevándorlási és Állampolgársági Hivatal,* C-364/11, Court of Justice of the European Union (2012), at para. 80f.

60 *Aydin Salahadin Abdulla, Kamil Hasan, Ahmed Adem, Hamrin Mosa Rashi, Dier Jamal v. Bundesrepublik Deutschland, supra* note 58.

by changing circumstances in the country of origin. Exclusion from refugee protection was another issue addressed in the subsequent jurisprudence of the CJEU. *Bolbol*,[61] delivered 17 June 2010, concerned the protection of Palestinian stateless persons by the United Nations Relief and Work Agency (UNWRA) in the light of Article 12 (1) (a) of the QD. The case of *B and D*,[62] delivered 9 November 2010, evaluated exclusion based on serious non-political crimes and membership of a terrorist organisation, in the light of Article 12 (2) (b) and (c) as well as the application of Article 3, which provides more favourable standards for individuals excluded from refugee protection. *El Kott and Others*[63] of 12 December 2012 addressed exclusion matters under Article 12 (1) (a) for situations involving the cessation of protection provided by other UN agencies. The qualification for refugee status was ruled on in *Y and Z*[64] of 5 September 2012 on Articles 2 (c) and 9 (1) (a) and persecution based on religious grounds. In *X, Y and Z*,[65] in November 2013, the persecution of homosexuals based on Article 9 (1) (a) in conjunction with 9 (2) (c) and 10 (1) (d) was examined and Shepard,[66] of 26 February 2015, established an interpretation of Article 9 (2) (b), (c) and (e) concerning a claimant who had refused military service in the context of international crimes being committed by the conflict parties. The 2012 *MM* judgement delivered by the CJEU explored the assessment of the facts and circumstances of a case-by-case evaluation following two distinct phases, with the first phase dedicated to the establishment of the factual circumstances as reflected by Article 4 (1), (3) and (5), while the second phase of the assessment entailed the legal examination of the facts against the eligibility criteria.[67] The assessment of the facts and circumstances under Article 4 and in conjunction with the Asylum Procedures Directive in *A, B and C*[68] concerned claims of homosexual orientation and disclosure of information, while the newest judgement in the case of *HT*[69] of 24 June 2015 considered the substance of international protection under Articles 21 (2)–(3) and 24 (1) on residence permits and the limitations of national security and public order.

61 *Bolbol v. Bevándorlási és Állampolgársági Hivatal, supra* note 58.

62 *Bundesrepublik Deutschland v. B and D*, C-57/09 and C-101/09, Court of Justice of the European Union (2010).

63 *Mostafa Abed El Karem El Kott and Others v. Bevándorlási és Állampolgársági Hivatal, supra* note 59.

64 *Bundesrepublik Deutschland v. Y and Z*, C-71/11 and C-99/11, Court of Justice of the European Union (2012).

65 *X, Y, Z v. Minister voor Immigratie en Asiel*, C-199/12 to C-201/12, Court of Justice of the European Union (2013).

66 *Andre Lawrence Shepherd v. Bundesrepublik Deutschland*, C-472/13, Court of Justice of the European Union (2015).

67 *M. M. v. Minister for Justice, Equality and Law Reform, Ireland, Attorney General*, C-277/11, Court of Justice of the European Union (2012), at para. 64.

68 *A, B, C v. Staatssecretaris van Veiligheid en Justitie*, C-148/13 to C-150/13, Court of Justice of the European Union (2014).

69 *H. T. v. Land Baden-Württemberg*, C-373/13, Court of Justice of the European Union (2015).

The CJEU's jurisprudence evidently shapes the interpretation and implementation of EU asylum law in the Member States. It has also examined the relationship between EU law and public international law generally. Considering the Union asylum laws, the court has addressed the integration of EU legislation into the wider human rights and refugee law framework, particularly by linking EU legislation to the jurisprudence of the European Court of Human Rights (ECtHR) concerning the integration of interpretations of the 1951 Convention and the guidance delivered by the UNHCR.

The requirement for EU law to be in accordance with the pertinent international and regional law instruments is enshrined in various legal sources: Article 78 (1) TFEU, Article 52 (3) Charter of Fundamental Rights or Recitals 2–4 and 17 of the Recast QD include references to the 1951 Convention, the European Convention on Human Rights (ECHR) and other relevant treaties. The selectivity of the court in actually applying references to or interpretations of these instruments has been criticised as "unnecessarily compartmentalizing international treaties, arguably leading to a gradual dissociation of EU asylum law from international human rights and refugee law".[70] Recent jurisprudence on the QD is referred to in this regard. Specifically, the case of *Y and Z* and the case of *X, Y and Z* on persecution can be read as such a renunciation of persecution based on homosexual orientation and religious freedom, as interpreted under the 1951 Convention. The bench delivered its ruling, ignoring the UNHCR's guidance and jurisprudence of the ECtHR on Article 3 ECHR.[71] The recent case of *M'Bodi* is yet another example in which the CJEU did not align its assessment with prior case law of the ECtHR on *refoulement* in medical cases. The UNHCR's position and interpretative assessment of rights under the Refugee Convention on exclusion from and cessation of protection was contradicted in the newest CJEU case *B and D* and in *El Kott*.[72] In the former, the court deviated from the traditional approach to assessing exclusion through the lens of proportionality, i.e. to balance the consequences of exclusion from refugee protection against the seriousness of the claimants acts pursuant to Article 12 (2), the commission of crimes against peace or humanity (para. a); serious non-political crimes outside the country of refuge (para. b) and acts contrary to the purposes and principles of the United Nations. In the latter, the bench took a deviating standpoint concerning the cessation of protection by the UNWRA.[73]

70 EDAL: Taylor, *The CJEU and its Interaction with International Law in the Qualification Directive: A Calculated Selectivity?* (2015), available online at http://www.asylumlawdatabase.eu/en/journal/cjeu-and-its-interaction-international-law-qualification-directive-calculated-selectivity (last visited 1 August 2018), at 1.

71 European Database of Asylum Law, *Summary* (2013), available online at http://www.asylumlawdatabase.eu/en/content/court-justice-european-union-delivers-judgment-joined-cases-c-19912-c-20012-and-c-20112-x-y (last visited 1 August 2018).

72 *Mostafa Abed El Karem El Kott and Others v. Bevándorlási és Állampolgársági Hivatal, supra* note 59.

73 See for a detailed analysis, EDAL: Taylor, *supra* note 70, at 5ff.

Despite ambiguous considerations on the role and the fulfilment of its role, the CJEU is the main authoritative source in interpreting EU law. Refugee status based on the QD, as such, has so far not been on its radar. In contrast, its interpretation of the QD in regard to subsidiary protection for persons fleeing conflict is of essence as an interpretative source to delimitate the scope of subsidiary protection status.

3.4 An interpretative overhaul – the (Recast) QD and international humanitarian law

The Recast QD is the legal basis for the Union's subsidiary protection status, which covers persons fleeing conflict. In contrast to the 1951 Convention, the Recast QD uses explicit wording on conflict-induced displacement and harm. Its precise scope of application has been greatly debated and still remains contested. Against the background of the special role of the CJEU in the interpretation of Union asylum law, its judgements concerning the QD and flight from conflict are emphasised in the interpretation of the (Recast) QD.

3.4.1 Missing clarity – the scope of application of Article 15 (Recast) QD

Turning to the legal basis itself, Member States grant subsidiary protection in accordance with Article 18 Recast QD,

> Member States shall grant subsidiary protection status to a third country national or a stateless person eligible for subsidiary protection

and Article 2 (f),

> who does not qualify as a refugee but in respect of whom substantial grounds have been shown for believing that the person concerned, if returned to his or her country of origin, or in the case of stateless persons, to his or her country of former habitual residence, would face a real risk of suffering serious harm as defined in Article 15.

Article 15 defines exhaustively three types of serious harm which can constitute the basis for a protection claim, whether individually or combined. Paragraph (c) is put at the centre of the following analysis:

> (c) consist[ing] of serious or individual threat to a civilian's life or person by reason of indiscriminate violence in situations of international or internal armed conflict.

The interpretation of the 1951 Convention in the context of conflict has generated significant debate, particularly due to its lack of explicit phrasing. One would imagine that the interpretation of Article 15 (c) (Recast) QD and its direct reference to conflict-induced displacement renders its application easier, but this is not so. The application of Article 15 (c) varies in national jurisprudence and the questions of what constitutes a conflict and who is eligible for subsidiary protection reflect this struggle to provide clarity.[74] As such, the scope of Article 15 (c) has been criticised as "highly problematical"[75] due to its "tortuous word[ing]".[76] Others stressed that "the ambiguities and the implicit or apparent inconsistencies are the (usual) outcome of negotiation and compromise."[77] Some years after the adoption of the original QD, the need for clarifying guidance by the CJEU became indispensable, according to the UNHCR, if the narrow interpretation of the terms were not to render it an "empty shell in protection terms".[78]

3.4.1.1 Interpreting the elements of "serious threat to a civilian's life or person by reason of indiscriminate violence in situations of international or internal armed conflict"

To clarify and delimit the scope of application of Article 15 (c), each of its constitutive elements is in need of examination. For this matter, the interpretative guidance of the CJEU, as delivered in a preliminary ruling on the QD, comes to the fore. This can equally be applied to the Recast instrument, as the regulations concerning beneficiaries of subsidiary protection were not revised in the recast process.[79]

The CJEU had only ruled on matters of asylum under EU law in two other cases by the time the Member States' judiciaries turned their attention to the QD. One case considered an annulment brought by the European Parliament,[80] and another

74 United Nations High Commissioner for Refugees, *UNHCR Manual on the Case Law of the European Regional Courts, 1st edition* (2015), available online at http://www.refworld.org/docid/558803c44.html (last visited 1 August 2018), at 91. United Nations High Commissioner for Refugees, 'UNHCR Intervention before the Upper Tribunal Immigration and Asylum Chamber of the United Kingdom in the Case of A and Others v. Secretary of State for the Home Department' (ANIJQ817/2008, AA/00688/2008, ANI0936/2008, AN01419/2007, 2010).

75 *QD (Iraq) v. Secretary of State for the Home Department; AH (Iraq) v. Secretary of State for the Home Department, supra* note 46, at 19.

76 *KH (Article 15(c) Qualification Directive) Iraq v. Secretary of State for the Home Department,* CG [2008] UKAIT 00023, United Kingdom: Asylum and Immigration Tribunal / Immigration Appellate Authority (2008), at 32.

77 Errera, R., 'The CJEU and Subsidiary Protection. Reflections on Elgafaji - and After', 23 *International Journal of Refugee Law* (2011) 93, at 104.

78 United Nations High Commissioner for Refugees, *Safe at Last? Law and Practice in Selected EU Member States with Respect to Asylum-Seekers Fleeing Indiscriminate Violence* (2011), available online at http://www.unhcr.org/protection/operations/4e2d7f029/safe-law-practice-selected-eu-member-states-respect-asylum-seekers-fleeing.html (last visited 1 August 2018), at 29.

79 Peers, Steve *et al. (eds.), EU Immigration and Asylum Law (text and commentary). Volume 3: EU Asylum Law* (2nd ed., 2015), at 84.

80 *European Parliament v. Council of the European Union,* C-133/06, Court of Justice of the European Union (2008).

was referred by a Swedish court on the implementation of Regulation EC 343/2003 (Dublin II) and its time limits for the suspensive effects of an appeal against Dublin transfers.[81] Subsidiary protection status has so far been addressed by the CJEU in four judgements, the latest being *M'Bodi,*[82] delivered on 18 December 2014, in a case concerning medical grounds as a basis for subsidiary protection, by virtue of Articles 2 (e) and (f) and 15 (b). Prior to this, the case of *Abdida*[83] of 18 December 2014 equally concerned medical grounds under Article 15 (b).

However, it was only in 2009 that the question of interpretation of the QD in the context of conflict was brought to the supranational level through a preliminary ruling in the cases of *Elgafaji* and later in *Diakité.* These two cases are so far the first and only attempts of the court to investigate and clarify particularities of the QD as they explicitly concerned the issue of Article 15 (c) and generalised situations of violence. As such, they constitute the starting point for a common interpretation of conflict-related subsidiary protection.

To turn to the first preliminary ruling of 2009: the claimant, Meki Elgafaji, had been employed by a British security company which provided for his safe travel between Baghdad Airport and the Green Zone. In 2006, he found a note at his door, accusing him of being a collaborator with the foreign troops. His uncle, employed by the same company, had already been killed. Of further cause for concern was the fact that he and his wife had a mixed Sunni-Shiite marriage. He and his wife fled from Iraq to the Netherlands, where they applied for temporary residency, citing the danger of indiscriminate violence in Iraq. The Dutch asylum authorities rejected their asylum claims and argued that Elgafaji had not established a real risk of serious and individual threat in his home country.[84] Elgafahi then appealed the decision of the governmental authorities before the District Court of The Hague, which declared the decision to be void. This decision was followed by a governmental appeal before the Dutch Council of State. The government argued that the applicants had failed to demonstrate an individualised threat by reasons of indiscriminate violence. He was not 'singled out' as required under Article 15 (a)–(c). They argued that the death penalty or execution were always directed at a particular individual according to the interpretation of Article 15 (b). Therefore, Article 15 (c) should also be interpreted as focusing on individualised threats, requiring a claimant to have been singled out as a target.[85] The claimants countered that argument by stressing the lack of an additional meaning of Article 15 (c) if it was simply mirroring the elements of its counterparts (a) and (b). The Dutch Council of State suspended its litigation and, based on Article 117 Treaty of Rome (former equivalent of Article

81 *Migrationsverket v. Edgar Petrosian, Nelli Petrosian, Svetlana Petrosian, David Petrosian, Maxime Petrosian,* C-19/08, Court of Justice of the European Union (2009).

82 *Mohamed M'Bodj v. État belge: Opinion of Advocate General, supra* note 13.

83 *Centre public d'action sociale d'Ottignies-Louvain-La-Neuve v. Moussa Abdida,* C-562/13, Court of Justice of the European Union (2014).

84 *Meki Elgafaji, Noor Elgafaji v. Staatssecretaris van Justitie,* C-465/07, Court of Justice of the European Union (2009), at 18.

85 Fullerton, Maryellen, *supra* note 5, at 124.

234 EC Treaty and current Article 267 TFEU),[86] referred the issue to the then European Court of Justice, requesting a preliminary ruling on a clarification of the disputed terms of Article 15, in particular subparagraph (c). The judgement in the preliminary ruling case provided for an authoritative interpretation of the pertinent EU legislation, which could then be applied to the pending case in the requesting Member States' court.

The Dutch Council of State requested the CJEU to consider two distinct and abstract legal questions:

1 Is Article 15 (c) [...] to be interpreted as offering protection only in a situation in which Article 3 of the (ECHR), as interpreted in the case law of the European Court of Human Rights, also has a bearing, or does Article 15 (c), in comparison with Article 3 of the (ECHR), offer supplementary or other protection?
2 If Article 15 (c) of the Directive, in comparison with Article 3 of the (ECHR), offers supplementary or other protection, what are the criteria in that case for determining whether a person who claims to be eligible for subsidiary protection status runs a real risk of serious and individual threat by reason of indiscriminate violence within the terms of Article 15 (c) of the Directive, read in conjunction with Article 2 (e) (now Article 2 (f) Recast QD) thereof?

Not only the Dutch government as party to the domestic case but also the UK, Sweden, France, Greece, Finland and Belgium submitted positions to the CJEU presenting their different interpretations of the scope of Article 15 (c) QD.[87] Sweden, Belgium and Greece advocated for a broad interpretation of the terms as an asylum law instrument with its own independent meaning, not simply to be read and understood in the light of the existing Article 3 ECHR case law. The Commission stated that it consisted of a lower standard, and France and the UK, by contrast, favoured a restrictive interpretation of the QD's scope.[88] The UNHCR argued (in a public statement) for a broad interpretation of Article 15 (c) and the "possibility for states to extend its application to people in need of international protection beyond the scope of the 'classical' refugee definition".[89]

86 "The Court of Justice shall have jurisdiction to give preliminary rulings concerning: a) the interpretation of this Treaty; b) the validity and interpretation of acts of the institutions of the Community and of the ECB; c) interpretation of the statutes of bodies established by an act of the Council where those statutes so provide. Where such a question is raised before any court or tribunal of a Member State, that court or tribunal may, if it considers that a decision on the question is necessary to enable it to give judgment, request the Court of Justice to give a ruling thereon. Where any such question is raised in a case pending before a court or tribunal of a Member State against whose decision there is no judicial remedy under national law, that court or tribunal shall bring the matter before the Court of Justice."

87 Errera, R., *supra* note 77, at 97.

88 *Ibid.*

89 United Nations High Commissioner for Refugees, *UNHCR Public Statement in Relation to Elgafaji v. Staatssecretaris van Justitie before the Court of Justice of the European Union* (2008),

The judgement in the case was delivered on 17 January 2009. The CJEU firstly criticised and rejected the phrasing of the question posed by the Dutch Council of State with reference to the ECHR. It emphasised the autonomy of EU law and denied any limitation of the QD's scope by reference to the ECHR.[90] Turning to the QD and based on the three diverging formulations of the paragraphs, the court analysed that each paragraph covered a different situation and different types of injuries.[91] Therefore, Article 15 (c) would indeed cover threats not included in paragraphs (a) and (b).[92] On the relationship between Article 3 ECHR and Article 15 QD, the court held that paragraph (c) would encompass matters not addressed by Article 3 ECHR and the individualised threat incorporated in the latter.[93]

Despite the first preliminary ruling on the interpretation of the QD, the national determining authorities and the courts tasked with asylum proceedings continued to express interpretative difficulties and obstacles. The major issue turned out to be the correct understanding of the conflict-related wording and the question of guidance from the field of IHL. Against this background, a second preliminary ruling was delivered in 2014 in the Belgian *Diakité* case. The claimant, a Guinean national, had applied for international protection in Belgium in 2008 and 2010, following his participation in protests against the ruling government in his country and the repression and threats he had faced. Belgium denied protection on the basis of Article 15 (c) and stated that Guinea was not considered as being in an armed conflict of a non-international character, as defined by IHL.[94] The applicant countered this determination, relying on the fact that the QD was part of EU asylum law and not IHL. Only the interpretation of the former, according to the claimant, would have relevance for this case. The Highest Court in Belgium, against the *Elgafaji* judgement delivered earlier, acknowledged the potential independent, autonomous classification under the QD[95] and submitted the case to the CJEU, asking for an interpretation of the term 'internal armed conflict' within the QD. The *Diakité* judgement then laid the foundation for a unique asylum law concept of internal armed conflict.

---

available online at http://www.refworld.org/cgi-bin/texis/vtx/rwmain?docid=479df7472 (last visited 1 August 2018), at 8.

90 *Meki Elgafaji, Noor Elgafaji v. Staatssecretaris van Justitie, supra* note 84, at 28.

91 *Id.*, at 36.

92 *Id.*, at 38.

93 *Id.*, at 28.

94 "La Guinée a [...] été confrontée à des tensions internes, des troubles intérieurs, des actes isolés et sporadiques de violence et autre actes analogues [...] Il n' existe pas acutellement [...] de conflict armé." *Arret No. 60972,* Belgium: Conseil du contentieux des étrangers (2011), at 3.

95 "Il ne peut extre exclus, comme le soutient le requérant, que cette notion, au sens de l'article 15, c), de la directive 2004/83/CE, puisse etre également interprétée de facon autonome, et revetir une signification spécifique au regard de celle issue de la jurisprudence du Tribunal pénal international sur l'ex-Yougoslavie", *Arret no 219.37,* France: Conseil D'Etat (2012), at 5.

The Conseil d'État posed the following two questions to the CJEU:

1 Must Article 15 (c) of Council Directive 2004/83/EC be interpreted as meaning that that provision offers protection only in a situation of "internal armed conflict", as interpreted by international humanitarian law and, in particular, by reference to Common Article 3 of the four Geneva Conventions of 12 August 1949?
2 If the concept of "internal armed conflict" referred to in Article 15 (c) of Directive 2004/83 is to be given an interpretation independent of Common Article 3 of the four Geneva Conventions of 12 August 1949, what, in that case, are the criteria for determining whether such an "internal armed conflict" exists?[96]

The CJEU examined several relevant issues on the interpretation of the QD's wording. On matters of the content of Article 15 (c), the court considered the specific phrasing of "serious harm consists of serious and individual threat to a civilian's life or person by reason of indiscriminate violence in situations of international or non-international armed conflict". The court understood the phrasing of paragraphs (a) and (b) relating to the specific acts of the death penalty or execution and torture, inhumane or degrading punishment or inhumane and degrading treatment as more narrow and specific types of harm to an individual.[97] On the contrary, the phrasing of paragraph (c)'s "serious threat to life or person" would refer to a broader interpretation of harm. This argumentation was supported by reference to situations of general conflict and threats of indiscriminate violence, which would reject a narrow interpretation of specific types of harm to individuals.[98] The court held that these situations would encompass general situations of threat without referring to individuals being targeted due to specific personal circumstances.[99] The bench stated that "by contrast, the harm defined in article 15 (c) of the Directive [...] covers a more general risk of harm."[100] And the term indiscriminate violence is "a term which implies that it may extend to people irrespective of their personal circumstances".[101] Furthermore, and as is addressed in detail below, the CJEU expressed its opinion on the relationship between EU asylum law and IHL.

3.4.1.2 A disputed relationship – between EU asylum law and international humanitarian law

The major distinct feature of Article 15 (c), which is the reason for the QD's close proximity to the regional extended refugee instruments, is the explicit link to indiscriminate violence in situations of international or internal armed

96 *Aboubacar Diakité v. Commissaire général aux réfugiés et aux apatrides*, C-285/12, Court of Justice of the European Union (2014), at 16.
97 *Meki Elgafaji, Noor Elgafaji v. Staatssecretaris van Justitie, supra* note 84, at 32.
98 *Id.*, at 33f.
99 *Id.*, at 34.
100 *Id.*, at 33.
101 *Id.*, at 34.

conflict. However, disappointingly, the EU secondary instrument does not include definitions of the terms, either in the defining section under Article 2, or in the pertinent Article 15. In particular, the two-tier reference to both international and internal armed conflict and the use of the term 'armed conflict' results in the direct association with the field of IHL. That proximity generated extensive legal debate between 2004 and 2014, both in courts and among scholars concerning the relevance of IHL for the interpretation of Article 15 (c) QD.[102] One approach would be to transfer of IHL definitions and classification onto the asylum law instrument, while a second approach would be the use of IHL as potential interpretive guidance. A third approach could be the rejection of IHL for the interpretation of asylum matters altogether.

In the latest judgement in *Diakité*, the court, while evaluating the concept of internal conflicts, ultimately decided on an autonomous interpretation and thereby put an end to the debate on the prerogative of IHL to distinguish armed conflicts from other situations of violence that climaxed in the interim of the *Elgafaji* and *Diakité* judgements. The assessment of the concept of conflict under asylum law offers the opportunity for legal clarification, but also an additional opportunity to (re-)consider the interrelation between the EU legal order and international law.[103] On a more abstract level, the decision of the court can also be taken to contribute to the debate about the (de-)fragmentation[104] of international law.

3.4.1.2.1 SEPARATING THE ASYLUM CONCEPT OF CONFLICT FROM THE LAWS OF ARMED CONFLICT

IHL has almost exclusively retained the prerogative to classify the existence and character of armed conflict and distinguish it from other situations of violence, in addition to further regulating any relevant conduct during hostilities in the light of the *lex specialis* rule. The concept of an international armed conflict (IAC) has, for a long time, dominated the field of IHL, as inter-state war has been the classical type of conflict and that for which states have allowed for some internationally binding rules. The recognition of NIACs as the object of

102 See as a broad analysis of domestic jurisprudence, Lambert, Hélène and Farrell, Theo, *supra* note 34. Lambert, Hélène, 'The EU Asylum Qualification Directive, Its Impact on the Jurisprudence of the United Kingdom and International Law', 55 *International and Comparative Law Quarterly* (2006) 161. For a discussion on the different usage of IHL concepts in procedures on subsidiary protection in the EU, see United Nations High Commissioner for Refugees, 'UNHCR Intervention before the Court of Appeal of England and Wales in the case of QD (Iraq) v. Secretary of State for the Home Department' (UN Doc. C5/2008/1706, 2009), at paras. 32–58.

103 Wouters, Jan, Nollkaemper, André and Wet, Erika de (eds.), *The Europeanisation of International Law. The Status of International Law in the EU and its Member States* (2008).

104 Defragmentation as harmonic coordination of various fields of international law, see van Aaken, Anne, 'Defragmentation of Public International Law Through Interpretation. A Methodological Proposal', 16 *Indiana Journal of Global Legal Studies* (2009) 483.

international law has been slow to take root since the Second World War, with NIACs, in contrast to IACs, still being much less regulated.[105] Also, the relevant definition of armed conflict not of an international character "proved elusive"[106] despite references to it in Common Article 3 of the Geneva Conventions and Article 1 AP II. Developments in international criminal law, particularly the jurisprudence of the ad hoc Tribunals, gave further content and form to NIACs under IHL.[107] While a detailed consideration of NIACs under IHL is not essential for this contribution, it remains clear that the non-international armed conflict under the Geneva Conventions and the APs, supported by jurisprudential elaboration[108] nowadays constitute a broadly acknowledged conceptualisation for IHL and criminal law settings. One has to question grounds upon which the CJEU rejected the usage of the broadly acknowledged IHL definition as a means of giving substance to the terms of the QD, instead opting for an autonomous classification of conflict and violence which is unique to the EU legal order.

Generally, the EU legal order's respect for public international law in its basic form is emphasised in Article 3 (5) TEU, which states that the EU shall adhere to "the strict observance and the development of international law".[109] IHL and the classification of armed conflict were confirmed by the ICJ as "intransgressible principles of international customary law",[110] and for these reasons, and although the EU itself is not a treaty party, the court, when interpreting EU

105 Dapo Akande, 'Classification of Armed Conflicts: Relevant Legal Concepts', in E. Wilmshurst (ed.), *International Law and the Classification of Conflicts* (Oxford University Press, 2012), at 59.

106 Sivakumaran, Sandesh, *The Law of Non-international Armed Conflict* (Oxford University Press, 2014), at 155.

107 David, Eric, 'Internal (Non-International) Armed Conflict', in A. Clapham and P. Gaeta (eds.), *The Oxford Handbook of International Law in Armed Conflict* (Oxford University Press, 2014), at 353f. Fleck, Dieter, 'The Law of Non-International Armed Conflict', in D. Fleck (ed.), *The Handbook of International Humanitarian Law* (3rd ed.: Oxford University Press, 2013), at 605.

108 Most relevant is the Tadić Case and subsequent cases such as Prosecutor v Haradinaj on the two criteria of intensity and organisation of the non-state armed conflict party, *Prosecutor v. Dusko Tadic aka "Dule" (Decision on the Defence Motion for Interlocutory Appeal on Jurisdiction),* IT-94-1; 94-I-AR72, International Criminal Tribunal for the former Yugoslavia, Appeals Chamber (1995), at para. 70f. *Prosecutor v. Dusko Tadic aka "Dule" (Opinion and Judgment),* IT-94-1-T, International Criminal Tribunal for the former Yugoslavia, Trial Chamber (1997), at 562. *Prosecutor v. Haradinaj et al. (Trial Judgment),* IT-04-84-T, International Criminal Tribunal for the former Yugoslavia, Trial Chamber I (2008), at para. 36.

109 Larik, Joris, 'Shaping the International Order as an EU Objective', in D. Kochenov and F. Amtenbrink (eds.), *The European Union's Shaping of the International Legal Order* (Cambridge University Press, 2013), 62, at 62. Interestingly debated in *Kadi v. Council of the European Union and Commission of the European Communities,* C-402/05 P and C-415/05 P, Court of Justice of the European Union (2008). *Kadi v. European Commission,* T-85/09, Court of Justice of the European Union (2010). *European Commission and Others v. Yassin Abdullah Kadi,* C-584/10 P, C-593/10 P and C-595/10 P, Court of Justice of the European Union (2013).

110 *Legality of the Threat or Use of Nuclear Weapons. Advisory Opinion,* International Court of Justice (1996), at para. 79.

law, could have firstly considered them in order to ensure the conformity of its interpretation of EU law.[111]

The (Recast) QD and its *travaux préparatoires* do not present a clear indication for choosing or rejecting an IHL-based notion of the terms. The (Recast) QD explicitly supports the integration of the instrument into the international law setting, as referenced in Recital 25 QD (adopted as Recital 34 Recast QD):

> It is necessary to introduce criteria on the basis of which applicants for international protection are to be recognized as eligible for subsidiary protection. Those criteria should be drawn from international obligations under human rights instruments and practices existing in Member States.

While it is evident that the Recital calls for an integration of the (Recast) QD into the broader field of international law, despite the explicit reference to human rights law, no reference is made to IHL anywhere, which is one indication for the pursued autonomous interpretation of the term. Also, when looking at the prior judgement of *Elgafaji*, the court did not examine the relationship between asylum law and IHL, even though it analysed it in the context of other fields of law, in particular the regional (European) human rights framework. The CJEU stipulated that the QD must be interpreted with "due regard for fundamental rights, as they are guaranteed under the ECHR",[112] underlining that "the interpretation of Article 15(c) [...] is fully compatible with the ECHR."[113] The omission of an explicit link to IHL in this important case can, in retrospect, be understood as foreshadowing the court's later, explicit rejection.

Turning to the drafting history of the QD, the *travaux préparatoires* for the QD illustrate the early considerations made with regard to its application in the conflict context.[114] The first draft, as proposed by the Legal Service of the Council, contained the following formulation within Article 15 (c): "[...] in accordance with the 1949 Convention relating to the protection of civilians in time of war".[115] As such, the original phrasing in the European Commission's proposal established a link to IHL and by implication, its thresholds, criteria and definitions. Again, however, this phrasing was later omitted, suggesting even more that this close reference to IHL is misleading. References to other fields of law, on the other hand, remained explicitly enshrined in the QD.

Therefore, while an interpretation based on the principle of conformity with international law is common practice, the court in *Diakité* followed Advocate General Mengozzi's opinion that such an interpretation would depend on the

111 *Diakité v. Commissaire général aux réfugiés et aux apatrides: Opinion of Advocate General*, C-285/12, Court of Justice of the European Union (2013), at para. 23.

112 *Meki Elgafaji, Noor Elgafaji v. Staatssecretaris van Justitie, supra* note 84, at para. 28.

113 *Id.*, at para. 44.

114 More on the drafting history, see also McAdam, Jane, *supra* note 26.

115 European Parliament, *supra* note 11, at 3.

hermeneutic coherence of the fields of law in question.[116] The court effectively put an end to the debate in its judgement of 30 January 2014, which also contained a discussion about the coherence in question. The first part of its decision considered whether the QD would only apply to internal conflicts as interpreted by IHL, particularly its Common Article 3.

The argumentation correctly circled around both the communalities and differences between the two distinct fields of law, specifically in regard to their fundamental object and purpose. The court found the meaning of armed conflict within the QD to be unique and independent from the IHL interpretation, as both fields of law must be understood as pursuing different teleological purposes.[117] While both IHL and asylum law are underpinned by decisive humanitarian principles, they nonetheless pursue different aims. IHL focuses on limiting the effects of armed conflict through the restriction of methods and means of warfare and the promotion of protection for those not or no longer participating in the hostilities. The protection of civilians in particular extends to their protection during an ongoing armed conflict classified as such under IHL.[118] Asylum law in general and the provision of international protection based on the (Recast) QD are activated following a flight from countries in which the applicant fears indiscriminate violence. This protection by substitution, according to the court, is by its very nature based on the principle of *non-refoulement* and cannot be provided in the country of origin or by the countries in conflict.[119] In reference to this inherent difference between the two fields of law, the Advocate General rightly held that "a hermeneutical coherence" of the two notions of, on the one hand, the (Recast) QD's internal armed conflict and, on the other, IHL's non-international armed conflict was not established.[120]

Following this argumentation, the court rejected the notion that "eligibility for subsidiary protection [is] conditional upon a finding that the conditions for applying international humanitarian law have been met."[121] In greater detail, it rejected an analogous interpretation of Article 15 (c):

> It is not necessary for that conflict to be categorised as 'armed conflict not of an international character' under international humanitarian law; nor is it necessary to carry out, in addition to an appraisal of the level of violence

116 *Diakité v. Commissaire général aux réfugiés et aux apatrides: Opinion of Advocate General, supra* note 111, at para. 24. Nicolosi, Salvatore F., *supra* note 40, at paras. 66–67.

117 On the influence of IHL in other areas of the EU legal order, see for instance Matera, Claudio, 'Another Parochial Decision? The Common European Asylum System at the Crossroad between IHL and refugee law in Diakité', 12 *Questions of International Law, Zoom-in* (2015) 3, at 8f.

118 *Diakité v. Commissaire général aux réfugiés et aux apatrides: Opinion of Advocate General, supra* note 111, at para. 66.

119 *Id.*, at para. 67f.

120 *Id.*, at para. 72.

121 *Aboubacar Diakité v. Commissaire général aux réfugiés et aux apatrides, supra* note 96, at para. 26.

present in the territory concerned, a separate assessment of the intensity of the armed confrontations, the level of organisation of the armed forced involved or the duration of the conflict.[122]

The CJEU clearly rejected the traditional IHL approach to defining and classifying armed conflicts in two ways: firstly, it refrained from applying its established definitions and criteria and, secondly, it even rejected IHL as a source of interpretative guidance. Instead, in its analysis of the QD and hence, the scope of subsidiary protection, it correctly opted for an interpretation of conflicts exclusively with reference to asylum law.

3.4.1.2.2 AN AUTHORITATIVE SHIFT – ASYLUM LAW'S AUTONOMOUS CONCEPT OF CONFLICT

With its authoritative judgement in *Diakité*, the CJEU developed a new concept of internal armed conflict for the determination of protection in asylum law, one that is distinct from classifications derived from IHL. The second question posed by the Belgium High Court in its reference initiated the elaboration of such a new concept and asked for the practical meaning of the term 'internal armed conflict' as set out in Article 15 (c).

The court considered, firstly, its "usual meaning in everyday language" and determined that "an internal armed conflict exists, for the purposes of applying that provision [of the Directive], if a state's armed forces confront one or more armed groups or if two or more armed groups confront each other."[123] Clearly, from this wording, the definition of an internal armed conflict as such does not deviate from the basic interpretation provided by the ICTY in the *Tadić* appeal judgement. In that appeal, the tribunal held that such a conflict exists "whenever there is a resort to armed force between states or protracted armed violence between governmental authorities and organized armed groups or between such groups within a state".[124] The exchange of hostilities between either a state and (an) armed non-state actor(s), or between two or more non-state armed groups

122 *Id.*, at para. 35. State practice in the identification of a conflict and the assessment of the level of indiscriminate violence has proven inconsistent. Some states did not consider the existence of an armed conflict but solely focussed on the assessment of the level of violence, "The focus is on the level of violence and not the nature of armed conflict, which is why the test set out by the court of appeal does not refer to an armed conflict. Not every situation of armed conflict will meet the threshold; the key issue in this regard is the level of violence", United Kingdom: Home Office, *UK Interim Asylum Instructions. Operational Policy and Rules Unit* (2013), available online at https://www.gov.uk/government/uploads/system/uploads/attachment_data/file/25741/huma-prot.pdf (last visited 1 August 2018), at 8.

123 *Aboubacar Diakité v. Commissaire général aux réfugiés et aux apatrides, supra* note 96, at para. 28.

124 *Prosecutor v. Dusko Tadic aka "Dule" (Decision on the Defence Motion for Interlocutory Appeal on Jurisdiction), supra* note 108, at para. 70.

in both fields of law constitutes the most basic definition of internal or non-international armed conflict.

In both fields of law, the broad notion of internal armed conflict, however, must be brought to life and, in this regard, EU asylum law has followed a different path from the one envisaged by IHL. The two basic IHL criteria, namely the level of intensity and the level of organisation, were explicitly rejected as having any bearing on the asylum law concept of internal conflict:

> [T]he finding that there is an armed conflict must not be made conditional upon the armed forces involved having a certain level of organization or upon the conflict lasting for a specific length of time.[125]

Instead, the CJEU referred to its own previous preliminary ruling, and argued that criteria such as the duration of conflict or organisational structure of the belligerents were irrelevant, as long as the level of indiscriminate violence is given: "[...] it is sufficient if the confrontations in which those armed forces are involved give rise to the level of violence referred to in paragraph 30."[126] The conflict setting is rather the context for an assessment of the level of indiscriminate violence which is seen as giving rise to a subsidiary protection claim.[127]

In comparison to the IHL classification of armed conflict, the definition provided by the CJEU entails two assessments: firstly, with regard to the classification of internal conflict between a state's armed forces and one or more non-state armed groups or between only non-state armed groups, and secondly, the assessment of the level of indiscriminate violence necessary for the protection claim. No separate consideration must be given concerning the intensity and duration of the hostilities or the nature of the non-state armed groups. In rejecting these criteria, the asylum definition deflects from IHL's classification of conflict. Overall, no explicit considerations must be made concerning the classification of a conflict – the level of violence is the decisive element. In contrast to IHL guided assessments, one can therefore imagine protection claims resulting from otherwise unrecognised internal conflicts, such as drug and cartel wars, or other violent disturbances that would not usually activate Common Article 3 of the Geneva Conventions or AP II coverage.[128] Violence arising in the context of transnational organised crime or violence arising in the urban context can be

125 *Aboubacar Diakité v. Commissaire général aux réfugiés et aux apatrides, supra* note 96, at para. 34.

126 *Ibid.*

127 The Advocate General presented at 18 July 2013, "l'examen relatif à l'intensité de la violence et au risque qui en découle pour le demandeur joue un rôle central, alors que l'identification et la qualification des faits qui sont à l'origine de cette violence revêtent une importance mineure." *Diakité v. Commissaire général aux réfugiés et aux apatrides: Opinion of Advocate General, supra* note 111, at para. 91.

128 Bauloz, Céline, 'The Definition of Internal Armed Conflict in Asylum Law. The 2014 Diakite Judgment of the EU Court of Justice', 12 *Journal of International Criminal Justice* (2014) 835, at 845.

of a level comparable to that of traditional conflicts, but would not engage the application of IHL. Statistical data, such as homicide rates and trafficking rates, or quantifiable indicators for drug violence suggest that "modern cities in countries at peace are often the theatres of de facto warfare."[129] While the application of IHL in these scenarios is heavily disputed, one can infer that asylum claims can in theory be activated by these situations. On the other hand, if one keeps in mind the restrictive interpretative practice concerning the classical conflict-related claims from Afghan or Iraqi citizens, where European Member States' courts refused to hold that the threshold had been reached, it seems unlikely that a high number of cases will be generated out of such contexts.

3.4.1.2.3 ASSESSING THE NEW APPROACH OF AN ASYLUM LAW-GENERATED NOTION OF CONFLICT

Critics have found fault with this new, autonomous EU law classification of conflicts based on various grounds. A combination of influences deriving from the EU legal order and IHL has been assumed to increase the fragmentation of public international law in general. Some scholars assessed the repercussions of eroding IHL's monopoly on the classification of armed conflicts,[130] while others are debating the consequences of the expansion of legal concepts of conflict in various fields of international law.[131]

A leading opponent, Hugo Storey, proclaimed the IHL-rejecting approach as autarkic, delivered in a vacuum and denying its relationship with other fields of international law.

> By [...] opt[ing] for an essentially autonomous interpretation of the term 'armed conflict' that rejects not only IHL but even IHRL as sources, the court has only thrown into sharp relief that when it comes to international protection law it is prepared to forget its own jurisprudence situating EU law within the broader framework of customary and treaty-governed international law. Its approach not only fails to enhance harmonisation within the EU [...] but it has likely increased fragmentation and divergence globally.[132]

129 Koonings, Kees, 'Definition and Trends of Urban Violence', in European Union Institute for Security Studies and International Committee of the Red Cross (eds.), *Urban Violence and Humanitarian Challenges: Joint Report* (ISS European Union Institute for Security Studies, 2012), 13, at 14.

130 Bauloz, Céline, *The Definition of Internal Armed Conflict in Asylum Law, supra* note 128, at 837.

131 Nicolosi, Salvatore F., *supra* note 40. The article addresses the defragmentation potential of an autonomous interpretation of different notions in different fields. On the concept of europeanisation of international law, see also Wouters, Jan, Nollkaemper, André and Wet, Erika de, *supra* note 103, at 3. Generally on the matter: van Aaken, Anne, *supra* note 104.

132 Storey, Hugo, 'The "War Flaw" and Why it Matters', in D. Cantor and J.-F. Durieux (eds.), *Refuge from Inhumanity? War Refugees and International Humanitarian Law* (Brill, 2014),

Some scholars have evaluated the court's simplistic notion of internal conflict as positive, the right way forward and in accordance with the general tendency not to overemploy IHL.[133] National determination authorities or national courts no longer have to examine the intensities or organisational levels of armed groups, but must only tackle the level of indiscriminate violence. Quite a positive consequence is the alignment of the judgement with parts of national case law, although some Member States are now required to adapt.[134] Unfortunately, the court has missed the chance to establish substantive guidance on that matter, again leaving considerable discretion and room for deviation to national determining authorities and courts.[135] Therefore, it is again up to the national level to fill the given definition with substance and the outcome for status determination procedures and harmony within the CEAS remains to be seen.

Yet, by rejecting the IHL-adapted interpretation, the judgement has enabled the instrument to activate a broad scope of protection and is as such a breakthrough for asylum protection purposes. The emphasis on an assessment of the level of indiscriminate violence as a determinative eligibility criterion, rather than a classification of the existence of an internal conflict as such, allows for a more lenient and adaptable approach to status determination. This is aligned with the objective and purpose of the instrument and the (Recast) QD's nature as a basis for subsidiary protection status. The transfer of IHL criteria to the (Recast) QD could have rendered its subsidiary protection scheme ineffective and incompatible with its objective.[136] It would have rendered protection claims dependent on the strict classical IHL assessment criteria, which can be of informative but not necessarily decisive relevance for the determination of risk of claimants. If this approach had

at 55. And in response countering: Durieux, Jean-Francois, 'Of War, Flows, Laws and Flaws. A Reply to Hugo Storey', 31 *Refugee Survey Quarterly* (2012) 161.

133 Carlier, Jean-Yves, 'Guerre et paix pour les demandeurs d'asile. À propos de l'arrêt Diakité de la Cour de justice', 14 *Journal des Tribunaux* (2014) 237, at 238.

134 National jurisprudence has been ambivalent since the adoption of the QD. Some courts made direct reference to IHL prior to the CJEU's preliminary rulings on the QD. See for instance, *Judgment of 24 June 2008,* 10 C43.07, Germany: Federal Administrative Court (2008)., paras. 19ff. Against this standard, for instance *Judgment of 04 February 2010,* AN 14K09.30354, Germany: Administrative Court Ansbach (2010). *Judgment of 12 August 2010*, A 2 S 1134/10, Germany: Higher Administrative Court Baden-Wuerttemberg (2010). The UK Court of Appeal in KH (Iraq) treated the fields of law separately because IHL is "a specific area of operation [...] defined and limited purposes which do not include the grant of refuge to people who flee armed conflict." *KH (Article 15(c) Qualification Directive) Iraq v. Secretary of State for the Home Department, supra* note 76, at 16. *QD (Iraq) v. Secretary of State for the Home Department; AH (Iraq) v. Secretary of State for the Home Department, supra* note 46, at 18.

135 Matera, Claudio, *supra* note 117, at 20.

136 Teffera, Almaz, *Diakité: The CJEU Interprets the Concept of 'Internal Armed Conflict' for the Purpose of Granting Subsidiary Protection under EU Law* (2014), available online at http://www.asylumlawdatabase.eu/en/journal/diakit%C3%A9-cjeu-interprets-concept-%E2%80%98internal-armed-conflict%E2%80%99-purpose-granting-subsidiary (last visited 1 August 2018). Bauloz, Céline, *The Definition of Internal Armed Conflict in Asylum Law, supra* note 128, at 840.

been pursued, persons fleeing indiscriminate violence serious enough to threaten life and limb would not have been protected. Certain IHL criteria, such as organisation or intensity of conflict, would not have been fulfilled and, as such, no armed conflict would have been determined, due to the divergent definitions in the IHL and EU asylum systems. In this respect, the CJEU rightly distinguished between the meaning of conflict for the purposes of protection from the respective considerations under IHL.

3.4.1.3 A threat to a civilian's life or person

The definition of conflict is only one of several elements of Article 15 (c) that have caused interpretative troubles over the last decade. 'Civilians', according to 15 (c), are the designated recipients of protection by the (Recast) QD. Prior to the CJEU judgement in the case of *Diakité*, a broad study by the UNHCR highlighted divergent national practices in the determination of civilians as beneficiaries of subsidiary protection. In some countries, the practice involves assessment by explicit reference to IHL.[137] When assessing a civilian's asylum claim, one has to consider what is encompassed by the term 'civilian' from an asylum law perspective. The Belgian appeal body, the Council for Aliens Law Litigation, for instance, referred to Article 50 (I) of the 1977 AP I which states that civilians are any persons not belonging to the armed forces of the conflict. When in doubt, it has tended to follow the general presumption of Article 50 (I) that an applicant is a civilian rather than a combatant. However, as the UNHCR has recognised, in a number of judgements, some dubious cases in other jurisdictions have been decided against the claimant.[138] In France, both the CNDA, the Cour nationale du droit d'asile, and the first instance authority, the OFPRA, Office français de protection des refugies et apatrides, linked the term 'civilian' to the concept of armed forces under the AP I, interpreting it broadly to include irregular forces as well. In interviews with the UNHCR, the French courts considered a claimant to be a member of the armed forces and therefore not a civilian, even in cases when the claimant had not directly participated in hostilities but had only indirectly supported the troops. In effect, they interpreted 'civilian' even more narrowly when they denied those individuals who worked for official decision-making departments involved in the conflict the right to make a claim as a civilian. Furthermore, they denied the right to informants providing information to conflict parties linked to military actions.[139]

137 United Nations High Commissioner for Refugees, *supra* note 78.

138 European Migration Network, *EU and Non-EU Harmonised Protection Statuses in Belgium* (2009), available online at https://emnbelgium.be/sites/default/files/publications/eu_and_non-eu_harmonised_protection_statuses_in_belgium_0.pdf (last visited 1 August 2018), at 29. United Nations High Commissioner for Refugees, *supra* note 78, at 57.

139 *Id.*, at 58.

In *Diakité*, the CJEU indirectly clarified the interpretation of the nature of a civilian claimant without explicitly addressing 'civilian' in the sense of the QD. The judges clearly opted for a generic asylum law interpretation and rejected an adaptation of the strict legal definitions and threshold codified in IHL. From this general assumption, one can deduce that the term 'civilian', as enshrined in the (Recast) QD, is understood according to its ordinary, everyday meaning,[140] constituting a broader personal scope that may but need not align with the preconceived legal status of a combatant or a civilian.[141] Similarly, the UNHCR has also considered a broader notion of civilian for asylum law more generally and subsidiary protection matters in particular. The Office considered it necessary to clarify that the status as civilian is a genuine renunciation of military activities.[142] An example of the discrepancies between the legal and factual status of civilian is the legal treatment of wounded combatants. Under IHL, they do not lose their combatant status and are not considered civilians. Under asylum law, on the other hand, they may be considered factual civilians who are not to be denied international protection, unless the exclusion clause of Article 17 (Recast) QD applies.

Another assumption one can infer from the general approach of the CJEU relates to NIACs and members of non-state armed forces. The IHL category of combatant is only constituted by the laws of IAC, which does not apply to NIACs and the non-state, belligerent parties involved. However, following the CJEU's reasoning, this distinction would also be irrelevant. Of importance is the factual determination whether the person has participated in the conflict, with indicators being, for instance, the existence of military ranks, the position of the person in relevant organisations such as the armed opposition, or duress.[143] In *B and D*, the CJEU considered exclusion from international protection and cautioned against oversimplified exclusion based solely on membership of a certain group. This reasoning can be transferred to interpret the scope of civilian under the inclusion clause: "[…] not justifiable for a competent authority when considering whether to exclude a person […] to base its decisions solely on that person's membership of an organisation".[144] The UNHCR supports this assessment, stating,

140 *Aboubacar Diakité v. Commissaire général aux réfugiés et aux apatrides, supra* note 96, at para. 27.

141 European Asylum Support Office, *Article 15(c) Qualification Directive (2011/95/EU). A judicial analysis* (2014), available online at https://www.easo.europa.eu/sites/default/files/public/Article-15c-Qualification-Directive-201195EU-A-judicial-analysis.pdf (last visited 1 August 2018), at 19.

142 UNHCR: ExCom, *Conclusion No. 94 (LIII) Conclusion on the Civilian and Humanitarian Character of Asylum* (2002), available online at http://www.refworld.org/pdfid/4b28bf1f2.pdf (last visited 1 August 2018), at para. (c)(vii). United Nations High Commissioner for Refugees, *supra* note 52, at 16.

143 European Asylum Support Office, *supra* note 141, at 21.

144 *Bundesrepublik Deutschland v. B and D, supra* note 62, at 89.

> [i]n this connection, the term 'civilian' in Article 15 (c) should not serve to exclude former combatants who can demonstrate that they have renounced military activities. The fact that an individual was a combatant in the past does not necessarily exclude him or her from international protection if he or she has genuinely and permanently renounced military activities.[145]

Furthermore, the Office illustrated its position in a written court submission:

> From the perspective of refugee/human rights law, the distinction between violence employed against military targets and civilians is a false one. The correct distinction is between violence giving rise to a well-founded fear of persecution and violence that does not, but which nonetheless gives rise to the need for international protection outside the regime of the 1951 Refugee Convention.[146]

The other element of the criterion, namely the threat to 'life or person', has not been addressed by the CJEU and is not further emphasised in the QD itself. Due to the lack of concrete interpretative guidance, national jurisprudence has generated a variety of understandings of what 'life or person' actually covers. The German Federal Administrative Court, for example, considered this element of the transposition as relating to "substantial individual danger to life or limb", such as death or bodily injury caused by indiscriminate violence. Through a General Administrative Regulation, i.e. a subordinate regulation, concerning the Residence Act, it specifically omitted the coverage of restrictive measures such as detention.[147] The UK, by contrast, considered the terms more broadly as extending to "significant physical injuries, serious mental traumas and serious threats to bodily integrity"[148] and other "indirect forms of violence, such as intimidation, blackmail, seizure of property, raids on homes and businesses, checkpoints and kidnapping".[149] These two examples mirror the divergent scope

145 United Nations High Commissioner for Refugees, *UNHCR Statement on Subsidiary Protection Under the EC Qualification Directive for People Threatened by Indiscriminate Violence* (2008), available online at http://www.unhcr.org/cgi-bin/texis/vtx/search?page=search&docid=479df9532&query=subsidiary%20protection%20Qualification%20Directive (last visited 1 August 2018), at 7.

146 United Nations High Commissioner for Refugees, *supra* note 102, at para. 45.2.

147 Allgemeine Verwaltungsvorschriften zum Aufenthaltsgesetz, Freizügigkeitsgesetz-EU und Ausländerzentralregistergesetz, No 60.7.2.5. United Nations High Commissioner for Refugees, *supra* note 78, at 59.

148 *HM and Others (Article 15(c)) Iraq v. Secretary of State for the Home Department,* CG [2010] UKUT 331 (IAC), United Kingdom: Upper Tribunal (Immigration and Asylum Chamber) (2010), at 76.

149 *HM and others (Article 15(c)) Iraq CG v. the Secretary of State for the Home Department,* [2012] UKUT 00409(IAC), United Kingdom: Upper Tribunal (Immigration and Asylum Chamber) (2012), at 114.

of protection attached to the interpretation. While the CJEU did not explicitly examine the wording, it provided guidance on the scope of the element from the context of subparagraph 15 (c). Paragraphs (a) and (b), respectively, refer to specific forms of harm, including the death penalty and summary execution as well as torture or inhumane or degrading treatment or punishment. In contrast to the preceding paragraphs, 15 (c) addresses a more general risk of harm:

> By contrast, the harm defined in Article 15(c) of the Directive as consisting of a 'serious and individual threat to [the applicant's] life or person' covers a more general risk of harm. Reference is made, more generally, to a 'threat … to a civilian's life or person' rather than to specific acts of violence.[150]

The broad consideration of the claimant's 'life or person' led to a conclusion that harm that arises during conflict in a more indirect form can also suffice as the necessary risk of harm to the civilian.[151]

3.4.1.4 "By reasons of" – nexus of harm, indiscriminate violence and the situation of conflict

With Article 15 (c), the (Recast) QD establishes a specific instrument to protect people who have experienced conflict-induced displacement. In comparison with the test required to activate refugee protection, where the threat must emanate from the discriminating persecutory act or fear thereof, the (Recast) QD does not require a specific association to the harm and an underlying motivation or rationale in order to justify subsidiary protection. On the contrary, it demands that the harm be the result of indiscriminate violence arising from conflict.[152]

In practice, national courts have struggled with this criterion. For instance, German courts have applied the nexus quite strictly, to include only violence generated by parties to the conflict and resulting in death or bodily injury.[153] General threats to life stemming from deteriorating living conditions, as

150 *Meki Elgafaji, Noor Elgafaji v. Staatssecretaris van Justitie, supra* note 84, at paras. 33f.

151 *HM and Others (Article 15(c)) Iraq v. Secretary of State for the Home Department, supra* note 148, at para. 114. United Nations High Commissioner for Refugees, *supra* note 78, at 60.

152 Lambert, Hélène, 'Causation in International Protection from Armed Conflict', in D. Cantor and J.-F. Durieux (eds.), *Refuge from Inhumanity? War Refugees and International Humanitarian Law* (Brill, 2014), at 7. For instance, "[d]er Kläger hat dem entsprechend bei seiner Anhörung durch die Beklagte auch keine Furcht wegen expliziter Furcht vor Verfolgung als Kurde durch den "IS" beschrieben ("[…] umzingelt von dem IS, der freien syrischen Armee und der Türkei"). Vielmehr schilderte der Kläger typische und jedermann drohende Gefahren im Zusammenhang mit einem innerstaatlichen bewaffneten Konflikt, wonach insbesondere das Risiko besteht, zwischen die Fronten der Konfliktparteien zu geraten bzw. mehr oder weniger zufällig Opfer kriegerischer Handlungen einer der Konfliktparteien zu werden."), *Judgment of 29 April 2016*, 5 K 725/16.A, Germany: Administrative Court Chemnitz (2016).

153 *Judgment of 24 June 2008, supra* note 134, at 24.

consequences of the conflict, have been excluded from the assessment.[154] This would exclude the lack of basic goods necessary for survival.[155] Other EU Member States have been more open. The Dutch Council of State stated that the humanitarian situation in the country would need to be taken into account.[156] Similarly, the UK's Asylum and Immigration Tribunal held:

> [W]e see no reason why criminal acts should not be included in the scope of indiscriminate violence and indeed, it is often difficult to separate armed conflict from a criminal act [...] It is a question of causation [...] There therefore needs to be causal link between the threat to life or person and the indiscriminate violence, but that indiscriminate violence does not need to be caused by one or more armed factions or the state.[157]

In adopting this perspective, the Tribunal agreed with decisions of the French Council of State that the threat would not need to emanate from actors of the conflict but could equally be caused by the breakdown of the state.[158] Sweden formulated a similar approach, stating that it does not consider it necessary for the threat to be solely the result of actions of the conflict parties, but that it could also be caused by other actors involved in a situation of state breakdown and conflict.[159]

Scholars have emphasised the necessity of interpreting the nexus requirement broadly, employing, as discussed under section 2.4.2.2 concerning refugee protection, a contributing-cause test. The complexity of conflict and the social context in which conflicts arise have an important impact on the analysis of the causation of threat. Lambert, in this regard, utilised the example of the 'night letters' in Afghanistan, where the Taliban threatened individuals and communities for supporting the government and 'Western' allied forces. The letters alone and their delivery to claimants of international protection, out of context, would itself not be considered a violent act. In the social context in Afghanistan, however, their threat is real; it can and was the reason for flight and subsequent asylum claims.[160]

154 *Id.*, at para. 35.

155 *Ibid.*

156 *200802709/1,* Netherlands: Council of State (2008). Awb 10/5495, Netherlands: Court of Arnhem (2010).

157 *GS (Article 15(c): Indiscriminate Violence) Afghanistan v. Secretary of State for the Home Department,* CG [2009] UKAIT 00044, United Kingdom: Asylum and Immigration Tribunal / Immigration Appellate Authority (2009), at 65.

158 *HM and Others (Article 15(c)) Iraq v. Secretary of State for the Home Department, supra* note 148, at 80. and *L'Office français de protection des réfugiés et apatrides (OFPRA) v. Baskarathas,* Decision No 320295, France: Council of State (2009).

159 United Nations High Commissioner for Refugees, *supra* note 78, at 61.

160 Lambert, Hélène, 'Causation in International Protection from Armed Conflict', *supra* note 152, at 8.

3.4.1.5 Serious and individual threat (by reason of) indiscriminate violence

While the (Recast) QD, as distinct from the 1951 Convention, explicitly covers indiscriminate violence, Article 15 (c) uses the phrasing "individual threat (by reason of) indiscriminate violence". This phrasing reflects the somewhat conflicted juxtaposition of an individualised and general risk or threat to which the claimant must be exposed.[161] Recital 26 QD, adopted as Recital 35 in the Recast QD, was intended to clarify the scope of application by stating that general risks would normally not create the individual threat required:

> Risks to which a population of a country or a section of the population is generally exposed do not normally create in themselves an individual threat which would qualify as serious harm.

The UNHCR commented on both Recital 26 and Article 15 (c), respectively, and promoted the broad scope of protection against generalised situations of violence: "The notion of 'individual' should not lead to an additional threshold and higher burden of proof. Situations of generalized violence are characterized precisely by the indiscriminate and unpredictable nature of the risk civilians may face."[162]

The relationship between the individualisation of threats and the situation of generalised violence seems contradictory, leading Advocate General Maduro to state, in 2008, that the court had to "reconcile what seemed *prima facie* irreconcilable".[163] The Advocate General linked the understanding of indiscriminate violence to the enjoyment of fundamental rights, stating "there might be circumstances in which a substantive breach of fundamental rights can occur

161 The relationship between those two counterparts caused divergent transposition practices, as already reflected in the wording employed by the different states. For instance, Germany and France did not transpose the term 'indiscriminate' into their national laws. While France used the term 'generalised violence' instead of 'indiscriminate violence', and the difference is not clarified, Germany used the term 'willkürliche Gewalt' in Sentence 2 of Section 60 (7) Residence Act. The Federal Administrative court stated in that regard: "Although this requirement is not mentioned explicitly in Section 60 (7) Sentence 2 Residence Act, the statement of that reason for the government's bill points out that the provision encompassed 'the distinguishing characteristics under Article 15 letter c of the Qualification Directive', which is to be implemented, the granting of subsidiary protection 'in cases of indiscriminate violence' in connection with armed conflict." *Judgment of 24 June 2008, supra* note 134, at 36.

162 United Nations High Commissioner for Refugees, *UNHCR Annotated Comments on the EC Council Directive 2004/83/EC of 29 April 2004 on Minimum Standards for the Qualification and Status of Third Country Nationals or Stateless Persons as Refugees or as Persons Who Otherwise Need International Protection and the Content of the Protection Granted (OJ L 304/12 of 30.9.2004)* (2005), available online at http://www.refworld.org/docid/4200d8354.html (last visited 1 August 2018), at 32.

163 *Elgafaji v. Staatssecretaris van Justitie: Opinion of Advocate General*, C-465/07, Court of Justice of the European Union (2008), at para. 31.

even in the absence of any discrimination."[164] The QD would aim at these circumstances. The CJEU, examining this relationship in *Elgafaji*, referred to the wording of the Recital and rejected a general limitation to individualised threats, in particular because of the use of the word 'normally'. Although generalised situations of violence would not *normally* amount to the necessary individual threat, under exceptional circumstances they would.[165]

In this context, the court determined the necessary threshold of indiscriminate violence to activate Article 15 (c) protection. There must be evidence of a high level of general risk to satisfy the requirement of individual threat.

> Exceptionally [is] established where the degree of indiscriminate violence characterising the armed conflict taking place [...] reached such a high level that substantial grounds are shown for believing that a civilian [...] would, solely on account of his presence [...] face a real risk of being subject to that threat.[166]

This statement ascertains that in situations of such exceptionally strong violence arising from a conflict, the claimant would only need to establish that he or she is a civilian.[167] Concerning the question of individualisation, the court linked the terms 'individual threat' to the occurrences of indiscriminate violence in conflict situations, where civilians would face serious risk solely because of their presence. This risk is therefore independent of the person's race, religion or political views, but exists because of the arbitrary nature of indiscriminate violence.[168] Therefore, the judgement stated that violence "may extend to people irrespective of their personal circumstances"[169] and "the existence of serious and individual threat [...] is not subject to the condition that that applicant adduces evidence that he is specifically targeted by reason of factors particular to his personal circumstances".[170]

The level of indiscriminate violence in this context is to be assessed for the region in which the claimant is situated and not for the specific country.[171] In contrast to the assessment of claims under the 1951 Convention, in which the claimant's individual persecutory experience and the identification of grounds for such (feared) persecution are central to the assessment, claims for subsidiary protection focus on the level of indiscriminate violence because of conflict.

164 *Id.*, at para. 34.
165 *Meki Elgafaji, Noor Elgafaji v. Staatssecretaris van Justitie, supra* note 84, at para. 37.
166 *Id.*, at para. 35.
167 Storey, Hugo, 'Art. 15', in K. Hailbronner and D. Thym (eds.), *EU Immigration and Asylum Law: A Commentary* (Beck/Hart/Nomos, 2016), at 1237.
168 *Meki Elgafaji, Noor Elgafaji v. Staatssecretaris van Justitie, supra* note 84, at paras. 34f.
169 *Id.*, at para. 34.
170 *Id.*, at para. 43.
171 "[T]he geographical scope of the situation of indiscriminate violence and the actual destination of the applicant in the event that he is returned to the relevant country, as is clear from Article 8(1) of the Directive", *id.*, at para. 40.

3.4.1.6 An assessment of the level of indiscriminate violence

Due to the lack of a legally defined threshold for the existence of a conflict and the rejection of the IHL-established threshold in the context of NIACs in particular, determining authorities need to clarify a new threshold for asylum law purposes. For a long time, the *Elgafaji* judgement provided the only guidance on the interpretation of the QD, but it has left much room for variety in application:

> [T]he Court's analysis, by failing to answer the question raised about what criteria should be used, if not IHL ones, and offering its own autonomous definition, has left national decision makers with no methodology or tools for going about the task of assessing Article 15 (c) claims.[172]

The test of whether the indiscriminate violence has reached or is likely to reach the threshold required to establish a real risk of harm to civilians is carried out in Germany, the Netherlands and the UK. Belgium, France and Sweden, in contrast, assess whether or not there is an IAC or a NIAC and evaluate the level of indiscriminate violence within that assessment.[173] During the timeframe of a UNHCR study, several countries in conflict were used as the focus of research.[174] The main question was whether the level of violence in the country was of such a level that no specific risk for the claimant must be brought forward. Around 2010, the UK government, for instance, considered that in

> none of the following countries (or in parts of the countries) would a claim based on indiscriminate violence automatically succeed: Iraq, Afghanistan; and Southern and Central Somalia. Therefore, a claim from any of these countries will only succeed if a sliding scale/enhanced risk is established.[175]

This evaluation is contrasted with practices observed in Sweden and Belgium, where a broader range of situations were considered as providing for a sufficiently high level of indiscriminate violence. On the one hand, the Belgian authorities included Baghdad, the five central governorates of Iraq, the eastern region of the Democratic Republic of the Congo, Darfur, Gaza, Southern and Central Somalia and Mogadishu in their list, while Sweden considered provinces in Afghanistan, the northeastern region of the Congo and Darfur to meet the threshold.[176] Another geographical example that has regularly been found to evince indiscriminate violence sufficient to activate Article 15 (c) is the city

172 Storey, Hugo, 'The "War Flaw" and Why it Matters', *supra* note 132, at 55.
173 United Nations High Commissioner for Refugees, *supra* note 78, at 32.
174 *Id.*, at 42.
175 Interim Asylum Instruction on Humanitarian Protection, September 2010 cited in *id.*, at 34.
176 *Id.*, at 35.

of Mogadishu around 2010. However, "very little reliable quantitative date is available due, in part, to the virtual absence of independent media and civil society."[177] Furthermore, the conflict often shifts during the course of a year, or several years, meaning that information on the conflict must constantly be updated.

> The irony is that we now know [in contrast to the information situation in 2007 when the AIT rejected claims based on indiscriminate violence in Mogadishu] that, even as the AIT was writing its judgments, conditions in Mogadishu were beginning to deteriorate and during 2008 became dramatically worse. The country guidance relating to Mogadishu is now such that most potential returnees will be entitled to subsidiary protection.[178]

The European Asylum Support Office (EASO)[179] conducted research which determined that at the end of 2014, thirteen EU Member States considered the Syrian conflict to be subsumed under Article 15 (c) and affecting the whole territory of the country. Following the intensification of the conflict in 2014, the numbers of asylum applicants under Article 15 (c) increased, which also led to more EU Member States considering the level of violence in Syria from 2013 to 2014 to be high enough to establish a real risk for civilians solely by their presence in the territory. Prior to that, a large number of states had, applying the sliding scale in the risk assessment, required additional individual predicaments in order to support the protection claim.[180]

Availability of information about the country of origin and the evaluation of the situation are both extremely difficult when guidance on criteria and thresholds is missing. What one can infer from national practices is the use of varying combinations of quantitative and qualitative data.[181] Quantitative data in this

177 *Id.*, at 46.

178 *HH (Somalia) & Others v. Secretary of State for the Home Department,* [2010] EWCA Civ 426, United Kingdom: Court of Appeal (2010).

179 EASO is an agency of the EU set up by Regulation (EU) 439/2010 of the European Parliament and of the Council, see for more, European Asylum Support Office, *About Us* (2017), available online at https://www.easo.europa.eu/about-us (last visited 1 August 2018).

180 European Asylum Support Office, *The Implementation of Article 15(c) QD in EU Member States. EASO Practical Guides Series* (2015), available online at https://www.easo.europa.eu/sites/default/files/public/EASO_The-Implementation-of-Art-15c-QD-in-EU-Member-States.pdf (last visited 1 August 2018), at 22.

181 The use of quantitative data leaves courts to calculate equations to determine the risk faced by the claimant: "The Petitioner comes from the Sheikan area. [...] While, based on the information submitted, no statements regarding the number of attacks and victims relative to the number of inhabitants can be made for this area [...], statements can be made about Ninewa province, within which most of the Sheikan area is located. [...] According to these statements, the statistical probability of falling victim to fatal attack in Ninewa or Mosul was approx. 0.03 percent in 2009. The court concurs with the conclusion drawn from this by the senate that, based on the current security situation, Iraqis returning to Mosul are generally not subject to

assessment most commonly includes the number of inhabitants in the area; the number of security incidents committed by the conflict parties against civilians; their intensity, methods and means of warfare employed and localities of those incidents; and the number of civilian deaths compared to the total population in the given area.[182] Quantitative data that have been considered were, for instance, the number of displaced persons and access to protection in the country of origin.[183] In particular, the inclusion of qualitative data is important for comprehensively assessing the conflict situation.

This approach is also in line with the broader (and more recent) refugee, human rights and asylum law development that takes into account the importance of socio-economic rights and specific human vulnerabilities and advocates for a more sensitive treatment of such cases. In the context of Article 15 (c) assessments, this includes considerations of foreseeable, broader socio-economic, political and security-related developments of the conflict, the humanitarian situation in the areas affected by the hostilities[184] and the nature of violence and violations of human rights and humanitarian law, short of death or life-threatening physical injuries. Part of the assessment involves psychological trauma,[185] rape, arbitrary arrest, or detention,[186] or the cumulative effects resulting from the protracted nature of the conflict.[187]

The wide discretion that EU Member States can exercise in their assessment of the situation curtails the granting of subsidiary protection and surely leads to legal uncertainty and arbitrariness in RSD.[188] However, the increasing recognition that conflict can only be evaluated broadly and holistically is, at the very least, a step in the right direction. Article 15 (c) "ordinarily requires decision-makers to adopt an inclusive approach when seeking to determine the levels and extent of indiscriminate violence"[189]; "our overall assessment of Article 15 c) risk has to be a holistic one looking at a range of variables."[190]

---

significant individual threat to life and limb according to Sec, 60 Para 7 Sentence 2 Residence Act", *Judgment of 28 April 2010,* RO 8K 09.30272, Germany: Administrative Court Regensburg (2010).

182 For instance *Judgment of 27 April 2010,* 10 C 4.09, Germany: Federal Administrative Court (2010), at 33.

183 European Asylum Support Office, *supra* note 180, at 3. See for Germany: *Judgment of 25 March 2010,* A 2 S 364/09, Germany: Higher Administrative Court Baden-Wuerttemberg (2010). and *Judgment of 12 August 2010, supra* note 134. On some IHL characteristics that are useful as indicators, *Judgment of 27 April 2010, supra* note 182, at 23.

184 United Nations High Commissioner for Refugees, *supra* note 78, at 42.

185 *HM and Others (Article 15(c)) Iraq v. Secretary of State for the Home Department, supra* note 148, at 76.

186 *Supra* note 156.

187 Storey, Hugo, 'Art. 15', *supra* note 167, at 1240.

188 Fullerton, Maryellen, *supra* note 5, at 130.

189 *HM and Others (Article 15(c)) Iraq v. Secretary of State for the Home Department, supra* note 148, at 239.

190 *Id.*, at 278 (ii).

3.4.1.7 The balance of the sliding scale

When examining the complexity of conflict situations *per se*, in particular when opting for a new autonomous notion of conflicts for asylum determination purposes, one requires a new tool. The tool chosen to evaluate the various types of conflict and levels of generalised violence is the so-called 'sliding scale'. It is employed to balance the element of individual threat and the contextual element of indiscriminate violence and was developed in the cases of *Elgafaji* and *Diakité*.

> The more the applicant is able to show that he is specifically affected by reason of factors particular to his personal circumstances, the lower the level of indiscriminate violence required for him to be eligible for subsidiary protection.[191]

The CJEU held that, in situations in which the level of indiscriminate violence was sufficiently high, there would be no further need to bring evidence to ascertain that the applicant has been specifically targeted or singled out – his or her mere presence would be enough to trigger protection. The sliding scale reflects the assessment that Article 15 (c) does not exclusively cover these situations of such a high level of generalised violence, but also more individualised threats resulting from conflict. In the case of an individualised threat, however, the individual must show an accordingly higher specific risk than that of others affected by the conflict.[192]

For assessing protection claims in a holistic and yet case-by-case manner, the sliding scale is one useful mechanism for considering threat accumulation. Even when risks exist which are below the exceptional level of risk identified by the court as directly activating international protection, the claimant can still be eligible when further risk-relevant characteristics support his or her claim, such as proximity to threat of hostilities or medical reasons increasing exposure to the risks. When combining these individual factors with the conflict context in the country of origin, the sliding scale is an appropriate instrument to fulfil the protection object and purpose of the (Recast) QD's Article 15 (c), while keeping the balance between the necessary individualistic approach and the context of general indiscriminate violence.

3.4.2 Separating grounds for protection – distinguishing between Article 15 (b) and Article 15 (c) (Recast) QD

Similar to the characterisation concerning grounds for protection in refugee protection claims under section 2.4.2.3, overlaps in protection grounds are equally

191 *Meki Elgafaji, Noor Elgafaji v. Staatssecretaris van Justitie, supra* note 84, at 39. *Aboubacar Diakité v. Commissaire général aux réfugiés et aux apatrides, supra* note 96, at 31.

192 Storey, Hugo, 'Art. 15', *supra* note 167, at 1237.

possible between the different bases of subsidiary protection.[193] The CJEU delivered some guidance in *Elgafaji* considering Article 15, in which it held that paragraph (c) covers more generalised forms of violence than those included in paragraphs (a) and (b):

> [...] Article 15 (a) and (c) of the Directive cover situations in which the applicant for subsidiary protection is specifically exposed to the risk of a particular type of harm. By contrast, the harm defined in Article 15 (c) of the Directive [...] covers a more general risk of harm.[194]

The court held further, as will be discussed in chapter 4 in more detail, that Article 15 (b) would, in essence, correspond to Article 3 ECHR. Starting from this assumption, one could infer that the scope of Article 15 (c) is different.[195] Similar arguments were rightly made, stating that Article 15 (c) must go beyond the scope of paragraphs (a) and (b) and have some "added value",[196] otherwise "[t]hat would have offended the EU principle of effet utile."[197] Yet, in status determination, the separation of grounds or the clear identification of the decisive ground is seldom practiced.[198]

3.4.3 The actors of serious harm

Article 6 of the (Recast) QD defines actors of persecution (for the determination of refugee claims) as well as actors of serious harm (for the determination of subsidiary protection). Standards with regard to refugee status have already been considered under section 2.4.2.4. They can, as such, be considered equally applicable in considerations of actors subject to serious harm. As Article 15 (c) also applies to internal armed conflicts between a state's armed forces and non-state armed actors, or solely between non-state armed forces, and Article 6 explicitly lists them as actors of serious harm, whose acts can undoubtedly

193 Practice in the assessment of the claims both with regard to the grounds for subsidiary protection but also the order of refugee protection and subsidiary protection assessments vary in the administrative practice of countries. For instance, comparative research on the application of the QD has shown that the different EU Member States apply Article 15 in hierarchical order from (a)-(c), while others do not order or use a pragmatic approach, in case information on the general situation in the country of origin indicates a general situation of violence. European Asylum Support Office, *supra* note 180, at 5.

194 *Meki Elgafaji, Noor Elgafaji v. Staatssecretaris van Justitie, supra* note 84, at paras. 33f.

195 *Id.*, at 28. With a different opinion, see minority view of Tiedemann, assessing that Article 15 (b) and (c) QD and Article 3 ECHR have the same scope of protection, only that Article 15 (c) limits its personal application to 'civilians', Tiedemann, Paul, 'Subsidiary Protection and the Function of Article 15(c) of the Qualification Directive', 31 *Refugee Survey Quarterly* (2012) 123, at 138.

196 *KH (Article 15(c) Qualification Directive) Iraq v. Secretary of State for the Home Department, supra* note 76, at paras. 28–31.

197 *Id.*, at para. 128.

198 European Asylum Support Office, *supra* note 180, at 5.

trigger protection claims and is acknowledged as such. Interestingly, in regard to Article 15 (c), the nexus between serious harm and indiscriminate violence resulting from the conflict is also established through the indirect effects of conflict, such as the disruption of the rule of law and the general breakdown of public order as result of a conflict. A direct link to single acts by the state or non-state parties to the conflict is, as such, not always decisive in the assessment of the level of harm as triggering Article 15 (c).[199]

3.4.4 The actors of protection

Article 7 concerning the actors of protection, that is, the actors responsible for providing protection against persecution or serious harm, lists the same actors as Article 6. This encompasses the state (Article 7 (1) (a)) and parties or organisations, including international organisations controlling the state or a substantial part of the territory of the state, provided that they are willing and able to offer protection in accordance with paragraph 2 (Article 7 (1) (b)). With the adoption of Article 7 (1) (b), the EU has explicitly introduced non-state actors as alternative providers of protection and thereby opted for a flexible protection concept.[200] But whether non-state actors can provide protection comparable to that which can (at least theoretically) be provided by states is rightfully a subject of debate. It must be considered as a step in the right direction that some safeguards have been explicitly codified or have been carved out by the CJEU in this respect. The requirements attached to the nature of the parties or organisations are listed under subparagraphs 2 and 3:

> Such protection is generally provided when the actors [...] take reasonable steps to prevent the persecution or suffering of serious harm, *inter alia*, by operating an effective legal system for the detection, prosecution and punishment of acts constituting persecution or serious harm, and when the applicant has access to such protection.

Protection according to the Recast QD must be "effective and of non-temporary nature", according to Article 7 (2). In this connection, in 2004 the Council of the EU stated that

> [f]or the purpose of applying Article 7, the Council, considering information from relevant international organisations, will endeavour to provide guidance on the question of whether an international organisation is

199 *Ibid.* EDAL Case summary non-state actor persecution and the QD, European Database of Asylum Law, *EDAL Case Summaries: Non-state Actors/ Agents of Persecution*, available online at http://www.asylumlawdatabase.eu/en/case-law-search?f[0]=field_keywords%3A50 (last visited 1 August 2018).

200 Dörig, Harald, 'Art. 7', in K. Hailbronner and D. Thym (eds.), *EU Immigration and Asylum Law: A Commentary* (Beck/Hart/Nomos, 2016), at 1153.

> actually in control of a State or a substantial part of its territory and whether this international organisation provides protection from persecution or suffering of serious harm.[201]

Most prominently, the UNHCR has criticised that parties or organisations holding either a different status or no status at all under international law and have different powers, including an (in)ability to enforce the law, together with a lack of any obligations under human rights law, are considered as actors of protection.[202] In its comments concerning the original QD, the Office underlined that non-state actors, in contrast to the state, could ensure neither permanent protection, nor the enforcement of the broader rule of law in the country.[203] The Recast QD has taken this critique on board, introducing the requirement that "they are willing and able to offer protection in accordance with paragraph 2" in Article 7 (1) (a). Meanwhile, the first sentence of paragraph 2 states that "[p]rotection against persecution or serious harm must be effective and of a non-temporary nature". In this respect, it has formally addressed the concerns issued by the UNHCR.

Through its case law, the CJEU has further expanded the understanding and importance of access to protection.[204] In the 2010 *Aydin Salahadin* case, the CJEU emphasised that the determining factors for refugee status are not a lack of protection in the country of origin, but rather the circumstances based on which he or she fears persecution for Convention reasons.[205] The CJEU elaborated on the elements of protection to include that the actors of protection

> have taken reasonable steps to prevent the persecution, that they therefore operate, *inter alia*, an effective legal system for the detection, prosecution and punishment of acts constituting persecution and that the national concerned will have access to such protection [...] the factors which formed the basis of the refugee's fear of persecution may be regarded to have

201 Council of the European Union, 'Addendum to Draft Minutes: 2579th meeting of the Council of the EU at 29 and 30 April 2004. Council Doc. No. 8990/04 ADD 1 REV 1' , at 9.

202 United Nations High Commissioner for Refugees, 'Guidelines on International Protection: Internal Flight or Relocation Alternative' within the Context of Article 1 A (2) of the 1951 Convention and/or 1967 Protocol relating to the Status of Refugees' (UN Doc. HCR/GIP/03/04, 2003), at 17. See for more Hailbronner, Kay and Alt, Simone, 'Art. 7', in K. Hailbronner (ed.), *EU Immigration and Asylum Law: Commentary on EU Regulations and Directives* (Beck/Hart/Nomos, 2010), at 1049. Dörig, Harald, *supra* note 200, at 1151ff.

203 United Nations High Commissioner for Refugees, *supra* note 162, at 18.

204 For a detailed discussion, O'Sullivan, Maria, 'Acting the Part: Can Non-State Entities Provide Protection Under International Refugee Law?', 24 *International Journal of Refugee Law* (2012) 85, at 94ff.

205 *Aydin Salahadin Abdulla, Kamil Hasan, Ahmed Adem, Hamrin Mosa Rashi, Dier Jamal v. Bundesrepublik Deutschland, supra* note 58, at paras. 57, 60.

> been permanently eradicated. The assessment of the significant and non-temporary nature of the change of circumstances thus implies that there are no well-founded fears [...].[206]

Actors widely recognised in this context include international organisations that offer protection. One example are multinational forces, such as KFOR or UNMIK, which had administrative authorities in Kosovo delegated by the Security Council.[207] The provision of protection by clans or national *de facto* authorities is much more disputed.[208] In accordance with Article 7, to act as an actor of protection, the organisation or entity in question must control at least a substantial part of the territory and be willing and able to provide protection of an effective and non-temporary nature. Some examples, such as clans and *de facto* authorities in Somalia, have already been examined in case law as being capable of providing protection and being the primary entity to do so, as they *de facto* constitute the government in areas such as Somaliland or Puntland.[209] In particular, when considering situations in the numerous failed or failing states, non-state actors of protection, provided they fulfil the respective requirements, can become practical surrogates for state protection. In this regard, the Recast QD attempts to accommodate factual conflict realities and legal requirements.

3.4.5 The concept of an internal flight alternative in the (Recast) QD

One part of the assessment of a protection claim concerns possible internal protection. The question whether such an option exists is evaluated through a distinct test. A factual assessment is required, including an assessment of the claimant's ability to travel to the designated area: "[H]e or she can safely and legally travel to and gain admittance to that part of the country and can reasonably be expected to settle there."[210]

The requirement is directly related to the question of availability of protection and actors of protection. Article 7 of the Recast QD on actors of protection

206 *Id.*, at paras. 69, 73.

207 Zimmermann, Andreas and Mahler, Claudia, 'Article 1 A, para. 2 1951 Convention', in A. Zimmermann (ed.), *The 1951 Convention Relating to the Status of Refugees and its 1967 Protocol: A Commentary* (Oxford University Press, 2011), at 359.

208 Dörig, Harald, *supra* note 200, at 1154.

209 *Ibid. AM & AM (Armed Conflict: Risk Categories) Somalia v. Secretary of State for the Home Department,* [2008] UKAIT 00091, United Kingdom: Asylum and Immigration Tribunal / Immigration Appellate Authority (2009), at para. 164.

210 Article 8 para. 1 Recast QD. Recital 27 specifies further: "Internal protection against persecution or serious harm should be effectively available to the applicant in a part of the country of origin where he or she can safely and legally travel to, gain admittance to and can reasonably expected to settle. Where the state or agents of the State are the actors of persecution or serious harm, there should be a presumption that effective protection is not available to the applicant".

elaborates that protection against persecution or serious harm can be provided by (a) the state or (b) parties or organisations that control substantial parts or the whole of the state's territory, and that protection must be effective and of a non-temporary nature.[211] In the EU asylum scheme, this is not a constitutive element but "part of the assessment of the application for international protection". One can equally deduce this interpretation from the fact that Article 8 on Internal Protection is an optional provision that did not have to be transposed by Member States.[212]

The Recast QD, in comparison to the original QD, contains clarifications on internal protection. The former expectation of the applicant to 'stay' in a certain part of the territory is displaced by the new expectation that the applicant can be expected to 'settle' in that respective part of the country. The change in terminology mirrors the approach of the ECtHR, as reflected in *Salah Seekh*, in which the presumption of safety in the respective part of the country is highlighted[213]:

> When referring to the relocation process itself, the Recast QD elaborates more on the reasonableness condition, by stating: '[...] and he or she (the applicant) can safely and legally travel to and gain admittance to that part of the country and can reasonably be expected to settle there'.[214]

The determination of the existence in another part of the country has proven difficult. The case of *AH (Sudan) and Others* is one example of the analysis of an IFA. Here, the UK's House of Lords argued that

> [t]he humanitarian object of the Refugee Convention is to secure a reasonable measure of protection for those with a well-founded fear of persecution in their home country or some parts of it; it is not to procure a general levelling-up of living standards around the world, desirable though of course that is.[215]

211 Article 7 para. 2.

212 See for information on the transposition in Member States, European Commission, *supra* note 50.

213 *Salah Sheekh v. The Netherlands*, App. No. 1948/04, European Court of Human Rights (2007), at para. 141.

214 With reference to the Recast QD and its Article 8, United Nations High Commissioner for Refugees, *The internal Flight Alternative Practices. A UNHCR Research Study in Central European Countries* (2012), available online at http://www.refworld.org/docid/4ffaabdf2.html (last visited 1 August 2018). This deviated from the former, more limited formulation of: "[T]he applicant can reasonably be expected to stay in that part of the country. [...] The former reading of "Member States shall at the time of taking the decision on the application have regard to the general circumstances prevailing in that part of the country and to the personal circumstances of the applicant." Article 8 QD.

215 *Secretary of State for the Home Department v. AH (Sudan) & Ors*, [2007] UKHL 49, United Kingdom: House of Lords (2007), at para. 5.

In this case, the refugee claims were finally rejected upon establishing the existence of an IFA. The judgement shows how difficult this balancing is. Baroness Hale of Richmond described the conditions in the part of the country being considered as an IFA as 'appalling':

> Yet the Tribunal concluded that because the conditions faced by returning Darfuris, however appalling, would be no worse than those faced by other Sudanese IDPs, it would not be not "unduly harsh" to expect them to return. The standard of comparison was not with their lives in Darfur before their persecution, not with the general run of ordinary lives in Sudan, not even with the lives of poor people in Sudan, but with the lives of the poorest of the poor, internally displaced victims of the civil war in the south, living in camps or squatter slums, and "subject from time to time to relocations, sometimes involving force and human rights violations" (para 244).[216]

By inserting the new requirement for states to ensure that precise and up-to-date information is obtained from relevant sources, hereby referencing explicitly the UNHCR and EASO, some safeguards are enshrined against a too broad discretion which would lead to variations in Member States' practices.[217] Article 8 paragraph 2 holds:

> To that end, Member States shall ensure that precise and up-to-date information is obtained from relevant sources, such as the United Nations High Commissioner for Refugees and the European Asylum Support Office.

3.5 Intermediate conclusion on the (Recast) QD and subsidiary protection for persons fleeing conflict and violence

The development of subsidiary protection as a complementary mechanism in the EU had raised the hopes of establishing a comprehensive and consistent asylum system, whose different categories cover the various kinds of people in need of international protection.

Unfortunately, since the adoption of the original QD in 2004 and even after the entry into force and transposition of the Recast QD, the legal basis for subsidiary protection for persons fleeing conflict has remained troublesome. Examples of the diverging national jurisprudence reflect the need for authoritative guidance from the supranational level on its own instrument. The instrument chosen by the EU legislator for the creation of a common protection status is a directive, which is, in contrast to a regulation, not self-executing. Rather than requiring one single, common way, the Directive requires states to pursue certain

216 *Id.*, at para. 28.
217 Article 8 para. 2 Recast QD.

broad aims. The differences in subsequent transposition laws are reflective of the discretionary nature of such an instrument. As such, it purports to protect the sovereignty of single Member States while paving the way for legal uncertainty and protection gaps among them. Consequently, the interpretation of the wording used in Directives is essential for creating harmonisation across the EU.

The interpretative approach is decisive when considering the single elements of Article 15 (c) of the (Recast) QD as well as its phrasing, in order to delineate the scope of the Article and, as such, protection in cases of conflict-induced flight. In this regard, the interaction between EU asylum law and IHL was examined, as the outcome decides the interpretation of the single elements of the eligibility test. With the *Diakité* judgement of 2014, following its prior approach in the 2009 case of *Elgafaji*, the CJEU put an end to the debate in the domestic courts and among scholars, opting instead for an approach unique to EU asylum law.

The wording of Article 15 (c), although limited, does not employ unique IHL terminology. When looking at the drafting history of the QD, further explicit links to IHL were, although included in discussion among the delegates, omitted from the proposal that would eventually be adopted as the QD. The context of Article 15, in particular when taking into account the Recitals of the QD, incorporated links to the field of human rights law. However, it also omitted explicit reference to the laws of armed conflict. While these arguments already strongly favour a rejection of IHL as a decisive source for the interpretation of the QD, the teleological approach provides the strongest argument for such an autonomous approach. The inherent differences in the natures of IHL and asylum law *qua* (Recast) QD provide the main justification. While the general protection purpose might overlap, the two specialised fields of law differ in terms of regulatory content, the form of protection granted, beneficiaries and geographical and temporal scopes of application. These differences are most clearly illustrated when one considers how determining authorities employ and courts interpret the QD and its terms independently, without following the predetermined definitions and criteria contained in IHL principles. In contrast to refugee protection in which violence by conflict only plays a role in status determination if it is the chosen means of persecution on the grounds of one or more Convention attributes, protection from conflict under the (Recast) QD is conceptualised differently. A preliminary understanding of the (Recast) QD's Article 15 (c) suggests eligibility for subsidiary protection from serious harm and simply justifies the claimant's flight from a country in conflict. However, if decision-makers are not using IHL classifications as a reference point for their decisions, the situation in the claimant's country of origin must be assessed differently.

The context of generalised and random violence of a conflict is explicitly recognised in the QD. However, the lexicon of 'serious and individual threat' has generated wide uncertainty on the construction of a subsidiary protection claim. It has been asked, for example, how much individualisation in a situation characterised by indiscriminate violence is necessary to support a subsidiary protection claim, and to what extent an individual must be singled out within the broader context of individualised violence of a conflict. Clearly, in contrast to the 1951

Convention, the element of singling out a target is not attached to the perpetrator's discriminatory motivation. However, balancing individualisation and generalisation is still important in determining eligibility. The indiscriminate violence of international and internal armed conflicts is the main criterion to activate subsidiary protection. Yet, as ruled by the CJEU, indiscriminate violence alone is only a trigger for this type of complementary protection in the most exceptional cases. It is only in those exceptional cases where the level of violence is so high that an applicant's mere presence in the affected (part of the) country raises a real risk of being subject to the serious threat envisaged in Article 15 (c). In cases of lower levels of indiscriminate violence, in order to be able to address the complexity of conflict scenarios and, finally, to balance the elements of individual threat and indiscriminate violence, the sliding scale is employed. The sliding scale is the tool to evaluate a claim in cases of diminishing levels of indiscriminate violence by considering the characteristics of the individual, his or her vulnerability, and taking an overall view of the different facets of risk.

The CJEU, through preliminary rulings, has provided the necessary interpretative instructions concerning the scope of the (Recast) QD, particularly with regards to eligibility for subsidiary protection of persons fleeing conflict and violence. Not only in clarifying specifics with regard to single elements, but in finally choosing an interpretative approach to do so, the court has ended a decade-long debate on the importance of IHL for asylum law matters. The court has rightly opted for a unique interpretative approach and, in doing so, has satisfied the protection objective of the (Recast) QD's Article 15 (c). The CEAS warrants a harmonised approach to, *inter alia*, refugee or subsidiary protection status, and the basis for such an assessment is, most prominently, 'serious threat by reason of indiscriminate violence in situations of international or internal armed conflict'. What remains unsatisfactory so far is that the court has not provided clearer indicators to assess levels of indiscriminate violence. Arbitrariness in the assessment of risks and the levels of violence in countries of origin might be the consequence. Therefore, one has to see whether asylum statistics continue to show differences in assessments, while political practices continue to lack consistency in the application of the legal framework. Furthermore, the impact of the CJEU's approach on the relationship between IHL and asylum law and on the broader question of whether the EU legal order is being integrated into or disconnected from international law remains to be seen.

References

Allgemeine Verwaltungsvorschriften zum Aufenthaltsgesetz, Freizügigkeitsgesetz-EU und Ausländerzentralregistergesetz, No 60.7.2.5.

Baldaccini, Anneliese, Guild, Elspeth and Toner, Helen (eds.), *Whose Freedom, Security and Justice? EU Immigration and Asylum Law and Policy* (Hart, 2007).

Bauloz, Céline, 'The (Mis)Use of International Humanitarian Law under Article 15(C) of the EU Qualification Directive', in D. Cantor and J.-F. Durieux (eds.), *Refuge from Inhumanity? War Refugees and International Humanitarian Law* (Brill, 2014).

Bauloz, Céline, 'The Definition of Internal Armed Conflict in Asylum Law. The 2014 Diakite Judgment of the EU Court of Justice', 12 (4) *Journal of International Criminal Justice* 835 (2014).

Arret No. 60972, Belgium: Conseil du contentieux des étrangers (2011).

Bouteillet-Paquet, Daphné and Hailbronner, Kay (eds.), *Subsidiary Protection of Refugees in the European Union: Complementing the Geneva Convention?* (Bruylant, 2002).

Bundesamt für Migration und Flüchtlinge, 'Das Bundesamt in Zahlen 2013. Asyl, Migration und Integration', July 2014, available online at http://www.bamf.de/SharedDocs/Anlagen/DE/Publikationen/Broschueren/bundesamt-in-zahlen-2013.pdf?__blob=publicationFile (last visited 1 August 2018).

Cantor, David and Durieux, Jean-François (eds.), *Refuge from Inhumanity? War Refugees and International Humanitarian Law* (Brill, 2014).

Carlier, Jean-Yves, 'Guerre et paix pour les demandeurs d'asile. À propos de l'arrêt Diakité de la Cour de justice', 14 *Journal des Tribunaux* 237 (2014).

Chetail, Vincent and Bauloz, Céline, *Research Handbook on International Law and Migration* (Edward Elgar, 2014).

Christian Kaunert and Sarah Leonard, 'The European Union Asylum Policy after the Treaty of Lisbon and the Stockholm Programme: Towards Supranational Governance in a Common Area of Protection', 31 (4) *Refugee Survey Quarterly* 1 (2012).

Clapham, Andrew and Gaeta, Paola (eds.), *The Oxford Handbook of International Law in Armed Conflict* (Oxford University Press, 2014).

Costello, Cathryn, *The Human Rights of Migrants and Refugees in European Law* (Oxford University Press, 2016).

Council of the European Union, 'Addendum to Draft Minutes: 2579th meeting of the Council of the EU at 29 and 30 April 2004. Council Doc. No. 8990/04 ADD 1 REV 1'.

Council Directive 2003/86/EC of 22 September 2003 on the Right to Family Reunification, 3 October 2003.

Federal Republic of Germany and Others v. Commission of the European Communities, C-281/85, Court of Justice of the European Union (1987).

European Parliament v. Council of the European Union, C-133/06, Court of Justice of the European Union (2008).

Kadi v. Council of the European Union and Commission of the European Communities, C-402/05 P and C-415/05 P, Court of Justice of the European Union (2008).

Elgafaji v. Staatssecretaris van Justitie: Opinion of Advocate General, C-465/07, Court of Justice of the European Union (2008).

Migrationsverket v. Edgar Petrosian, Nelli Petrosian, Svetlana Petrosian, David Petrosian, Maxime Petrosian, C-19/08, Court of Justice of the European Union (2009).

Meki Elgafaji, Noor Elgafaji v. Staatssecretaris van Justitie, C-465/07, Court of Justice of the European Union (2009).

Aydin Salahadin Abdulla, Kamil Hasan, Ahmed Adem, Hamrin Mosa Rashi, Dier Jamal v. Bundesrepublik Deutschland, C-175/08, C-176/08, C-178/08 and C-179/08, Court of Justice of the European Union (2010).

Bolbol v. Bevándorlási és Állampolgársági Hivatal, C-31/09, Court of Justice of the European Union (2010).

Court of Justice of the European Union, *Kadi v. European Commission*, T-85/09 (2010).

Court of Justice of the European Union, *Bundesrepublik Deutschland v. B and D*, C-57/09 and C-101/09 (2010).

Court of Justice of the European Union, *Bundesrepublik Deutschland v. Y and Z*, C-71/11 and C-99/11 (2012).

Court of Justice of the European Union, *M. M. v. Minister for Justice, Equality and Law Reform, Ireland, Attorney General,* C-277/11 (2012).
Court of Justice of the European Union, *Mostafa Abed El Karem El Kott and Others v. Bevándorlási és Állampolgársági Hivatal,* C-364/11 (2012).
Court of Justice of the European Union, *Diakité v. Commissaire général aux réfugiés et aux apatrides: Opinion of Advocate General,* C-285/12 (2013).
Court of Justice of the European Union, *European Commission and Others v. Yassin Abdullah Kadi,* C-584/10 P, C-593/10 P and C-595/10 P (2013).
Court of Justice of the European Union, *X, Y, Z v. Minister voor Immigratie en Asiel,* C-199/12 to C-201/12 (2013).
Court of Justice of the European Union, *Aboubacar Diakité v. Commissaire général aux réfugiés et aux apatrides,* C-285/12 (2014).
Court of Justice of the European Union, *H. N. v. Minister for Justice, Equality and Law Reform, Ireland, Attorney General,* C-604/12 (2014).
Court of Justice of the European Union, *Mohamed M'Bodj v. État belge: Opinion of Advocate General,* Case C-542/13 (2014).
Court of Justice of the European Union, *A, B, C v. Staatssecretaris van Veiligheid en Justitie,* C-148/13 to C-150/13 (2014).
Court of Justice of the European Union, *Centre public d'action sociale d'Ottignies-Louvain-La-Neuve v. Moussa Abdida,* C-562/13 (2014).
Court of Justice of the European Union, *Andre Lawrence Shepherd v. Bundesrepublik Deutschland,* C-472/13 (2015).
Court of Justice of the European Union, *H. T. v. Land Baden-Württemberg,* C-373/13 (2015).
Dapo Akande, 'Classification of Armed Conflicts: Relevant Legal Concepts', in E Wilmshurst (ed.), *International Law and the Classification of Conflicts* (Oxford University Press, 2012).
David, Eric, 'Internal (Non-International) Armed Conflict', in A. Clapham and P. Gaeta (eds.), *The Oxford Handbook of International Law in Armed Conflict* (Oxford University Press, 2014).
Donadio, Rachel, 'Italy Lashes Out at European Union Over Immigrants' (New York Times, 2011).
Dörig, Harald, 'Art. 7', in K. Hailbronner and D. Thym (eds.), *EU Immigration and Asylum Law: A Commentary* (Beck/Hart/Nomos, 2016).
Durieux, Jean-Francois, 'Of War, Flows, Laws and Flaws. A Reply to Hugo Storey', 31 (3) *Refugee Survey Quarterly* 161 (2012).
E Wilmshurst (ed.), *International Law and the Classification of Conflicts* (Oxford University Press, 2012).
EDAL: Taylor, 'The CJEU and its interaction with international law in the Qualification Directive: a calculated selectivity?', 12 February 2015, available online at http://www.asylumlawdatabase.eu/en/journal/cjeu-and-its-interaction-international-law-qualification-directive-calculated-selectivity (last visited 1 August 2018).
Errera, R., 'The CJEU and Subsidiary Protection. Reflections on Elgafaji - and After', 23 (1) *International Journal of Refugee Law* 93 (2011).
European Asylum Support Office, 'Article 15(c) Qualification Directive (2011/95/EU). A Judicial Analysis', December 2014, available online at https://www.easo.europa.eu/sites/default/files/public/Article-15c-Qualification-Directive-201195EU-A-judicial-analysis.pdf (last visited 1 August 2018).
European Asylum Support Office, 'The Implementation of Article 15(c) QD in EU Member States. EASO Practical Guides Series', July 2015, available online at

https://www.easo.europa.eu/sites/default/files/public/EASO_The-Implementation-of-Art-15c-QD-in-EU-Member-States.pdf (last visited 1 August 2018).

European Asylum Support Office, 'About Us', 8 March 2017, available online at https://www.easo.europa.eu/about-us (last visited 1 August 2018).

Commission Directive 85/381/EEC of 14 December 1984 amending Annexes I and II to Council Directive 66/401/EEC on the Marketing of Fodder Plant Seed, 14 December 1984.

European Commission, 'Proposal For A Council Directive on Minimum Standards for the Qualification and Status of Third Country Nationals And Stateless Persons as Refugees or as Persons Who Otherwise Need International Protection' (COM(2001)510 final, 2001).

European Commission, 'Communication from the Commission to the European Parliament, the Council, the European Economic and Social Committee and the Committee of Region, Policy Plan on Asylum. An Integrated Approach to Protection Across the EU' (COM(2008)360 final, 2008).

European Commission, 'Proposal for a Directive of the European Parliament and of the Council on Minimum Standards for the Qualification and Status of Third Country Nationals or Stateless Persons as Beneficiaries of International Protection and the Content of the Protection Granted' (COM(2009)551 final, 2009/0164 (COD), 2009).

European Commission, 'Report from the Commission to the European Parliament and the Council On the Application of Directive 2004/83/EC of 29 april 2004 on Minimum Standards for the Qualification and Status of Third Country Nationals or Stateless Persons as Refugees or as Persons who Otherwise Need International Protection and the Content of the Protection' (COM(2010)314 final, 2010).

European Council, 'Action Plan on how to best implement the provisions of the Amsterdam Treaty establishing an Area of Freedom, Security and Justice, Part II. A' (1999/C 19/01, 1998).

European Council, 'The Hague Programme: Strengthening Freedom, Security and Justice in the European Union' (2005/C 53/01, OJ C 53/1, 2004).

European Council on Refugees and Exiles, 'Comments from the European Council on Refugees and Exiles on the European Commission Proposal to Recast the Qualification Directive', March 2010, available online at http://www.ecre.org/wp-content/uploads/2016/07/ECRE-Comments-on-the-Commission-Proposal-to-Recast-the-Qualification-Directive_March-2010.pdf (last visited 1 August 2018).

European Council on Refugees and Exiles, 'Asylum on the Clock? Duration and Review of International Protection Status in Europe', June 2016, available online at http://www.ecre.org/wp-content/uploads/2016/07/AIDA-Briefing-Asylum-on-the-Clock-duration-and-review-of-international-protection-status-in-Europe_-June-2016.pdf (last visited 1 August 2018).

European Court of Human Rights, *Salah Sheekh v. The Netherlands,* App. No. 1948/04 (2007).

European Database of Asylum Law, 'EDAL Case Summaries: Non-State Actors/ Agents of Persecution', available online at http://www.asylumlawdatabase.eu/en/case-law-search?f[0]=field_keywords%3A50 (last visited 1 August 2018).

European Database of Asylum Law, 'Summary', 18 November 2013, available online at http://www.asylumlawdatabase.eu/en/content/court-justice-european-union-delivers-judgment-joined-cases-c-19912-c-20012-and-c-20112-x-y (last visited 1 August 2018).

European Migration Network, 'EU and Non-EU Harmonised Protection Statuses in Belgium', 2011, available online at https://emnbelgium.be/sites/default/files/

publications/eu_and_non-eu_harmonised_protection_statuses_in_belgium_0.pdf (last visited 1 August 2018).

European Parliament, 'Presidency Conclusions, Tampere European Council 15 and 16 October 1999. Towards a Union of Freedom, Security and Justice: The Tampere Milestones', 1999, available online at http://www.europarl.europa.eu/summits/tam_en.htm (last visited 1 August 2018).

European Parliamentary Research Service Blog, 'Justice and Home Affairs after the Stockholm Programme', 25 June 2014, available online at https://epthinktank.eu/2014/06/25/justice-and-home-affairs-after-the-stockholm-programme/ (last visited 1 August 2018).

European Union, 'The History of the European Union: 1980–1989, Official European Union Site', available online at https://europa.eu/european-union/about-eu/history/1980-1989_en (last visited 1 August 2018).

European Union Institute for Security Studies and International Committee of the Red Cross (eds.), *Urban Violence and Humanitarian Challenges. Joint Report* (ISS European Union Institute for Security Studies, 2012).

Eurostat, 'Asylum Applicants 2013', March 2014, available online at http://ec.europa.eu/eurostat/documents/4168041/5948933/KS-QA-14-003-EN.PDF/3309ae42-431c-42d7-99a3-534ed5b93294 (last visited 1 August 2018).

Fiddian-Qasmiyeh, Elena *et al. (eds.), The Oxford Handbook of Refugee and Forced Migration Studies* (Oxford University Press, 2014).

Fleck, Dieter (ed.), *The Handbook of International Humanitarian Law* (3rd ed.: Oxford University Press, 2013).

Fleck, Dieter, 'The Law of Non-International Armed Conflict', in D. Fleck (ed.), *The Handbook of International Humanitarian Law* (3rd ed.: Oxford University Press, 2013).

France: Conseil D'Etat, *Arret no 219.37* (2012).

France: Council of State, *L'Office français de protection des réfugiés et apatrides (OFPRA) v. Baskarathas,* Decision No 320295 (2009).

Fullerton, Maryellen, 'A Tale of Two Decades: War Refugees and Asylum Policies in the European Union', 10 (1) *Washington University Global Studies Law Review* 87 (2011).

Germany: Administrative Court Ansbach, *Judgment of 04 February 2010,* AN 14K09.30354 (2010).

Germany: Administrative Court Chemnitz, *Judgment of 29 April 2016,* 5 K 725/16.A (2016).

Germany: Administrative Court Chemnitz, *Judgment of 28 April 2010,* RO 8K 09.30272 (2010).

Germany: Federal Administrative Court, *Judgment of 24 June 2008,* 10 C43.07 (2008).

Germany: Federal Administrative Court, *Judgment of 27 April 2010,* 10 C 4.09 (2010).

Germany: Federal Administrative Court, *Judgment of 17 June 2014,* BVerwG 10 C 7.13 (2014).

Germany: Higher Administrative Court, *Judgment of 25 March 2010,* A 2 S 364/09 Baden-Wuerttemberg (2010).

Germany: Higher Administrative Court, *Judgment of 12 August 2010,* A 2 S 1134/10 (2010).

Gil-Bazo, María-Teresa, 'Refugee Status and Subsidiary Protection under EC Law: The Qualification Directive and the Right to Be Granted Asylum', in A. Baldaccini, E. Guild and H. Toner (eds.), *Whose Freedom, Security and Justice? EU Immigration and Asylum Law and Policy* (Hart, 2007).

Hailbronner, Kay (ed.), *EU Immigration and Asylum Law. Commentary on EU Regulations and Directives* (Beck/Hart/Nomos, 2010).

Hailbronner, Kay and Alt, Simone, 'Art. 7', in K. Hailbronner (ed.), *EU Immigration and Asylum Law: Commentary on EU Regulations and Directives* (Beck/Hart/Nomos, 2010).

Hailbronner, Kay and Thym, Daniel (eds.), *EU Immigration and Asylum Law. A Commentary* (Beck/Hart/Nomos, 2016).

International Court of Justice, 'Legality of the Threat or Use of Nuclear Weapons', Advisory Opinion, (1996).

Prosecutor v. Dusko Tadic aka "Dule" (Decision on the Defence Motion for Interlocutory Appeal on Jurisdiction), IT-94-1; 94-I-AR72, International Criminal Tribunal for the former Yugoslavia, Appeals Chamber (1995).

Prosecutor v. Dusko Tadic aka "Dule" (Opinion and Judgment), IT-94-1-T, International Criminal Tribunal for the former Yugoslavia, Trial Chamber (1997).

Prosecutor v. Haradinaj et al. (Trial Judgment), IT-04–84-T, International Criminal Tribunal for the former Yugoslavia, Trial Chamber I (2008).

Jakulevičienė, Lyra, 'Is there a Need for an Extension of Subsidiary Protection in the European Union Qualification Directive', 2 (120) *Jurisprudencjia* 215 (2010).

Joanne van Selm (ed.), *Kosovo's Refugees in the European Union* (Pinter, 2000).

Kochenov, Dimitry and Amtenbrink, Fabian (eds.), *The European Union's Shaping of the International Legal Order* (Cambridge University Press, 2013).

Koonings, Kees, 'Definition and Trends of Urban Violence', in European Union Institute for Security Studies and International Committee of the Red Cross (eds.), *Urban Violence and Humanitarian Challenges: Joint Report* (ISS European Union Institute for Security Studies, 2012).

Lambert, Hélène, 'The EU Asylum Qualification Directive, its Impact on the Jurisprudence of the United Kingdom and International Law', 55 (1) *International and Comparative Law Quarterly* 161 (2006).

Lambert, Hélène, 'Causation in International Protection from Armed Conflict', in D. Cantor and J.-F. Durieux (eds.), *Refuge from Inhumanity? War Refugees and International Humanitarian Law* (Brill, 2014).

Lambert, Hélène and Farrell, Theo, 'The Changing Character of Armed Conflict and the Implications for Refugee Protection Jurisprudence', 22 (2) *International Journal of Refugee Law* 237 (2010).

Larik, Joris, 'Shaping the International Order as an EU Objective', in D. Kochenov and F. Amtenbrink (eds.), *The European Union's Shaping of the International Legal Order* (Cambridge University Press, 2013).

Matera, Claudio, 'Another Parochial Decision? The Common European Asylum System at the Crossroad between IHL and Refugee Law in Diakité', 12 *Questions of International Law, Zoom-in* 3 (2015).

McAdam, Jane, 'The European Union Qualification Directive. The Creation of a Subsidiary Protection Regime', 17 (3) *International Journal of Refugee Law* 461 (2005).

McAdam, Jane, *Complementary Protection in International Refugee Law* (Oxford University Press, 2007).

Migration Policy Institute, 'The European Union's Stockholm Program: Less Ambition on Immigration and Asylum, But More Detailed Plans', 12 January 2010, available online at http://www.migrationpolicy.org/article/european-unions-stockholm-program-less-ambition-immigration-and-asylum-more-detailed-plans (last visited 1 August 2018).

Netherlands: Council of State, *200802709/1* (2008).

Netherlands: Court of Arnhem, Awb 10/5495 (2010).

Nicolosi, Salvatore F., 'Disconnecting Humanitarian Law from EU Subsidiary Protection. A Hypothesis of Defragmentation of International Law', 29 (02) *Leiden Journal of International Law* 463 (2016).

O'Sullivan, Maria, 'Acting the Part: Can Non-State Entities Provide Protection under International Refugee Law?', 24 (1) *International Journal of Refugee Law* 85 (2012).

Peers, Steve, 'Analysis. The Next Multi-Year EU Justice and Home Affairs Programme Views of the Commission and the Member States', 12 March 2014, available online at http://www.statewatch.org/analyses/no-238-new-jha-programme.pdf (last visited 1 August 2018).

Peers, Steve *et al. (eds.), EU Immigration and Asylum Law (Text and Commentary). Volume 3: EU Asylum Law* (2nd ed.: Brill, 2015).

Ramet, Sabrina P., 'War in the Balkans', 71 (4) *Foreign Affairs* (1992).

Sandra Lavenex, 'France: International Norms, European Integration and State Discretion', in Joanne van Selm (ed.), *Kosovo's Refugees in the European Union* (Pinter, 2000).

Simeon, James C. (ed.), *Critical Issues in International Refugee Law. Strategies Toward Interpretive Harmony* (Cambridge University Press, 2010).

Sivakumaran, Sandesh, *The Law of Non-International Armed Conflict* (Oxford University Press, 2014).

Spijkerboer, Thomas, 'Subsidiarity in Asylum Law. The Personal Scope of International Protection', in D. Bouteillet-Paquet and K. Hailbronner (eds.), *Subsidiary Protection of Refugees in the European Union: complementing the Geneva Convention?* (Bruylant, 2002).

Storey, Hugo, 'The "War Flaw" and Why it Matters', in D. Cantor and J.-F. Durieux (eds.), *Refuge from Inhumanity? War Refugees and International Humanitarian Law* (Brill, 2014).

Storey, Hugo, 'Art. 15', in K. Hailbronner and D. Thym (eds.), *EU Immigration and Asylum Law: A Commentary* (Beck/Hart/Nomos, 2016).

Teffera, Almaz, 'Diakité: The CJEU Interprets the Concept of 'Internal Armed Conflict' for the Purpose of Granting Subsidiary Protection Under EU Law', 22 March 2014, available online at http://www.asylumlawdatabase.eu/en/journal/diakit%C3%A9-cjeu-interprets-concept-%E2%80%98internal-armed-conflict%E2%80%99-purpose-granting-subsidiary (last visited 1 August 2018).

Tiedemann, Paul, 'Subsidiary Protection and the Function of Article 15(c) of the Qualification Directive', 31 (1) *Refugee Survey Quarterly* 123 (2012).

Tsourdi, Evangelia, 'What Protection for Persons Fleeing Indiscriminate Violence? The Impact of the European Courts on the EU Subsidiary Protection Regime', in D. Cantor and J.-F. Durieux (eds.), *Refuge from Inhumanity? War Refugees and International Humanitarian Law* (Brill, 2014).

UNHCR: ExCom, 'Conclusion No. 94 (LIII) Conclusion on the Civilian and Humanitarian Character of Asylum', 8 October 2002, available online at http://www.refworld.org/pdfid/4b28bf1f2.pdf (last visited 1 August 2018).

United Kingdom: Asylum and Immigration Tribunal/ Immigration Appellate Authority, *KH (Article 15(c) Qualification Directive) Iraq v. Secretary of State for the Home Department,* CG [2008] UKAIT 00023 (2008).

United Kingdom: Asylum and Immigration Tribunal/ Immigration Appellate Authority, *AM & AM (Armed Conflict: Risk Categories) Somalia v. Secretary of State for the Home Department,* [2008] UKAIT 00091 (2009).

United Kingdom: Asylum and Immigration Tribunal / Immigration Appellate Authority, *GS (Article 15(c): Indiscriminate Violence) Afghanistan v. Secretary of State for the Home Department,* CG [2009] UKAIT 00044 (2009).

United Kingdom: Court of Appeal, *HH (Somalia) & Others v. Secretary of State for the Home Department,* [2010] EWCA Civ 426 (2010).

United Kingdom: Court of Appeal (England and Wales), *QD (Iraq) v. Secretary of State for the Home Department; AH (Iraq) v. Secretary of State for the Home Department,* [2009] EWCA Civ 620 (2009).

United Kingdom: Court of Appeal (England and Wales), *Secretary of State for the Home Department v. HH (Iraq),* [2009] EWCA Civ 727 (2009).

United Kingdom: Home Office, 'UK Interim Asylum Instructions. Operational Policy and Rules Unit', May 2013, available online at https://www.gov.uk/government/uploads/system/uploads/attachment_data/file/25741/huma-prot.pdf (last visited 1 August 2018).

United Kingdom: House of Lords, *Secretary of State for the Home Department v. AH (Sudan) & Ors,* [2007] UKHL 49 (2007).

United Kingdom: Upper Tribunal (Immigration and Asylum Chamber), *HM and Others (Article 15(c)) Iraq v. Secretary of State for the Home Department,* CG [2010] UKUT 331 (IAC) (2010).

United Kingdom: Upper Tribunal (Immigration and Asylum Chamber), *HM and others (Article 15(c)) Iraq CG v. the Secretary of State for the Home Department,* [2012] UKUT 00409(IAC) (2012).

United Nations High Commissioner for Refugees, 'Guidelines on International Protection: Internal Flight or Relocation Alternative within the Context of Article 1 A (2) of the 1951 Convention and/or 1967 Protocol relating to the Status of Refugees' (UN Doc. HCR/GIP/03/04, 2003).

United Nations High Commissioner for Refugees, 'UNHCR Annotated Comments on the EC Council Directive 2004/83/EC of 29 April 2004 on Minimum Standards for the Qualification and Status of Third Country Nationals or Stateless Persons as Refugees or as Persons Who Otherwise Need International Protection and the Content of the Protection Granted (OJ L 304/12 of 30.9.2004)', 28 January 2005, available online at http://www.refworld.org/docid/4200d8354.html (last visited 1 August 2018).

United Nations High Commissioner for Refugees, 'Asylum in the European Union. A Study of the Implementation of the Qualification Directive', November 2007, available online at http://www.refworld.org/docid/473050632.html (last visited 1 August 2018).

United Nations High Commissioner for Refugees, 'UNHCR Public Statement in Relation to Elgafaji v. Staatssecretaris van Justitie Before the Court of Justice of the European Union', January 2008, available online at http://www.refworld.org/cgi-bin/texis/vtx/rwmain?docid=479df7472 (last visited 1 August 2018).

United Nations High Commissioner for Refugees, 'UNHCR Statement on Subsidiary Protection Under the EC Qualification Directive for People Threatened by Indiscriminate Violence', January 2008, available online at http://www.unhcr.org/cgi-bin/texis/vtx/search?page=search&docid=479df9532&query=subsidiary%20protection%20Qualification%20Directive (last visited 1 August 2018).

United Nations High Commissioner for Refugees, 'UNHCR Intervention before the Court of Appeal of England and Wales in the Case of QD (Iraq) v. Secretary of State for the Home Department' (UN Doc. C5/2008/1706, 2009).

United Nations High Commissioner for Refugees, 'UNHCR Intervention before the Upper Tribunal Immigration and Asylum Chamber of the United Kingdom in the Case of A and Others v. Secretary of State for the Home Department' (ANlJQ817/2008, AA/00688/2008, ANl0936/2008, AN01419/2007, 2010).

United Nations High Commissioner for Refugees, 'Submission by the Office of the United Nations High Commissioner for Refugees in the Case of S.A. v. Section for Asylum, Ministry of Interior of the Former Yugoslav Republic of Macedonia' (2010).

United Nations High Commissioner for Refugees, 'UNHCR Comments on the European Commission's Proposal for a Directive of the European Parliament and of the Council on Minimum Standards for the Qualification and Status of Third Country Nationals or Stateless Persons as Beneficiaries of International Protection and the Content of the Protection Granted (COM(2009)551, 21 October 2009)', 29 July 2010, available online at http://www.refworld.org/docid/4c503db52.html (last visited 1 August 2018).

United Nations High Commissioner for Refugees, 'Safe at Last? Law and Practice in Selected EU Member States with Respect to Asylum-Seekers Fleeing Indiscriminate Violence', July 2011, available online at http://www.unhcr.org/protection/operations/4e2d7f029/safe-law-practice-selected-eu-member-states-respect-asylum-seekers-fleeing.html (last visited 1 August 2018).

United Nations High Commissioner for Refugees, 'Ministerial Communiqué' (UN Doc. HCR/MINCOMMS/2011/6, 2011).

United Nations High Commissioner for Refugees, 'The Internal Flight Alternative Practices. A UNHCR Research Study in Central European Countries', June 2012, available online at http://www.refworld.org/docid/4ffaabdf2.html (last visited 1 August 2018).

United Nations High Commissioner for Refugees, 'UNHCR Manual on the Case Law of the European Regional Courts, 1st edition', June 2015, available online at http://www.refworld.org/docid/558803c44.html (last visited 1 August 2018).

van Aaken, Anne, 'Defragmentation of Public International Law Through Interpretation. A Methodological Proposal', 16 (2) *Indiana Journal of Global Legal Studies* 483 (2009).

Vedsted-Hansen, Jens, 'Complementary or Subsidiary Protection? Offering an Appropriate Status without Undermining Refugee Protection' (UNHCR Working Paper No. 52, 2002).

Wouters, Jan, Nollkaemper, André and Wet, Erika de (eds.), *The Europeanisation of International Law. The Status of International Law in the EU and Its Member States* (T.M.C. Asser Press, 2008).

Zimmermann, Andreas (ed.), *The 1951 Convention Relating to the Status of Refugees and its 1967 Protocol. A Commentary* (Oxford University Press, 2011).

Zimmermann, Andreas and Mahler, Claudia, 'Article 1 A, para. 2 1951 Convention', in A. Zimmermann (ed.), *The 1951 Convention Relating to the Status of Refugees and its 1967 Protocol: A Commentary* (Oxford University Press, 2011).

4 European human rights law protection for persons fleeing conflict and violence

The European Convention on Human Rights (ECHR) and the court ultimately responsible for its enforcement, the European Court of Human Rights (ECtHR), constitute the most renowned regional instrument of human rights protection. In particular, the court's jurisprudence on the human rights of migrants has become very prominent over the last years and has shaped the asylum system in Europe, due to its standard-setting character. While the previous two chapters of this book addressed the two positive protection statuses for persons fleeing from violence in their countries, their protection under the ECHR is established by virtue of protection against expulsion. The *non-refoulement* obligation is analysed in a twofold manner and the chapter follows this structure. Firstly, as an omnibus clause, it offers protection from forcible return. This prohibition against return in certain scenarios applies to persons already within the territorial scope of the ECHR, meaning that they are already in Europe and under the full and the indisputable jurisdiction of the ECHR Contracting Parties, which includes not just the EU Member States but all members of the Council of Europe. It applies to those persons not eligible for either refugee or subsidiary protection status, or those falling under the respective exclusion clauses of the protection statuses. This complementary protection scheme residing within European human rights law does not grant a protection status, but only a temporary suspension from return and therefore provides less comprehensive support and protection than refugee status and subsidiary protection.

Secondly, the implementation of the principle of *non-refoulement* in border situations and outside of state territory is put into focus. The *non-refoulement* obligation of regional human rights law has been subject to a long-established jurisprudential debate about the scope of its application with regard to its beneficiaries, subject matter and its territorial and extraterritorial boundaries. In the context of migration and immigration, the *non-refoulement* obligation has emerged as a primary protection instrument for those persons reaching the borders of Europe over land or sea. It enshrines the prohibition against forcibly returning persons to situations of distress and offers protection from *refoulement* as soon as a claimant is within the state's territorial borders. State practice varies considerably in terms of both expulsion practices and border control mechanisms. For these reasons, the interpretation of the principle by the ECtHR can be seen as setting important standards vis-à-vis the interpretation and application of the norm by the Contracting Parties to the ECHR.

The following chapter analyses the *non-refoulement* obligation both within and outside European territory, with particular focus given to individuals fleeing countries in conflict. The main question to be considered here is whether the contextual element of conflict and violence influences the prohibition against return. Similar to the debate on subsidiary protection in the light of Article 15 (c) of the (Recast) QD, in regard to Article 3 ECHR it also needs to be examined which level of generalised violence in a country precludes deportation by the host state. Given the extensive Article 3 jurisprudence of the court, this chapter focuses only on cases dealing with the principle of *non-refoulement* and return to countries in conflict. As claimants of ECHR protection often encounter and claim violations even before entering European territory, hence beyond the traditional territorial scope of application of the ECHR, in the final part of this chapter the extraterritorial application of the principle of *non-refoulement* is analysed.

4.1 Complementary protection in Europe – turning to the ECHR

Complementary protection in Europe and around the globe is not a legal term, but a catch-all phrase for a variety of different protection schemes conferred on persons who, for various reasons, cannot be returned to their country of origin or former habitual residence.[1] This prohibition against return, known as the principle of *non-refoulement*, forms the basis for various complementary protection schemes ranging from simple prohibition against deportation to the granting of a minimum set of substantive rights. The primary point of reference for the principle of *non-refoulement* in the context of refugeehood stems from Article 33 of the 1951 Convention. While enshrined in the 1951 Convention, *non-refoulement* has also been repeatedly affirmed as an important principle "whose applicability is embedded in customary international law"[2] and as a peremptory international norm by the ICJ in the *North Sea Continental Shelf* case.[3] The 1951 Convention is an international treaty, widely ratified, but its Article 33 obligation is constrained by the eligibility criteria for refugee protection of Article 1 A (2). As such, it only applies to those fulfilling the exclusive Convention

1 UNHCR: Mandal, 'Protection Mechanisms Outside of the 1951 Convention ("Complementary Protection")' (UN Doc. PPLA/2005/02, 2005), at viii.

2 Ministerial Meeting of States Parties to the 1951 Convention and/or Its 1967 Protocol relating to the Status of Refugee, 'Declaration of States Parties to the 1951 Convention and or its 1967 Protocol Relating to the Status of Refugees' (UN Doc. HCR/MMSP/2001/09, 2002).

3 *North Sea Continental Shelf Cases (Federal Republic of Germany v. Denmark; Federal Republic of Germany v. Netherlands)*, [1969], International Court of Justice (1969), at para. 42. Lauterpacht, Elihu and Bethlehem, Daniel, 'The Scope and Content of the Principle of Non-Refoulement: Opinion', in E. Feller, V. Türk and F. Nicholson (eds.), *Refugee Protection in International Law: UNHCR's Global Consultations on International Protection* (Cambridge University Press, 2003), 87, at 143.

refugee criteria. However, it is important to bear in mind that persons fleeing conflict might be, but may not necessarily be eligible for refugee status. For this reason, the wider *non-refoulement* obligation of regional human rights law is of essence when considering their protection.

A single principle of *non-refoulement* does not exist, as it exists in different facets, depending on the various legal sources in which it is enshrined. As such, it varies with regard to its territorial scope, its content, the group of beneficiaries and the addressees of its obligatory nature.[4] Provisions of *non-refoulement*, either explicitly or implicitly phrased, can be found in a number of human rights treaties. Article 7 (a) of the International Covenant on Civil and Political Rights prohibits torture or cruel, inhumane treatment or punishment[5], Article 3 of the UN Convention against Torture and Other Cruel, Inhumane or Degrading Treatment or Punishment encompasses the prohibition against expulsion, return or extradition of a person to another state where there is fear of one of these, the African Charter on Human and People's Rights, the American Convention on Human Rights as well as the EU Charter of Fundamental Rights, to name the most prominent examples, enshrine versions of 'the principle' of *non-refoulement.*[6]

The principle of *non-refoulement*, in the context of mixed migration movements and increasingly restrictive border management measures, has resulted in more than one negative obligation not to return individuals to their home countries. It has become the most important first-stage and final protection instrument in the context of migration and refugeehood. It provides the basis a) to prohibit general return at the first moment a migrant or refugee encounters a European border[7] and b) to provide minimum protection for those not eligible or excluded from either refugee or subsidiary protection status. It is minimal in the sense that it entails the temporary negative obligation not to deport.

In contrast to the allocation of refugee or subsidiary protection status, in most countries, protection from expulsion varies considerably from the aforementioned protection status in terms of substance. Beneficiaries of complementary protection schemes have only a few basic positive rights, as their protection stems from a 'negative' obligation not to return, rather than from a 'positive' allocation of protection rights. This distinction becomes evident in relation to social security standards, lower standards of medical care, no options for family reunification and a lack of access to the labour market.[8]

4 Messineo, Francesco, 'Non-Refoulement Obligations in the Public International Law: Towards a New Protection Status?', in S. S. Juss (ed.), *The Ashgate Research Companion to Migration Law, Theory and Policy* (Ashgate, 2013), at 4.

5 See discussion of the Human Rights Committee in the General Comments No. 6 (2005), No. 31 (2004) and No. 20 (1992) and for a comparison of the different scope of application, Wouters, Kees, *International Legal Standards for the Protection from Refoulement* (Intersentia, 2009).

6 See Article 12 African Charter, Article 22 American Convention, Article 4 and 19 (2) EU Charter.

7 Strengthened by the prohibition of collective expulsion Article 4 of Protocol 4, minimum procedural standards for expulsion in Article 1 Protocol 7.

8 European Council on Refugees and Exiles, *Complementary Protection in Europe* (2009), available online at https://www.ecre.org/wp-content/uploads/2016/07/ECRE-Complementary-Protection-in-Europe_July-2009.pdf (last visited 1 August 2018), at 9.

Under European human rights law, the principle of *non-refoulement* is most prominently codified in the ECHR, albeit not explicitly in the pertinent provision itself, namely Article 3. That being said, the ECtHR's interpretation of the legal provision has created an implicit, but nonetheless, nowadays undisputed *non-refoulement* obligation. In various cases, the court has recognised that other Convention rights, namely Articles 2, 5 and 6 ECHR, also implicitly establish *non-refoulement* obligations. Violations of Article 6, for instance, would arise in exceptional cases, e.g. 'flagrant denial of justice', in a case of *refoulement*, as was established in *Othman v. UK*, a case concerning evidence obtained through torture.[9] In other cases concerning Articles 8 and 9, the bench argued that any violation would naturally be included in a violation of Article 3.[10] Despite the theoretical conceptualisation of *non-refoulement* in the other Articles, over the years the ECtHR has established Articles 2 and 3 as the most prominent foundations for a clear *non-refoulement* obligation. Article 2 reads "Everyone's right to life shall be protected by law" and Article 3, "No one shall be subjected to torture or to inhuman or degrading treatment or punishment". The principle of *non-refoulement* is considered to be an inherent part of both Articles:

> If article 3 may be engaged it is difficult to follow why, as a matter of logic, article 2 could be peremptorily excluded. There may well be cases where article 3 is not applicable but article 2 may be.[11]

While the *non-refoulement nature* is recognised as inherent in both Articles, Article 2 on its own has, so far, only been used successfully to prevent deportation in the case of *Bader*.[12] The only other cases were *Tatete v. Switzerland*,[13] in which a settlement was reached, and *D. v. UK*,[14] in which the ECtHR assessed the *non-refoulement* obligation following a deferral to Article 3. For these reasons, and since the *non-refoulement* jurisprudence of the court in the context of migration centres around Article 3, this Article and the respective case law are examined in detail. Firstly, the application to persons excluded from protection status in Europe, facing deportation to countries in conflict, is analysed, before the chapter turns to assessments of extraterritorial applications of the Convention. In this second step, it examines jurisdiction in the light of Article 1 ECHR beyond the states' territory, i.e. in cases of border control.

9 *Othman (Abu Qarada) v. The United Kingdom*, App. No. 8139/09, European Court of Human Rights (2012), at para. 282.

10 *N. v. Finland*, App. No. 38885/02, European Court of Human Rights (2005). In Z and T v UK, the court endorsed the stand taken by the House of Lords in the *Ullah* decision that "it would be difficult to visualise a case in which a flagrant violation of Article 9 would not also involve treatment in violation of Article 3", *Z and T v. The United Kingdom*, App. No. 27034/05, European Court of Human Rights (2006), at para. 7.

11 *Regina v. Special Adjudicator, Ex parte Ullah; Do (FC) v. Secretary of State for the Home Department, Lord Steyn*, [2004] UKHL 26, United Kingdom: House of Lords (2004), at para. 40.

12 *Bader and Others v. Sweden*, App. No. 13284/04, European Court of Human Rights (2005).

13 *Tatete v. Switzerland*, App. No. 41874/98, European Court of Human Rights (2000).

14 *D v. The United Kingdom*, App. No. 30240/96, European Court of Human Rights (1997).

4.2 The scope of the Convention's Article 3 of non-refoulement

Article 3 ECHR prohibits the return of anyone to a place where persons face a 'real and substantiated' risk of ill-treatment and thereby constrains the parties to the ECHR from expelling aliens from their state's territory.[15] In contrast to the 1951 Convention, the Article's personal scope of protection is not restricted to a distinct group, such as the refugee defined by Article 1 A (2) of the 1951 Convention, but grants protection for every person within the Convention's (extra-)territorial scope of application. Article 3 ECHR has been subject to several judgements by the ECtHR, clarifying the nature, scope and content of the prohibition, including in the context of conflict and violence.

4.2.1 The absolute nature of the prohibition

The political developments in Europe over the last years have shown that debates about migration and immigration policies mostly encompass considerations about national security. These have repeatedly been the reason for the closure of borders and the reactivation of border controls in the otherwise border-free Schengen area. Considerations of state sovereignty, domestic states of emergency and national security concerns in situations of a mass influx of migrants have even been enshrined as situations allowing for derogations, among others in chapter II, Articles 23 onwards of the Schengen Border Code on the Temporary Reintroduction of Internal Controls at Internal Borders. In cases in which derogations are permitted, it is important to identify the minimum and most fundamental protection standards. The ECHR's human rights obligation of *non-refoulement* is such a fundamental protection.[16]

Article 3 ECHR establishes a very broad, non-derogable prohibition against ill-treatment.[17] This is buttressed by Article 15 ECHR, concerning derogations in times of emergency, which highlights in paragraph 2 that "[n]o derogation [...] from Articles 3, 4 (paragraph 1) and 7 shall be made under this provision." Already in 1978, the court affirmed the non-derogable nature of Article 3 by stressing that

> the Convention prohibits in absolute terms torture and inhuman or degrading treatment or punishment, irrespective of the victim's conduct. [...] Article 3 makes no provisions for exception [...] there can be no derogation

15 Mole, Nuala and Meredith, Catherine, *Asylum and the European Convention on Human Rights* (5th ed., Council of Europe Publ, 2010), at 18ff.

16 Reidy, Aisling, *The Prohibition of Torture: A Guide to the Implementation of Article 3 of the European Convention on Human Rights. Human Rights Handbooks, No. 6* (2003), available online at http://www.refworld.org/docid/49f1829b2.html (last visited 1 August 2018), at 8.

17 *Chahal v. The United Kingdom*, App. No. 70/1995/576/662, European Court of Human Rights (1996), at para. 78ff. Mavronicola, Natasa, 'What is an 'Absolute Right'? Deciphering Absoluteness in the Context of Article 3 of the European Convention on Human Rights', 12 *Human Rights Law Review* (2013) 723, at 736f.

> therefrom even in the event of a public emergency threatening the life of the nation.[18]

Also, more recently, the ECtHR strongly reaffirmed the absolute nature explicitly in regard to the principle of *non-refoulement* established by Article 3. In the case of *Saadi v. Italy*, concerning the relevance of *non-refoulement* in the context of international terrorism, the Grand Chamber stated that while "States face immense difficulties [...] this must not call into question the absolute nature of article 3"[19].

In this regard, the contrast with the more restrictive Article 33 of the 1951 Convention and hence, the importance of a parallel human rights application, becomes apparent. The drafting history of the 1951 Convention reflects the drafters' assessment, as brought forward by a Dutch delegate, that "the Conference was in agreement with the interpretation that the possibility of mass migration across frontiers or of attempted mass migration was not covered by Art. 33."[20] Under the ECHR, however, no exceptions are permitted;[21] its *non-refoulement* prohibition is absolute and non-derogable in times of mass influx. It creates the fundamental and basic protection for asylum seekers before any status determination procedure commences. Nonetheless, states have repeatedly challenged, both politically and legally, the interpretation of Article 3 through their practices in the area of border control and through the expulsion of rejected asylum seekers. Therefore, in order to ensure legal certainty, it is essential to clarify the scope of the Article in such situations and to pursue the harmonisation of state practice with respect to expulsion procedures.

4.2.2 Treatment generally proscribed by the Convention's Article 3

Article 3 ECHR encompasses the prohibition of three elements, namely torture, inhumane and degrading treatment or punishment, which have been considered as distinct but related:

> It is plain that there may be treatment to which all these descriptions apply, for all torture must be inhumane and degrading treatment, and inhumane treatment also degrading.[22]

18 *The Republic of Ireland v. The United Kingdom*, App. No. 5310/71, European Court of Human Rights (1978), at para. 163.

19 *Saadi v. Italy*, App. No. 37201/06, European Court of Human Rights (2008), at para. 137.

20 Statement of Baron van Boetzelaer, the Netherlands, United Nations General Assembly, 'Conference of Plenipotentiaries on the Status of Refugees and Stateless Persons: Summary Record of the Thirty-fifth Meeting' (UN Doc. A/CONF.2/SR.35, 1951), at 21f.

21 United Nations Committee Against Torture, 'Gorki Ernesto Tapia Paez v. Sweden' (UN Doc. CAT/C/18/D/39/1996, 1997), at para. 14.5. Concerning Article 13 as implicitly prohibiting collective expulsion, Human Rights Committee, 'General Comment No. 15: The Position of Aliens Under the Covenant' (1986), at 18, para. 10.

22 *The Greek Case*, Appl. No. 3321/67, 3322/67, 3323/67 and 3344/67, Council of Europe; European Commission on Human Rights (1969) YB XII.

While Article 3 does not give any indication of a hierarchical relationship between the three, but addresses them on equal footing, courts have often analysed them as constituting a hierarchy:[23]

> The notion of inhuman treatment covers at least such treatment as deliberately causing severe suffering, mental or physical, which, in a particular situation, is unjustifiable. The word 'torture' is often used to describe inhuman treatment, which has a purpose, such as the obtaining of information or confession, or the infliction of punishment, and is generally an aggravated form of inhuman treatment. Treatment or punishment of an individual may be said to be degrading if it grossly humiliates him before others or drives him to act against his will or conscience.[24]

As the European Convention on Human Rights has been acknowledged as a 'living instrument',[25] its scope, including Article 3, has been developed further to reflect factual necessities of its protection. The prohibition of ill-treatment has also evolved and is not limited to an exhaustive and predefined conduct. "Certain acts which were classified differently in the past as inhuman and degrading treatment as opposed to torture could be classified differently in the future."[26] This assessment is considered to be of special importance, in particular in the context of migration, where different forms of prohibited ill-treatment can arise than those which had been envisaged at the time of drafting.

In contrast to the original Article 3 cases concerning the prohibition of torture, inhumane or degrading treatment or punishment, the ECtHR has refrained from distinguishing between the three distinct subject matters,[27] as "in the extraterritorial context, a prospective assessment is required [and] it is not always possible to determine whether the ill-treatment which may ensue in the receiving state will be sufficiently severe as to qualify as torture."[28] The ill-treatment, as prohibited under Article 3, has to attain "a minimum level of severity in order to be within

23 Tiedemann, Paul, 'Subsidiary Protection and the Function of Article 15(c) of the Qualification Directive', 31 *Refugee Survey Quarterly* (2012) 123, at 130.

24 *The Greek Case, supra* note 22.

25 *Selmouni v. France*, App. No. 25803/94, European Court of Human Rights (1999). William Rehnquist, 'The Notion of a Living Constitution' *Texas Law Review* (1976) 693. George Letsas, 'Strasbourg's Interpretive Ethic: Lessons for the International Lawyer', 21 *European Journal of International Law* (2010) 509. George Letsas, *The ECHR as a Living Instrument: Its Meaning and its Legitimacy* (2012), available online at https://ssrn.com/abstract=2021836 (last visited 1 August 2018).

26 *Selmouni v. France, supra* note 25, at para. 101.

27 *Chahal v. The United Kingdom, supra* note 17, at para. 79. *Mamatkulov and Askarov v. Turkey*, App. No. 46827/99 and 46951/99, European Court of Human Rights (2005), at para. 67. *Saadi v. Italy, supra* note 19, at para. 125. Schabas, William, *The European Convention on Human Rights* (Oxford University Press, 2015), at 195.

28 *Babar Ahmad and Others v. The United Kingdom*, App. No. 23027/07, 11749/08, 36742/08, 66911/09 and 67354/09, European Court of Human Rights (2012), at para. 170.

the scope of Art. 3 ECHR".[29] Similarly to the discussed assessments of refugee and subsidiary protection, an individual's vulnerabilities and predicaments are recognised as strong influences on the nature of the ill-treatment and its effects. For this reason, "[t]he assessment of this minimum is, in the nature of things, relative; it *depends on all the circumstances of the case*",[30] such as duration of the treatment, the nature of its execution, its physical or mental effects and/or personal attributes such as sex, age and state of health.[31] These individual circumstances have greatly influenced the court's assessment in *non-refoulement* cases, which is also reflected in its considerations concerning involuntary expulsion to countries in conflict.

4.2.3 The Convention's non-refoulement and countries in conflict

A variety of claimants, including persons from countries affected by conflict, have pursued Article 3 ECHR cases. While the Article itself neither entails an explicit or implicit reference to situations of violent conflict, the case law of the ECtHR shows the debate about forcible returns to countries in conflict. For these reasons, the court's reference to the concept of conflict and the potential incorporation of IHL as source of interpretation is taken into consideration in the following.

4.2.3.1 The actors and sources of ill-treatment

The classical state centricity of human rights law, with states and their organs as holders of the respective human rights obligation, could cause difficulties when one assesses conflict-related risk in the country of return. In relation to protection claims by persons fleeing conflict, two distinct developments concerning Article 3 ECHR are decisive: firstly, harm traditionally stems from human conduct. The acceptance of the conduct of non-state actors, prominently non-state armed groups, is a prerequisite for a comprehensive coverage of protection claims, otherwise many cases would remain unheard. Secondly, harm following conflict can arise from the broader conflict-related shutdown of social, medical and economic facilities. One must consider whether the scope of Article 3 equally covers these sources of harm.

While refugee and subsidiary protection both explicitly require human conduct as a source of (the risk of) ill-treatment, the ECHR itself is silent on the actors of ill-treatment. Nonetheless, the developing case law of the ECtHR has interpreted the scope in this regard. The following chapter analyses the various sources of conflict-related risk in the light of Article 3 and *non-refoulement.*

29 *The Republic of Ireland v. The United Kingdom, supra* note 18, at para. 162. Regular scenarios would for instance include the prohibition to return persons fleeing execution or death penalty. In this case for instance a Syrian applicant who was sentenced to death *in absentia*, *Bader and Others v. Sweden, supra* note 12.

30 *The Republic of Ireland v. The United Kingdom, supra* note 18, at 162.

31 See for instance *Vilvarajah and Others v. The United Kingdom*, App. No. 13163/87, 13164/87, 13165/87, 13447/87 and 13448/87, European Court of Human Rights (1991), at para. 107. *Yassar Hussain v. The United Kingdom*, App. No 8866/04, European Court of Human Rights (2006), at para. 53.

4.2.3.1.1 STATE AND NON-STATE ACTORS OF ILL-TREATMENT

The traditional case law on Article 3 focused on state-derived ill-treatment. The ECtHR follows a more general trend, which has the effect of detaching sources of harm from the state-centric approach.[32] Landmark cases, such as *Soering v. UK*, paved the way in interpreting the Convention state's obligation to protect individuals from such ill-treatment, since they addressed not only ill-treatment arising in the contemporary state of residence, but equally in the state of destination following expulsion or extradition. This line of argumentation, both with regard to state and non-state actors, has been pursued in the light of return to countries in conflict.

Two prominent, early cases from the ECtHR's discussion on non-state actor ill-treatment in relation to *non-refoulement* are *Ahmed v. Austria* and *H.L.R. v. France*. In *Ahmed*, the court regarded the situation in Somalia as a state of civil war, characterised by continued fighting for control over territory between different clans. It was first assessed that the risk of ill-treatment of the applicant would not stem from state conduct. The court further argued that, given the absolute character of Article 3, expulsion would not be "invalidated by the applicant's criminal conviction or the current lack of state authority in Somalia" and analysed the risk of ill-treatment by the different warring non-state parties of the civil war.[33]

In *H.L.R. v. France*, again the source of harm did not lie with state authorities, but rather arose in the context of drug trafficking. The French government argued that the expulsion of a Colombian who had been convicted for drug trafficking would not amount to a violation of Article 3 ECHR, as any danger upon return did not emanate from state actors.[34] The ECtHR did not follow that line of argumentation. The bench clarified how harm by non-state actors should be assessed. Firstly, the harm had to be real, not merely a possibility, secondly, it had to be severe, as in the meaning of Article 3, and thirdly, authorities in the country of return had to be unable or unwilling to preclude the risk:

> Owing to the absolute character of the right guaranteed, [...] Article 3 of the Convention [...] may also apply where the danger emanates from persons or groups of persons who are not public officials. However, it must be shown that the risk is real and that the authorities of the receiving State are not able to obviate the risk by providing appropriate protection.[35]

While the court has continuously strengthened the application of Article 3 ECHR to include non-state actors as a source of the proscribed ill-treatment, some extension of state responsibility for acts committed by non-state actors remains necessary to engage the Article's protection, i.e. the state's failure to

32 Nykänen, Eeva, *Fragmented State Power and Forced Migration* (Martinus Nijhoff Publishers, 2012), at 297. Wouters, Kees, *supra* note 5, at 244.

33 *Ahmed v. Austria*, App. No. 25964/94, European Court of Human Rights (1996), at para. 46.

34 *H.L.R. v. France*, App. No. 24573/94, European Court of Human Rights (1997), at para. 39.

35 *Id.*, at para. 40.

provide adequate protection against the prohibited treatment or punishment. This follows from the fact that the ECHR does not hold non-state actors accountable although it encompasses them as direct source of harm. Adequate protection could, for instance, mean preventive steps (not) taken in situations in which the authorities had or ought to have had knowledge of ill-treatment.[36]

These examples of cases, read in the light of the general positive development of jurisprudence concerning non-state actor ill-treatment, is a necessary precondition for the ECtHR's comprehensive examination of protection from return to countries in conflict and the various sources of harm arising in this context. When considering conflict-related risks of individuals, direct harm resulting from human conduct is the first thing that comes to mind. However, the broader consequences of violence, the breakdown of state governance, infrastructure, or the provision of the basic necessities for life for the affected population lead to further indirect harm.

4.2.3.1.2 NATURALLY OCCURRING HARM

Conflict in countries of origin is not solely characterised by direct harm caused by state and non-state actors, but can also be caused more indirectly by the shutdown of social, medical and economic facilities and a decay of the overall humanitarian situation. Interestingly, jurisprudence on Article 3 has considered this path. The second major development concerning conflict-related harm under Article 3 emanates from considerations about non-human sources of harm, i.e. 'naturally occurring harm'.[37] Here, the ECtHR's jurisprudence concerning the 'medical cases' will be considered and adapted to the conflict scenario. Naturally occurring harm originally gained prominence in relation to terminal diseases such as HIV/AIDS, in which the state itself can neither directly, nor indirectly, be held responsible for the harm. The most prominent and, so far only successful case of *non-refoulement* based on the expected violation of socio-economic rights in the receiving country is the case of *D. v. UK*. This case provides the cornerstone for any legal argument in favour of the prohibition of return to countries where the claimant fears that his or her socio-economic rights will be violated by naturally occurring harm. In *D. v. UK*, the scope of ill-treatment in the country of destination, St Kitts, was analysed. The ECtHR evaluated the level and quality of domestic health care systems as well as income and social security.[38] The exceptional circumstances in this particular case included poor medical conditions

36 *A v. The United Kingdom*, App. No. 100/1997/884/1096, European Court of Human Rights (1998). A v UK (1998), 27 EHRR, 611 or *Z and Others v. The United Kingdom*, App. No. 29392/95, European Court of Human Rights (2001), at para. 73.

37 The term is chosen as it has been used earlier with regard to the medical cases addressed here, which lay the foundation for the following argumentation. Naturally-occurring harm in this context not only covers harm caused as a direct result of human conduct but also, and in contrast to its original context (i.e. medical cases or natural disasters), the indirect effects of conflict and violence, including socio-economic deprivation.

38 *D v. The United Kingdom*, *supra* note 14, at 53f.

in St Kitts, no reliable access to a hospital bed and the resultant risks of further infection if the applicant, who was suffering from AIDS, were unable to access shelter and proper nutrition or palliative care. These circumstances were further aggravated by the lack of familial or social support and the general poor health and sanitation situation in the country. Taken together, a return would "subject him to acute mental and physical suffering".[39] The ECtHR stressed that

> the court must *reserve to itself sufficient flexibility to address the application of that article in other contexts which might arise.* It is not therefore prevented from scrutinising an applicant's claim under article 3 where *the source of the risk of proscribed treatment in the receiving country stems from factors which cannot engage either directly or indirectly the responsibility of the public authorities of that country, or which, taken alone, do not in themselves infringe the standards of that article.* To limit the application of article 3 in this manner would be to undermine the absolute character of its protection.[40]

In the light of the absolute character of the protection envisaged under Article 3, the ECtHR broadened its scope, firstly to harm that does not result from direct or indirect responsibilities of public authorities. Secondly, the article was held to be infringed by cumulative, individual forms of ill-treatment that would not, however, constitute violations on their own.

Despite this positive outcome and the general openness towards claims on the grounds of naturally occurring harm, the court established a high threshold of both "very exceptional circumstances" and "compelling humanitarian considerations" necessary to trigger Article 3.[41] Thus far, *D. v. UK* is the only judgement in which the court's assessment of the situation reached this threshold of extreme exceptional circumstances sufficiently serious to constitute a violation of Article 3 in case of return.

N. v. UK was a comparable case concerning the return of an HIV/AIDS infected person to Uganda. The ECtHR held, in contrast to *D. v. UK*, that the circumstances were not sufficiently exceptional so as to entail a violation of Article 3. The bench decided that the return of the applicant, as she was not in the last stages of illness and could find adequate care with her family in Uganda, was not sufficient to amount to a breach of Article 3. Distinguishing the case from their earlier decision in *D. v. UK*, the court applied the following general principles and opined that "[t]he fact that the applicant's circumstances, including his life expectancy, would be significantly reduced if he were to be removed from the contracting state is not sufficient in itself to give rise to breach of article 3."[42] They explicitly referred to the limits of protection of socio-economic

39 *Id.*, at 52.
40 *Id.*, at paras. 48f. (emphasis added by the author).
41 *Id.*, at 54.
42 *N. v. The United Kingdom*, App. No. 26565/05, European Court of Human Rights (2008), at para. 42.

rights under the ECHR as the treaty was "essentially directed to protect civil and political rights".[43] The bench stressed further that varying conditions in the expelling state and country of destination could not be balanced by the court:

> Advances in medical science, together with social and economic differences between countries, entail that the level of treatment available in the Contracting State and the country of origin may vary considerably. [...] Article 3 does not place an obligation on the Contracting State to alleviate such disparities through the provision.[44]

Similarly, in the latter case of *F. v. UK*, the court clearly emphasised that "[o]n a purely pragmatic basis, it cannot be required that an expelling Contracting State only return an alien to a country which is in full and effective enforcement of all the rights and freedoms set out in the Convention."[45]

While one can follow the court's argumentation concerning violations of socio-economic rights, in particular when considered cumulatively, as amounting to similar levels of ill-treatment as other forms of violations of civil and political rights, the inclusion of naturally occurring harm within the ambit of harms proscribed by Article 3 reflects the very progressive nature often found in ECtHR judgements. It is probably the case that, upon reflection on contemporary state practice and willingness, as well as practicability in implementing these interpretations, the court has restricted its theoretical progressive approach to the necessity of a threshold of extreme circumstances. So far, only the case of *D. v. UK* has successfully established protection from forcible return to countries in cases of naturally occurring harm, including the risk of the most severe violations of socio-economic rights. Ultimately, however, what can be observed in the judgements discussed above is a strong reluctance to find violations of Article 3 for both socio-economic matters and on the basis of naturally occurring harm. As such, the ECtHR's theoretical openness will probably not be followed by significant implications for state practice. Restrictive state interests might still be reconcilable with the high

43 *Id.*, at para. 44.

44 *Ibid.*

45 *F. v. The United Kingdom*, App. No. 17341/03, European Court of Human Rights (2004), at 12. Similarly, in 2011, the court delivered its judgment in *Yoh-Ekale Mwanje v. Belgium* concerning the detention of an HIV woman from Cameroon, and although her Article 3 complaint was dismissed, 6 out of 7 judges called for the Grand Chamber to revise the ruling in N. v. UK. The extreme severity of the threshold was not considered consistent with the object and purpose of Article 3, establishing a fundamental human right, *Yoh-Ekale Mwanje v. Belgium*, Application No. 10486/10, European Court of Human Rights (2011), at 6. In *Bensaid v. UK*, a comparable threshold to that of *D. v. UK* was again not reached. This case examined the refoulement of a schizophrenic applicant and his return to Algeria. The judgment states the circumstances were "less certain and more speculative". However, also in this case, the separate opinion stressed that there was "considerable hesitation" and "powerful and compelling humanitarian considerations in the present case which would justify and merit reconsideration by the national authorities of the decisions to remove the applicant to Algeria". *Bensaid v. The United Kingdom*, App. No. 44599/98, European Court of Human Rights (2001).

threshold and resulting isolated cases of application for some time. Nonetheless, the ECtHR has taken a highly progressive approach to *non-refoulement* cases. This has laid further groundwork for a comprehensive evaluation of claims against forcible return to countries affected by violence and conflict.

4.2.3.2 The risk of ill-treatment and the necessity of being singled-out

Expulsion may give rise to claims under Article 3 where substantial grounds have been shown for believing that the applicant faces a real risk of being subjected to torture or inhumane and degrading treatment in the destination country.[46] In *Soering*, the ECtHR had already established that a "mere possibility of ill-treatment is not enough", but an aggravated risk must be evident.[47] Comparable to the debate on refugee and subsidiary protection, the ECtHR also concerned itself with risk considerations in the context of generalised situations of violence, in particular the relevance of the risk, a different risk, for the specific individual applicant.

The case of *Vilvarajah and others v. UK* has, for some years, led the interpretation in this context. The introduction of the 'Vilvarajah criterion' has severely destabilised the application of Article 3 to persons fleeing countries in conflict and violence, as it opened up the discussion on the necessary level of individualisation of the claimant's risk in relation to others. Sri Lanka, as the claimants' country of origin, was regarded as a country negatively affected by "civil disturbances"[48] that had direct consequences for its population. The Vilvarajah criterion introduced by the ECtHR established the necessity of a 'special distinguishing feature' of the claimant, setting him or her apart from others in the same context of conflict.[49] Being at risk of ill-treatment, but 'only' in the same way as others in the situation, would not trigger the application of Article 3. With this judgement, the personal nature of the risk and the singling-out of the victim from the general population became constitutive criteria for subsequent Article 3 risk assessments. In its judgement in 1991, the court ruled that the claimants would not face a real risk of violation of Article 3 when forcibly returned.[50]

> The evidence before the court concerning the background of the applicants, as well as the general situation, *does not establish that their personal position was any worse than the generality of other members of the Tamil community or other young male Tamils who were returning to their country* [...] mere possibility of ill-treatment [...] is not sufficient [...] there existed *no special*

46 *Cruz Varas and Others v. Sweden*, App. No. 15576/89, European Court of Human Rights (1991), at 69f.

47 *Soering v. The United Kingdom*, App. No. 14038/88, European Court of Human Rights (1989), at 94.

48 *Vilvarajah and Others v. The United Kingdom, supra* note 31, at para. 110.

49 *Id.*, at para. 111f.

50 *Id.*, at para. 115.

> *distinguishing features* in their cases that could or ought to have enabled the Secretary of State to foresee that they would be treated in this way.[51]

Venkadajealasarma v. the Netherlands also decided upon the threat to Tamils in Sri Lanka. In this case, the bench upheld that risks stemming from situations of conflict and violence in the country did not necessarily lead to exposure to a real risk of proscribed ill-treatment under Article 3. Also, in the same year in *H.L.R. v. France*, which concerned the risk for a claimant from Sri Lanka which stemmed from drug trafficking violence, the court denied that a violation of Article 3 would result from the general situation of violence in the event of deportation.[52]

The ECtHR, however, has since then changed its ruling with regards to the determination of special distinguishing features of claimants in the context of conflict. The *Salah Sheekh v. the Netherlands* and *Saadi v. Italy* judgements are examples of this change concerning the involuntary return of claimants to countries in conflict. Of essence in both cases was the fact that the respective claimants were members of groups systematically exposed to ill-treatment in their country of origin. In these specific cases, the court decided that the requirement of individual claimants' special distinguishing features would not need to be proven.[53]

In 2007, the case of *Salah Sheekh* examined the circumstances of a member of the Somali Ashraf minority. When considering the generally unsafe situation for this specific minority and minorities in general, the court departed from the formerly established Vilvarajah criterion. The threshold for showing special distinguishing features which set the applicant apart from others in the same context was clearly lowered:

> The court would add that, in its opinion, *the applicant cannot be required to establish the existence of further special distinguishing features concerning him personally* in order to show that he was, and continues to be, personally at risk. [...] It might render the protection offered by that provision illusory if, in addition to the fact that he belongs to the Ashraf [...], the applicant be required to show the existence of further special distinguishing features.[54]

The same argumentation was subsequently employed in *Saadi v. Italy*:

> In cases where an applicant alleges that he or she is a member of a group systematically exposed to a practice of ill-treatment, the court considers that the protection of Article 3 of the Convention enters into play when the applicant established where necessary on the basis if the sources mentioned

51 *Id.*, at paras. 248ff. (emphasis added by the author).

52 *Venkadajalasarma v. The Netherlands*, App No. 58510/00, European Court of Human Rights (2004), at para. 68. and *H.L.R. v. France, supra* note 34, at para. 41.

53 *Salah Sheekh v. The Netherlands*, App. No. 1948/04, European Court of Human Rights (2007), at para. 148.

54 *Ibid.* (Emphasis added by the author)

> in the previous paragraph, that there are serious reasons to believe in the existence of the practice in question and his or her membership of the group concerned.[55]

Between the early case law of 1991 and the shift seen in *Salah Sheekh* in 2007, the requirement that the individual applicant be singled out as being in particular danger was upheld. The claimant needed to substantiate the claim that he or she, in contrast to others in the same or comparable situation, faced a higher risk. The *Salah Sheek* and *Saadi* judgements revised this aggravated risk, assessing that, if the claimant belongs to a group that is ill-treated, such as a minority, he or she would not need to present evidence of his or her personal additional features that aggravate the risk over that of other members of such group. This balancing element closely resembles the sliding-scale test that was established by the Court of Justice of the European Union (CJEU) in the *Elgafaji* judgement (and part of the discussion of section 3.4.1.7). The CJEU has established the need to show special factors particular to his or her personal circumstances. For both assessments, when the level of violence was not exceptional, the individual and the particular situation would need to be considered. For the ECtHR, however, membership of a group that is systematically exposed to ill-treatment already fulfils this requirement.

4.2.3.3 Determining conflict and the level of generalised violence

The ECtHR, when considering claims of *non-refoulement* against forcible return to countries in conflict, faces more abstract legal questions concerning the relationship with International Humanitarian Law (IHL) in the interpretation of the ECHR. Is the classification of an armed conflict as being either of an international or a non-international nature, per IHL, a prerequisite for the assessment under Article 3? Similarly to the previous chapter, the question is whether the ECtHR has established its own unique definition and classification of conflict, or that defining armed conflict according to certain criteria is actually irrelevant for Article 3 claims.

4.2.3.3.1 THE ECHR'S VIEW ON INTERNATIONAL HUMANITARIAN LAW AND THE CLASSIFICATION OF CONFLICTS

In contrast to the CJEU's task of clarifying the interpretation of the explicit 'armed conflict' terminology under Article 15 (c) of the (Recast) Qualification Directive (QD), the ECtHR has no specific conflict-related provisions to refer to when evaluating *non-refoulement* claims brought under Article 3 ECHR. Nonetheless, factual realities have required the court to examine appeals against forcible

55 *Saadi v. Italy, supra* note 19, at para. 132. *Y v. Russia*, App. No. 20113/07, European Court of Human Rights (2008). *Muminov v. Russia*, App. No. 42502/06, European Court of Human Rights (2008).

returns to countries affected by conflict and/or different levels of violence. Given this background, one needs to consider the relevance of IHL in the determination of conflicts in the ECtHR setting. Conflicts or other situations of violence, ranging from the conflicts between Cyprus and Turkey, between Turkey and the Workers' Party of Kurdistan, concerning North Atlantic Treaty Organisation (NATO) engagement in former Yugoslavia, Iraq, Russia or the Ukraine have, so far, all been issues that concerned the court. In most cases, it was considered whether a combination of both human rights law and IHL should be applied, or alternatively whether a choice should be made between the two frameworks. Further, the question of how to assess single attacks or rights violations under either field of law were in focus. For the purposes of this chapter, however, the usage of IHL definitions and criteria of classification by the court is of primary interest in the matter of forcible returns to conflict zones. Prior case law suggests that the ECtHR has refrained from classifying situations of violence as Non-International Armed Conflicts (NIACs)[56] and, in doing so, seldom has occasion to resort to IHL explicitly.

The court's last strand of jurisprudence concerning its Chechnyan and Kurdish cases reflects its consideration of conflict for matters of *non-refoulement.* Most of these former cases concern assessments of violations of the right to life under Article 2 ECHR in situations of violence, potentially in NIACs. What becomes obvious is that the court has consistently refrained from classifying violent situations according to IHL terminology, arguably to circumvent involvement in the political tug-of-war.[57] The application of either humanitarian or human rights law, complementary or using the former to the exclusion of the latter, however, is essential for determinations of the legality of violations of the right to life. This is because the approaches under the two distinct fields of law diverge significantly. And yet, the court had positioned itself only indirectly. In both the Chechnyan and Kurdish situations, Russia and Turkey, respectively, rejected the classification of the conflicts as IHL-governed NIACs, but referred to them as internal anti-terror law enforcement operations. Additionally, they did not engage derogations in accordance with Article 15 (II) ECHR for cases of armed conflict. That left the court to decide whether to make use of IHL or not. In two prominent Kurdish cases before the ECtHR,[58] the court seemed to refer to IHL targeting assessments, but without explicitly naming the principle of precaution,[59] the principle of proportionality in attack and prohibitions on

56 Abresch, William, 'A Human Rights Law of Internal Armed Conflict: The European Court of Human Rights in Chechnya', 16 *European Journal of International Law* (2005) 741, at 741.

57 Heintze, Hans-Joachim, 'Zum Verhältnis von Mernschenrechtsschutz und humanitärem Völkerrecht', 16 *Humanitäres Völkerrecht - Informationsschriften* (2003) 172, at 187.

58 Simsek, Cilem, 'Kurden- und Tschechenenfälle vor dem Europäischen Gerichtshof für Menschenrechte', 28 *Humanitäres Völkerrecht - Informationsschriften* (2015) 171, at 172ff.

59 The court, for instance, held that "[the responsibility of the State] may also be engaged where they fail to take all feasible precautions in the choice of means and methods of a security operation mounted against an opposing group with a view to avoiding and, in any event, to minimising, incidental loss of civilian life." *Ergi v. Turkey*, App. No. 66/1997/850/1057, European Court of Human Rights (1998), at para. 79. The indirect and close link to the principle of precaution

indiscriminate attacks.[60] Similar, tacit consideration of IHL principles can be found in the cases concerning Chechnya.[61]

While some scholars argue that the close terminological proximity to IHL principles or definitions in the ECtHR's wording does not constitute the actual use of IHL,[62] others consider it an application of IHL as *lex specialis,* albeit lacking direct reference.[63] These judgements provide an interesting basis for further examinations of the application of and relationship between IHL and human rights law in the jurisprudence of the court. For the question here, the focus lies on the court's practice in using IHL. The cases concerning Article 2 have illustrated that the ECtHR, even when appearing to apply IHL examinations, has refrained from directly relying on this specialised field of law. Even more so, the court has refrained from engaging in a classification debate on the occurrence of IHL-governed armed conflicts. In particular, the public announcement of NIACs has not lost any political brisance since 1949 and the regional human rights court, correctly, has not got itself further involved in a debate about the application of a different field of law beyond its own jurisdiction.

Instead, the ECtHR has consistently based its decisions on the particular field of law and treaty upon which its jurisdiction is based, namely the ECHR and its jurisprudence. IHL as such is not its applicable field of law. Nonetheless, in certain individual cases concerning armed conflict, it should be recognised that the court has taken some guidance from IHL principles. However, this is not representative of its usual practice in cases concerning *non-refoulement* to countries in conflict. The threshold for determining prohibitions of return to countries in conflict instead follows an assessment of the divergent levels of violence in the country or parts of the country. Of interest and need for further examination is whether the court implicitly uses IHL criteria to assess the level of violence and conflict, or employs a unique, solely human rights-governed perspective. This matter is addressed in the examination below.

---

as enshrined in Article 57 II (a) (ii) AP I is obvious: "With respect to attacks, the following precautions shall be taken: (a) those who plan or decide upon an attack shall: (ii) take all feasible precautions in the choice of means and methods of attack with a view to avoiding, and in any event to minimizing, incidental loss of civilian life [...]".

60 Cases of indiscriminate attacks and prohibition thereof are among others, *Benzer and Others v. Turkey*, App. No. 23502/06, European Court of Human Rights (2013).

61 As examples of the courts consideration, *Isayeva v. Russia; Yusupova v. Russia; Bazayeva v. Russia*, App No. 57947/00, 57948/00 and 57949/00, European Court of Human Rights (2005), at para. 157. *Isayeva v. Russia*, App. No. 57950/00, European Court of Human Rights (2005), at para. 198.

62 Moir, Lindsay, 'The European Court of Human Rights and International Humanitarian Law', in R. Kolb and G. Gaggioli (eds.), *Research Handbook on Human Rights and Humanitarian Law* (Edward Elgar, 2013), at 481. Abresch, William, *supra* note 56, at 746.

63 See prominently in this regard, Krieger, Heike, 'A Conflict of Norms: The Relationship Between Humanitarian Law and Human Rights Law in the ICRC Customary Law Study', 11 *Journal of Conflict and Security Law* (2006) 265, at 265.

4.2.3.3.2 EXAMINING THE INTENSITY OF GENERALISED VIOLENCE

In the 1990s in its *H.L.R.* judgement concerning deportation to Colombia, the ECtHR still took the position that it "can but note the general situation of violence existing in the country of destination. It considers, however, that this circumstance would not in itself entail, in the event of deportation, a violation of Article 3".[64] In various subsequent judgements, this strict position has been softened and situations of generalised violence considered, albeit without determining a level of violence high enough to prohibit expulsion.[65] Cases in which the court reviewed situations of violence in countries of origin were *Sultani*,[66] and the referred cases of *Afghanistan*, *Thampibillai* and *Venkadajalasarma* concerning Sri Lanka. In regard to Sri Lanka, the court considered the local context in more detail and held that, due to the improvement in the general security situation and the progress made in the peace process, the situation at the given time would not deliver substantial grounds for believing that the applicants would face a real risk of ill-treatment contrary to Article 3, were they to be returned.[67] The court at that point had never ascertained that the threshold was reached, despite its openness towards generalised violence arising in conflict as a ground to halt deportation.

In *NA v. UK*, concerning the feared ill-treatment of a Sri Lankan by Tamil Tigers, the court found that a situation of violence and conflict in the country of origin would normally not be a violation of Article 3.[68] However, it proceeded and emphasised that preclusion from return in case of widespread violence could, in theory, be covered by the Article:

> [T]he Court has never excluded the possibility that a general situation of violence in a country of destination will be of a sufficient level of intensity as to entail that any removal to it would necessarily breach Article 3 of the Convention.[69]

Violence of such severity that it functions as the sole trigger for a *non-refoulement* case could only be affirmed in the most extreme and extraordinary circumstances.[70] The level of violence in this case would need to be exceptionally high:

> [T]he Court would adopt such an approach only in the most extreme cases of general violence, where there was a real risk of ill-treatment simply by virtue of an individual being exposed to such violence on return.[71]

64 *H.L.R. v. France*, *supra* note 34, at para. 41.

65 *Müslim v. Turkey*, App. No. 53566/99, European Court of Human Rights (2005), at para. 70.

66 *Sultani v. France*, App. No. 45223/05, European Court of Human Rights (2007), at para. 67.

67 *Thampibillai v. The Netherlands*, App. No. 61350/00, European Court of Human Rights (2004), at paras. 64f. *Venkadajalasarma v. The Netherlands, supra* note 52, at paras. 66f.

68 *NA. v. The United Kingdom*, App. No. 25904/07, European Court of Human Rights (2008), at para. 114.

69 *Id.*, at paras. 115ff.

70 *Id.*, at paras. 114 f. *Salah Sheekh v. The Netherlands, supra* note 53 (emphasis added by the author).

71 *NA. v. The United Kingdom, supra* note 68, at paras. 115ff.

Laying its theoretical groundwork, the court, in its renowned 2011 case of *Sufi and Elmi*, finally pursued its preparatory earlier paths. It followed the applicant's argument "that the indiscriminate violence in Mogadishu was of a sufficient level of intensity to pose a real risk to the life or person of any civilian in the capital"[72] and against the background of various human rights and news reports, which "overwhelmingly indicates that the level of violence in Mogadishu is of sufficient intensity to pose a real of treatment reaching Article 3 threshold to anyone in the capital".[73] On this basis, it ruled that removal to Somalia would be a violation of Article 3 ECHR.

The *Sufi and Elmi* case was again revived and reflected upon two years later in *K.A.B. v. Sweden*, which again concerned the comparable question of return to Somalia. The court emphasised the importance of assessing the situation in the country at the time of the judgement and therefore considered how circumstances in Somalia had changed, if at all.[74] In doing so, the court acknowledged the ongoing fragile security situation in Mogadishu, but it argued that as Al Shabbab was no longer in power and the general situation had improved, it was time to take a new view:

> Lastly, the Court notes that the applicant does not belong to any group that is at risk of being targeted by al-Shabaab and that allegedly he has a home in Mogadishu, where his wife lives. Having regard to the above, the court concludes that the applicant has failed to make it plausible that he would face a real risk of being killed or subjected to ill-treatment upon return to Somalia. Consequently, his deportation to that country would not involve a violation of Article 2 or 3 of the Convention.[75]

The judgements represent the ECtHR's analysis of *non-refoulement* and its risk assessment in the context of violence. While the general assessment has changed throughout its jurisprudence and, more recently, the court has recognised generalised situations of violence as a possible sole ground for prohibiting involuntary return in the most extreme circumstances, it has not defined its assessment criteria clearly.

The ongoing conflict in Syria has also fuelled the debate. The first case concerning the assessment of Syria under the ECHR was the case of *L.M. and Others v. Russia*, which addressed violations of Article 2 and/or 3 ECHR when expelling two Syrian nationals and a stateless Palestinian who had had their habitual residence in Syria. All three claimants had entered Russia in 2013. The court referred to the *Sufi and Elmi* case for guidance in assessing the intensity of the conflict in the country of return.[76] It underlined that, while not exhaustive,

72 *Sufi and Elmi v. The United Kingdom*, App. No. 8319/07 and 11449/07, European Court of Human Rights (2011), at para. 241.

73 *Id.*, at para. 248.

74 *K.A.B. v. Sweden*, App. No. 886/11, European Court of Human Rights (2013), at paras. 87–91.

75 *Id.*, at paras. 96f.

76 "[F]irst, whether the parties to the conflict were either employing methods and tactics of warfare which increased the risk of civilian casualties or directly targeting civilians; secondly, whether

the criteria provided the appropriate yardstick to assess violence. The ECtHR observed that it had not been concerned with the Syrian conflict, particularly due to the fact that most countries have, upon their own discretion, adopted non-return policies in relation to Syria. In reference to the United Nations High Commissioner for Refugees' (UNHCR) and the UN reports on Syria and, in view of the facts that the applicants originated from Aleppo and Damascus, two particularly affected cities, that their relatives had been killed and that the stateless refugee was particularly vulnerable, there was enough evidence to conclude that their return would violate Articles 2 and 3 of the Convention.[77]

In the case of *H.S. and Others v. Cyprus* of 2015, the ECtHR examined claims by a group of Syrian nationals of Kurdish origin and two stateless Kurds who had been denied protection status in Greece.[78] Here, the court considered whether Article 3 was violated in the case of expulsion to Syria. The deportation of the applicants had taken place in 2010 before the so-called Syrian uprisings which had preceded the start of the conflict. Furthermore, the applicants had not been able to substantiate any *sur place* claims for activities conducted in Cyprus. Therefore, the court held that:

> at the relevant time there was no indication that the general situation in Syria for Kurds was so serious that the return of the applicants would constitute, in itself, a violation of Article 3 of the Convention (para.275).

The ECtHR has, in recent years, clearly adopted a conflict-sensitive approach to Article 3 assessments. This assessment does not include a classification of conflicts comparable to an IHL approach as such, but centres on the level of violence in the country of return and the subsequent risk for the claimant. In this regard, the court has opened up the possibility of precluding return, regardless of the claimant's special vulnerabilities or possible exposure to targeted ill-treatment. If the level of violence reaches an exceptionally high threshold of general violence

---

the use of such methods and/or tactics was widespread among the parties to the conflict; thirdly, whether the fighting was localised or widespread; and finally, the number of civilians killed, injured and displaced as a result of the fighting", *AM & AM (Armed Conflict: Risk Categories) Somalia v. Secretary of State for the Home Department*, [2008] UKAIT 00091, United Kingdom: Asylum and Immigration Tribunal / Immigration Appellate Authority (2009), at para. 241.

77 *L.M. and Others v. Russia*, App. No. 40081/14, 40088/14 and 40127/14, European Court of Human Rights (2015), at paras. 123ff. In reference to the ECtHR assessment on Syria, see for instance the case of *X v. State Migration Service of Ukraine*, Case 815/3681/13-a, Ukraine: Odessa Administrative Court of Appeal (2013). Here the Appellate Court referred to the criteria used by the ECtHR to conclude that the intensity of violence in Syria would preclude forcible returns. Concerning the appeal against the dangers of chain refoulement from the UK to Algeria and from there to Syria as violation of Article 3, see *RR (Refugee - Safe Third Country) Syria v. Secretary of State for the Home Department*, [2010] UKUT 422 (IAC), United Kingdom: Upper Tribunal (Immigration and Asylum Chamber) (2010).

78 *H.S. and Others v. Cyprus*, App. No. 41753/10, 41786/10, 41793/10, 41794/10, 41796/10, 41799/10, 41807/10, 41811/10, 41812/10, 41815/10, 41820/10, 41824/10, 41919/10 and 41921/10, European Court of Human Rights (2015).

that the person would be exposed to simply by being present, returns would be in violation of Article 3. This approach can be seen as a practical reflection of the dangers arising in situations of conflict and violence, in which the individual and his or her situation might have neither increased nor decreased chances of being harmed. It is simply the individual's mere presence in the conflict or violence context that gives rise to such a claim. The high threshold of violence is again the practical limitation of the court which is set to avoid stretching the burden of host states, since generally the responsibility to protect from violence lies with the home state. In this context, it will be interesting to follow up on the contemporary debate and practice of states in returning rejected asylum seekers from Afghanistan, which increased in 2017. Given the federal structure of Germany, for instance, the common position on returning persons to Afghanistan or safe areas in Afghanistan has come under fire by some federal states that consider the level of violence in Afghanistan to be too high to proceed with involuntary returns. So far, these decisions are taken in a political arena, but legal claims on the national and regional levels are likely to follow. They will again offer the chance to clarify the court's approach to the assessment of suspensions from return to violence and conflict.

4.2.3.3.3 GENERALISED VIOLENCE OF A MOST EXTREME NATURE

In the ECtHR's jurisprudence concerning countries in conflict, determination of the intensity of violence is at the centre of the analysis.[79] In this regard and similarly to the CJEU, the court has worked with different indicators in order to assess the level of violence.[80] To determine what level of violence is necessary to preclude an applicant's involuntary return, it has developed two different

79 General developments in recent jurisprudence with regard to Article 3 were the rigorous scrutiny of the examination characterised by the obligation of the expelling state to verify the authenticity of core documents, *Singh and Others v. Belgium*, App. No. 33210/11, European Court of Human Rights (2012), at 104. See also Art. 4(1) QD and *M. M. v. Minister for Justice, Equality and Law Reform, Ireland, Attorney General*, C-277/11, Court of Justice of the European Union (2012). An obligation to examine medical claims and attach significant weight to medical findings, in particular concerning potential cases of torture was discusses, *R.C. v. Sweden*, App. No. 41827/07, European Court of Human Rights (2010), at 53 ff. The obligation to gather COI (reliable and objective other than domestic sources) which would be applied in the individual case was addressed in *M.S.S. v. Belgium and Greece*, App. No. 30696/09, European Court of Human Rights (2011), at para. 359. and *Salah Sheekh v. The Netherlands, supra* note 53, at para.136.

80 *Saadi v. Italy, supra* note 19, at para. 142. The 'close scrutiny' with which the court must make its assessment covers an analysis of reliable information from reliable sources, including UNHCR, human rights organisations such as Human Rights Watch or Amnesty International to consider past and the risk of potential ill-treatment, the situation in the country of origin and the possibility of an IFA, or chain refoulement risk. "(I)t must be satisfied that the assessment made by the authorities of the Contracting State is adequate and sufficiently supported by domestic materials as well as by materials originating from other reliable and objective sources such as, for instance, other Contracting or non-Contracting States, agencies of the United Nations and reputable non-governmental organisations." *Salah Sheekh v. The Netherlands, supra* note 53, at para. 136.

approaches that will be referred to here as 'the predominant-harm approach' and 'the exceptionality approach'. The judgements that gave rise to these two assessment approaches are the cases of *MSS v. Belgium and Greece* and *N. v. UK*. Both approaches, which originally did not concern violence in the applicants' home countries, were later transferred to cases concerning (involuntary) return to countries in conflict and the associated risks.

In *Salah Sheekh* in 2007, the ECtHR had held that socio-economic and humanitarian conditions in the country of destination do not have a decisive influence on the substantiation of an Article 3 violation.[81] The 2008 case of *N. v. UK* deviated from this consideration, albeit restricting its theoretical openness with an exceptionally high threshold. The case is part of the court's aforementioned 'medical cases' whose reasoning was later transferred to wider considerations on living conditions in countries of return. The court famously stated that, despite the ECHR's emphasis on the protection of civil and political rights, socio-economic rights violations were not outside its scope:

> The fact that the applicant's circumstances, including his life expectancy, would be significantly reduced if he were to be removed from the Contracting State is not sufficient in itself to give rise to breach of Article 3 [...] In the D. v. the United Kingdom case the very exceptional circumstances were that the applicant was critically ill and appeared to be close to death, could not be guaranteed any nursing or medical care in his country of origin and had no family there willing or able to care for him or provide him with even a basic level of food, shelter or social support. *The court does not exclude that there may be other very exceptional cases where the humanitarian considerations are equally compelling*.[82]

This judgement is one of the few that take into account the humanitarian conditions in the country of return. Following the quoted argumentation, the court found that the expulsion of the Somali asylum seeker would constitute a violation of Article 3, since returning a member of the Ashraf minority to the unsafe areas of Somalia rendered exposure to ill-treatment a foreseeable risk and not a mere possibility.

The second main approach to the assessment of living conditions stems from the case of *MSS v. Belgium and Greece*. In this case, the compatibility of the Dublin II Regulation with the ECHR, concerning transfers of asylum seekers to Greece, was at issue. In this regard, the court assessed, among other things, the applicant's living conditions in Greece and characterised these as involving serious deprivation. Since the asylum seeker was forced to live on the streets for several months, he was "unable to cater for his most basic needs: food, hygiene and a place to live".[83] Additionally, he had been attacked and robbed and his situation was considered unlikely to improve in a reasonably foreseeable time-

81 *Id.*, at 136ff.

82 *N. v. The United Kingdom, supra* note 42, at paras. 42f. (emphasis added by the author).

83 *M.S.S. v. Belgium and Greece, supra* note 79, at para. 254.

frame.[84] In reference to its prior decision in *Budina v. Russia*, the court held that the state's responsibility was engaged under Article 3 when an applicant, wholly dependent on state support, was confronted by government indifference in a situation of serious deprivation which was incompatible with human dignity.[85] These considerations led the court to find, among others, a violation of Article 3 by Greece due to the serious deficiencies in its asylum procedures which led to the hardship in which the applicant had been forced to live, as well as violations of Article 3 by Belgium, which was responsible for transferring the applicant to Greece and had knowingly exposed him to the ill-treatment.[86] These two approaches developed by the court have subsequently shaped its analysis of contemporary circumstances in countries of return, including those affected by violence and conflict.

In *Sufi and Elmi*, the court was confronted with a deteriorating humanitarian situation of a comparable severity to the ongoing conflict in Somalia and Kenya. The court considered sources of ill-treatment to develop indicators for the assessment of the level of violence in those countries. In this context, it turned to criteria that had been identified by the UK Asylum and Immigration Tribunal (AIT) in the case of *AM and AM (Somalia)*.[87] The ECtHR's reliance on national decisions for guidance illustrates an example of vertical judicial dialogue between the European and domestic level which has been for particular relevance in asylum cases.[88] The criteria identified are as follows:

- Whether the conflict parties were employing methods and tactics of war that increase the risk of civilian casualties or directly target civilians;
- Whether these methods and tactics were widespread among the parties;
- Whether the fighting was widespread or localised; and
- The number of civilians killed, injured or displaced as a result of the fighting.

The court further underlined that "[...] these criteria are not to be seen as an exhaustive list to be applied to all future cases [...] they form an appropriate yardstick by which to assess the level of violence".[89] The range of indicators represents a broader assessment of the consequences of conflict and violence on individuals which not only takes into account the direct physical effects associated with conflict, but also indirect effects resulting from the more general disintegration of the state's structures.[90]

84 *Ibid.*

85 *Antonina Dmitriyevna Budina v. Russia*, App. No. 45603/05, European Court of Human Rights (2009).

86 *M.S.S. v. Belgium and Greece, supra* note 79, at 100 and 107ff.

87 *Sufi and Elmi v. The United Kingdom, supra* note 72, at para. 226. See further Edwards, Alice, 'Human Security and the Rights of Refugees: Transcending Territorial and Disciplinary Borders', 30 *Michigan Journal of International Law* (2009) 763, at 763.

88 Extensively Baldinger, Dana, *Vertical Judicial Dialogues in Asylum Cases* (Brill, 2015).

89 *Sufi and Elmi v. The United Kingdom, supra* note 72, at para. 241.

90 *AM & AM (Armed Conflict: Risk Categories) Somalia v. Secretary of State for the Home Department, supra* note 76.

In the case at hand, the situation in refugee camps in Somalia, as well as in the neighbouring Kenya, were evaluated as so poor that deportation would be intolerable. In more detail, the court distinguished between, firstly, the dire humanitarian situation attributable to poverty or to a lack of resources caused by natural phenomena such as drought and, secondly, the humanitarian crisis that was caused predominantly by the direct and indirect actions of the parties to the conflict. In this regard, the court considered not only the physical integrity of persons, but also personal dignity when discussing the effects of violence on individuals. It took into account a wide range of qualitative and quantitative factors in order to create a comprehensive assessment of the risks faced by the applicants upon return.

When evaluating the background information, the court held that it was not the effects of naturally occurring harm but rather the deliberate actions and inaction of the multiple actors in the conflict, including the Ethiopian forces and Al-Shabaab, which caused the humanitarian crisis. These included the indiscriminate methods of warfare, the resulting widespread displacement and social, political and economic downfall. These were further aggravated by the fact that Al-Shabaab denied access to humanitarian organisations to provide aid to the affected civilians. The court applied its predominant-harm approach from *MSS* to the examination of the situation of violence in Somalia.

> *If the dire humanitarian conditions in Somalia were solely or even predominantly attributable to poverty or to the state's lack of resources to deal with a naturally occurring phenomenon, such as a drought, the test in* N. v. the United Kingdom *may well have been considered to be the appropriate one.* However, it is clear that while drought has contributed to the humanitarian crisis, the crisis is predominantly due to the direct and indirect actions of the parties to the conflict.[91]

The court held that returning an applicant to a country affected by drought would not generally amount to a violation of Article 3, but if the 'predominant harm' is caused by the actions of the parties to the conflict, then it is not necessary to apply the exceptionally high threshold test. For the predominant harm approach, the humanitarian situation, however, would need to be characterised by an inability to cater for the most basic needs, vulnerability to ill-treatment and the weak prospects of the situation improving in the near future. In *Sufi and Elmi*, the court found these criteria to have been fulfilled, as there was only limited access to food and water, and the IDPs were a) at risk of being exploited by landlords and b) vulnerable with regard to violent crime, exploitation, abuse and forced recruitment in the camps. Additionally, c) they were without much prospect of improvement within a reasonable timeframe.[92]

91 *Sufi and Elmi v. The United Kingdom, supra* note 72, at para. 281 (emphasis added by the author).
92 *Id.*, at para. 291.

SHH and *K.A.B.* are the two ECtHR cases that followed the *Sufi and Elmi* judgement, in which the court deviated from its previously established guidance in order to assess the levels of indiscriminate violence in return countries. In *SHH*, the bench was tasked with determining the level of indiscriminate violence in Afghanistan. The court contrasted conditions in Afghanistan with the situation assessed in Somalia and held that, while the country was suffering from ongoing conflict, in contrast to Somalia, it had a functioning central government and infrastructure in place. Specifically, in Kabul, the city to which the applicant was to be returned, the government was in control, in contrast to the parts of Somalia that were under control of Islamic insurgents in *Sufi and Elmi*. Despite a diminishing humanitarian area in Afghanistan, international aid organisations operated in Afghanistan and provided relief. Finally, the court considered whether the special vulnerabilities of the claimant, who had been disabled by a rocket launch some years earlier, warranted a different assessment. The court held that the inadequacies of care in Afghanistan were the result of a lack of resources rather than result of deliberate actions or omissions of the Afghan authorities. The examination, which identified the situation without a dominant focus on the actions or inactions of state or non-state actors led the court to employ the aforementioned exceptionality approach.

> *The Court therefore considers that, in the circumstances of the present case where the problems facing the applicant would be largely as a result of inadequate social provisions through a want of resources, the approach adopted by the Court in* N. v. the United Kingdom, *cited above, is more appropriate.* The Court will therefore need to determine whether or not the applicant's case is a very exceptional one where the humanitarian grounds against removal are compelling.[93]

In *K.A.B. v. Sweden* of 2013, the court again examined the level of violence and its effects on the humanitarian situation in order to evaluate whether an expulsion would be a violation of Article 3.

> Exact figures about civilian casualties do not appear to be readily available but sources indicate that the number of civilian casualties has decreased because frontline fighting has moved out of the city […] in particular the fact that al-Shabaab is no longer in power in the city, there is no front-line fighting or shelling any longer and the number of civilian casualties has gone down, it finds that the available country information does not indicate that the situation is, at present, of such a nature as to place everyone who is present in the city at a real risk of treatment contrary to Article 3 of the Convention.[94]

93 *S.H.H. v. The United Kingdom*, App. No. 60367/10, European Court of Human Rights (2013), at para. 92.

94 *K.A.B. v. Sweden, supra* note 74, at paras. 88ff.

In the joint dissenting opinion of Judges Power-Forde and Zupancic, the narrow approach to the assessment of violence was criticised:

> To my mind, there is a deficiency in the majority's approach in this regard which can be seen, for example, in its failure to examine a number of important factors to which the court had regard in Sufi. In departing from the court's earlier finding, the majority has considered, briefly, only the general level of violence and the numbers of civilian casualties in Mogadishu (§§ 88, 89). It has failed to include in its assessment the reality of massive internal displacement of persons and the unpredictability of the still volatile situation in the Somali capital.[95]

The court chose its assessment tool on the basis of a *prima facie* assessment concerning the nature of generalised violence, with regard to both direct and indirect effects of such violence. The assessment criteria used encompass both qualitative and quantitative elements and allow for the inclusion of cumulative harm amounting to a violation of Article 3. As such, the court chose its tools wisely to reflect the comprehensiveness and complexity of harm and sources of harm arising in situations of violence and conflict. Then again, stipulating a high threshold to preclude return, or requiring the applicant to show special vulnerabilities are the tools the court has used to prevent a proliferation of appeals against deportation orders, commonly known as the 'floodgates argument'. Legal theoretical assumptions on the nature of *non-refoulement* and Article 3 should, in this manner, be reconciled with practicality and the realistic responsibilities of host states towards rejected asylum seekers. Nonetheless, due to the ever-evolving legal background and the complex factual context, the use of the given criteria in single conflicts rightfully generated criticism for being wrongfully or incompletely employed and for not having taken into account all the relevant negative consequences of violence and conflict for the claimant. Furthermore, the required individual assessment of each situation of violence at the given time and for the respective claimant severely hinders the courts' and the states' options for developing some form of index or generalising assessment schemes for conflict countries. While respecting and protecting the individual's rights, it also further contributes to both the court's increasing caseload and to divergent state practices.

4.2.4 The concept of an internal flight alternative in the Convention's treatment of non-refoulement

Expulsion or deportation following the rejection of an Article 3 ECHR claim necessitates the assessment and feasibility of an existing IFA. If ill-treatment, as prohibited under Article 3, is geographically localised, or if relocation within the country is possible, a return would not violate Article 3. Similar analyses have taken place

95 *Id.*, Joint Dissenting Opinion.

with regard to refugee and subsidiary protection. In contrast to Article 3 ECHR, which gives no direct reference to IFAs, the 1951 Convention definition makes an indirect reference to an IFA. Furthermore, in Europe, both refugee and subsidiary protection statuses based on the QD contain explicit regulations of such an IFA, as presented in sections 2.4.2.6 and 3.4.5. Against this background, one needs to look for guidance within the ECtHR's jurisprudence, instead of in the ECHR text itself.

The case of *Chahal* is one major point of reference. It concerned a Sikh activist from Punjab who feared ill-treatment by security forces within the region. The ECtHR considered a combination of different factors before finally ruling that no other part of India would offer an adequate IFA. These factors included the 'high profile' of the applicant as a leading activist, the bad reputation and human rights profile of the Punjab security forces, both in the region as well as in neighbouring regions, and the general lack of Indian authority to provide protection for him.[96]

The assessment of an IFA, particularly within a country affected by conflict, has, since then, been shaped further, including in the aforementioned cases of *Salah Sheek v. The Netherlands*, *Sufi and Elmi v. UK*, *K.A.B. v. Sweden* and *A.A. v. Sweden*. In both *Salah Sheekh* and *Sufi and Elmi*, the order of assessment taken by the court was, firstly, to assess the risk, and, secondly, to determine the existence of an alternative. In both *K.A.B. Sweden* and in *A.A. v. Sweden*, the court followed these steps in reverse order.

In *Salah Sheek*, the practicality of the IFA was brought into focus:

> [T]he Court considers that as a precondition for relying on an internal flight alternative certain guarantees have to be in place: the person to be expelled must be able to travel to the area concerned, gain admittance and settle there.[97]

Sufi and Elmi affirmed the requirement of safe travel to a given area, but also assessed the existence of social ties in the proposed internal protection area:

> [I]n view of the humanitarian crisis and the strain that it has placed both on individuals and on the traditional clan structure, in practice the court does not consider that a returnee could find refuge support in an area where he has no close family connections (see para. 115, 119, 138). If a returnee either has no such connections or if he could not safely travel to an area where he has such connections, the Court considers it reasonably likely that he would have to seek refuge in an IDP settlement or refugee camp.[98]

96 "Though the Court does not doubt the good faith of the Indian Government in providing the assurances mentioned above (paragraph 92), it would appear that, despite the efforts of that Government, the NHRC and the Indian courts to bring about reform, the violation of human rights by certain members of the security forces in Punjab and elsewhere in India is a recalcitrant and enduring problem", *Chahal v. The United Kingdom, supra* note 17, at paras. 103ff.

97 *Salah Sheekh v. The Netherlands, supra* note 53, at para. 141.

98 *Sufi and Elmi v. The United Kingdom, supra* note 72, at para. 267.

The court explicitly considered the conditions in Daadab to be below the acceptable standard, notwithstanding humanitarian relief delivered by the UNHCR and international organisations.

> The refugees in the Dadaab camps are not permitted to leave and would therefore appear to be trapped in the camps until the conflict in Somalia comes to an end. In the meantime, the camps are becoming increasingly overcrowded as refugees continue to flee the situation in Somalia. Although the IDPs in the Afgooye Corridor are permitted to leave, in reality the only place they are able to return to is Mogadishu, which the court has found not to be a safe place for the vast majority of civilians. Consequently, there is also little prospect of their situation improving while the conflict continues.[99]

Apart from practical issues, such as safe access, this part of the ECtHR's analysis also includes considerations on chain *refoulement*, which is the return of a person to a safe third country from which it might be refouled to another – unsafe – country. Similar to the duty to ascertain that no chain *refoulement* would take place as considered above, the ECtHR argued along the same lines that the state would not only carry the duty to ascertain that no risk of ill-treatment arises upon return, but equally that no chain removal from the safe area to the unsafe areas would take place:

> [A] returnee with no recent experience of living in Somalia would be at real risk of being subjected to treatment proscribed by Article 3 in an al-Shabaab controlled area. Accordingly, if a returnee's home area is in an al-Shabaab controlled area, the Court does not consider that he could relocate within Somalia without being exposed to a real risk of Article 3 ill-treatment.[100]

In line with this determination of the situation at hand, and comparable to the argumentation concerning (chain) *refoulement*, which holds that the simple ratification, for example of the 1951 Convention in the case of Libya, is not a sufficient guarantee of safety and security in the case of return, the court had already debated removal to Kazakhstan in 2010 and assessed reliance on governmental assurances.

99 *Id.*, at para. 291. "In light of the above, the Court considers that the conditions both in the Afgooye Corridor and in the Dadaab camps are sufficiently dire to amount to treatment reaching the threshold of Article 3 of the Convention. IDPs in the Afgooye Corridor have very limited access to food and water, and shelter appears to be an emerging problem as landlords seek to exploit their predicament for profit. Although humanitarian assistance is available in the Dadaab camps, due to extreme overcrowding access to shelter, water and sanitation facilities is extremely limited. The inhabitants of both camps are vulnerable to violent crime, exploitation, abuse and forcible recruitment. Moreover, the refugees living in – or, indeed, trying to get to – the Dadaab camps are also at real risk of refoulement by the Kenyan authorities. Finally, the Court notes that the inhabitants of both camps have very little prospect of their situation improving within a reasonable timeframe."

100 *Id.*, at paras. 272–277.

State assurances that the applicant would not be exposed to harm in violation of Article 3 could not be grounds for proceeding with the expulsion, due to the lack of any effective system to prevent torture.[101] In the 2012 judgement of *Othman (Abu Qatada) v. UK* concerning expulsion to Jordan, the court decided differently and found no violation of Article 3. In this case, the court engaged in a lengthy assessment of how to consider and assess safeguards and assurances given by the Jordanian government and ultimately evaluated these as sufficient. The UK and Jordan had reached a Memorandum of Understanding, which included detailed assurances such as the regular visits of the detained returnee by the Adaleh Center for Human Rights Studies, a non-governmental, non-profit organisation. The ECtHR further took into account the long-standing bilateral relations between the UK and Jordan; the fact that the assurances had been given in good faith by the highest levels in the Jordan government was seen as a further and sufficient safeguard.[102]

4.2.5 *The relation of Article 3 ECHR and Article 15 (b) and (c) of the (Recast) QD*

Subsidiary protection status based on the (Recast) QD and protection from *non-refoulement* based on the ECHR vary considerably with regard to the bundle of substantive rights attached to the protection status, on the one hand, and the prohibited removal on the other. In three more general points, the ECHR's *non-refoulement* deviates from protection under the QD. Firstly, a clear distinction lies in the absolute nature of Article 3 in contrast to the provisions of the (Recast) QD. The (Recast) QD contains limitations, i.e. the grounds for exclusion from subsidiary protection, enshrined in Article 17.[103] Secondly, the personal scope differs, as the (Recast) QD's subsidiary protection status only applies to third-country nationals, while the personal scope of Article 3 ECHR covers anyone within the jurisdiction of the High Contracting Parties. Thirdly, both the incorporation of Actors of Persecution and Serious Harm in Article 6 (Recast) QD and the lack of an equivalent provision in the context of Article 3 ECHR, together with the subsequent jurisprudence of the ECtHR, has clarified that only Article 3 offers protection in situations of naturally occurring harm, while the serious harm under the Recast QD requires human conduct as the causal factor. In the case of *Mohamed M'Bodj v. Council of Ministers*, the CJEU affirmed these differences:

> Article 6 of Directive 2004/83 sets out a list of those deemed responsible for inflicting serious harm, which supports the view that such harm must take the form of conduct on the part of a third party and that it cannot

101 *Baysakov and Others v. Ukraine*, App. No. 54131/08, European Court of Human Rights (2010), at para. 51.

102 See in particular para. 76 and the following.

103 See for national case concerning rejection from protection based on 1951 Convention Article 1 F and reliance on Article 3, *MH (Syria) v. Secretary of State for the Home Department; DS (Afghanistan) v. Secretary of State for the Home Department*, [2009] EWCA Civ 226, United Kingdom: Court of Appeal (England and Wales) (2009).

> therefore simply be the result of general shortcomings in the health system of the country of origin.[104]

These differences render the two instruments quite different in their overall scope. However, in the context of violence and conflict, they do share some commonalities, which is why a comparative analysis of Article 3 ECHR and Article 15 (b) and (c) (Recast) QD is offered in the following.

During the drafting procedures of the original QD, the overlaps in the wording of Article 3 ECHR, "No one shall be subjected to torture and inhuman or degrading treatment or punishment", and Article 15 (b), "Torture or inhuman or degrading treatment or punishment of an applicant in the country of origin", were already being discussed, leading the European Commission to state in 2004 that Article 15 (b)'s content would "reflect […] the content of Article 3 of the ECHR".[105]

The Commission further stated:

> This subparagraph relates to torture, inhuman or degrading treatment or punishment, reflecting the content of Article 3 of the ECHR. In establishing whether an applicant qualifies according to these criteria Member States should not apply a greater threshold of severity than is required by the ECtHR.[106]

These early references indicate that the European legislator had already assumed that Article 3 ECHR and the QD would include similar provisions.

Recital 34 of the Recast QD[107] reflects the close relationship between asylum law and regional human rights law, as it underlines that the criteria of eligibility

104 *Mohamed M'Bodj v. État belge: Opinion of Advocate General*, Case C-542/13, Court of Justice of the European Union (2014), at para. 35. "None the less, the fact that a third country national suffering from a serious illness may not, under Article 3 ECHR as interpreted by the European Court of Human Rights, in highly exceptional cases, be removed to a country in which appropriate treatment is not available does not mean that that person should be granted leave to reside in a member state by way of subsidiary protection under Directive 2004/83. In the light of the foregoing, Article 15 (b) of Directive 2004/83 must be interpreted as meaning that serious harm, as defined by the directive, does not cover a situation in which inhuman or degrading treatment, such as that referred to by the legislation at issue in the main proceedings, to which an applicant suffering from a serious illness may be subjected if returned to his country of origin, is the result of the fact that appropriate treatment is not available in that country, unless such an applicant is intentionally deprived of health care." *id.*, at paras. 42f.

105 European Commission, 'Proposal for a Council Directive on minimum standards for the qualification and status of third country nationals and stateless persons as refugees or as persons who otherwise need international protection. COM(2001)510 final' (2001), at 26.

106 *Ibid.*

107 "It is necessary to introduce common criteria on the basis of which applicants for international protection are to be recognised as eligible for subsidiary protection. Those criteria should be drawn from international obligations under human rights instruments and practices existing in Member States. It is necessary to introduce criteria on the basis of which applicants for international protection are to be recognised as eligible for subsidiary protection. Those criteria

should be drawn from international obligations in the latter. Both the CJEU and the ECtHR have considered their relationship, both in general and against the background of the pertinent articles. In *Sufi and Elmi*, the ECtHR expressed its view of a comparable protection offered by Article 3 ECHR and Article 15 (Recast) QD. While it had no jurisdiction to consider the scope of Article 15 (c),[108] it stated that there was no reason not to consider that comparable protection would be offered by the (Recast) QD.[109] It elaborated that:

> based on the ECJ's interpretation in Elgafaji, the Court is not persuaded that Article 3 of the Convention, as interpreted in NA, does not offer comparable protection to that afforded under the Directive. In particular, it notes that the threshold set by both provisions may, *in exceptional circumstances, be attained in consequence of a situation of general violence of such intensity that any person being returned to the region in question would be at risk simply on account of their presence there.*[110]

The CJEU has, on several occasions, equally examined the relationship between the different paragraphs of Article 15 and their relationship to Article 3 ECHR. Similar to the characterisation concerning grounds for refugee protection claims under section 2.4.2.3, overlaps on protection grounds are equally possible between refugee status and subsidiary status, as well as between the different grounds for subsidiary protection.[111] For the former, the aforementioned primacy of the 1951 Convention and its protection status must be kept in mind and assessed accordingly. For potential overlaps concerning subsidiary protection grounds, the CJEU delivered some guidance in *Elgafaji* considering Article 15. The judges underlined that, in contrast to paragraphs (a) and (b) that concern individual harm, paragraph (c) addresses more generalised forms of violence.

> [...] Article 15 (a) and (c) of the Directive, cover situations in which the applicant for subsidiary protection is specifically exposed to the risk of a particular type of harm. By contrast, the harm defined in Article 15 (c) of the Directive [...] covers a more general risk of harm.[112]

---

should be drawn from international obligations under human rights instruments and practices existing in Member States", Recital 25 QD.

108 *Sufi and Elmi v. The United Kingdom, supra* note 72, at para. 226.

109 *Ibid.*

110 *Ibid.* (Emphasis added by the author)

111 Comparative research by UNHCR on the application of the QD to situations of conflict has shown that the different EU Member States apply Article 15 in a hierarchical order from a-c, while other do not order or use a pragmatic approach, European Asylum Support Office, *The Implementation of Article 15(c) QD in EU Member States. EASO Practical Guides Series* (2015), available online at https://www.easo.europa.eu/sites/default/files/public/EASO_The-Implementation-of-Art-15c-QD-in-EU-Member-States.pdf (last visited 1 August 2018), at 5.

112 *Meki Elgafaji, Noor Elgafaji v. Staatssecretaris van Justitie*, C-465/07, Court of Justice of the European Union (2009), at paras. 33f.

In this decisive judgement, the court elaborated that, while Article 15 (b) in essence corresponds to Article 3, the general scope of Article 15 was larger than the comparable Article 3 scope, due to the inclusion of its additional and more general paragraph (c).[113] In the light of this difference, Article 15 (c) would need to be autonomously assessed, despite the general adherence to the fundamental rights guaranteed by the ECHR.[114]

The debates arising over subparagraph 15 (c) (Recast) QD also address the broader relationship between EU law and regional human rights law. The autonomous character[115] of EU law has been pursued by Advocate General Poiares Maduro:

> [T]he real point of the debate [...] concerns, in actual fact, the scope of the protection which must be afforded to applicants for asylum on the basis of Community law [...] the answer to that question cannot be inferred from Article 3 of the ECHR but must be sought principally through the prism of Article 15 c) of the Directive.[116]

Furthermore, he held that

> [c]ommunity provisions, irrespective of which provisions are concerned, are given an independent interpretation which cannot therefore vary to and/or be dependent on developments in the case law of the European Court of Human Rights[117]... It is not for the Community courts to determine the interpretation of article 3 of the Convention which prevails.[118]

In 2011, the *N.S.* judgement again focused on the relationship between European human rights and EU law. The CJEU stated that, as the EU itself is not party to the ECHR, the latter is not Union law itself, but a source of inspiration.[119] While the CJEU, as seen in section 3.4.1.2, has a particular tendency to emphasise its autonomous standing, the influence of human rights law should not be disregarded. The ECHR has an important place in EU law, as is also guaranteed by Article 52 (3) Charter of Fundamental Rights:

> In so far as this Charter contains rights which correspond to rights guaranteed by the Convention for the Protection of Human Rights and Fundamental Freedoms, the meaning and scope of those rights shall be the same as those laid down by the said Convention. This provision shall not prevent Union law providing more extensive protection.[120]

113 *Id.*, at paras. 28f.
114 *Id.*, at para. 28.
115 See discussion Errera, R., 'The CJEU and Subsidiary Protection. Reflections on Elgafaji - and After', 23 *International Journal of Refugee Law* (2011) 93, at 97f.
116 *Meki Elgafaji, Noor Elgafaji v. Staatssecretaris van Justitie, supra* note 112, at paras. 17, 19.
117 *Id.*, at para. 19.
118 *Id.*, at para. 20.
119 Peers, Steve *et al. (eds.), The EU Charter of Fundamental Rights. A Commentary* (2014), at 1581.
120 *Meki Elgafaji, Noor Elgafaji v. Staatssecretaris van Justitie, supra* note 112, at para. 20.

The CJEU stated in *Salahadin Abdulla and Others* and similarly in *Bolbol* concerning the QD and human rights law:

> The provisions of that Directive must for that reason be interpreted [...] in the light of [...] other relevant treaties referred to in point 1 of the first subparagraph of Article 63 EC [now Article 78(1) TFEU]. Those provisions must also, as is apparent from recital 10 in the preamble to that directive, be interpreted in a manner which respects the fundamental rights and the principles recognized in particular by the Charter of Fundamental Rights of the European Union.[121]

While the autonomous character of both fields of law is underlined, the interpretation "must be carried out independently with due regard, of course, for fundamental rights as they are guaranteed under the ECHR".[122] The scope of this book does not allow for a more abstract examination of the relationship between the pertinent fields of law and their individual provisions, but the lines of argumentation brought forward by the regional human rights court of Europe and the supranational court of the EU reflect their understanding of the position of their respective field of law. The CJEU has continued to stress the autonomy and independence of the EU law framework when interpreting its individual instruments and has only *in abstracto* referred to European human rights law as its benchmark. The ECtHR, in turn, has argued for a stronger position of the ECHR and its respective interpretation as the reference point and guardian of fundamental rights in the region. The human rights court has, as such, no formal mechanism to review decisions taken by the EU court, but it has nonetheless made efforts to compare and analyse its regulations and decisions implicitly.[123] So far, both courts, while referencing each other, have not yet provided clarity on

121 *Bolbol v. Bevándorlási és Állampolgársági Hivatal*, C-31/09, Court of Justice of the European Union (2010), at paras. 36–38. Article 78 (1) holds "1. The Union shall develop a common policy on asylum, subsidiary protection and temporary protection with a view to offering appropriate status to any third-country national requiring international protection and ensuring compliance with the principle of non-refoulement. This policy must be in accordance with the Geneva Convention of 28 July 1951 and the Protocol of 31 January 1967 relating to the status of refugees, and other relevant treaties." Article 52(3)(1) Charter of Fundamental Rights: "In so far as this Charter contains rights which correspond to rights guaranteed by the Convention for the Protection of Human Rights and Fundamental Freedoms, the meaning and scope of those rights shall be the same as those laid down by the said Convention. This provision shall not prevent Union law providing more extensive protection." And Article 53: "Nothing in this Charter shall be interpreted as restricting or adversely affecting human rights and fundamental freedoms as recognized, in their respective fields of application, by Union law and international law and by international agreements to which the Union or all the Member States are party, including the European Convention for the Protection of Human Rights and Fundamental Freedoms, and by Member States' constitutions."

122 *Meki Elgafaji, Noor Elgafaji v. Staatssecretaris van Justitie, supra* note 112, at para. 28.

123 Tsourdi, Evangelia, 'What Protection for Persons Fleeing Indiscriminate Violence? The Impact of the European Courts on the EU Subsidiary Protection Regime', in D. Cantor and

their exact interaction and it will be of interest in the future to see how the more general relationship of human rights law and EU asylum law will develop, especially when considering obligations that must be in accordance with international law, such as refugee law.[124]

4.3 Extraterritorial application of European human rights law

Persons fleeing conflict often cross various jurisdictions on their way to their destination country. In classical refugee law, the flight from their country of origin is *per definitionem* characterised by flight from their national sovereign and finally into another sovereign's jurisdiction.[125] Despite the lack of citizenship, transit states or the state of destination (which is a potential host state) are bound to extend protection for aliens in their jurisdiction from various obligations stemming, *inter alia*, from human rights law. The last few years in Europe, and equally in other regions or popular countries of destination, have shown that governments have attempted to circumvent their obligations towards asylum seekers, by heavily restricting and diffusing their entry into state territories. To enhance control of entry through the major flight routes and to limit irregular migration, the EU and the Member States have collectively and individually employed increasingly restrictive border security and migration control mechanisms. Methods to circumvent states' obligations include involuntary return to ports of departure, deterrence of passage on the High Seas, pushbacks to the territorial waters of other states or cooperation with third states in order to prevent departure in the first place.[126] As long as preventive measures are conducted beyond states' borders – taken 'offshore' – traditionalists have characterised them as being outside the states' jurisdictions and therefore outside their sphere of accountability. However, with states' growing attempts to restrict access to territory and asylum procedures by pushing their *non-refoulement* obligations offshore,[127] the growing relevance of extraterritorial application of protection provisions, including the pertinent treaties, must be put into focus.

J.-F. Durieux (eds.), *Refuge from Inhumanity? War Refugees and International Humanitarian Law* (Brill, 2014), 270, at 284f.

124 *Id.* Moreno-Lax, Violeta, 'Of Autonomy, Autarky, Purposiveness and Fragmentation: The Relationship between EU Asylum Law and International Humanitarian Law', in D. Cantor and J.-F. Durieux (eds.), *Refuge from Inhumanity? War Refugees and International Humanitarian Law* (Brill, 2014). This is particularly interesting, as the CJEU has rejected the EU's attempt to accede to the ECHR, which was envisaged in the Lisbon Treaty.

125 Goodwin-Gill, Guy S., *The Refugee in International Law* (2nd ed., Clarendon Press, 1996), at 40.

126 Goodwin-Gill, Guy S., 'The Right to Seek Asylum. Interception at Sea and the Principle of Non-Refoulement', 23 *International Journal of Refugee Law* (2011) 443, at 450.

127 Gammeltoft-Hansen in his contribution not only considers in detail the issue of off-shoring immigration control but also of out-sourcing it. Especially within the EU, with its already complex EU and Member States relations and respective issues of accountability, privatising

The pertinent question in this context is whether fundamental human rights obligations end at states' borders. Against this background, the following section will examine the extraterritorial application of *non-refoulement* by virtue of Article 3 ECHR, which, as seen above, establishes the minimum protection for asylum seekers and migrants when intercepted on their flight and before entering Europe's territory.

4.3.1 Human rights beyond states' borders

Human rights obligations for asylum seekers and migrants oscillate "between two opposing poles – on the one hand the universal claim underpinning both refugee and human rights law, on the other, principles of national sovereignty anchoring responsibility to the state and its territory".[128] While human rights law holds a special position in this regard, the broader issue at stake is the general understanding and application of treaties beyond the traditional limit, namely the states' borders. The question of the application of protection obligations is raised by the tension between the universal normative idea, on the one hand, that constraints must be engaged where power is exercised and, on the other hand, the understanding that state responsibility follows legal positivist constructions of treaty application.[129] The *Lotus* case established the general rule that no executive jurisdiction can legally be exercised in the territory of another state without its consent.

> Now, the first and foremost restriction imposed by international law upon a state is that – failing the existence of a permissive rule to the contrary – it may not exercise its power in any form in the territory of another state. In this sense jurisdiction is certainly territorial.[130]

The development of international human rights law has questioned the principle of territoriality and challenged the prior approach as the sole basis for the jurisdiction of states. Instead, it has been suggested that human rights law applies beyond the national territories of states even when acts are committed outside of the territory. This shift from a *de jure* to a *de facto* determination of the exercise of authority is *inter alia* underlined in the ICJ's advisory opinion on South West Africa:

> The fact that South Africa no longer has any title to administer the Territory does not release it from it's obligations and responsibilities under international law towards other States in respect of the exercise of its powers in

---

immigration control further aggravates the legal determination of state responsibility and jurisdiction. Gammeltoft-Hansen, Thomas, *Access to Asylum: International Refugee Law and the Globalisation of Migration Control* (Cambridge University Press, 2011).

128 *Id.*, at 23.

129 *Id.*, at 24.

130 *Case of the S.S. "Lotus" (France vs. Turkey)*, (1927) PCIJ Series A No. 10, Permanent Court of Justice (1927), at para. 19.

> relation to this Territory. *Physical control of a territory, and not sovereignty or legitimacy of title, is the basis of State liability* for acts affecting other States.[131]

Higgins, Kooijmans and Buergenthal, in their joint separate opinion of the ICJ's Arrest Warrant Case, emphasised the special role of human rights law for the individual and the international community as changing the traditional territorial premises of treaty application.

> [A] gradual movement towards bases of jurisdiction other than territoriality can be discerned. This slow but steady shifting to a more extensive application of extraterritorial jurisdiction by States reflects the emergence of values which enjoy an ever-increasing recognition in international society.[132]

International human rights treaties do not necessarily contain explicit provisions on their scope of application *ratione loci*. Their potential extraterritorial application is therefore attached to the interpretation of their jurisdictional clauses.[133] While the literal interpretation of the wording of 'jurisdiction' does differ between general public international law and human rights law, and its context mostly does not indicate any extraterritorial connotations, the object and purpose of human rights treaties can result in a decisive change in the interpretation of the term jurisdiction. The ICJ examined the object and purpose of human rights law in its Advisory Opinion on the Legal Consequences of the Construction of a Wall concerning the International Covenants and highlighted,

> [...] while the jurisdiction of States is primarily territorial, it may sometimes be exercised outside the national territory. *Considering the object and purpose of [the ICCPR]*, it would seem natural that, even when such is the case, States parties to the Covenant should be bound to comply with its provisions [...].[134]

131 *Legal Consequences for States of the Continued Presence of South Africa in Namibia (South West Africa) notwithstanding Security Council Resolution 276 (1970)*, International Court of Justice (1971), at para. 113 (emphasis added by the author).

132 *Arrest Warrant of 11 April 2000 (Democratic Republic of the Congo v. Belgium), Joint separate opinion of Judges Higgins, Kooijmans and Buergenthal*, International Court of Justice (2002), at 73.

133 Concerning the extraterritorial application of the CAT and the criterion of effective control over persons, the Committee Against Torture stressed with reference to Article 2 CAT "'any territory' includes all areas where the State arty exercises, directly or indirectly, in whole or in part, de jure or de facto effective control, in accordance with international law. The reference to 'any territory' refers to prohibited acts committed not only on board a ship or aircraft registered by a State party, but also during military occupation or peacekeeping operations and in such places as embassies, military bases, detention facilities, or other areas over which a State exercises factual or effective control." United Nations Committee Against Torture, 'General Comment No. 2: Implementation of Article 2 by States Parties' (UN Doc. CAT/C/GC/2, 2008), at 16.

134 *Legal Consequences of the Construction of a Wall in the Occupied Palestinian Territory. Advisory Opinion*, International Court of Justice (2004), at para. 109 (emphasis added by the author).

Hence, the court established that "it is not to be excluded that (the ICESCR) applies both to territories over which a State party has sovereignty",[135] but "that the State party's obligations under the Covenant apply to all territories and populations *under its effective control*".[136] Similar developments can be traced to the regional level.

4.3.2 The extraterritorial application of the ECHR

The ECHR contains its jurisdictional clause in Article 1: "The High Contracting Parties shall secure to everyone within their jurisdiction the rights and freedoms defined in Section I of this Convention." These "apparently simple words have proven to be remarkably troublesome".[137] The following section highlights the prolific jurisprudential development of the ECtHR concerning the Convention's application outside its High Contracting Parties' state territories.[138]

Establishing *de facto* control as a rightful equivalent to *de jure* jurisdiction in human rights law has been repeatedly confirmed, although not without facing resistance.[139] Already in a number of judgements by the ECtHR's predecessor, the European Commission of Human Rights (ECommHR), a different approach alongside *de jure* jurisdiction, that is *de facto* control, was examined as a basis for jurisdiction. This approach was employed in cases concerning diplomatic and consular authorities,[140] cases involving arrest or detention of persons

135 *Id.*, at para. 112.

136 *Ibid.* (Emphasis added by the author)

The Human Rights Committee supported this reading of the ICCPR's jurisdictional clause of Article 2(1) by stating that "1. Each State Party to the present Covenant undertakes to respect and to ensure to all individuals within its territory and subject to its jurisdiction the rights recognized in the present Covenant […]", and explicitly held in the General Comment No 31. (2004) "A State party must respect and ensure the rights laid down in the Covenant to anyone within the power or effective control of that State Party, even if not situated within the territory of the State Party […] This principle also applies to those *within the power or effective control of the forces of a State Party acting outside its territory*", Human Rights Committee, 'General Comment No. 31: The nature of the general legal obligation imposed on States Parties to the Covenant' (UN Doc. CCPR/C/21/Rev.1/Add.13, 2004). The HRC stated further that "not to be manifestly absurd or unreasonable", under Article 3 of the ICCPR it would be a violation of the norm if a state party is permitted to unlawfully perpetrate violations of the Covenant on the territory of another State", Human Rights Committee, 'Sergio Euben Lopez Burgos v. Uruguay, Communication No. R.12/52' (UN Doc. Supp. No. 40 (A/36/40), 176 (1981), 1979), at para. 12.3.

137 Lord Dyson, *The Extraterritorial Application of the European Convention on Human Rights: Now on a Firmer Footing, but is it a Sound One?* (2014), available online at https://www.judiciary.gov.uk/wp-content/uploads/JCO/Documents/Speeches/lord-dyson-speech-extraterritorial-reach-echr-300114.pdf (last visited 1 August 2018), at 1.

138 Wouters, Kees, *supra* note 5, at 140ff.

139 Wilde, Ralph, 'Triggering State Obligations Extraterritorially: The Spatial Test in Certain Human Rights Treaties', 40 *Israel Law Review* (2007) 503, at 526.

140 See for instance *X v. Federal Republic of Germany*, App. No. 1611/62, European Court of Human Rights (1965).

abroad,[141] exercise of public powers abroad[142] and cases involving the presence of troops abroad.[143] The ECommHR's test to constitute jurisdiction by virtue of Article 1 was 'authority and control over persons and property' by agents of the state and in the aforementioned scenarios.[144]

The ECtHR has since underlined that, by virtue of Article 1, circumventing human rights obligations by moving the respective conduct beyond the states' territorial borders does not relieve the state of its obligations. In the case of *Issa*, the judges stressed that:

> [...] Article 1 of the Convention cannot be interpreted so as to allow a State party to perpetrate violations of the Convention on the territory of another State, which it could not perpetrate on its own territory.[145]

The jurisprudence of the court can be divided into cases in which extraterritorial jurisdiction was examined under the 'spatial approach' concerning control over territory or under the 'effective control over persons approach'. For some years, the jurisprudence of the court has been progressively broadening the extraterritorial interpretation of Article 1 ECHR.[146] This practice came to a harsh (but only temporary) halt with the prominent case of ***Banković et al v. Belgium et al*** concerning NATO airstrikes. The case completely destabilised a previously straightforward evolution towards a broad, territorially detached notion of human rights and is, as a result, often understood as a relapse of the court's position. Its emphasis on the ordinary meaning of jurisdiction, instead of the broader object and purpose of Article 1 and the ECHR as a whole, is detrimental to the contemporary understanding of human rights law.[147]

141 See for instance *Hess v. The United Kingdom*, App. No. 6231/73, European Court of Human Rights (1975).

142 *X and Y v. Switzerland*, App. No. 7289/75 and 7349/76, European Court of Human Rights (1977).

143 See the later discussed *Cyprus v. Turkey*, App. No. 6780/74 and 6950/75, Council of Europe; European Commission on Human Rights (1975). For a general overview of the cases before the ECommHR, see da Costa, Karen, *The Extraterritorial Application of Selected Human Rights Treaties* (Martinus Nijhoff Publishers, 2013), at 96ff.

144 *Id.*, at 109.

145 *Issa and Others v. Turkey*, App. No. 31821/96, European Court of Human Rights (2004), at para. 71.

146 The case leading to an inadmissibility decision that concerned claimed violations of Articles 2, 10 and 14 ECHR emphasised that the jurisdiction of the ECHR Member States would not extend to aerial bombardment in non-Member States' territory. "Article 1 of the Convention must be considered to reflect this ordinary and essentially territorial notion of jurisdiction, other bases of jurisdiction being exceptional and requiring special justification in the particular circumstances of each case." *Banković and Others v. Belgium and Others*, App. No. 52207/99, European Court of Human Rights (2001), at paras. 61f. While the court had been more flexible in earlier cases, Banković was understood as being detrimental to the human rights core; the idea that states could not be supported in violating rights outside their territory that would be impermissible if committed within their territory.

147 Altiparmak, Kerem, 'Bankovic. An Obstacle to the Application of the European Convention on Human Rights in Iraq?', 9 *Journal of Conflict and Security Law* (2004) 213, at 223.

The classical conception of the territorial or spatial approach usually covers control over territory, such as during situations of occupation or other forms of territorial military control. EU or Member States border control personnel or other migration management personnel, if deployed extraterritorially, are likely to establish control over persons rather than over territory. Even if one considers the idea of establishing transit or reception centres in African states, an idea that has repeatedly been raised by single EU states as well as in the EU institutions themselves, such centres would operate in cooperation with the respective state. Also, in such cases, the EU or Member State personnel would not be able to establish jurisdiction through territorial control but rather via the control-over-persons approach. Therefore, the following discussion centres around the evolving jurisprudence of this approach.

Cases of control over persons have traditionally covered issues of detention or arrest.[148] The Human Rights Committee, in a comparable context, asserts the approach as relating

> not to the place where the violation occurred, but rather to the relationship between the individual and the State in relation to a violation of any of the rights [...] wherever they occurred.[149]

In the case of *Öcalan v. Turkey*, the ECtHR acknowledged and applied the 'authority and control over persons test', stating that the applicant was "physically forced to return to Turkey by Turkish officials and was subject to their authority and control".[150] It eventually held:

> It is common ground that, directly after being handed over to the Turkish officials by the Kenyan officials, the applicant was effectively under Turkish authority and therefore within the "jurisdiction" of that State for the purposes of Article 1 of the Convention, even though in this instance Turkey exercised its authority outside its territory.[151]

While most of the jurisprudence discussed concerns the assessment of the *de facto* jurisdiction of one state in an area of competing sovereignty, namely another state's territory, the determination of jurisdiction on the High Seas is essential in the context of a mixed migration movement and protection from *refoulement*. Several ECtHR cases from the last few years are of interest here. The extraterritorial application through jurisdiction over flagged state vessels was debated in the Grand Chamber decision on *Medvedyev* concerning arbitrary detention at sea. Nine claimants in *Medvedyev*, namely the crew of the Cambodian-flagged vessel 'Winner', had been taken into custody by the French

148 Among others Human Rights Committee, *supra* note 136.
149 *Id.*, at para. 12.2.
150 *Öcalan v. Turkey*, App. No. 46221/99, European Court of Human Rights (2005), at para. 93.
151 *Id.*, at para. 91.

authorities, which had suspected drug smuggling offences and intercepted the cargo vessel. The court had to address the facts of the case and consider whether the events, from intercepting the Winner on the High Seas and subjecting the claimants to thirteen days of alleged deprivation of liberty until the ship reached Brest, brought the applicants within French jurisdiction.[152] It held that interception and additional escort by two warships, the use of warning shots and the boarding by a special forces team amounted to the exercise of full and exclusive *de facto* control over the foreign state vessel and its crew.[153]

In 2011, the court in *Al-Skeini* again highlighted several scenarios establishing extraterritorial jurisdiction and thereby the scope of application of the ECHR. This is particularly the case due to its refinement of the notion that jurisdiction is exercised when, in an extraterritorial setting, "public powers normally to be exercised by a sovereign government" are displayed.[154] The court referred to the case of *Medvedyev* and considered this "exercise of physical power and control over persons"[155] to be decisive in establishing extraterritorial jurisdiction. In such a scenario, one must raise the question whether asylum seekers interacting with state officials are protected from *refoulement* in the light of Article 3 ECHR and, additionally, whether procedural human rights guarantees apply.

This matter has been answered in the affirmative by the ECtHR in the leading (and first) case on this matter, *Hirsi Jamaa and Others v. Italy.*[156] The case concerned a mixed group of Somali and Eritrean migrants whose boat was intercepted by Italian authorities south of Lampedusa in 2009. They were transferred onto an Italian military ship and transported back to Libya.[157] In this case, the vessel sailing under the Italian flag on the High Seas, according to the court, exercised exclusive *de facto* and *de jure* jurisdiction under Article 1 ECHR. Parallel to the finding of violations of Article 3 *refoulement* and the risk of secondary refoulement, as well as the prohibition of collective expulsion under Article 4 Protocol No. 4, the Grand Chamber held that the claimants must have access to an individualised procedure and that, if not, as in the case at hand, their rights to an effective remedy were equally infringed, as they "had no access to a procedure to identify them and to assess their personal circumstances"[158] before they were

152 *Medvedyev and Others v. France*, App. No. 3394/03, European Court of Human Rights (2010), at para. 62.

153 *Id.*, at para. 67.

154 *Al-Skeini and Others v. The United Kingdom*, App. No. 55721/07, European Court of Human Rights (2011), at para. 149.

155 *Hirsi Jamaa and Others v. Italy*, App. No. 27765/09, European Court of Human Rights (2012), at para. 80.

156 Moreno-Lax, Violeta, 'Hirsi Jamaa and Others v Italy or the Strasbourg Court versus Extraterritorial Migration Control?', 12 *Human Rights Law Review* (2012) 574.

157 The basis for these push backs was the bilateral cooperation agreement of Italy and Libya concluded in December 2007 and its Additional Protocol of February 2009, containing the transit state's obligation to take back migrants that had left its shore to support the Italian authorities against irregular migrations in exchange for money and training.

158 *Hirsi Jamaa and Others v. Italy, supra* note 156, at paras. 196–207.

returned.[159] Against this background, the judgement, unanimously delivered on all counts, rendered the variety of measures to intercept migrants at sea as unlawful and in breach of various obligations and rights contained in the ECHR.[160]

The latest challenge will be the progressive externalisation of the EU's borders policy, which has been observed since the 2000s.[161] The externalisation of the migration policy involves practices that lead to the shifting of migration management to countries of departure or transit[162] and is included, albeit still vague and weakly developed, in the new European Agenda on Migration[163] adopted on 13 May 2015. Border controls on the High Seas or in other states' territories might be examined as establishing jurisdiction for the controlling state via the effective control over persons or 'public authority approach' of the ECtHR. This will depend on the levels of authority and control of the acting ECHR Member State official and their cooperation with the home country. The *Hirsi* concurring opinion already foreshadows the consequences of developing Articles 1 and 3 jurisprudence in this regard.

> [T]he full range of conceivable immigration and border policies, including denial of entry to territorial waters, denial of visa, denial of pre-clearance embarkation or provision of funds, equipment or staff to immigration-control operations performed by other States or international organisations on behalf of the Contracting Party, remain subject to the Convention standard. They all constitute forms of exercise of the State function of border control and a manifestation of State jurisdiction, wherever they take place and whoever carries them out.[164]

159 Written submissions were provided in this case by the UNHCR, Human Rights Watch, the AIRE Centre and Amnesty International.

160 The court stated "is also immaterial whether the immigration or border control takes place on the land or maritime territory of a State, its diplomatic missions, warships, ships registered in the State or under its effective control, a navy of another State or a facility placed on the territory of another State or a territory leased from another State, as long as the border control is performed on behalf of the Contracting Party". A State cannot evade its treaty obligations in respect of refugees by using the device of changing the place of determination of their status." *id.*, at para. 76.

161 Red Cross EU Office (ed.), *Shifting Borders. Externalising Migrant Vulnerabilities and Rights?* (2013).

162 United Nations General Assembly, 'Report of the Special Rapporteur on the human rights of migrants, François Crépeau. Regional study: management of the external borders of the European Union and its impact on the human rights of migrants' (UN Doc. A/HRC/23/46, 2013). See also *Regina v. Immigration Officer at Prague Airport and Another, Ex parte European Roma Rights Centre and Others,* [2004] UKHL 55, United Kingdom: House of Lords (2004). Here the House of Lords recognised that pre-clearance operations on foreign territory "purported to exercise governmental authority" over those targeted, *id.*, at para. 45.

163 European Commission, 'Communication from the Commission to the European Parliament, the Council, the European Economic and Social Committee and the Committee of the Regions: A European Agenda on Migration' (COM(2015)240 final, 2015).

164 *Hirsi Jamaa and Others v. Italy, supra* note 156, at para. 76.

This far-reaching interpretation will surely place other immigration control mechanisms, such as prominent Frontex missions and reception centres in non-EU states, into a human rights law straitjacket. One potential, yet highly controversial, practical consequence that can follow from the above-discussed interpretation of the ECHR in the context of extraterritorial immigration control is the development of a (temporary) right to access.[165] The court, however, has not gone this far and states will surely resist such a weakening of their sovereignty in determining the right to enter their territory in the long run. And yet, for now, all future immigration control mechanisms cannot be implemented unless they can be reconciled with the fundamental obligations, first and foremost deriving from European human rights law and more particularly, from its principle of *non-refoulement*.

4.4 Intermediate conclusion on the ECHR's non-refoulement and countries in conflict

The ECHR has evolved into the primary protection instrument in the broader mixed migration context, particularly in the light of its jurisprudence on the principle of *non-refoulement*, which is only implicitly codified, yet widely recognised in Article 3 ECHR. The undisputed interpretation of Article 3 offers a suspension from involuntary return in two ways – firstly, for asylum seekers whose application for refugee or subsidiary protection status has been rejected, but who are already on the soil of one of the ECHR's Contracting Parties and, secondly, for individuals who have not arrived yet, such as migrants and potential refugees who have been intercepted at sea or confronted with border controls. The jurisprudence of the ECtHR has interpreted the Article as safeguarding the first insurances for irregular migrants, such as when intercepted on the High Seas. On this basis, the principle must be considered as the first protection mechanism for those arriving at Europe's borders without a valid entry visa. In contrast to the refugee and subsidiary protection statuses, the principle of *non-refoulement* ensures only minimal substantive rights. Ultimately, it does not give rise to a protection status with a bundle of 'positive' rights, but provides merely 'negative' protection against involuntary return. As such, it is the protection mechanism of last resort for those not eligible or excluded from protection status. In the light of the diverging state practices regarding both the expulsion of rejected asylum seekers and border control practices, legal certainty in the interpretation of the Article is essential. To examine these two functions of Article 3, as interpreted by the ECtHR, this chapter firstly analysed the scope of protection against involuntary return to a country in conflict, before examining the extraterritorial application of the principle in the context of migration management.

165 Noll assessed the "impressive inherent right to access", Noll, Gregor, *Negotiating Asylum* (Martinus Nijhoff Publishers, 2000), at 454. See also Costello, Cathryn, *The Human Rights of Migrants and Refugees in European Law* (Oxford University Press, 2016), at 231ff.

The first scenario concerns mostly rejected asylum seekers in Europe who have not been granted a protection status. Undeniably, within the jurisdiction of their current host state, the question at issue is the extent of the host state's responsibilities under the ECHR in cases of involuntary return to countries in conflict. Two distinct questions address the source or actor of the foreseeable ill-treatment in case of return and the level of violence in the country of origin required in order to preclude a return. The absolute nature of the principle of *non-refoulement*, as affirmed in the jurisprudence, is the main reason for explaining the broadening approach concerning the actors of ill-treatment triggering Article 3. In the context of flight from conflict, the concept of actors of ill-treatment is essential to cover the risks arising from violence and conflict in a comprehensive manner, as conflict parties are not the only actors who might cause harm to returnees and citizens. The traditional state-centricity of human rights law has given way to include the recognition of risks stemming from non-state actors, such as non-state armed forces or individuals. Interestingly, the court has progressively concerned itself with harm arising naturally, such as through disease. It has even included violations of social and economic rights in assessments of violations of Article 3 – albeit only in special circumstances. Yet, this broadening of sources of ill-treatment must be considered the necessary basis for a full consideration of appeals against return to countries affected by violence and conflict, where there may be multiple sources posing a risk to the applicant's safety and wellbeing.

Before analysing the different approaches of the ECtHR, the potential intersection with IHL and the definition of conflict envisaged under Article 3 was brought into focus in order to determine whether it could be used as a tool to assess conflict and violence in the country of return. One had to consider if reference to IHL and its classification of conflict serves to simplify this assessment and whether the court has taken a consistent approach in this respect. Previous case law, particularly in the Kurdish and Chechnyan cases, was taken as evidence illustrating the court's reluctance to engage in classification debates over IHL and the nature of conflicts. In this chapter, the *non-refoulement* cases involving return to countries affected by violence were seen to have followed this path. That being said, the ECtHR does not require a conflict classification synonym or its own assessment of conflict comparable to IHL in order to make a risk assessment. In its sensible refusal to enter into IHL-guided debates on IACs, NIACs and targeting decisions, the court has highlighted its unique nature as a human rights court governed by human rights considerations.

In the context of involuntary returns, this has led the court to engage in individual assessments of the risk of ill-treatment stemming from violence. In carrying out such individual assessments, the court has reverted to domestic jurisprudence to establish quantitative and qualitative criteria, such as the number of civilians killed, injured or displaced, the methods and means employed, or the extent of direct targeting of civilians by the different parties to the conflict. The ECtHR has carved out two approaches which its employs to assess the level of general violence in the country of return and the triggering of protection against *refoulement*, namely the exceptionality and the predominant-harm approach. Under very exceptional circumstances and in the light of compelling humanitarian considerations, the exceptionality approach can be taken to trigger Article 3 protection, even when the harm does not stem from direct or indirect human conduct. This could provide protection against the general consequences of hostilities, including the social and economic breakdown of the state or natural disasters. Despite its existence, in practice it is almost impossible to reach this threshold and therefore, so far, it is of theoretical rather than practical value. The second, 'predominant-harm approach' requires a lesser degree of harm if it is predominantly caused by, or a result, of the hostilities of state and non-state actors. Both approaches provide the judges with a tool to consider the effects of violence and conflict comprehensively. For claims arising in such a context, the evolution of the treatment of individualisation was of great significance. For a long time, the court necessitated a special distinguishing feature that singled-out the claimant from a group of equally affected individuals. More recent jurisprudence has established that, under special circumstances and in cases of extreme levels of violence, return is prohibited as a violation of Article 3, irrespective of the returnee's further individual characteristics. Through these jurisprudential developments, the court has developed its protection of last resort for persons facing expulsion to countries in conflict, at least from a theoretical point of view.

State practice in this regard, including decisions taken by national courts, varies considerably and is usually guided by contemporary return policies concerning specific countries. The court itself shot its bolt in order to avert a flood of positive decisions by introducing a high threshold for suspensions from return. Nonetheless, the divergent approaches of European states, based on assumptions regarding the countries that produce asylum-seekers and migrants, conflict with the individual approach to rights-based decision-making, specifically on Article 3. Both require an individual assessment of the claimant's specific situation as well as circumstances in (the relevant parts of) his or her country of origin at the given time. Yet, this individual and case-by-case approach clearly lacks practicability when faced with situations of mass influx or huge numbers of rejected asylum-seekers. While theoretically gratifying as a progressive development of human rights protection in Europe, its practical implementation is questionable.[166]

166 So far, Article 3 claims have been in focus in the migration context. Future applications causing a comparable divergence might also be based on Article 8 of the Convention, concerning private and family life. Nuala Mole, *Asylum and the European Convention on Human Rights* (2003), available online at http://www.echr.coe.int/LibraryDocs/DG2/HRFILES/DG2-EN-HRFILES-09(2000).pdf (last visited 1 August 2018), at 25. *Bensaid v. the United Kingdom*, App. No. 44599/98, European Court of Human Rights (2000). On family reunification, Daniel Thym, 'Respect for Private and Family Life Under Article 8 ECHR in Immigration Cases: A Human Right to Regularize Illegal Stay?' *International and Comparative Law Quarterly* (2008) 87. Philip Czech, *A Right to Family Reunification for Persons Granted International Protection? The Strasbourg Case-law, State Sovereignty and EU Harmonisation* (2016), available online at http://eumigrationlawblog.

The principle of *non-refoulement* in the European context has developed a second major function over the years which goes beyond the conflict context. As interpreted by the ECtHR, Article 3 offers a first protection for irregular migrants, as it expands protection under the ECHR beyond the territorial borders of the High Contracting Parties. For this reason, the extraterritorial application of the ECHR was brought into focus to consider potential *non-refoulement* obligations for persons at European borders, in foreign territories or interacting with border controls on the High Seas.

Both in Europe and elsewhere, human rights law has in recent years been challenging the traditional conceptualisation of jurisdiction as solely based on territory. While the effective control approach theoretically broadens the geographic scope of human rights protection, the entanglements of jurisprudence have led to legal uncertainty, both for those subject to law and those applying it in their executive functions. The complex, highly politicised field of migration control, with contesting legal positions on states' powers and obligations, has not established a clear way ahead in either case law, state practice or academic debate. Often, successive judgements by the ECHR oscillating between restrictive and expansive interpretations was considered unsatisfactory, leading to arbitrary results,[167] resulting in confusion and ambiguity[168] and generally being of lesser value as a judicial construction.[169] Furthermore, it was cautioned that "[a]uthority and control over individuals as a basis for state jurisdiction simply boils down to the proposition that a state has obligations under human rights treaties towards all individuals whose human rights it is able to violate."[170]

The last few years of ECtHR jurisprudence on the extraterritorial application of the Convention has attempted to deliver a consistent threshold for the establishment of jurisdiction under Article 1. As case-by-case decisions, these interpretations have shaped subsequent state practice, mostly through their political influence and the ECtHR's underlying fear of future negative decisions if other states do not follow. While case law is still vulnerable to fluctuation between progress and regression, three bases for jurisdiction have been reaffirmed over the years, namely effective control over territory, effective control over persons, and lately also the exercise of the public powers approach. When imagining scenarios of extraterritorial immigration control, the second and third approach are particularly likely to trigger

---

eu/a-right-to-family-reunification-for-persons-under-international-protection-the-strasbourg-case-law-state-sovereignty-and-eu-harmonisation-2/ (last visited 1 August 2018).

167 Shany, Yuval, 'Taking Universality Seriously. A Functional Approach to Extraterritoriality in International Human Rights Law', 7 *The Law & Ethics of Human Rights* (2013) 47, at 47.

168 Miltner, Barbara, 'Revisiting Extraterritoriality after Al-Skeini: The ECHR and its Lessons', 33 *Michigan Journal of International Law* (2012) 693, at 694f.

169 Dennis, Michael J., 'Application Of Human Rights Treaties Extraterritorially To Detention Of Combatants And Security Internees: Fuzzy Thinking All Around?', 12 *ILSA Journal of International & Comparative Law* (2006) 459, at 462.

170 Scheinin, Martin, 'Extraterritorial Effect of the International Covenant on Civil and Political Rights', in F. Coomans and M. T. Kamminga (eds.), *Extraterritorial Application of Human Rights Treaties* (Intersentia, 2004), 73, at 76.

jurisdiction under Article 1 and thereby potential bases for *non-refoulement* under Article 3. *Non-refoulement* cases have so far been established for scenarios concerning control over vessels upon being intercepted and escorted to a specific harbour,[171] when persons have been taken aboard in rescue operations[172] and when vessels are prevented from entering territorial waters of the respective state by its organs.[173] This development has led scholars to ascertain that "in that sphere (of human rights law) the movement towards acceptance of the extraterritorial application of Human rights obligations is slow but apparently inexorable."[174] The latest and most influential judgement, *Hirsi Jamaa*, has rightly clarified which requirements and prohibitions, in more practical terms, flow from the principle of (individual and collective) *non-refoulement*, which can even lead to an evolution of the principle towards a (temporary) right of access. And yet, neither the court, nor state practice so far shows any indication that such a right is to be made explicit in the near future. Even the broad interpretation of *non-refoulement* in ECtHR jurisprudence will likely remain a theoretical exercise until further cases are brought to the court and a consistent interpretative practice is established. The new externalisation of border control policies of the EU and its Member States provide no indication that state practice will be willing to follow this interpretation.

In today's world, where states can easily project their powers and authorities beyond their borders, a paradigm shift might be needed to follow this factual expansion across the globe. If sovereign powers and functions are outsourced and off-shored, do they not lead to an expansion of the application of the relevant legal instruments (and obligations)?[175] Judge Bonello wrote in this regard:

> I think poorly of an esteem for human rights that turns casual and approximate depending on geographical coordinates. Any state that worships fundamental rights on its own territory but then feels free to make a mockery of them anywhere else does not, as far as I am concerned, belong to that comity of nations for which the supremacy of human rights is both mission and clarion call.[176]

The extraterritorial application of human rights law has gradually followed the exercise of authority beyond state borders, beyond their territorial waters and on the High Seas. When considering the pertinent laws in total, taking into account European human rights, EU legislation, the 1951 Convention and international principles of state responsibility, it is clear that states cannot bypass the human rights of migrants simply by moving them beyond their own borders.

171 *Medvedyev and Others v. France, supra* note 153.
172 *Hirsi Jamaa and Others v. Italy, supra* note 156.
173 *Women on Waves and Others v. Portugal*, App. No. 31276/05, European Court of Human Rights (2009).
174 Gallagher, Anne T. and David, Fiona, *The International Law of Migrant Smuggling* (Cambridge University Press, 2014), at 272.
175 Gammeltoft-Hansen, Thomas, *supra* note 127, at 19. Scheinin, Martin, *supra* note 171, at 73ff.
176 *Al-Skeini and Others v. The United Kingdom, supra* note 155, at para. 18.

References

Abresch, William, 'A Human Rights Law of Internal Armed Conflict: The European Court of Human Rights in Chechnya', 16 (4) *European Journal of International Law* 741 (2005).

Altiparmak, Kerem, 'Bankovic. An Obstacle to the Application of the European Convention on Human Rights in Iraq?', 9 (2) *Journal of Conflict and Security Law* 213 (2004).

Baldinger, Dana, *Vertical Judicial Dialogues in Asylum Cases. Standards on Judicial Scrutiny and Evidence in International and European Asylum Law* (Brill, 2015).

Cantor, David and Durieux, Jean-François (eds.), *Refuge from Inhumanity? War Refugees and International Humanitarian Law* (Brill, 2014).

Coomans, Fons and Kamminga, Menno T. (eds.), *Extraterritorial Application of Human Rights Treaties* (Intersentia, 2004).

Costello, Cathryn, *The Human Rights of Migrants and Refugees in European Law* (Oxford University Press, 2016).

Council of Europe; European Commission on Human Rights, *The Greek Case*, Appl. No. 3321/67, 3322/67, 3323/67 and 3344/67 (1969) YB XII.

Council of Europe; European Commission on Human Rights, *Cyprus v. Turkey*, App. No. 6780/74 and 6950/75 (1975).

Court of Justice of the European Union, *Meki Elgafaji, Noor Elgafaji v. Staatssecretaris van Justitie*, C-465/07 (2009).

Court of Justice of the European Union, Bolbol v. Bevándorlási és Állampolgársági Hivatal, C-31/09 (2010).

Court of Justice of the European Union, *M. M. v. Minister for Justice, Equality and Law Reform, Ireland, Attorney General*, C-277/11 (2012).

Court of Justice of the European Union, *Mohamed M'Bodj v. État belge: Opinion of Advocate General*, Case C-542/13 (2014).

Czech, Philip, 'A Right to Family Reunification for Persons Granted International Protection? The Strasbourg Case-Law, State Sovereignty and EU Harmonisation', 17 January 2016, available online at http://eumigrationlawblog.eu/a-right-to-family-reunification-for-persons-under-international-protection-the-strasbourg-case-law-state-sovereignty-and-eu-harmonisation-2/ (last visited 1 August 2018).

da Costa, Karen, *The Extraterritorial Application of Selected Human Rights Treaties* (Martinus Nijhoff Publishers, 2013).

Daniel Thym, 'Respect for Private and Family Life Under Article 8 ECHRin Immigration Cases: A Human Right to Regularize Illegal Stay?' (57) *International and Comparative Law Quarterly* 87 (2008).

Dennis, Michael J., 'Application of Human Rights Treaties Extraterritorially to Detention of Combatants and Security Internees: Fuzzy Thinking All Around?', 12 (2) *ILSA Journal of International & Comparative Law* 459 (2006).

Edwards, Alice, 'Human Security and the Rights of Refugees: Transcending Territorial and Disciplinary Borders', 30 (3) *Michigan Journal of International Law* 763 (2009).

Errera, R., 'The CJEU and Subsidiary Protection. Reflections on Elgafaji - and After', 23 (1) *International Journal of Refugee Law* 93 (2011).

European Asylum Support Office, 'The Implementation of Article 15(c) QD in EU Member States. EASO Practical Guides Series', July 2015, available online at https://www.easo.europa.eu/sites/default/files/public/EASO_The-Implementation-of-Art-15c-QD-in-EU-Member-States.pdf (last visited 1 August 2018).

European Commission, 'Proposal for a Council Directive on Minimum Standards for the Qualification and Status of Third Country Nationals and Stateless Persons as Refugees or as Persons Who Otherwise Need International Protection' (COM(2001)510 final, 2001).

European Commission, 'Communication from the Commission to the European Parliament, the Council, the European Economic and Social Committee and the Committee of the Regions: A European Agenda on Migration' (COM(2015)240 final, 2015).

European Council on Refugees and Exiles, 'Complementary Protection in Europe', July 2009, available online at https://www.ecre.org/wp-content/uploads/2016/07/ECRE-Complementary-Protection-in-Europe_July-2009.pdf (last visited 1 August 2018).

European Court of Human Rights, *X v. Federal Republic of Germany*, App. No. 1611/62 (1965).

European Court of Human Rights, *Hess v. The United Kingdom*, App. No. 6231/73 (1975).

European Court of Human Rights, *X and Y v. Switzerland*, App. No. 7289/75 and 7349/76 (1977).

European Court of Human Rights, *The Republic of Ireland v. The United Kingdom*, App. No. 5310/71 (1978).

European Court of Human Rights, *Soering v. The United Kingdom*, App. No. 14038/88 (1989).

European Court of Human Rights, *Cruz Varas and Others v. Sweden*, App. No. 15576/89 (1991).

European Court of Human Rights, *Vilvarajah and Others v. The United Kingdom*, App. No. 13163/87, 13164/87, 13165/87, 13447/87 and 13448/87 (1991).

European Court of Human Rights, *Costello-Roberts v. the United Kingdom*, App. No. 89/1991/341/414 (1993).

European Court of Human Rights, *Loizidou v. Turkey*, App. No. 15318/89 (1995).

European Court of Human Rights, *Chahal v. The United Kingdom*, App. No. 70/1995/576/662 (1996).

European Court of Human Rights, *Ahmed v. Austria*, App. No. 25964/94 (1996).

European Court of Human Rights, *D. v. The United Kingdom*, App. No. 30240/96 (1997).

European Court of Human Rights, *H.L.R. v. France*, App. No. 24573/94 (1997).

European Court of Human Rights, *Ergi v. Turkey*, App. No. 66/1997/850/1057 (1998).

European Court of Human Rights, *A v. The United Kingdom*, App. No. 100/1997/884/1096 (1998).

European Court of Human Rights, *Selmouni v. France*, App. No. 25803/94 (1999).

European Court of Human Rights, *Bensaid v. the United Kingdom*, App. No. 44599/98 (2000).

European Court of Human Rights, *Tatete v. Switzerland*, App. No. 41874/98 (2000).

European Court of Human Rights, *Bensaid v. The United Kingdom*, App. No. 44599/98 (2001).

European Court of Human Rights, *Z and Others v. The United Kingdom*, App. No. 29392/95 (2001).

European Court of Human Rights, *Banković and Others v. Belgium and Others*, App. No. 52207/99 (2001).

European Court of Human Rights, *Thampibillai v. The Netherlands*, App. No. 61350/00 (2004).

European Court of Human Rights, *Venkadajalasarma v. The Netherlands*, App No. 58510/00 (2004).

European Court of Human Rights, *F. v. The United Kingdom*, App. No. 17341/03 (2004).

European Court of Human Rights, *Issa and Others v. Turkey*, App. No. 31821/96 (2004).

European Court of Human Rights, *Mamatkulov and Askarov v. Turkey*, App. No. 46827/99 and 46951/99 (2005).

European Court of Human Rights, *Isayeva v. Russia*, App. No. 57950/00(2005).

European Court of Human Rights, *Isayeva v. Russia; Yusupova v. Russia; Bazayeva v. Russia*, App No. 57947/00, 57948/00 and 57949/00 (2005).

European Court of Human Rights, *Müslim v. Turkey*, App. No. 53566/99 (2005).

European Court of Human Rights, *Öcalan v. Turkey*, App. No. 46221/99 (2005).

European Court of Human Rights, *N. v. Finland*, App. No. 38885/02 (2005).

European Court of Human Rights, *Bader and Others v. Sweden*, App. No. 13284/04 (2005).

European Court of Human Rights, *Z and T v. The United Kingdom*, App. No. 27034/05 (2006).

European Court of Human Rights, *Yassar Hussain v. The United Kingdom*, App. No 8866/04 (2006).

European Court of Human Rights, *Salah Sheekh v. The Netherlands*, App. No. 1948/04 (2007).

European Court of Human Rights, *Sultani v. France*, App. No. 45223/05 (2007).

European Court of Human Rights, *Saadi v. Italy*, App. No. 37201/06 (2008).

European Court of Human Rights, *N. v. The United Kingdom*, App. No. 26565/05 (2008).

European Court of Human Rights, *NA. v. The United Kingdom*, App. No. 25904/07 (2008).

European Court of Human Rights, *Y v. Russia*, App. No. 20113/07 (2008).

European Court of Human Rights, *Muminov v. Russia*, App. No. 42502/06 (2008).

European Court of Human Rights, *Women on Waves and Others v. Portugal*, App. No. 31276/05 (2009).

European Court of Human Rights, *Antonina Dmitriyevna Budina v. Russia*, App. No. 45603/05 (2009).

European Court of Human Rights, *Baysakov and Others v. Ukraine*, App. No. 54131/08 (2010).

European Court of Human Rights, *R.C. v. Sweden*, App. No. 41827/07 (2010).

European Court of Human Rights, *Medvedyev and Others v. France*, App. No. 3394/03 (2010).

European Court of Human Rights, *M.S.S. v. Belgium and Greece*, App. No. 30696/09 (2011).

European Court of Human Rights, *Sufi and Elmi v. The United Kingdom*, App. No. 8319/07 and 11449/07 (2011).

European Court of Human Rights, *Al-Skeini and Others v. The United Kingdom*, App. No. 55721/07 (2011).

European Court of Human Rights, *Yoh-Ekale Mwanje v. Belgium*, Application No. 10486/10 (2011).

European Court of Human Rights, *Othman (Abu Qarada) v. The United Kingdom*, App. No. 8139/09 (2012).

European Court of Human Rights, *Hirsi Jamaa and Others v. Italy*, App. No. 27765/09 (2012).

European Court of Human Rights, *Babar Ahmad and Others v. The United Kingdom*, App. No. 23027/07, 11749/08, 36742/08, 66911/09 and 67354/09 (2012).

European Court of Human Rights, *Singh and Others v. Belgium*, App. No. 33210/11 (2012).

European Court of Human Rights, *S.H.H. v. The United Kingdom*, App. No. 60367/10 (2013).

European Court of Human Rights, *K.A.B. v. Sweden*, App. No. 886/11 (2013).

European Court of Human Rights, *Benzer and Others v. Turkey*, App. No. 23502/06 (2013).

European Court of Human Rights, *H.S. and Others v. Cyprus*, App. No. 41753/10, 41786/10, 41793/10, 41794/10, 41796/10, 41799/10, 41807/10, 41811/10, 41812/10, 41815/10, 41820/10, 41824/10, 41919/10 and 41921/10.

European Court of Human Rights, *L.M. and Others v. Russia*, App. No. 40081/14, 40088/14 and 40127/14 (2015).

Feller, Erika, Türk, Volker and Nicholson, Frances (eds.), *Refugee Protection in International Law. UNHCR's Global Consultations on International Protection* (Cambridge University Press, 2003).

Gallagher, Anne T. and David, Fiona, *The International Law of Migrant Smuggling* (Cambridge University Press, 2014).

Gammeltoft-Hansen, Thomas, *Access to Asylum: International Refugee Law and the Globalisation of Migration Control* (Cambridge University Press, 2011).

George Letsas, 'Strasbourg's Interpretive Ethic: Lessons for the International Lawyer', 21 (3) *European Journal of International Law* 509 (2010).

George Letsas, 'The ECHR as a Living Instrument: Its Meaning and its Legitimacy', 15 March 2012, available online at https://ssrn.com/abstract=2021836 (last visited 1 August 2018).

Goodwin-Gill, Guy S., *The Refugee in International Law* (2nd ed.: Clarendon Press, 1996).

Goodwin-Gill, Guy S., 'The Right to Seek Asylum. Interception at Sea and the Principle of Non-Refoulement', 23 (3) *International Journal of Refugee Law* 443 (2011).

Heintze, Hans-Joachim, 'Zum Verhältnis von Mernschenrechtsschutz und humanitärem Völkerrecht', 16 (4) *Humanitäres Völkerrecht - Informationsschriften* 172 (2003).

Human Rights Committee, 'Sergio Euben Lopez Burgos v. Uruguay, Communication No. R.12/52' (UN Doc. Supp. No. 40 (A/36/40), 176 (1981), 1979).

Human Rights Committee, 'General Comment No. 15: The Position of Aliens Under the Covenant' (1986).

Human Rights Committee, 'General Comment No. 31: The Nature of the General Legal Obligation Imposed on States Parties to the Covenant' (UN Doc. CCPR/C/21/Rev.1/Add.13, 2004).

North Sea Continental Shelf Cases (Federal Republic of Germany v. Denmark; Federal Republic of Germany v. Netherlands), [1969], International Court of Justice (1969).

Legal Consequences for States of the Continued Presence of South Africa in Namibia (South West Africa) notwithstanding Security Council Resolution 276 (1970), International Court of Justice (1971).

Arrest Warrant of 11 April 2000 (Democratic Republic of the Congo v. Belgium), Joint separate opinion of Judges Higgins, Kooijmans and Buergenthal, International Court of Justice (2002).

Legal Consequences of the Construction of a Wall in the Occupied Palestinian Territory. Advisory Opinion, International Court of Justice (2004).

Juss, Satvinder S. (ed.), *The Ashgate Research Companion to Migration Law, Theory and Policy* (Ashgate, 2013).

Kolb, Robert and Gaggioli, Gloria (eds.), *Research Handbook on Human Rights and Humanitarian Law* (Edward Elgar, 2013).

Krieger, Heike, 'A Conflict of Norms: The Relationship Between Humanitarian Law and Human Rights Law in the ICRC Customary Law Study', 11 (2) *Journal of Conflict and Security Law* 265 (2006).

Lauterpacht, Elihu and Bethlehem, Daniel, 'The Scope and Content of the Principle of Non-Refoulement: Opinion', in E. Feller, V. Türk and F. Nicholson (eds.), *Refugee Protection in International Law: UNHCR's Global Consultations on International Protection* (Cambridge University Press, 2003).

Lord Dyson, 'The Extraterritorial Application of the European Convention on Human Rights: Now on a Firmer Footing, but is it a Sound One?', 30 January 2014, available online at https://www.judiciary.gov.uk/wp-content/uploads/JCO/Documents/Speeches/lord-dyson-speech-extraterritorial-reach-echr-300114.pdf (last visited 1 August 2018).

Mavronicola, Natasa, 'What is an 'Absolute Right'? Deciphering Absoluteness in the Context of Article 3 of the European Convention on Human Rights', 12 (4) *Human Rights Law Review* 723 (2013).

Messineo, Francesco, 'Non-Refoulement Obligations in the Public International Law: Towards a New Protection Status?', in S. S. Juss (ed.), *The Ashgate Research Companion to Migration Law, Theory and Policy* (Ashgate, 2013).

Miltner, Barbara, 'Revisiting Extraterritoriality after Al-Skeini: The ECHR and Its Lessons', 33 (4) *Michigan Journal of International Law* 693 (2012).

Ministerial Meeting of States Parties to the 1951 Convention and/or Its 1967 Protocol relating to the Status of Refugee, 'Declaration of States Parties to the 1951 Convention and or Its 1967 Protocol relating to the Status of Refugees' (UN Doc. HCR/MMSP/2001/09, 2002).

Moir, Lindsay, 'The European Court of Human Rights and International Humanitarian Law', in R. Kolb and G. Gaggioli (eds.), *Research Handbook on Human Rights and Humanitarian Law* (Edward Elgar, 2013).

Mole, Nuala and Meredith, Catherine, *Asylum and the European Convention on Human Rights* (5th ed.: Council of Europe Publ, 2010).

Moreno-Lax, Violeta, 'Hirsi Jamaa and Others v Italy or the Strasbourg Court versus Extraterritorial Migration Control?', 12 (3) *Human Rights Law Review* 574 (2012).

Moreno-Lax, Violeta, 'Of Autonomy, Autarky, Purposiveness and Fragmentation: The Relationship between EU Asylum Law and International Humanitarian Law', in D. Cantor and J.-F. Durieux (eds.), *Refuge from Inhumanity? War Refugees and International Humanitarian Law* (Brill, 2014).

Noll, Gregor, *Negotiating Asylum. The EU Acquis, Extraterritorial Protection and the Common Market of Deflection* (Martinus Nijhoff Publishers, 2000).

Nuala Mole, 'Asylum and the European Convention on Human Rights', 2003, available online at http://www.echr.coe.int/LibraryDocs/DG2/HRFILES/DG2-EN-HRFILES-09(2000).pdf (last visited 1 August 2018).

Nykänen, Eeva, *Fragmented State Power and Forced Migration. A Study on Non-State Actors in Refugee Law* (Martinus Nijhoff Publishers, 2012).

Peers, Steve *et al. (eds.)*, *The EU Charter of Fundamental Rights. A Commentary* (Hart, 2014).

Case of the S.S. "Lotus" (France vs. Turkey), (1927) PCIJ Series A No. 10, Permanent Court of Justice (1927).

Red Cross EU Office, *Shifting Borders. Externalising Migrant Vulnerabilities and Rights?* (Red Cross EU Office; International Federation of Red Cross and Red Crescent Societies, 2013).

Reidy, Aisling, '*The Prohibition of Torture: A Guide to the Implementation of Article 3 of the European Convention on Human Rights*, Human Rights Handbooks, No. 6, July 2003, available online at http://www.refworld.org/docid/49f1829b2.html (last visited 1 August 2018).

Schabas, William, *The European Convention on Human Rights. A Commentary* (Oxford University Press, 2015).

Scheinin, Martin, 'Extraterritorial Effect of the International Covenant on Civil and Political Rights', in F. Coomans and M. T. Kamminga (eds.), *Extraterritorial Application of Human Rights Treaties* (Intersentia, 2004).

Shany, Yuval, 'Taking Universality Seriously. A Functional Approach to Extraterritoriality in International Human Rights Law', 7 (1) *The Law & Ethics of Human Rights* 47 (2013).

Simsek, Cilem, 'Kurden- und Tschechenenfälle vor dem Europäischen Gerichtshof für Menschenrechte', 28 (4) *Humanitäres Völkerrecht - Informationsschriften* 171 (2015).

Tiedemann, Paul, 'Subsidiary Protection and the Function of Article 15(c) of the Qualification Directive', 31 (1) *Refugee Survey Quarterly* 123 (2012).

Tsourdi, Evangelia, 'What Protection for Persons Fleeing Indiscriminate Violence? The Impact of the European Courts on the EU Subsidiary Protection Regime', in D. Cantor and J.-F. Durieux (eds.), *Refuge from Inhumanity? War Refugees and International Humanitarian Law* (Brill, 2014).

X v. State Migration Service of Ukraine, Case 815/3681/13-a, Ukraine: Odessa Administrative Court of Appeal (2013).

UNHCR: Mandal, 'Protection Mechanisms Outside of the 1951 Convention ("Complementary Protection")' (UN Doc. PPLA/2005/02, 2005).

AM & AM (Armed Conflict: Risk Categories) Somalia v. Secretary of State for the Home Department, [2008] UKAIT 00091, United Kingdom: Asylum and Immigration Tribunal / Immigration Appellate Authority (2009).

MH (Syria) v. Secretary of State for the Home Department; DS (Afghanistan) v. Secretary of State for the Home Department, [2009] EWCA Civ 226, United Kingdom: Court of Appeal (England and Wales) (2009).

Regina v. Special Adjudicator, Ex parte Ullah; Do (FC) v. Secretary of State for the Home Department, Lord Steyn, [2004] UKHL 26, United Kingdom: House of Lords (2004).

Regina v. Immigration Officer at Prague Airport and Another, Ex parte European Roma Rights Centre and Others, [2004] UKHL 55, United Kingdom: House of Lords (2004).

RR (Refugee - Safe Third Country) Syria v. Secretary of State for the Home Department, [2010] UKUT 422 (IAC), United Kingdom: Upper Tribunal (Immigration and Asylum Chamber) (2010).

United Nations Committee Against Torture, 'Gorki Ernesto Tapia Paez v. Sweden' (UN Doc. CAT/C/18/D/39/1996, 1997).

United Nations Committee Against Torture, 'General Comment No. 2: Implementation of Article 2 by States Parties' (UN Doc. CAT/C/GC/2, 2008).

United Nations General Assembly, 'Conference of Plenipotentiaries on the Status of Refugees and Stateless Persons: Summary Record of the Thirty-fifth Meeting' (UN Doc. A/CONF.2/SR.35, 1951).

United Nations General Assembly, 'Report of the Special Rapporteur on the Human Rights of Migrants, François Crépeau. Regional Study: Management of the External Borders of the European Union and its Impact on the Human Rights of Migrants' (UN Doc. A/HRC/23/46, 2013).

Wilde, Ralph, 'Triggering State Obligations Extraterritorially: The Spatial Test in Certain Human Rights Treaties', 40 (2) *Israel Law Review* 503 (2007).

William Rehnquist, 'The Notion of a Living Constitution' (54) *Texas Law Review* 693 (1976).

Wouters, Kees, *International Legal Standards for the Protection from Refoulement. A Legal Analysis of the Prohibitions on Refoulement Contained in the Refugee Convention, the European Convention on Human Rights, the International Convenant on Civil and Political Rights and the Convention Against Torture* (Intersentia, 2009).

5 Conclusion

Flight from conflict and other situations of generalised violence is a major reason for overall global displacement. Persons flee or leave their countries for various reasons, and only some are considered worthy of protection in legal terms. The determination of statuses and allocation of protection claims is based on a strict separation into different legal categories of protection status and sets of substantive rights. Even for those entitled to protection, hardly any legal channels of entry are available, hardly any legal channels of entry are available. Thus, migrants and refugees, regardless of the later acquired status, travel in large-scale mixed movements. Identifying individuals arriving at host states' or host regions' borders is wrought with obstacles. On the one hand, there are the factual difficulties of mixed movements and flights in such numbers seen in 2010–2016, including a lack of documentation, lack of capacity to determine status and a lack of logistics to accommodate and organise the first phase of entry. On the other, there is the legal question of who is deserving and eligible for which kind of protection. How does one clearly distinguish between the divergent statuses of refugee protection, subsidiary protection and those who, although lacking a claim to a protection status, still cannot be returned to their countries of origin because of either their personal vulnerabilities or the serious risks they would face upon return?

This book has brought into focus the legal protections and determination of status for persons fleeing to Europe from violence and conflict. Clarification of the scope of the respective protection status and the legal interpretation of the applicable instruments in the context of conflict is the first step in the correct determination and consistent implementation of the law in the host country. With a focus on asylum applications in Europe, the book examined the main statuses of refugee protection, subsidiary protection and the prohibition of *refoulement* in the context of flight from violence and conflict. The courts' changing interpretation of the terminology of the protection pillars and thereby their scope of protection became apparent, yet inconsistencies in the interpretation and implementation unfortunately remain.

5.1 Conflict displacement and the challenge of status determination

People applying for asylum in a foreign country often encounter ambiguity and uncertainty in the allocation of a protection status. The claims of those fleeing violence and conflict still struggle, firstly, with divergent or inconsistent interpretations of the pertinent legal instruments, and secondly, obstacles in national implementation and practice. Despite the progressive development of a unique and common asylum system in the last 25 years, decision-makers in Europe still struggle to allocate the correct status to its rightful holder. Despite the goal to harmonise legal statuses and implement them in a uniform manner, the lack of consistency in recognition rates clearly shows that practice has fallen short of this aim. Asylum applications from contemporary conflict areas, such as in Syria, have highlighted the legal uncertainty about the assignment of protection status and suspension of involuntary return. Difficulties regarding specific groups of asylum seekers are enhanced by the politicisation of the migration topic in general and the handling of country-specific situations in particular. Legal uncertainty, however, furthers politicisation and discretion in the determination of status and, for this reason, the interpretation and correct application of the pertinent protection instruments is essential.

Additionally, and following a clear interpretation of the scope of the respective protection status, identifying the appropriate status for an asylum seeker is another challenge. "While the extremes of voluntary migrant and refugee may be sufficiently clear-cut, they define two ends of a spectrum in which voluntary migration gradually merges into forms of migration that are increasingly recognizable as forced."[1] Flight from conflict is one facet of forced migration. The allocation of the appropriate type of legal protection has proved challenging, as often both the factual and the legal assessment can appear different at first glance or potentially overlap, which makes the identification of the decisive criteria vital. For these reasons, the hierarchy in assessments of claims and the determination of status must also be emphasised and adhered to.

The conflict context or high levels of violence in the country of return pose a practical challenge to the identification and application of the different fields of law and their respective protection mechanisms. Eligibility for either refugee status or subsidiary protection is based, first and foremost, on a legal assessment of the nature of violence encountered by the claimant. Individualised persecution based on an exhaustive number of discriminatory reasons is decisive to trigger the protection of the 1951 Convention, while indiscriminate violence stemming from conflict mandates considerations of subsidiary protection. For beneficiaries of subsidiary protection, as well as rejected asylum seekers, the level of violence is the decisive element in substantiating their claim. The factual situation of conflict, however, impedes exactly these considerations. Changing allegiances, power and control dynamics hinder a clear demarcation between indiscriminate and discriminate warfare or harm. Moreover, where violence is not directed at one specific group, for instance a minority, but at broader parts of a society, linkages are blurred by the number of actors, motives and incidents. In the light

1 Zetter, Roger, 'Protecting Forced Migrants. A State of the Art Report of Concepts, Challenges and Ways Forward' (Federal Commission on Migration, 2014), at 22.

of the complexity of conflict and violence, as well as the contemporary situation of migration to Europe, providing legal clarity on the interpretation of the respective instruments is essential, not only for the individual claimant, but for the legal regimes governing flight and migration and their consistent implementation by host states.

5.2 Refugee law, Europe's complementary protection scheme and the role of international humanitarian law

The conflict context in the determination of protection claims, whether explicitly or implicitly, requires a consideration of the role of International Humanitarian Law (IHL). While the protection of civilians under IHL in countries affected by conflict was not of relevance for this book, it was, necessary to examine whether IHL would influence the neighbouring fields of refugee-, asylum- and human rights law when analysing conflict-induced displacement through their different lenses.

The three major fields of public international law which are pertinent to the protection of conflict-induced displaced persons has undergone a rapid evolution.[2] Following the atrocities of the Second World War and the consequences of massive forced displacement, IHL, human rights law and refugee law evolved as distinct fields of law, choosing different paths and institutional parameters, despite sharing an overall protection goal. Some have argued that the "artificial separation [...] has steadily eroded. Efforts to bridge perceived doctrinal gaps, to synthesise these bodies of law and to coordinate implementing bodies [...] have begun to produce concrete results."[3] While one can support the overall assessment when looking at the development of the three fields from a broader protection angle, there are limits to the qualities they share. Considering the different relationships between IHL and the other pertinent fields of law, the experience of recent years, seen in the light of judicial interpretative practices have, so far, put an end to a merging of refugee and migration matters with the laws of armed conflict.

5.2.1 To include or not to include the laws of armed conflict

IHL, with its distinct classifications of International Armed Conflicts (IACs) and Non-International Armed Conflicts (NIACs) and the different thresholds required to meet each classification,[4] is still the main source of international

2 Fitzpatrick, Joan, 'Human Rights and Forced Displacement: Converging Standards', in A. F. Bayefsky and J. Fitzpatrick (eds.), *Human Rights and Forced Displacement* (Martinus Nijhoff Publishers, 2001), at 3.

3 *Ibid.*

4 Common Article 2 Geneva Conventionss and Article 1 (iii) and (iv) AP I for IAC, in Common Article 3 and Article 1 (i) and (ii) AP II for NIAC and as further interpreted in jurisprudence of international courts and tribunals, particularly the ICTY in its Tadić or Limaj judgments.

law for designating armed conflicts. However, the laws of armed conflict are not of primary interest to the matter of which forms of protection are available to people fleeing a conflict when they have already crossed an international border. Nonetheless, the conflict context remains. Given its close proximity to the subject-matter, it was hypothesised that IHL could offer some simplifications when interpreting the other fields of law. This seems even more compelling when one observes the shared lexicon between IHL and the Common European Asylum System (CEAS), as enshrined in the (Recast) Qualification Directive (QD). For these reasons, the relevance of IHL was discussed with reference to the determination and interpretation of relevant protection regimes. Why not make use of IHL, seeing as it is the one framework that has codified binding definitions and established criteria and indicators for the classification and existence of armed conflicts? Why not incorporate these existing tools into other fields of law that struggle with comparable terminology? Despite some years of uncertainty and recourse to IHL by different national determining authorities and courts, a clear, negative answer has emerged only in recent years.

Firstly, international refugee law and status determination, in the light of the Convention refugee definition, do not establish a terminologically explicit link to conflicts. By means of treaty interpretation, the relevance of conflict context as a criterion in status determination was denied. Therefore, the incorporation of IHL as an interpretative tool was rejected. Secondly, the legal basis for the determination of subsidiary protection status in EU asylum law, the (Recast) QD, is a different matter. The Directive itself explicitly links the determination of status to, *inter alia*, the existence of "(c) […] indiscriminate violence in situations of international or internal armed conflict". The usage of IHL definitions and thresholds of armed conflict, while for some years controversial, has recently been rejected in the interpretation and application of the (Recast) QD. The Court of Justice of the European Union (CJEU), in its preliminary rulings in the case of *Diakité*, clearly denied any reliance on IHL in the interpretation of asylum law terminology, particularly emphasising the divergent development histories and purposes of the two fields of law. The classification of an armed conflict under IHL is therefore not decisive for the determination of a claim of subsidiary protection and was replaced by violence as decisive element. One could, in protection terms, consider this rejection of an IHL approach as a softening of the rather high IHL threshold criteria. No formal criteria concerning the nature of actors, motives or methods and means used are required, but solely a risk assessment on the level of violence. However, examples of national decision-making indicate that the asylum law determination of violence, as stipulated by the QD's Article 15 (c), is in practice no more lenient – states often consider the level of violence to be too low to trigger the protection claims, even if the conflicts would, under IHL, be classified as NIACs. Thirdly, regional human rights law, in the form of Article 3 European Convention on Human Rights (ECHR) *non-refoulement*, does not contain an explicit link to conflicts. Nevertheless, the principle has been activated to protect claimants facing expulsion to home countries in conflict. In these cases, the ECtHR did not consider the classification of conflicts according to the IHL definitions as a decisive factor in the activation of a *non-refoulement* prohibition. The risk assessment in cases of forcible return to countries in conflict followed their own assessments of the level of violence, rather than a predetermined criterion to assess conflict. While one can generally support the merging of neighbouring fields of international law and, specifically, a more consistent interpretation of synonymous terms as a way of countering fragmentation tendencies, this merging is rightly limited by divergences in the object and purpose of different fields of law. The different approaches to protection, particularly in IHL, refugee law, EU complementary protection and European human rights law, merit a divergence of interpretation of treaty law terminology. What all three fields of law share is the general renunciation of a conflict assessment or classification in favour of an independent determination of the existence of violence and, specifically, the level of violence. However, national divergences in interpretation and application of a particular legal framework remain problematic, and therefore an analysis of the legal norms and their interpretation must follow.

5.2.2 The determination of protection under the 1951 Convention, the (Recast) QD and Article 3 ECHR

When interpreting the eligibility criteria for a particular protection status and *non-refoulement*, the conflict context poses an additional challenge. Normative considerations must be put into focus to resolve whether the conflict context changes the interpretation or application of the legal instruments. An additional general shortcoming is the divergence in state practice. On the one hand, this arises through the transposition of primary international legal sources into national legal systems and, on the other, through the prevailing divergent interpretations concerning the respective instrument. For these reasons, treaty interpretation and analysis of pertinent and authoritative jurisprudence was employed to provide clarity on the scope of the legal instruments, their inclusion clauses and their interpretation of conflict-induced displacement. While this book did not focus on the various interpretations and asylum jurisprudence of individual states, the interaction of national courts, both vertically and horizontally, with neighbouring states' judicial counterparts or regional courts, has opened the door for further research on this new topic. Literature on judicial dialogue has more recently been published, providing a bigger picture of interpretative practice and interaction in the European states and beyond.[5]

5 Müller, Amrei and Kjos Hege Elisabeth (eds.), *Judicial Dialogue and Human Rights* (2017). Baldinger, Dana, *Vertical Judicial Dialogues in Asylum Cases* (Brill, 2015). Arnull, Anthony, 'Judicial Dialogue in the European Union', in J. Dickson and P. Eleftheriadis (eds.), *Philosophical Foundations of European Union Law* (Oxford University Press, 2012). Aust, Helmut P. and Nolte, Georg, *The Interpretation of International Law by Domestic Courts* (Oxford University Press, 2016). Of overall importance for this topic, albeit not part of this book, is the broader

5.2.2.1 International refugee law and the 1951 Convention definition

International refugee law, as based on the 1951 Convention and its refugee definition inclusion clause in Article 1 A (2), was created in the aftermath of the Second World War. Yet, its application to persons fleeing consequences of hostilities and violence has, since then, been disputed and inconsistently applied. In its first chapter, the book brought the analysis of the inclusion clause in the context of violence into focus. The UNHCR, with its Handbook in 1979, has to some extent fuelled the controversies over the application of refugee protection status to persons fleeing conflict. It stated that "Persons compelled to leave their country of origin because of international or national armed conflicts are not normally considered refugees under the 1951 Convention or 1967 Protocol". While this statement does not *per se* exclude persons fleeing persecution during conflict from its protection, but only those fleeing as a direct result of conflict, it has, for a long time, been interpreted as rejecting the application of the 1951 Convention to conflict-induced displacement. Since then, the UNHCR has published further guidance, including on the application of the primary instrument to conflicts, substantively changing the Office's position and reflecting the interpretative reorientation and clarification. The new Guidelines No. 12 on Claims for Refugee Status Related to Situations of Armed Conflict and Violence, published on 6 December 2016, illustrate the last change in its analysis. Volker Türk, Assistant High Commissioner for Protection, in this context underlined:

> What the new guidelines actually show is that it is not about a broadening of the refugee definition. It is really about explaining and updating our understanding of the definition in today's context. [...] What the guidelines are doing is to bring forward the understanding amongst states and judiciaries that the definition that was drafted then is as relevant today as it was at the time.[6]

Despite the new broad interpretation promoted by the Office, the nature of the UNHCR and the value of its interpretation and guidance can be debated. Between the 1979 Handbook and the Guidelines of 2016, various guidance documents were published by the UNHCR, differently labelled and with different focus, and these could be considered as hampering, even contradicting

debate about fragmentation and coherence in the international and European legal framework. Risks of fragmentation through divergent interpretative practices, cross fertilisation and matters of autonomy are discussed further in Moreno-Lax, Violeta, 'Of Autonomy, Autarky, Purposiveness and Fragmentation: The Relationship between EU Asylum Law and International Humanitarian Law', in D. Cantor and J.-F. Durieux (eds.), *Refuge from Inhumanity? War Refugees and International Humanitarian Law* (Brill, 2014).

6 Electronic Immigration Network, *New UNHCR Guidelines on Claims for Refugee Status Related to Situations of Armed Conflict and Violence* (2016), available online at http://www.ein.org.uk/news/new-unhcr-guidelines-claims-refugee-status-related-situations-armed-conflict-and-violence (last visited 1 August 2018).

and opposing one strong consistent doctrinal position of the Office with regard to interpretative questions. Not only is it possible that the number of various documents generates confusion on the Office's position, but also that the nature of the different documents remains, to some extent, unclear. The UNHCR's interpretation and guidance have considerable weight, but their exact authority as a source of soft law, or rather a strong political instrument, remains disputed. To assess in detail its role in the interpretation of the Convention and its interpretative documents, the UNHCR's legal role and attached state obligations were analysed before tracing the Office's policy development concerning the protection of persons fleeing conflict.

The UNHCR's role in refugee protection stems from three main sources: firstly, its nature as a subsidiary organ of the General Assembly and resulting states' obligations to cooperate, secondly, its own mandate, and thirdly, the refugee and asylum law instruments that explicitly contain references to the work of the UNHCR, most prominently, the 1951 Convention, the regional refugee law instruments and the instruments of the CEAS. The UNHCR itself understands its interpretative guidance, taking various forms, as an embodiment of its supervisory role. Therefore, its weight is based on states' obligations to cooperate with the UNHCR by virtue of the obligations from the three sources addressed above. While the obligations of states towards refugees form the basis on which the UNHCR engages with states, including advising or collaboration in status determination, these obligations do not endow the UNHCR's guidance document with binding legal value. As such, the cooperation obligations are too weak and too general to empower the Office as a doctrinal interpreter of the norms. Nonetheless, the political weight of the UNHCR and its instruments must not be disregarded and has been affirmed by judicial practices of referencing. Assessments towards certain groups of asylum seekers or country-specific analyses by the Office often guide political decisions on status determination as well as general trends and changes in state practice. Its interventions in individual asylum proceedings often, but not always, have an impact on the legal outcome. This power and influence derive from the special position of the Office and its nature *sui generis*. As an independent expert advocate for refugees, supervisor of the 1951 Convention and regional instruments and an organ of the UN, mandated by the UNGA and formally led by the intergovernmental Executive Committee, the Office has continuously strengthened its leading position in refugee protection with (but sometimes also against) states.

The 1951 Convention and its inclusion clause are the basis for refugee protection claims. For this reason, and to clarify the position of the primary refugee law instruments in the context of violence, this book took two research steps. Firstly, the overall applicability of the 1951 Convention was considered and assessed for the conflict context. Secondly, attention was paid to the inclusion clause as the basis for refugee claims. Only a legal interpretation of Article 1 A (2) based on the established process of treaty interpretation could provide clarification of its application to persons fleeing conflict and violence. This book argues that the prevalence of a conflict in the country of origin and a flight across its borders does not suffice to activate eligibility under Article 1 A (2). The 1951 Convention itself is, from a doctrinal point of view, not an adequate instrument to address displacement resulting from purely generalised situations of violence and mass flight from conflict, as the definition of refugee enshrines the requirement of (fear of) individual persecution on a number of possible grounds. This wrongly leads political decision makers to restrict asylum and refugee procedures, precluding the application of refugee law at all. Conflict, however, does not preclude the Convention from being applied at all. Whenever the fear felt or harm suffered is not indiscriminate, but suffered by certain targeted groups or individuals, the refugee definition and its refugee status protection are engaged. While the conflict context (in practice) does create undesirable obstacles, such as uncertainty about events, difficulties in obtaining or assessing evidence and information, the conflict does not create an additional legal criterion for the refugee definition. The threshold of harm feared or felt, the assessment of the risk, the identification of Convention grounds remain the same, regardless of the context.

Normative gaps in the application of the 1951 Convention to persons fleeing violence and conflict are therefore not the issue – it is rather the implementation of the Convention's criteria to applicants (and the consistency of that implementation) which is inadequate, creating serious defects and hence a lack of effective protection. While this book did not undertake a general analysis of states' practice in their application of the Convention in the context of violence, harmonised interpretative practices by the different courts, however, cannot yet be identified in Europe. As such, uniform interpretation going beyond case-by-case decision is not clearly noticeable either. A progressive interpretation paralleled by the UNHCR policies has been adopted on some occasions. Whether this trend will prevail will be driven by future status determination practices. From a purely normative point of view, as based on treaty interpretation, the 1951 Convention definition of a refugee is also fully applicable for persons fleeing conflict, as long as they are otherwise deemed eligible – not more and not less.

5.2.2.2 European Union asylum law and the (Recast) QD

The EU, as a supranational organisation, has since 1999 actively promoted and pursued the creation of a CEAS to harmonise national asylum practices and create a unified asylum status determination and implementation scheme. In comparison with regional developments in Africa and Latin America, which resulted in the adoption of extended regional refugee definitions, the EU chose a different path to include other categories of forced persons, including those fleeing the indiscriminate harm of conflicts. For this reason, it created its unique complementary protection status: subsidiary protection based on the (Recast) QD. The (Recast) QD, in accordance with its Article 15 (c), explicitly links subsidiary protection to violence resulting from conflict situations, without requiring one or more discriminatory factors. As such, subsidiary protection is commonly considered less individualised than its refugee law counterpart:

> the existence of a serious and individual threat to the life and person of an applicant for subsidiary evidence is not subject to the condition that that applicant adduce evidence that he is specifically targeted by reason of factors particular to his personal circumstances.[7]

The mere thirteen years since the adoption of the original QD have seen the transposition the 2004 QD and its Recast version into national legislation. Already, the choice of a Directive instead of the directly applicable EU Regulation would augur inconsistencies and divergence in the national context. Despite not having eradicated these implementation issues, the CJEU has recently started to provide assistance to the Member States in interpreting the EU instrument. In contrast to chapter 2, chapter 3 could turn to authoritative guidance in the interpretation of the scope of subsidiary protection and its legal basis, the QD and the Recast QD. The CJEU, whose role in adjudicating asylum law matters was initially assessed, delivered two preliminary rulings on the QD's eligibility for persons fleeing conflict in the *Elgafaji* and *Diakité* cases in 2009 and 2014. Of particular interest in the preliminary rulings was the understanding of what constitutes a conflict within meaning of the QD and how individualised must the harm have been in order to trigger subsidiary protection claims. The CJEU in this regard established the so-called sliding-scale: the lower the level of indiscriminate violence as such, the more the claimant needs to prove his or her special vulnerabilities.

Prior to the two rulings, divergent national asylum practices had rendered the determination a highly incoherent procedure, in which national decision makers employed various ways to assess the risk and the existence of conflicts in home countries, including those based on IHL criteria. In these last two judgements, the CJEU put an end to at least this dispute, rejecting the use of IHL criteria in favour of a unique asylum law determination of conflict and intensity of violence. The CJEU, however, while rightly rejecting an IHL-guided assessment of armed conflicts and thereby clarifying this interpretative dispute, failed to establish a unique scheme that the individual Member States could apply consistently. Hence, it is likely that the risk assessment of conflict-related claims will remain divergent and incoherent throughout the Union and claimants from one country will continue to be awarded different protection statuses, depending on the country in which they first arrived.

5.2.2.3 European human rights law and the ECHR

In the case of denial of international or regional protection status, rejected asylum seekers can turn to other forms of regional or national protection from expulsion under international and regional human rights law. In Europe, the most prominent protection from forcible return stems from the *non-refoulement* treaty obligation of the ECHR. Article 3 ECHR, however, contains no explicit reference to

7 *Meki Elgafaji, Noor Elgafaji v. Staatssecretaris van Justitie*, C-465/07, Court of Justice of the European Union (2009), at 45.

either *non-refoulement* or conflict. The prohibition to return claimants in specific cases is, rather, based on an interpretation of the norm in the judgements of the ECtHR. The fourth chapter of the book analysed the jurisprudence of the ECtHR in migration matters, specifically in the context of conflict. The ECtHR has developed a long-standing history of progressively developing and expanding the principle of *non-refoulement.* The conflict context, however, requires the detailed collection of the court's rulings on various implicit and explicit aspects of Article 3 claims, including considerations of the source of ill-treatment, state and non-state actors as well as challenges of naturally occurring harm. Like assessments under the QD, the ECtHR considered a potential requirement of individualisation, the necessity of being 'singled out'. The higher the overall level of violence, the less individualised the harm faced by the claimant needed to be. When assessing the intensity of indiscriminate violence in the country of destination, comparable obstacles to those discussed in chapter 3 arise, the lack of a defined threshold and the different indicators used by the court to consider the level of violence that is needed to preclude any return to the given area. It is, however, far from constituting a clear analytical scheme to determine the risk so far.

The role of the regional, treaty-based *non-refoulement* principle in the context of migration and flight to Europe has been characterised by one other important adaptation in the ongoing factual development: the broadening jurisprudence of the ECtHR on the extraterritorial application of the Convention. Seen against a background of numerous human rights enforcement bodies and courts, one must value the court's progressive interpretation and approach to human rights protection in general. Its openness to considering naturally occurring harm as a (potential) source of ill-treatment, or violations of socio-economic rights as triggering human rights protection under the ECHR, can also be criticised in practical terms for overwhelming the courts and the signatory states with responsibilities that once originated in the claimants' home countries. Some of the court's judgements have led to adjustments in national policies with their combination of role model and deterrence effect. While one context of Article 3 is the suspension from forcible return for rejected asylum seekers in Europe, the second major scenario is that of border control as means of preventing the arrival of potential asylum seekers who have not yet set foot on European territory. Particularly in the context of mixed migration travels, including over High Seas, *non-refoulement* constitutes the basis on which claims can be pursued further. As such, it can be considered both as protection of last and first resort. In times of outsourcing and off-shoring migration control, the "classical dictum that a state's executive power is to be exercised by its own officials and confined within the scope of its territorial borders can no longer be asserted with the same rigor".[8] The question at issue is whether the most fundamental obligations, such as the principle of *non-refoulement*, particularly the first encounter of

8 Gammeltoft-Hansen, Thomas, *Access to Asylum: International Refugee Law and the Globalisation of Migration Control* (Cambridge University Press, 2011), at 3.

mixed migrant groups with Member States' or EU officials, also apply beyond the Member States' borders. This all depends on the first legal determination of jurisdiction and the interpretation of Article 1 ECHR in the context of extraterritorial application. With the departure from territory being the sole basis of jurisdiction towards a broader approach, including effective control over persons and the exercise of public powers, the ECtHR has laid the groundwork for the application of the ECHR beyond European borders and when interacting with irregular migrants. ECtHR jurisprudence has also become increasingly explicit, e.g. prohibiting formerly employed measures such as pushbacks at sea.

Current plans of European states, specifically within the forum of the EU, include further developments of extraterritorial transit or reception centres and the deployment of border control personnel at transit states or at exit points in states of origin. These plans will all have to be examined for their compliance with obligations under European human rights law. The division of authority between the EU and the Member States will be decisive for such considerations of where the lines of jurisdiction and obligations are drawn. The evolution of the *non-refoulement* obligation has led to considerations of an implicit right to (temporary) access, at least to ensure that, upon removal, *non-refoulement* obligations will be adhered to. This is likely to continue. However, the ECtHR has not yet ventured to declare such an access right as the next evolutionary step in the interpretation of Article 3 ECHR. The divergent but fairly restrictive legal opinions of states on the interpretation of the principle of *non-refoulement* will clearly reject such an interpretation, meaning that the voluntary adoption of such practices by states is highly unlikely. Any consideration of such a right to access remains theoretical.

5.3 Concluding remarks

The willingness of states to commit themselves to higher human rights standards is low. Meanwhile, new, expansive legal developments in the field of refugee or asylum law are, realistically, nowhere to be seen. Flight from violence and conflict challenges the broad field of refugee and migration law, not only due to the complexity of the conflict context in asylum seekers' countries of origin, but also because their entitlement to protection by host states has, for a long time, been disputed. Both normative and interpretative gaps might be generating these obstacles in the context of migration and flight. This book did not examine implementation gaps, although national practices illustrate them clearly. Rather, the focus was the analysis of possible normative gaps in the application of the legal instruments to conflict-induced displacement. The 1951 Convention, which is at the centre of the most well-established refugee protection regime in the world, has not been reopened for adaptations or revisions regarding its refugee definition and eligibility criteria since the adoption of the 1967 Protocol. While this prevents states from renegotiating and thereby lowering existing protection standards, it is equally representative of their unwillingness to broaden the existing concept of a Convention refugee specifically and international refugee law more generally. This refusal or reluctance mirrors the fear of mass influx and is based on a political decision, just like the one taken in 1950, when the 'role model refugee', worthy of protection by foreign states, was invented – at least in Europe. On other continents, extended refugee definitions have been adopted, broadening the category of refugees to include those fleeing from conflict and violence. In Europe, the broadening of protection for persons fleeing to the continent has taken a different route, one that follows Europe's progressive human rights developments. Complementary schemes of protection were envisaged and have been adopted. Fortunately, these are more encompassing than the exclusive Convention refugee. In the special architecture of the EU, this notion was incorporated through a unique and newly created protection status of subsidiary protection, which includes persons fleeing conflict and violence within its ambit. Within Europe and the EU, this development evolved quite progressively, yet it currently struggles with the last years' forced migration movements. The EU has opted for a middle way, based on a positive and commendable approach to the protection of aliens in its territory. Taking this middle way has, unfortunately, increased legal inconsistencies in both the interpretation of norms and in their practical implementation. Despite the demand for harmonisation in the Common European Asylum System, discretion to deviate from the minimum standards set by EU instruments together with the ongoing political tensions between providing the envisaged broad protection and reducing the number of entitled beneficiaries generates further uncertainty about the protection status and its associated bundle of rights.

Europe's human rights regime, with its enforcement mechanisms, parallels the EU's steps in its development of a broader interpretation of state obligations. However, more often than not, these obligations exceed what states currently support, as is seen in the interpretation of their obligations and their deviating practices. As such, the ECtHR has manoeuvred itself into a position enabling it to monitor European states' performance of their rights obligations, and to interact with the EU's organs tasked with implementing human rights protection. And yet, EU asylum law is a distinct and independent field with its own monitoring and enforcement mechanisms. Vertical and horizontal dialogues between the regional and supranational judicial organs and Member States are the positive outcome of this interrelationship, while tensions over jurisdiction, sovereignty and divergent approaches are its downside.

An approach to the protection of persons fleeing conflict which is driven by human rights law presents a practical dilemma. Human rights and its protection mechanisms is a field of law which has at its heart the individual as its beneficiary. Asylum protection claims and remedies are always awarded on the basis of individual, case-by-case assessments and procedures. In this way, human rights and refugee law are equal. A more generalising approach to the determination of protection in both fields is not inherent and would only follow political, but not legal incentives. The core difficulty is that flights from violence and conflict generate mostly mass movement, leaving states to follow individual procedures while processing large numbers of asylum claims.

The analysis has shown that, although the context of violence and conflict affects large numbers of people, the single claimant can be eligible for refugee status, subsidiary protection or simply protection from *refoulement.* A thorough assessment of the specific claim is required, as one cannot simply generalise the claims of persons stemming from the same country of origin. This would severely impede their entitlements and legal standing, which sits uneasily with the fact that the pertinent fields of law explicitly enshrine rights and obligations to prevent their position as subjects and rights-holders from being undermined. In this regard, the legal framework is difficult to reconcile with the demands of politics in Europe. Realistically, a group-based assessment of claims arising from contexts of violence and conflict would facilitate a smoother and more expedient process. The admission or allocation of quotas of asylum-seekers, or accelerated determination processes, would equally simplify the process. However, a renunciation of the individual and thorough assessment of protection claims based on the individual rights of the claimants cannot be an option. A solution that strikes the correct balance between both perspectives is still not found.

People fleeing conflict and violence have a valid and individual claim for protection, irrespective of how many are in a similar situation. The pioneering role of a common asylum system, however, requires burden-sharing mechanisms to redistribute the burden borne by border states with those states which are economically stronger, yet relatively unaffected due to their geographic location. In the EU, the Dublin System creates a format to distribute the processing of asylum applications, one that has failed to survive the so-called refugee crisis and currently threatens the existence of the European Union as such. Despite the codification of the principles of solidarity and the fair sharing of responsibility in Article 80 of the Lisbon Treaty, genuine solidarity among the different Member States and true political commitment to the EU, its legal framework and practical needs, has not been evident. States' reluctance to comply with the protection obligations to which they have voluntarily committed themselves has thwarted the underlying aspiration of the CEAS to become an encompassing and unique protection regime.

The result is that the EU's asylum regime mirrors both the advantages and the drawbacks of consensus-based decision making between sovereign nation states. Since the central problem lies in the implementation of asylum management, not in its normative bases, concerted efforts at both national and regional levels are necessary to achieve the uniform application of the law. Despite contemporary political and legal hurdles, the development of a common area of asylum entailing shared responsibilities is still the right answer to the tension inherent in mixed migration movements expanding beyond national borders. Outside Europe, tackling the root causes of conflict-induced displacement is equally essential if we are ever to master mixed migration movements in the future. This goal must become a constant consideration in future political and legal developments. Ultimately, demanding and supporting good governance in countries of origin will only succeed – and achieve legitimacy – if the demanding states or regions themselves are ready to practise what they preach. This means, above all, honouring the obligations of their own protection regimes, but also refraining from short-term thinking and politicised reactions to perceived crises and change.

References

Arnull, Anthony, 'Judicial Dialogue in the European Union', in J. Dickson and P. Eleftheriadis (eds.), *Philosophical Foundations of European Union Law* (Oxford University Press, 2012).

Aust, Helmut P. and Nolte, Georg, *The Interpretation of International Law by Domestic Courts. Uniformity, Diversity, Convergence* (Oxford University Press, 2016).

Baldinger, Dana, *Vertical Judicial Dialogues in Asylum Cases. Standards on Judicial Scrutiny and Evidence in International and European Asylum Law* (Brill, 2015).

Bayefsky, Anne F. and Fitzpatrick, Joan (eds.), *Human Rights and Forced Displacement* (Martinus Nijhoff Publishers, 2001).

Cantor, David and Durieux, Jean-François (eds.), *Refuge from Inhumanity? War Refugees and International Humanitarian Law* (Brill, 2014).

Dickson, Julie and Eleftheriadis, Pavlos (eds.), *Philosophical Foundations of European Union Law* (Oxford University Press, 2012).

Electronic Immigration Network, 'New UNHCR Guidelines on Claims for Refugee Status Related to Situations of Armed Conflict and Violence', 6 December 2016, available online at http://www.ein.org.uk/news/new-unhcr-guidelines-claims-refugee-status-related-situations-armed-conflict-and-violence (last visited 1 August 2018).

Fitzpatrick, Joan, 'Human Rights and Forced Displacement: Converging Standards', in A. F. Bayefsky and J. Fitzpatrick (eds.), *Human Rights and Forced Displacement* (Martinus Nijhoff Publishers, 2001).

Gammeltoft-Hansen, Thomas, *Access to Asylum: International Refugee Law and the Globalisation of Migration Control* (Cambridge University Press, 2011).

Meki Elgafaji, Noor Elgafaji v. Staatssecretaris van justitie, C-465/07, Court of Justice of the European Union (2009).

Moreno-Lax, Violeta, 'Of Autonomy, Autarky, Purposiveness and Fragmentation: The Relationship between EU Asylum Law and International Humanitarian Law', in D. Cantor and J.-F. Durieux (eds.), *Refuge from Inhumanity? War Refugees and International Humanitarian Law* (Brill, 2014).

Müller, Amrei and Kjos Hege Elisabeth (eds.), *Judicial Dialogue and Human Rights* (Cambridge University Press, 2017).

Zetter, Roger, 'Protecting Forced Migrants. A State of the Art Report of Concepts, Challenges and Ways Forward' (Federal Commission on Migration, 2014).

Index

actors of persecution 96, 104, 142, 171, 215; non-state actors of persecution 101, 105, 107; state actors of persecution 101, 174
actors of protection 104–5, 172–4
aggravated risk *see* differentiated risk
Area of Freedom, Security and Justice 132

Banković and Others v. Belgium and Others (Judgment of the ECtHR) 224
border control 187, 190–2, 225–8, 232, 248–9

CEAS *see* Common European Asylum System (CEAS)
cessation 69, 105–6, 143–5
chain *refoulement* 206, 207, 214; *see also* secondary refoulement
children 54, 85, 95
civilians 60, 67, 77, 82, 89, 99, 160–9, 214, 229, 241; as collateral damage 8, 80, 87; not as combatants 160–2; as particular social group 94–5
classification of conflict 153, 157, 201, 229
combatant 94, 160–2
Common European Asylum System (CEAS) 10, 13, 53–4, 69, 104, 129, 131–4, 142, 178, 242, 245, 246, 251
complementary protection 7, 13, 18, 129, 137–8, 178, 188–90, 241–9

Diakité, A. v. Commissaire général aux réfugiés et aux apatrides (preliminary ruling of the CJEU) 130, 137, 148–56, 160, 170, 177, 242, 247
differentiated risk 73–5, 77, 91, 96, 110, 199, 201

effective control 222, 223, 224, 227, 231, 249
Elgafaji, M., Elgafaji, N. v. Staatssecretaris van Justitie (preliminiary ruling of the CJEU) 130, 143, 148–54, 166, 167, 171, 177, 217, 218
exceptionality approach 62, 208, 211, 230
exclusion 3, 6, 41, 69–70, 124, 144–5, 161, 187, 202, 215
expulsion 187–95, 199, 204–12, 215, 226–30, 242, 247
extended refugee definition 7, 19, 23–6, 54, 60, 107
extended refugee instruments 24, 129, 151, 250; *see also* extended refugee definition
extraterritorial application 13, 187–90, 220–6, 228, 231–2, 248–9

generalised situations of violence 2, 7–8, 22–5, 50–5, 61, 68, 73–4, 88, 107, 148, 165–6, 170, 171, 177, 188, 199, 201–12, 239, 246

The Hague Programme 133, 148
High Seas 220, 225–8, 231–2, 248
Hirsi Jamaa and Others v. Italy (Judgment of the ECtHR) 226, 227, 232

IAC *see* international armed conflict (IAC)
IFAs *see* internal flight alternatives (IFAs)
immigration control 220–1, 227–8, 231; *see also* border control
imputation 98–101
inclusion clause 13, 69, 130, 161, 244–5
indiscriminate violence 8, 51–2, 99, 137, 148, 162, 242, 247–8; level of indiscriminate violence 156–60, 163–78; by reason of indiscriminate violence 139, 146–51

internal armed conflict 52, 62, 139, 150–9, 178–9, 242
internal conflict 55, 103, 157, 159; *see also* internal armed conflict; non-international armed conflict (NIAC)
internal flight alternatives (IFAs) 41, 105–7, 174–6, 207, 212–15
international armed conflict (IAC) 152, 161, 167, 241

membership of a particular social group (MPSG) 21, 70, 86, 89, 92–6
mixed migration 1, 3–4, 189, 225–9, 248–51
MPSG *see* membership of a particular social group (MPSG)
M.S.S. v. Belgium and Greece (Judgment of the ECtHR) 208–10

nationality 2, 22–3, 45, 70–9, 89–92, 105–6
national practices 37, 108, 168, 176, 187, 192, 227–8, 247, 249, 250; interpretative practices 43, 101, 131, 241–6; status determination practices 86, 101, 130, 140, 160, 167, 178, 246
naturally occurring harm 196–8, 210, 215, 248
nexus 13, 86, 89, 99, 163–4, 172
NIAC *see* non-international armed conflict (NIAC)
non-international armed conflict (NIAC) 52, 53, 102, 151–3, 167, 241
non-refoulement 7, 139, 155, 187, 199–205; and Article 33 1951 Convention 71, 78; CJEU, scope of 41; protection from expulsion 19, 25, 200–8, 224–33, 244, 248–9
non-state armed group 21, 103, 156–7
N. v. The United Kingdom (Judgment of the ECtHR) 197, 208, 210–11

political opinion 2, 45, 70, 86, 89–91, 96, 98–9, 101
political opposition 96–100, 161
predominant harm approach 208–10, 230
protection claims 24, 44, 50–5, 67–8, 80, 90–7, 130, 134, 157–9, 170–2, 194, 239–42, 245, 247, 250–1
protection gaps 21, 177
push back operations 226

race 2, 45, 70, 79, 86, 89–91, 166
rape 84–5, 169
religion 2, 41, 45, 70, 79, 86, 89–91, 166

Saadi v. Italy (Judgment of the ECtHR) 192, 200–1, 207
Salah Sheek v.The Netherlands (Judgment of the ECtHR) 175, 200–8, 213
secondary refoulement 6; *see also* chain refoulement
serious harm 82; in accordance with the QD 100–2, 139–46, 151, 171–7, 215–16; as persecution 52, 76
singling out 74–5, 87, 148, 170, 177–8, 199, 201, 230, 248
sliding scale 167–70, 178, 201, 247
spatial approach 224–5
special distinguishing features 199, 230
state practice *see* national practices
status determination procedures 2–4, 10–11, 23–5, 40–2, 55–61, 72–7, 83, 89, 98, 107, 138, 159, 171–7, 192, 239–46; *see also* status determination practices
Stockholm Programme 132–4
Sufi and Elmi v. The United Kingdom (Judgment of the ECtHR) 205, 209–17

Tampere Programme 132

UNHCR mandate 7, 19, 26, 28–35, 42, 44–8, 51, 55–7, 59–60, 106, 245
UNHCR Statute 27–9, 31, 45–6

Vilvarajah criterion 199, 200

warfare 74, 86–8, 110, 155, 158, 169, 210, 240
well founded fear 45, 48, 52–3, 70–1, 100–1, 162, 175